MW00331830

Ambush

Dolon flanked by Odysseus and Diomedes. Red-figured calyx-krater, The Dolon Painter. British Museum B8168

Ambush

Surprise Attack in Ancient Greek Warfare

by

Rose Mary Sheldon

Frontline Books, London

Ambush: Surprise Attack in Ancient Greek Warfare

This edition published in 2012 by Frontline Books,
an imprint of Pen & Sword Books Ltd,
47 Church Street, Barnsley, S. Yorkshire, S70 2AS
www.frontline-books.com

ISBN: 978-1-84832-592-0

For more information on our books, please visit
www.frontline-books.com, email info@frontline-books.com
or write to us at the above address.

Printed and bound by CPI Group (UK) Ltd, Croydon, CR0 4YY

Typeset in 11/14 point Garamond in Edinburgh by Wordsense Ltd

In Memoriam

Inge Hynes
Incomparable mother and friend

4 November 1922, Gleiwitz, Silesia
– 28 July 2003, Arlington, Virginia

Contents

List of Maps

Abbreviations

ABSA   *Annual of the British School at Athens*. London, Institute of
           Classical Studies
AC   *Antiquité Classique*. Louvain-la-Neuve, Institut d'Archéologie,
           Collège Erasme
AE   *L'année Épigraphique*. Paris, Presses Universitaires
AFLS   *Annali della Facoltà di Lettere e Filosofia*. Perugia, Università degli
           Studi
AHB   *Ancient History Bulletin*. Calgary, Alberta, Department of Classics
AHR   *American Historical Review*. Washington, DC, American Historical
           Association
AJA   *American Journal of Archaeology*. Boston, Archaeological Institute
           of America
AJAH   *American Journal of Ancient History*. Cambridge, Massachusetts,
           Harvard University
AJPh   *American Journal of Philology*. Baltimore, Johns Hopkins
           University Press
AncW   *Ancient World*. Chicago, Ares Publishers
AntCl   *L'Antiquité Classique*. Louvain-la-Neuve
ANRW   *Aufstieg und Niedergang der Römischen Welt*. Geschichte und
           Kultur Roms in Spiegel der neueren Forschung, Berlin,
           de Gruyter
Athenaeum *Athenaeum Studi Periodici de Letteratura e Storia dell'Antichità*.
           Università di Pavia
ATINER   Athens Institute for Education and Research
AW   *Antike Welt*. Zürich
BCE   Before the Common Era

BCH   *Bulletin de Correspondence Hellénique.* Paris, de Boccard

BG   Caesar, *De Bello Gallico.* Julius Caesar, *The Gallic War*

BJ   *Bonner Jahrbücher* des Rheinischen Landesmuseums in Bonn und des Vereins von Altertumsfreunden im Rheinlande, Köln, Böhlau

Boreas   *Boreas.* Münstersche Beiträge zur Archaeologie, Münster, Archaeologischen Seminar der Universität

BSA   *The Annual of the British School at Athens.* London

BSAF   *Bulletin de la Société Nationale des Antiquaires de France.* Paris, Klincksieck

ByzZeit   *Byzantinische Zeitschrift.* Munich, Beck

CAH   *Cambridge Ancient History.* Lewis, I. E. S. et al. (eds), London: Cambridge University Press, 1970

CAH²   *Cambridge Ancient History.* J. B. Bury, S. A. Cook, F. E. Adcock *et al.* (eds), New York: Macmillan, 1924–1966

CB   *The Classical Bulletin.* St Louis, Missouri, Department of Classical Languages at Saint Louis University

Chiron   *Chiron Mitteilungen der Kommission für Alte Geschichte und Epigraphik des Deutschen Archaeologischen Instituts.* Munich, Beck

CHGRW   *Cambridge History of Greek and Roman Warfare.* Sabin, P., Wees, H. van and Whitby, M. (eds)

CJ   *The Classical Journal.* Athens, Georgia, University of Georgia

CIL   *Corpus Inscriptionum Latinarum*

ClAnt   *Classical Antiquity.* Berkeley, University of California Press

C&M   *Classica et Mediaevalia.* Révue danoise d'Histoire et de Philologie, Copenhagen, Gyldendal

CP   *Classical Philology.* Chicago, University of Chicago Press

CQ   *Classical Quarterly.* Oxford University Press

CR   *Classical Review.* Oxford University Press

CRAI   *Comptes Rendus de l'Academie des Inscriptions et Belles Lettres.* Paris: de Boccard

CW   *The Classical World.* Pittsburgh, Pennsylvania, Duquesne University

DHA   *Dialogues d'Histoire Ancienne.* Paris

DOP   *Dumbarton Oaks Papers.* New York

Eranos   *Eranos.* Acta Philologica Suecana, Uppsala, Eranos Förlag

FM	US Army Field Manual
Germania	*Germania.* Anzeiger der Röm-Germ, Kommission des Deutschen Archaeologischen Instituts, Mainz, von Zabern
G&R	*Greece & Rome.* Oxford, The Clarendon Press
Gnomon	*Gnomon Kritische Zeitschrift für die Gesamte Klassische Altertumswissenschaft.* Munich, Beck
GRBS	*Greek, Roman and Byzantine Studies.* Durham, North Carolina, Duke University
HCT	*A Historical Commentary on Thucydides.* A. W. Gomme
Hellénica	*Recueil d'Eprigraphie de Numismatique et d'Antiquités Grecques.* Paris' Librairie d'Amérique et d'Orient Adrien-Maisonneuve
Hermes	*Zeitschrift für klassische Philologie.* Wiesbaden, Steiner
HSCPh	*Harvard Studies in Classical Philology.* Cambridge, Massachusetts, Harvard University Press
Historia	*Historia.* Révue d'Histoire Ancienne, Wiesbaden, Steiner
IJIC	*International Journal of Intelligence and Counterintelligence*
ILS	*Inscriptiones Latinae Selectae.* Hermann Dessau (ed.)
JHS	*Journal of Hellenic Studies.* London
JRS	*Journal of Roman Studies.* London
Klio	*Klio. Beiträge zur alten Geschichte.* Berlin, Akademie Verlag
Latomus	*Latomus Révue d'Études Latines.* Brussels
LCM	*Liverpool Classical Monthly.* University of Liverpool
MAAR	*Memoirs of the American Academy in Rome.* Rome, American Academy
MEFR	*Mélanges d'Archéologie et d'Histoire de l'École Française de Rome.* Paris, de Boccard
NYRB	*New York Review of Books*
PBA	*Proceedings of the British Academy.* Oxford University Press
PEQ	*Palestine Exploration Quarterly*
Phoenix	*The Phoenix.* The Journal of the Classical Association of Canada, Toronto, University of Toronto Press
PP	*La Parola del Passato.* Rivista di Studi antichi, Napoli, Macchiaroli
P&P	*Past and Present. A Journal of Historical Studies.* Kendal, Wilson
RA	*Revue Archéologique.* Paris: Presses Universitaires

R-E	*Real-Encyclopädie der Klassischen Altertumswissenschaft*. Pauly–Wissowa (eds)
REG	*Revue des Études Grecques*. Paris, Les Belles Lettres
REL	*Révue des Études Latines*. Paris, Les Belles Lettres
RhM	*Rheinisches Museum*. Frankfurt, Saverländer
RömMitt	*Mitteilungen des deutschen Archaeologischen Instituts*, Römische Abteilung
RSA	*Rivista Storica dell'Antichità*. Bologna, Patron
SHA	*Scriptores Historiae Augustae*
TAPA	*Transactions and Proceedings of the American Philological Association*
Thuc.	Thucydides, *The Peloponnesian War*
YCS	*Yale Classical Studies*. New Haven, Yale University Press
ZPE	*Zeitschrift für Papyrologie und Epigraphik*. Bonn, Habelt

Acknowledgements

E VERY PROJECT FINDS ME in debt to friends and colleagues. This one is no exception. My research depends on the friendly and knowledgeable help of librarians like Janet Holly, Megan Newman and Tom Panko of the Virginia Military Institute who help search down materials and get them sent here to our little corner of Virginia. Elizabeth Teaff at Washington and Lee was particularly helpful with those last few works that just seem to disappear just when you needed them. The staff at the Alderman Library at the University of Virginia was as professional as always. The maps were done by Michele Angel with help from Michael Brickler and Cathy Wells of the VMI Media Services.

I thank my readers especially John Karras, Jeff Aubert, M. Brian Phillips and the late John MacIssac, who each in their own way saved me from errors of fact or interpretation. I am indebted to the anonymous reader who politely took me to task over several entries. The errors that remain are mine and mine alone.

I am grateful to Michael Leventhal at Frontline Books for believing in the project and to my editors Deborah Hercun and Stephen Chumbley for seeing the manuscript through the publication process. The editorial staff, especially Joanna Chisholm, has helped put together a beautiful and accurate volume, and it is for that reason and their professionalism that I keep coming back to them with my book projects.

During the time it takes to produce a book, one must work through the material by giving public lectures before various audiences who can provide useful feedback. Chapter 8 of this book was presented as a paper* at the 2007 Athens

---

* The paper was published in 'The Odysseus syndrome: Ambush and surprise in ancient Greek warfare', in Gregory T. Papanikos and Nicholas C. J. Pappas (eds), *European History: Lessons for the Twenty-First Century*, essays from the Third International Conference on European History (Athens: ATINER, 2007), ch. 8.

Institute for Education and Research (ATINER) in Athens, Greece. The editor for that article was particularly helpful. I also presented papers to the Virginia Social Science Association and Roman Army School of the Hadrianic Society in Durham. I thank the students in my Greek military history class whose military training gave me a great sounding board for my thesis.

I was exceedingly fortunate in getting an advanced copy of Casey Dué and Mary Ebbott's ground-breaking book *Iliad 10 and the Poetics of Ambush* from the authors. It helped me clarify many points in chapter 2. I thank the authors for their help, and I cannot recommend their book highly enough for those interested in the poetics of the *Doloneia*.

The 1,000 or so endnotes will prove my indebtedness to the scholars who have come before me. I hope that I have cited them correctly and have been gracious in my disagreements.

Finally, and on a more personal note, I thank Katherline Vergolias whose hard work buys me the time to sit and think and write, and Jeffrey Aubert who not only graciously tolerated my insanity throughout the struggles of book production, but also had the generosity and good taste to take me to Venice when it was all over.

Preface

BOOKS ON WARFARE IN ancient Greece are plentiful these days but they continue to leave out discussions of intelligence, ambush and irregular warfare even though solid research has been done on this subject. One only has to look at the recent *Cambridge History of Greek and Roman Warfare* (*CHGRW*) to see that neither volume has a special section on any of these topics, nor does the introduction by Victor Davis Hanson even mention intelligence among the topics needing more research.[1] Previous works on intelligence gathering in ancient Greece have either not discussed military intelligence or, if they included it, did not discuss its use in ambushing. Chester Starr's *Political Intelligence in Classical Greece*,[2] as the title would suggest, was limited to political intelligence. Frank Santi Russell's *Information Gathering in Classical Greece*[3] had no section on ambushing, and much of the remaining literature on ancient intelligence gathering concerns the Roman period.[4]

When W. K. Pritchett first collected a list of Greek ambushes in 1974, he found no secondary literature on the subject and he called out for more studies on the concept of *apaté* in Greek society.[5] Neither did he find any mention of ambush in the standard works on Greek warfare of ambushes or surprise attacks. There have been precious few since then.[6] Everett Wheeler's study of the vocabulary of military trickery did not specifically discuss *lochos*, *enedra* or their Latin equivalent *insidia*.[7] Not even a heading (*lemma*) on the subject of ambush appeared in the major Classical encyclopedias.[8] Since the 1970s, several smaller studies have appeared including Joseph Roisman's *The General Demosthenes and His Use of Military Surprise*, Edmund Heza's 'Ruse de guerre – trait caracteristique d'une tactique nouvelle dans l'oeuvre de Thucydide,[9] and a chapter in Hans van Wees' *Greek Warfare*.[10]

Since ambush depends on the gathering of advanced intelligence the discussion of the two must go hand in hand. Ambush is also accomplished best by the use of light-armed troops. The standard work on light-armed troops is still O. Lippelt's *Die Griechischen Leichtbewaffneten bis auf Alexander den Grossen*,[11] and although it lists all the ancient sources it is hardly available to monolingual readers with no access to a large research library.

The biggest problem one encounters in doing research on ambush is the paucity of sources. As Everett Wheeler points out in the *CHGRW*, no detailed account of a Greek battle exists before Herodotus' description of Marathon,[12] a clash between Greeks and barbarians which is steeped in Athenian propaganda. No detailed account of a Greek vs. Greek battle appears in a contemporary source until Thucydides writes on Delium,[13] a contest during the Peloponnesian war. Only in the first Athenian battle at Syracuse[14] does Thucydides[15] present the pre-battle etiquette: a skirmish with missile weapons, sacrifice and infantry charge. Ambushes, unlike major battles or sieges of cities, do not leave archaeological evidence so we have to rely entirely on literary sources. The accuracy of these is always questionable, especially when using writers such as Polyaenus and Diodorus for example.[16] By the time we get to the fourth century and beyond, there is the added risk of seeing Archaic and Classical events through the lenses of fourth-century, pan-Hellenic propaganda and Hellenistic military practices.[17]

This brings up the subject of the bias of both the ancient sources and modern commentaries. Generalisations abound in the traditional view of Greek combat. The open-pitched battle, devoid of trickery or manoeuvre and decided by the head-on clash of rival phalanxes, is interpreted by historians as not only an idealistic norm but also a portrayal of Greek military reality. They do not seem to notice the rules being broken before the Peloponnesian war. Yet it remains a fact that not all areas of Greece practised phalanx combat and the Peloponnesian war did not initiate the concept of stratagem in Greek warfare. A view slanted towards hoplite battle is caused by the fact that much of what is written about Greek warfare, especially in the Archaic and Classical periods, comes from a point of view that privileges the practices of the major mainland powers as reported in ethnocentric literary sources.[18] We must remember, however, that the Greek world as a whole did not experience uniform, simultaneous military development. The heavy-infantry phalanx, around which the traditional view of Greek tactics revolves, did not develop in Thessaly and Thrace where they were famous for fighting with cavalry and light infantry respectively. Nor did Macedonia develop a phalanx before the early fourth century BCE. We do not have much information to tell us how the Greeks of Asia Minor or the Aegean islands fought. They may have been users of hoplite equipment, but whether they employed the phalanx is unknown. In rugged northwest Greece the Aetolians and Acarnanians had little use for the heavy-infantry phalanx. On the other hand Arcadia exported mercenaries of heavy infantry. As scholars have pointed out, a phalanx may denote the existence of a polis, but the converse may not be true.[19]

When looking for the diversity of military development one only need look as far as Sicily. This island was often on the 'cutting edge' of Greek intellectual as well as military affairs. Long before Dionysius I (405–367) developed a true war machine, Gelon of Syracuse (c.480) boasted of the first major Greek army using combined arms, a possible precursor to Philip II's army. Against the Persians he offered the mainland Greeks 20,000 heavy infantry, 2,000 cavalry, 2,000 archers, 2,000 slingers and 2,000 *hamippoi* – light infantry in close co-ordination with cavalry. But the tradition never took root and only seventy-five years later a democratic Syracuse would hardly know how to fight in a phalanx, although its cavalry was still to be feared.[20]

The chronological coverage of this book is from the Homeric Age (eighth century BCE) to the Hellenistic East before the coming of Rome. (I have eliminated BCE since all dates in this book fall Before the Common Era.) Because of space limitations, my intent is merely to show relevant examples of ambush and put them into the military context of their age. The historicity of some of these examples may be questioned, but the fact that military writers thought them important enough to mention, and then collected them in handbooks, is important. Not every topic in Greek military history could be treated in detail, but there are serious studies on these other topics and I have guided readers to them in my footnotes. For a full treatment on peltasts, for example, one can still refer to the work of J. G. P. Best,[21] for light-armed infantry one can reference Lippelt[22] and for mercenaries there are the works of Griffth, Baker, Bettalli, Parke and Trundle listed in the bibliography. Generals such as Demosthenes and Brasidas have had separate studies.[23] My discussion of the Hellenistic is perhaps the most abbreviated because a full treatment of Hellenistic warfare would have required another book-length manuscript, and Chaniotis has written extensively on the subject. It was an age when most scholars agree ambush was a regular part of warfare and yet that is exactly when our sources fail us. I have concentrated most of my attention on earlier periods when scholars suggest ambush did not exist. Furthermore, it is an age of propaganda. Both the Greeks and Romans of the Hellenistic Age looked back to a simpler time when they claimed treachery, ambush and surprise attack did not occur because their ancestors were too honest. What I hope to show with this book is that this sentiment, while comforting to many modern authors, is a myth. The age that made them nostalgic was perhaps simpler, but not less likely to stage an ambush.

This book, as with my previous works, is aimed at a general audience of intelligence professionals, military historians and classicists. Since the book was not written for a professional audience of Greek and Latin scholars, Greek technical terms have been kept to a minimum and have been transliterated. I have used the more familiar Latin spellings rather than the Greek more popular among classicists today, and thus: Polybius, not Polybios. I have written the narrative for the general reader, but the footnotes should provide both the ancient sources and the modern works upon which my research is based.

A word is needed on the mechanics of translation and citation. The line numbers in the book will be to the Greek text. The only exception to this rule is on the few occasions when I have use Robert Fagles' translation. While this is not a word-for-word rendition of the poem, its poetic qualities recommend it to general readers with no knowledge of Greek. When using this translation I have given Fagles' line numbers in the text and footnoted the Greek line numbers since they are substantially different. All translations are given proper attribution, and my debt to the many great scholars who came before me will be obvious from the size of the bibliography. I hope this small contribution to the history of Greek warfare will help to highlight some interesting, but frequently overlooked, incidents that involved deadly fighting on the part of many courageous Greeks. They, too, deserve to have their story told. I have stopped the narrative at the coming of the Romans for purely selfish reasons; I am leaving the Romans for another book.

INTRODUCTION

The Odysseus Syndrome

THERE ARE TWO IMAGES of warfare that have dominated Greek history. One is the figure of Achilles, the Homeric hero skilled in face-to-face combat to the death. He is a warrior who is outraged by deception on the battlefield. The alternative model, yet equally Greek and also taken from Homeric epic, is Odysseus, 'the man of twists and turns' and the hero of the *Odyssey*.[1] To him, winning by stealth, surprise or even deceit was his foremost skill.[2]

While there are certainly exceptions to these paradigms, these polar opposites have been used in every discussion of intelligence and ambush in ancient Greek warfare. Homer introduced these twin models himself, and the tension between these rival approaches continues, not only in the study of Greek warfare but all of Western warfare as well. The debate over the respective virtues of bravery and trickery raged in antiquity as one side supported its views with moral posturing about honesty and fairness, while the other side pointed out that alternative methods offered a more economic and easier avenue to victory.[3]

Greek warfare always consisted of many varieties of fighting, and yet an inordinate amount of attention has been given to the hoplite phalanx, as if this were the only mode of warfare used by the Greeks. The use of spies, intelligence gathering, ambushing and surprise attacks were a part of Greek warfare as well, and while they were not the supreme method of defeating an enemy, such tactics always found their place when the correct motive, terrain or opportunity presented itself. Acknowledging the use of these stratagems does not discredit the conventions governing set-piece battles of the major mainland *poleis*; it merely completes the picture of the fighting life of the Greeks.

While everyone agrees that a system of limited warfare prevailed among the major *poleis* as an ideal in the Classical era, the origin of such rules and the frequency of observance are still hotly debated.[4] There have always been codes of honour and unwritten rules that have affected military operations. While Alexander the Great's refusal to launch a surprise nocturnal attack on Darius III's Persian army at Gaugamela may be an example of a general choosing to conform to the old ethos of Achilles, it is also true that the Greeks recognised two types of fighting. One type was the *polemos*, i.e. agonal warfare fought by the rules; the other was *polemos akeryktos* or *aspondos*, which meant war without herald or without truce. In the latter form of warfare any kind of ferocity or trickery was possible.[5] We are not suggesting cynically that belligerents always resorted to any means to win, but the element of surprise was never entirely absent. In their study of *Greek Diplomacy*, Adcock and Mosley were correct when they wrote: 'Although surprise attacks were made it was the habit of the Greeks to make a formal declaration of war.'[6] What the authors are commenting on, however, is the idea of strategic surprise. My topic in this book is rather tactical ambush that can be achieved in an appropriate situation once the war has been declared.

This prejudice against any fighting that did not involve hand-to hand combat to the death between heavily armed spearmen certainly is not a modern invention. The Greeks themselves expressed the idea. They glorified physical prowess, courage, readiness to die rather than yield even to overwhelming odds. In the Classical era hoplite warfare, the clash of two massed and disciplined phalanxes on level ground was certainly the way to glory and it received the most praise. Brasidas, for example, recommended it as the *only* way of testing one's courage.[7] Hoplite warfare was not, however, universally praised. The Persian, Mardonius, saw it as senseless[8] and Herodotus refers to it as 'suicidal madness'.[9] Although Greek literature is replete with disdain for peltasts, slingers, javelin men and archers who killed men from afar, these weapons continued to be used alongside of, or in place of, hoplite armour. The prejudice came about because missiles were for common folk or auxiliaries who could not afford hoplite armour. The poor were, therefore, accused of lacking the courage for direct combat. We will see, however, that ambushing requires courage too, and that in most cases it involves hand-to-hand combat at close quarters. Thucydides may lament the loss of good men to javelins,[10] but having them dead in hoplite combat is no less a disadvantage in the end. Thucydides comments bitterly that arrows do not discriminate between brave men and cowards.[11] They kill, nevertheless, and in the end, unless we are discussing a Pyrrhic victory, the winner is the side with the lower mortality rate.

The existence of a sense of 'fair play' in Greek warfare was thus a controversial idea even in ancient times.[12] The hoplite ideal was just that – an ideal. Letting the opposing army gather and having a battle on the plain between the full forces of each side, almost as if by appointment, probably originates in the same thought process we see in Roman writers. They believed that the desired state of mind in the defeated could only be achieved by such 'a fair and open' battle.[13] As Herodian writes: 'You will . . . prove to Rome and the world . . . that you did not violate a truce unjustly by trickery or deceit but that you won by superior force of arms.'[14]

Something of the same spirit is revealed by Alexander as reported by Quintus Curtius Rufus.[15] Parmenion 'gave it as his opinion that surprise was better than open battle. In the dead of night the foe could be overwhelmed.' Alexander replied:

> The craft which you recommend to me is that of petty robbers and thieves; for their sole device is to deceive. I will not suffer my glory always to be impaired by the absence of Darius, or by confined places, or by deceit by night. I am determined to attack openly by daylight; I prefer to regret my fortune rather than be ashamed of my victory.[16]

This attitude has been picked up by modern writers and used as an argument in favour of not only a 'Greek Way of War' but also, by extension, a 'Western Way of War'. Such commentators characteristically prove their case by taking selective quotations from Greek writers; they seem loathe to recognise any evidence that ascribes sneaky behaviour to the Greeks. This is a prejudice that has recently been described by Patrick Porter as 'military orientalism'.[17] This skewed approach is based on a stereotype that portrays the Greeks as 'us' (read Western and civilised), i.e. people who do not stoop to such behaviour, as opposed to 'them', the 'other' (easterners, barbarians or savages) who used such tactics because they are culturally or genetically disposed to being cowards, cheaters or back-stabbers. There are numerous examples of this prejudice in military writings. To give just a few examples, M. R. Davie writes: 'The essence of savage warfare is treachery and ambush. Primitive military tactics consist of stratagem and surprise in attack.'[18] Similarly, the French officer Ardant du Picq in his military classic *Battle Studies* states: 'War between savage tribes, between Arabs even today, is a war of ambush by small groups of men of which each one, at the moment of surprise, chooses not his adversary, but his victim, and is an assassin.'[19]

Indeed, he felt that Arabs were not capable of 'chivalrous warfare', only 'night surprise and sack of a camp'.[20] Oman writes of the Franks: 'To win by ambushes, night attacks and surprises seem despicable to the Frankish mind.'[21]

Americans during and after the American Revolution showed the same Western prejudice. During the War of Independence, Francis Marion was the laughing stock of the regular troops when he presented the guerrilla unit he had recruited to General Gates. The British, however, soon realised the strength of Marion's troops and they denounced him as a 'criminal' and blamed him for his 'ungentlemanlike' methods of fighting. Yet not long after, James Fenimore Cooper in *The Deerslayer* (chapter 3) discusses ambushes on the American frontier and claims that while white men could not ambush women and children in war it was a signal virtue in an Indian.[22] He conveniently forgets the Americans during their own revolution fighting with surprise attacks and ambushes as a motley collection of guerrilla frontiersmen. Indeed, the Declaration of Independence itself brands natives as barbarians and describes their warfare as 'the undistinguished destruction of all ages, sexes and conditions'.[23]

European texts on colonial warfare were replete with generalisations about 'Orientals', and freely used terms like 'savages', 'natives' and 'coloured peoples', interchangeably.[24] Alfred Ditte, in his *Observations sur les Guerres dans les Colonies*, writes:

> Savage wars are waged by alien cultures operating by different rules. Savages are easily impressed by bold and immediate procedure. Because Asiatics were unable to fight in more limited, conventional ways, and were readily coerced by shows of vigour, it was necessary to abandon norms of restraint to subdue them. The linkage is direct between a society's mode of war and its degree of civilisation.[25]

These examples of 'Orientalism' are not out-dated aberrations of an earlier age, and they continue to affect the writing of Greek history. Victor Davis Hanson in his 1989 work, *The Western Way of War*, describes non-hoplite soldiers as: 'Guerrilla and loosely organised irregular forces, the neo-terrorists who for centuries have been *despised* [italics mine] by Western governments and identified with the ill-equipped, landless poor.'[26] He then goes on to assume that we all share this attitude. He claims: 'There is in all of us a repugnance, is there not, for hit-and-run tactics, for skirmishing and ambush?'[27] He describes this revulsion as a 'burdensome legacy of the West that battle under any other guise except head to head confrontation is unpalatable' and then he proceeds to blame this attitude on the Greeks. Hanson indicts the Greeks for developing in us a distaste for the terrorist, the guerrilla or the irregular warrior who chooses to wage war differently, and is unwilling to die on the battlefield in order to kill his enemy. Such stereotypes of East and West never hold up to scrutiny for long. They are not useful in research and should by now be a thing of the past.[28] Yet as recently as 2004, H. John Poole wrote: 'Since the Crusades, Westerners have noticed how differently *those who live East of Constantinople* [italics mine] fight . . . Eastern adversaries routinely avoid set-piece battles.'[29]

The same cultural stereotypes are seen again in John Keegan's *History of Warfare*. He argues that 'Oriental' warfare is 'different and apart from European warfare'. It was characterised by traits peculiar to itself, foremost among these were 'evasion, delay and indirectness'.[30] If this generalisation were true, how would we then explain Attila, Genghis Khan and Tamerlane? Christopher Coker similarly generalises that Westerners historically preferred direct battle fought without guile to smash the enemy, whereas the 'Islamic' way of war was based on deceit.[31] Paul Bracken in his chapter 'Is there an Eastern way of war?' claims Eastern warfare was 'embodied by the stealthy archer', unlike the archetypal Western swordsman 'charging forward, seeking a decisive showdown, eager to administer the blow that will obliterate the enemy'.[32] Robert Cassidy sees the Eastern way of war as unorthodox, asymmetrical, indirect and rooted in perfidy.[33] H. John Poole writes about the 'Eastern thought process' which caused them to fight indirectly and use trickery.[34] William Lind speaks of the Oriental propensity for trickery and deception.[35] One need only look at the American Marine Corps's *Small Wars Manual* which urges the study of natives' 'racial characteristics'.[36] All of these interpretations have one thing in common. They completely ignore the long Western tradition of Western commanders using deception, ambush and indirect methods.[37] This includes ignoring such tactics among the Greeks. Walter Kaegi had already pointed out this lack of interest in ambush and surprise attack among historians already in 1981.[38]

The debate over the relationship of culture and warfare has been masterfully outlined by Patrick Porter in his book, *Military Orientalism*, where he correctly observes that war is a medium through which we have traditionally judged the calibre of our own and other civilisations.[39] Armed conflict has become an expression of identity as well as a means to an end.[40] John Keegan calls war 'culture by other means'.[41] Many have come to believe that how people fight reflects who they are.[42] The issue, however, is not that simple, and the relationship of culture to warfare is still a contested, ambiguous and politicised concept.[43] The legacy of the nineteenth-century, imperialist mind-set, and the attitudes that go with it, distort twenty-first-century scholarship and they affect the classics because the debate always begins with the Greeks. We hear the strains of these attitudes in W. K. Pritchett's *The Greek State at War* when he claims that the ancients, both Greeks and Romans, were: 'far removed from such malpractices as plotting mischief against their friends with the purpose of aggrandising their own power, and that they would not even consent to get the better of their enemies by fraud'.[44]

Many still believe the Greeks regarded no success as brilliant or secure unless they crushed the spirit of their adversaries in open battle, and that the Romans felt the same way.[45] There is no lack of quotations from ancient sources supporting this view. Both the Greeks and Romans themselves often claimed that only a hand-to-hand battle at close quarters was truly decisive, and that it was a sign of poor generalship to do anything except openly during warfare.[46] The truth is, however, that they would take a victory any way they could get it. While warfare without trickery is a nice ideal, fighting without using surprise to one's advantage simply does not represent the military history of Greece.

In short, there has been a tendency to lump the Greeks and Romans together, and quote liberally from Roman authors whose propaganda tried to tar and feather their enemies with charges of 'bad faith' when irregular tactics were used successfully against them. It was these same Roman writers and their Greek admirers, such as Polybius, who gave us this legacy of moralising propaganda and it has been picked up by Western defenders of empire ever since.[47] It is important not to fetishise certain Greek military tactics while ignoring the rest of the evidence.[48] The fact is that the Greeks constantly used irregular tactics, and they had few moral qualms about it. They were realists, not hypocrites, and the Classical Greeks certainly did not will this attitude to us. By showing how well and how often the Greeks used surprise in their tactics, and ambushed their enemies, we see that Western civilisation did not begin with a pure and untainted method of warfare that was somehow corrupted with time. In the same way there is no genetic propensity for sneakiness on the part of 'easterners' (whoever these turn out to be). Rather everyone's fighting formations are a reflection of their political and economic systems and all armies use regular formations or irregular forces as the situation requires. There is much to be done in the way of research on many periods of history to add a corrective to the stereotypes that have persisted over the centuries among historians. This is merely an attempt to give a more accurate portrait of how the Greeks fought.

Maps

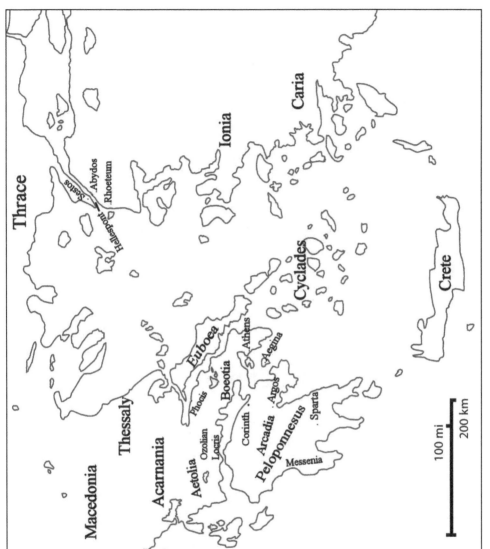

MAP 1 *Ancient Greece*

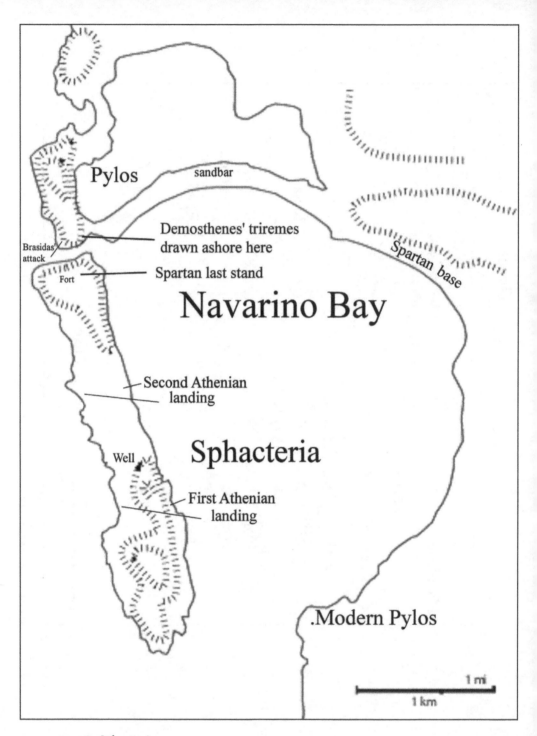

Pylos

sandbar

Demosthenes' triremes
drawn ashore here

Brasidas'
attack

Spartan last stand

Fort

Spartan base

Navarino Bay

Second Athenian
landing

Sphacteria

Well

First Athenian
landing

.Modern Pylos

1 mi

1 km

MAP 2 *Sphacteria*

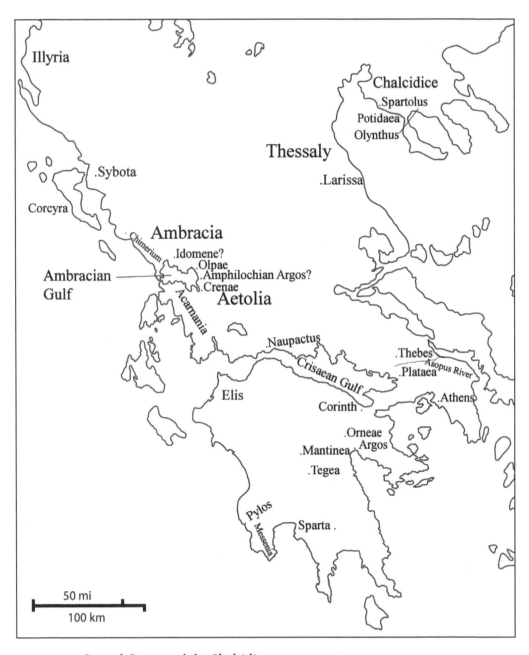

Illyria

Chalcidice

.Spartolus

Potidaea

Olynthus

Thessaly

.Sybota

.Larissa

Corcyra

Ambracia

Chimerium

.Idomene?

.Olpae

Ambracian
Gulf

.Amphilochian Argos?

.Crenae

Acarnania

Aetolia

.Naupactus

.Thebes

Asopus River

Crisaean Gulf

.Plataea

Elis

.Athens

Corinth .

.Orneae

Argos

.Mantinea

.Tegea

Pylos

Messenia

Sparta .

50 mi

100 km

MAP 3 *Central Greece and the Chalcidice*

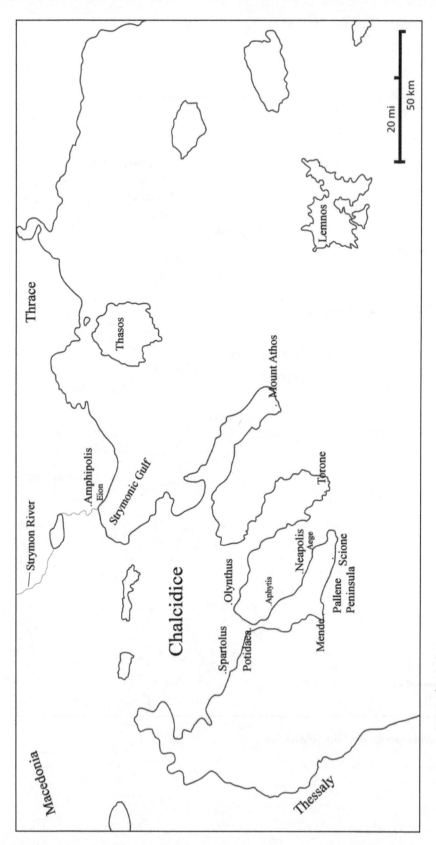

MAP 4 *Northern Greece*

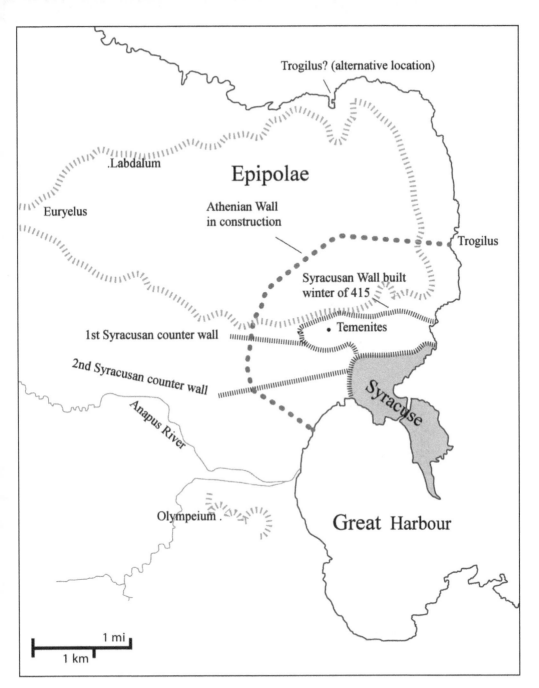

Trogilus? (alternative location)

Labdalum

Epipolae

Euryelus

Athenian Wall
in construction

Trogilus

Syracusan Wall built
winter of 415

1st Syracusan counter wall

Temenites

2nd Syracusan counter wall

Anapus River

Syracuse

Olympeium

Great Harbour

1 mi

1 km

MAP 5 *The Athenian attack on Syracuse*

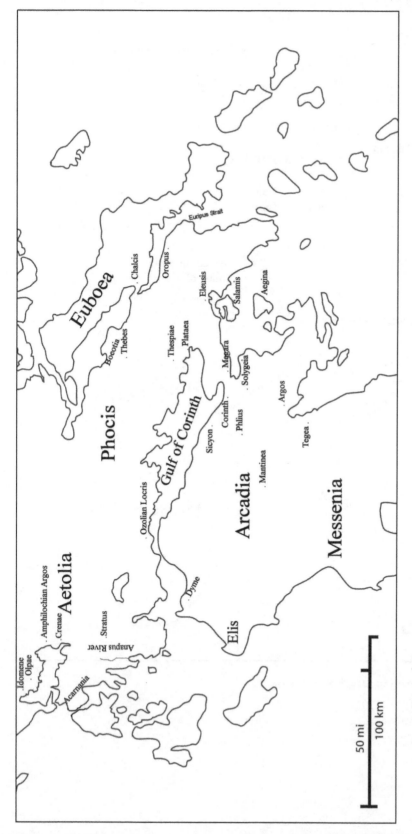

MAP 6 *Central Greece*

Locri

Rhegium

Messana

Naxos

Catana

Syracuse

Plemmyrium

Aeolian Islands

Symaethus River

Leontini

Sicily

Himera

Agrigentum

50 mi

100 km

MAP 7 *Sicily*

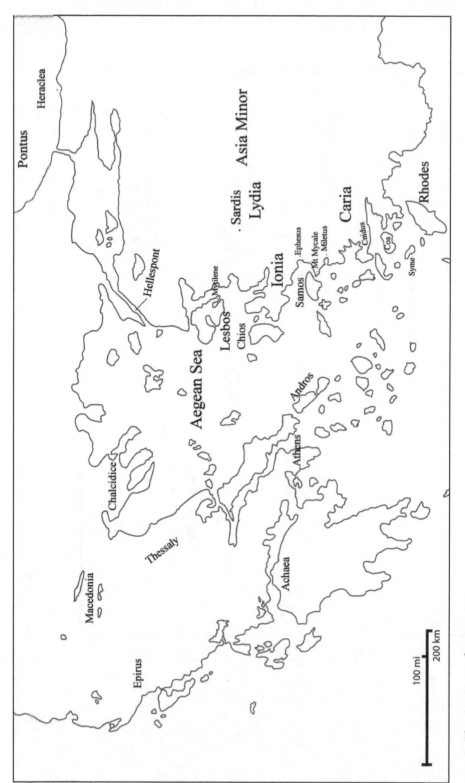

MAP 8 *The Aegean and Asia Minor*

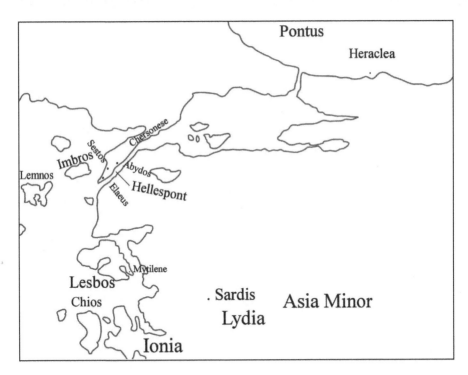

MAP 9 *The Hellespont*

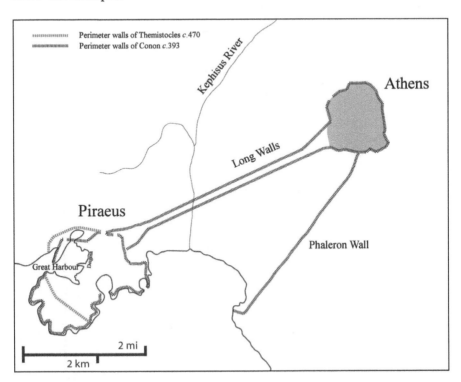

MAP 10 *Athens and Piraeus*

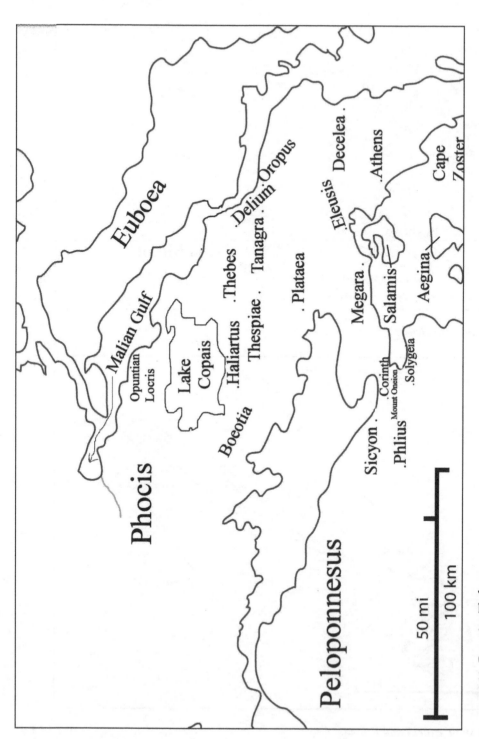

MAP 11 *Boeotia, Thebes*

CHAPTER 1

Ambush in the Iliad

War in the world of Homer is fought differently than in Classical Greece or the modern world.[1] War in the *Iliad* is conducted essentially in one spot, the plains of Troy, and the fighting is done by pairs of individual warriors.[2] It has been written that Homeric warriors had their own unique code of military behaviour, and their goal was to perform courageous deeds publicly in order to win glory that survived long after their death. According to this belief, the attainment of fame and glory (*kleos*) had to be achieved by a public action in the daytime that could be seen by all.[3] At first glance this would make the *Iliad* a strange place to start searching for information on ambushes, night attacks or any activity that was secretive or devious rather than in public. Some scholars still think we cannot find examples of intelligence activities, including ambush, in this quintessential war poem. Some have actually asserted that, with the exception of Book 10, no one in the *Iliad* does anything secret, devious or not able to be foreseen, and no forms of attack involve intelligence gathering, planning or very much skill.[4] This is patently false. If we accept the Trojan War as historical (and this is not universally accepted), then we might expect to find all the activities that occur in real wars. The fact is Homeric warriors happily deceived their enemies all the time and give praise to those who successfully staged ambushes.[5]

Traces of all the standard activities of military intelligence such as reconnaissance, signalling, espionage and counterintelligence can be found in the poem.[6] The fact that Homer includes them has led some scholars to suggest that these sophisticated techniques were added later to the poem and are indications of new forms of military strategy which gradually developed in the Dark and Archaic Ages.[7] The question of the historicity of Homeric society as described in the poem is, of course, still a thorny issue. There are still arguments over what age the poem represents – is it the Bronze Age of Mycenaean Greece or Homer's eighth century?[8]

1

Whatever age is being described, what we can say definitively is that as soon as the Greeks started writing about their own military activities, ambush and deception were a part of them.

Scholars continue to cling to the notion that there was no place for the sneaky, the deceptive or the treacherous in Homeric military action since these activities did not befit the heroic, courageous Greek warrior.[9] This is a subjective attitude, not based on the evidence. Ambush appears in the *Iliad* very clearly along with other examples of intelligence activities, and the Greeks show a very realistic attitude towards the strength and bravery needed to mount such operations. Ambush was certainly not the premier way of fighting or gaining glory, but the Greeks knew the appropriate time to use an ambush with the dangers it entailed. Although some scholars characterise an ambush as 'nothing more than an unexpected, tricky attack', we suggest the skills involved were honed by some of the greatest Greek warriors.[10]

The most frequently mentioned ambushes in the *Iliad* are not military operations at all, but attacks of wild beasts on domestic animals 'in the dead of night'. There is no clear division between lions and warriors – both are imagined as going 'through the night, slaughter, corpses, war-gear, black blood'.[11] Heroic warriors do not disdain such raids and ambushes; even the great Achilles himself takes part in such activities.[12]

Another context for ambush is the border raids that are frequently mentioned.[13] Paris began the Trojan–Achaean hostilities with a domestic raid.[14] While not quite as complicated as an ambush on humans, these raids acquire an attitude of ambush toward enemies. Once a war had begun, warriors could not merely live the life of heroic confrontations. Armies needed supplies to sustain themselves. We hear of Achilles' exploits and of cattle raids by Nestor and Achilles who saw these forays as an opportunity to win glory.[15] A recent study has shown the thematic connections between spying missions, cattle raids, horse rustling and ambush.[16]

There is no denigration of those who take part in an ambush in Homer where the motifs of hardship, victory and the single hero are so important. And although one scholar claims that ambush is on the lower end of Homer's 'ethical priorities', I suggest that in real warfare this is merely a distinction between fighting techniques. There may be more prestige in fighting like Achilles, but Greek armies knew when to use the wiles of an Odysseus when the situation required it. Certainly there were value judgements made against those who ambushed. The victim always accuses the successful ambusher of being sneaky and cowardly. The winner, however, take the victory as a sign of skill.

In Homeric warfare, the ambush was regarded as even demanding special courage and it was done by the best warriors. In the *Iliad* Achilles accuses Agamemnon of being a coward:

> You drunkard, with a dog's eyes and a deer's heart,
> Whenever it comes to arming yourself for war with the rest of the warriors
> Or going on an ambush with the champions of the Achaeans,
> You don't have the heart to endure it. That looks like death to you.[17]

There is no opposition formulated here between combat on the open battlefield by massed infantry formations and ambush.[18] It takes courage to do both. In the *Iliad*, the ambush is usually composed entirely of nobles.[19] It is done with a small ambushing party, and it calls for the highest daring and endurance. Homer does not distinguish between large battles or ambushes as far as courage is concerned. In fact, he implies ambushing takes far more courage. Ambush is simply a stratagem 'employing a small number of picked men and relying upon planning and dissimulation rather than speed or force'.[20] It also required advance intelligence. All the planning and dissimulation will do you no good if you do not locate the enemy first – before they locate you.

There are eight different ambushes described in the *Iliad*. Of these eight, five are indirect references which discuss the theme in a general way without recounting any particular ambush. The three remaining ambushes, which the *Iliad* presents directly, give the poem's particular view of such activities. There is no one single ambush that incorporates all of the motifs associated with that theme in the poem, and the examples of ambush can require complicated and lengthy episodes to describe them. The ambush is most explicitly described in 13.275–86, where it is stated that the ambush is where 'true valour' (*arête*) is most clearly displayed. Idomeneus, leader of the Cretans and one of the chief heroes, provides the most explicit description of ambush warfare in Homeric epic:

> I know what manner of men you are in valour; what need have you to tell the tale
> of it? For if now all the best of us were being chosen beside the ships for an ambush,
> *in which the valour of men is best discerned* [italics mine] – there the coward comes
> to light and the man of valour, for the colour of the coward changes ever to another

3

hue, nor is the spirit in his breast checked so that he sits still, but he shifts from knee to knee and rests on either foot, and his heart beats loudly in his breast and he imagines death, and his teeth chatter; but the colour of the brave man changes not, nor does he fear excessively when once he takes his place in the ambush of warriors, but he prays to mix immediately in woeful war – not even then, I say, would any man make light of your courage or the strength of your hands. For if you were stricken by an arrow in the toil of battle, or struck with a thrust, not from behind in neck or back would the missile fall; but your chest would it hit or your belly, as you were pressing on into the dalliance of the foremost fighters.[21]

Notice that Idomeneus believes it takes courage to fight face to face, and that it is in an ambush where 'a fighter's mettle is shown'.[22] He goes on to specify the process by which the bravest are selected. There are several examples of the best men going on ambush in Homeric epic.[23] Since it is necessary for an ambusher to assume a crouching position and wait patiently for the enemy, the ambush reveals what a man is made of. While the coward succumbs to fear, the brave man calmly awaits the desired moment of attack. The coward's loss of self-control is caused by the psychological hardship of remaining motionless in an enclosed space until the enemy is within striking distance. The attack must be held until the right moment.[24] Such concealment involves both physical and psychological hardship while holding back the attack until the right moment. The ambushers could be aided by scouts (skopoi) who would warn them of the enemy's approach. The victim was taken by surprise. The final stage of the ambush was the attack and vicious hand-to-hand combat that ensured.[25] We can see why advanced planning was needed to stage an ambush like the one related in Iliad 7.142. Nestor tells the story of Lycurgus and Areithous where Lycurgus confronts Areithous in narrow quarters so he will not be able to swing his mace. Such advanced planning to manipulate the scene of battle is not a form of trickery, but rather just good strategy.[26]

Another lengthy description of an ambush is given in Iliad 18.516ff., where it is portrayed on the shield of Achilles. Two armies of warriors are encamped around the city trying to decide between whether to lay waste to the town or to let themselves be bought off by a ransom of half the possessions of the townsfolk. The besieged, meanwhile, reject the idea of a ransom, and arm themselves with a plan to ambush the foe. The walls were left under the guard of the women, children and old men of the city. The able-bodied men went out, led by Ares and Pallas Athena.

4

They came to a place, a riverbed, which seemed to them a good place to set up the ambush. It was a good watering place for cattle and sheep, and so they waited there for the enemy to arrive with their flocks and herds. As they settled in, concealed, they sent out two scouts to watch for the approaching sheep and cattle. Within a short time, two herdsmen came by with their flocks, with no foreknowledge of the trap. They were speedily killed, but when the besiegers heard the noise made by the animals, they rushed to their defence and a battle ensued.[27]

The one ambush chosen most frequently by scholars to show the Greek disdain for ambushers is Paris' ambush of Diomedes in Book 11.369–95. Diomedes had just wounded Hector in a mighty display of his valour (*aristeia*), when Paris, concealed behind a grave stone, wounds Diomedes with an arrow. Paris leaps from behind cover[28] and takes advantage of the opportunity to make an appropriate boast. Diomedes, who has been fighting as the Achaean's foremost man or front-line fighter (*promos aner*), shouts back that Paris' bow attack is 'cowardly and womanish'. If Paris would only meet him openly in a spearfight, it would go much differently.[29] Part of this has to do with the character of Paris whom the audience knows is a lover, not a fighter. 'Arrow-fighter' may be a term of abuse to some, but archers in the *Iliad* are not ashamed of their craft. Paris taunts Diomedes: 'You are hit, and my arrow flew not in vain.'

Although there are associations drawn by some between archery and ambush, Paris has not waited for a group of soldiers to march past him and then fought them hand to hand. He is just shooting arrows at someone from behind cover, which is the standard way an archer fights.[30] This is shown well in the description of how Teucer shoots his arrows while he is protected by the shield of his brother Ajax in *Iliad* 8.266–272.[31] This pose can be seen in many sculptures and vase paintings, most notably the west pediment of the Temple of Aphaia at Aegina. There are no feminine connotations connected with using this weapon when Odysseus, at the end of the *Odyssey*, needs great strength to string his own mighty bow.[32] Because Paris is never really in danger, however, he comes in for the usual criticism levelled by front-line fighters against those who use long-distance weapons. Both archery and ambush have been understood and interpreted negatively in modern scholarship, but as Steven Farron argues there is no evidence in the *Iliad* that military archery was ineffectual or lower class.[33] He points out that insults to archers come not from the narrator but from the words of men such as Diomedes who have just been wounded, demonstrating that these are indeed effective weapons.[34] The value judgements made by modern commentators usually reflect their own attitudes or they exploit ambiguities in the epic.[35] Different outlooks, however, can simply motivate different passages in the text. There is no hint of cowardice when Teucer – 'the best of the Achaeans in archery' – shoots down many Trojans and brings glory to his absent father Telamon. Archery is, after all, one of the events at Patroclus' funeral games. The poem needs to present fighters with bows, fighters with swords and fighters with spears. All can be shown in an heroic light.[36]

Ambushes set for heroes are obviously going to be portrayed as sneaky and underhanded. The ambush set for Tydeus mentioned in Book 4.376–400 is an example. When the army of Polyneices reached Thebes, Tydeus was sent to the city as an ambassador. He challenged the Cadmeians to an athletic competition, and defeated them all, whereupon they decided to get even by ambushing him on his way home. Tydeus, however, slew all of his foes save one, whom he allowed to flee home. The attack on the Thebans is presented as treacherous and cowardly, while Tydeus' victory is portrayed as a mark of divine protection.[37] This fits the usual pattern. Ambush by the enemy is sneaky, but ambush by your own men is clever and brave.

Similarly in Book 6.155–95 Glaucus tells how his grandfather, Bellerophon, was falsely accused by Anteia who told her husband, King Proteus of Ephyre, that he was attempting to seduce her. Proteus laid a trap for Bellerophon by sending him to his father-in-law in Lycia with 'fatal tokens' (*seimata lugra*) commanding the bearer's death. After Bellerophon had successfully performed the third of the tasks set to test him him, the Lycian king decided in desperation to ambush him. The hero foiled the ambush, and revealed that he was the offspring of a god.[38] The king bestowed his daughter and a share of the kingdom upon him. The ambush in this narrative is associated with the deceit of the queen, while Bellerophon's triumph is linked to his divine race.[39]

The accusation of cowardice is made by anyone caught in a surprise that his own intelligence gathering did not anticipate. If these same men were participating in an ambush and killing the enemy, they would make no such value judgement against themselves or their men.[40] Rather they would judge themselves brave and clever.

The Narrative Pattern

The Homeric ambush, as a narrative pattern in the *Iliad*, was identified by A. T. Edwards as having the following stages.[41]

Planning

Before the ambush is set there must be a planning stage. The ambushers must collect intelligence on the enemy, and choose a proper place to set the ambush. These men are described as the *aristoi* (the best men). There are usually two leaders.

Concealment

The men must hide themselves in such a way that they can see the approaching enemy, but the enemy cannot see them and be forewarned of the ambush. The place is selected because the enemy is expected to march by. Very often it is the victim's route home. Concealment usually requires a crouching position. Often there is a density of the crowd of men hiding together in a cramped space. Remaining in this pose involves physical and psychological hardship. There is also the necessity of not falling asleep.[42] Enduring this hardship distinguishes the cowardly from the brave. The attack must be withheld until the right moment. The ambushers may be aided by scouts (*skopoi*).[43]

The Attack

If the hero is staging the ambush, it is usually successful. If the villain of the story is staging the ambush, then the ambushers are taken by surprise, join battle in hand-to-hand combat and are defeated by a single hero. The victim then denounces the ambush as cowardly.

This schematic is repeated throughout the poem and represents in broad outline how an ambush is set. There can be, of course, many variations on the theme in any military situation, but this basic pattern certainly captures the essence of the idea, as do many activities in the *Iliad*.

Another frequent accusation levelled against ambush is that it is of less strategic importance than the standing battle. This is simply restating the obvious; no one would argue otherwise. Characterising ambush as 'mere harassment of the enemy' or 'the assassination of a particular foe', however, is to minimise both its difficulty and its importance. Certainly, ambush in the *Iliad* is meant to be a contrast to the tactics characteristic of infantry combat. Obviously, the hardship of the ambush is not the same kind of trial as the spearfight, but it does require enduring intense psychological pressure and physical discomfort while waiting under difficult conditions and then fighting, possibly to the death, in close quarters. The charge of cowardice which the victim of an ambush is liable to direct at his assailants is not the same as that insult hurled in infantry combat where flight, not attack, earns one the charge of cowardice. The ambush requires planning and preparation in order to control space, time and the element of surprise in order to maximise the advantage of the ambushers. Ambushes are used when large battles are not possible. They are meant to gain small advantages, capture intelligence or demoralise a small force (see chapter 10).

Combat Versus Ambush

The salient characteristics of infantry combat in Homer are:[44]

- the spatial context of the battlefield where the ground itself grants an advantage to neither side, but is neutral;[45]
- the open nature of the spearfight in which a hero is free to withdraw before the advance of a stronger opponent, and where speeches and taunts are exchanged prior to joining battle;
- the pre-eminence of a single hero who is able to put the enemy formations to flight;
- the decisive role of force.

In contrast, the characteristics of the ambush are quite the reverse:

- since the aim of the ambush is to set up to control the scene of the fighting in advance, the locale is extremely important to the ambusher;
- the victim is given no opportunity to retreat and his enemies, of course, do not identify themselves beforehand;
- the ambush comprises a select group of the best men rather than a single hero;
- the success of the ambush is the effect of planning, concealment and sometimes (but not always) superior numbers.

While Edwards believes that the ambush illustrated the Homeric contrast of trickery (*dolos*) and force (*kratos*), I believe they illustrate two aspects of Greek warfare, not two ends of a moral spectrum.[46] Both the *Iliad* and the *Odyssey* acknowledge the place of the ambush in the repertoire of battle stratagems. In view of Idomeneus' speech and the comments of Achilles quoted above, it is clear that the *Iliad* conceives of the ambush as one aspect of heroic action. And as we shall see in chapter 3, the role of the ambush is central to the *Odyssey*. The continuity exhibited by the two poems suggests that the theme of the ambush was a conventional feature of the Greek epic tradition.

The Value Judgements

Whereas Edwards views ambush in the *Iliad* as a strategy employed by the weak and cowardly, when the *Iliad* discusses an actual ambush in real time we find that ambushers can be heroes, too.[47] Too many scholars have made the generalisation that all ambushes are portrayed negatively and assert that the Greeks considered them to be cowardly, treacherous or, in Paris' case, 'womanly' actions. Quite the contrary, Homer records an accurate view of what an ambush entails. He displays no moral taboo whatsoever against it, and sees it as something requiring courage and the best-trained men.[48] Thus in *Iliad* 6.189 King Proteus sets an ambush using 'the best men of Lycia',[49] and in the *Odyssey* Odysseus himself claims that Ares and Athena gave him the courage and strength that 'breaks the ranks of men', but that he chooses '*the best warriors for an ambush*' [italics mine].[50] Certainly they expect a soldier who wants to make a name for himself to win glory by fighting 'like men' face to face. In spite of these protestations, however, it is still a soldier's job to ward off 'treacherous ambushes'.

The Wooden Horse

While commentators continue to contrast the brave and honourable spearfighter to the sneaky and immoral ambusher, the fact remains that the great Trojan war ends in victory for the Greeks because of the most famous ambush in literature.[51] The story of the wooden horse does not appear in the *Iliad* (although it may be alluded to at 15.69ff.), and it was probably part of a pre-Homeric tradition about Troy.[52] The incident is mentioned three times in the *Odyssey*.[53] It stands out as the greatest of Odysseus' exploits at Troy and is identified with his heroism.[54] The stratagem is the final action of the war. In *The Little Iliad* by Lesches, the story is told as follows:

> The Trojans are now closely besieged and Epeius, by Athena's instruction, builds the Wooden Horse. Odysseus disguises himself and goes inside Ilium as a spy, and there being recognised by Helen, plots with her for the taking of the city; after killing certain Trojans, he returns to the ships . . . then after putting their best men into the Wooden Horse and burning their huts, the main body of the Hellenes sail to Tenedos. The Trojans, supposing their troubles are over, destroy a part of the city wall and take the Wooden Horse into their city and feast as though they had conquered the Hellenes.[55]

The rest of the story is told by Arctinus in *The Sack of Ilium*, more or less as we know it, and also from Vergil's *Aeneid*. Vergil gives us the fullest account we have of the ultimately successful nocturnal ambush tactics by which the Greeks finally sack Troy.[56]

> The Trojans were suspicious of the Wooden Horse and standing round it debated what they ought to do. Some thought they ought to hurl it down from the rocks, others to burn it up, while others said they ought to dedicate it to Athena. At last this third opinion prevailed. Then they turned to mirth and feasting believing the war was at an end ... and those in the Wooden Horse came out and fell upon their enemies, killing many and storming the city.[57]

The Trojan war, where so many Achaeans won glory and fame as champions and fighters, is concluded, therefore, through an ambush. In the *Odyssey's* proem [preface] we are told that Odysseus, along with the other Greeks, sacked Troy. It is the greatest of his victories and the wooden horse serves as the backdrop for the events following upon his return to Ithaca. Surely this belies Edwards' characterisation of the ambush as 'a tactic of only minor significance – suited to assassination or harassment'.[58] How ironic also that, in the *Odyssey*, ambush is elevated to a magnitude exceeding all other deeds of strength and courage at Troy. If this is the tactic that will win the war, then the best thing to do is use it and win.

The narrow view of 'heroic combat' has finally begun to be questioned in recent scholarship. Hans van Wees points out that, although the ideal of open and fair combat certainly exists in the *Iliad*, it seems to appear only in the formal duels, but not in the battle itself. For example, when Ajax is about to fight Hector he offers him the advantage of making the first move. Hector repays this compliment by warning Ajax to be on his guard: 'I do not want to look for an opportunity to hit a great man like you by stealth, but will hit you openly if I can.'[59] Duellists who decline such an advantage are not simply obeying some universal 'heroic code' but showing off their exceptional courage.[60] Hector knows the temptations of stealth and guile. Ajax is so dangerous, the prospect of attacking him stealthily is extremely attractive. Heroes do not display such chivalry anywhere else in the *Iliad*, and poetic vision and heroic ideal are not reality. Quite different behaviour is expected of warriors in regular battle. There, one eliminates the enemy by whatever means possible and no one seems to insist that the fight be open or fair, except for the restriction that leaders fight leaders. Most fights take the form of hit-and-run attacks rather than face-to-face confrontations. According to van Wees, only about one in six of the fights described in the *Iliad* involve opponents who deliberately seek out one another, or at least stand their ground when they come face to face. Five out of six times when a warrior does fight in the *Iliad*, he attacks his opponent without warning, often catching him off-guard. The single most common action in the *Iliad* is a single shot or blow which kills an enemy who is evidently caught unawares. Some men are hit while still dismounting from their chariots. Others struggle with one opponent only to fall victim to another who creeps up on him unnoticed. In retreat and flight men are hit and stabbed in the back without any attempt to make them stand and fight. A few are slaughtered while in a helpless state of shock.[61] Not only will a Homeric hero kill a man by stealth and surprise but he will also mock the man he has just killed and then strip and even mutilate the dead body. Warriors make jokes about the manner of the victim's collapse[62] or about what he can do with the spear that killed him.[63] They mock his deluded hopes of victory and warn that his body will be savaged by wild dogs or vultures.[64]

Ambush and Attitude in the *Iliad*

It is clear from the examples we have given that the *Iliad* acknowledges the place of ambush in warfare. Homer's heroes compete not only in open battle but also in ambushes and spying expeditions. Attacks by night can test bravery and strength as well as fleetness of foot and cunning intelligence of which Odysseus is the avatar.[65] Homer's warriors recognise the skill and bravery it takes to stage an ambush against the enemy, and they do not disdain such activities.[66] Homer often uses ambush as an effective means for an outnumbered, isolated hero to fight a just combat against scheming, unethical adversaries.[67] Using an ambush as a force multiplier is a well-known concept even in modern military strategy. In Homeric ambushes, the number of attackers and attacked is usually unequal, but the numerical advantage can be on either side and does not ensure success. As one recent study puts it: 'The decision to undertake a spying mission or an ambush is often born of a situation of desperation or the need to defeat an enemy who was not or cannot be beaten in conventional battle.'[68]

Although ambush is only one method in the repertoire of a warrior, it is the one that eventually wins the Trojan war. Ambush is certainly not what Edwards labels it: 'a strategy employed by the weak and cowardly'.[69] Facing an enemy in an ambush takes as much courage as facing an enemy while fighting in a massed formation. Lying in wait alone in an ambush may take even more courage. Most importantly,

11

both methods are well attested in Greek literature and each represents a facet of the historical ideology of Greek warfare.[70] Indeed, the fighting in Homer was so varied, and the author endorses so many possible ways of fighting, that scholars could pick and choose whatever passages supported their theory.[71] We must, however, view all the evidence. Looking at Greek epic tradition as a whole, and taking into account what we know of the now lost poems of the Epic Cycle, we find that there are no really discreet categories. Spearfighters such as Diomedes and Odysseus also traditionally excel at the kind of ambush warfare depicted in *Iliad* 10. Diomedes is a stellar fighter in the *polemos*, but he is equally good at the *lochos* (ambush). The sack of Troy is the ultimate night ambush, and both Odysseus and Diomedes are involved in several nighttime escapades leading up to and during its fall.

When we look closer at the descriptions of war in Homer, therefore, what we see is a very realistic view of a useful military technique. Ambush missions achieve what conventional battle cannot.[72] What we must avoid is the modern moralising about it, especially when it is based on stereotypes of Greek behaviour and attitudes.

CHAPTER 2

The Ill-fated Trojan Spy

THE ENTIRE TENTH BOOK of Homer's *Iliad* is the story of an ambush. A Trojan spy named Dolon is captured by Diomedes and Odysseus in one of the most famous intelligence operations in Greek literature.[1] Yet scholars have not only ignored the importance of ambush in the story they have also condemned it.[2] One study of the *Doloneia*, or 'Story of Dolon', refers to it as the 'most doubted, ignored and even scorned book of the Epic'.[3] The condemnation of the book has been almost universal until a recent study has resuscitated *Iliad* 10 so that it will 'no longer lie buried below a cairn heaped up to keep its unclean spirit out of the Homeric World . . .'[4] Another important task should be to liberate it from aesthetic judgements and intuitive responses that have nothing to do with the evidence of the poem or the realities of warfare.

The *Doloneia* occupies a peculiar place in the *Iliad* because it is a complete incident in itself and could be removed from the epic without leaving any trace. Even ancient critics believed that the poem was a separate composition by Homer, and not included by him in the *Iliad*, but added to the epic later on.[5] Modern scholars, too, have noted its lack of organic connection with the rest of the poem. Even the so-called 'Unitarians', i.e. those who believe the *Iliad* and *Odyssey* were composed by a single, literary genius named Homer, accept that it could have been a later addition.[6] Bernard Fenik put the question to rest in 1988 when he showed that, however little the *Iliad* needed the *Doloneia*, the *Doloneia* had been definitely crafted to fit into its place in the *Iliad*. It is not an independent lay, or what the Germans call an *Einzellied*, arbitrarily added.[7]

Based on the pioneering work of Milman Parry, recent scholarship has also shown that the *Iliad* is the product of oral tradition. In the earliest stages of development of the poem there was a great deal of multiformity in the Greek oral epic tradition. Countless variations on the story of the Trojan war, and episodes within it, are known to have been current in different times and different places.[8] One of the traditional attacks on *Iliad* 10 is that it is Odyssean, i.e. it shows themes that are more typical of the *Odyssey* than the *Iliad*.[9] *Iliad* 10 is also the only surviving example of an extended narrative about a night raid in Homeric poetry. This has led to the charge that the *Doloneia* was a later addition to the poetic tradition. Shewan argues, in contrast, that Book 10 was no more Odyssean than any other book and that we should understand that the poet was drawing on a variety of traditions, some older than others. Any affinity between the two epics can be explained by the fact that Odysseus appears as a character in both poems.[10] Material or themes that seems 'different' are not necessarily late or inferior. We should be careful of making these kinds of judgements based on what little epic literature has survived.[11] There were other traditions that dealt with the theme of ambush and nighttime action from which the poet of the *Iliad* could have drawn. A theme that is merely uncommon in the surviving epics might not seem so unusual if more of this other literature had survived.[12] As it turns out, there was indeed a traditional theme of the night raid, with its own traditional language, subthemes, conventions and poetics, and this was a part of the same system of oral poetry to which the *Iliad* belongs. In fact, the theme of *lochos* (ambush) with its traditional structure and diction long predates our received text of the *Iliad*.[13]

This Morally Sordid Business

Part of the shunning of this text has to do with a strategy employed by Classical scholars who feel they have to ignore it so as not to incur the charge of making arguments about Homer based on an 'interpolated', problematic text.[14] There is another reason, however, why the text is disliked. The very theme of ambush is anathema to some, because of what some have labelled the vile, underhanded tactics described in the *Doloneia*. Such tactics seemed to some readers completely out of line with their own conception of what the noble Greeks should be doing: i.e. fighting in the daylight as heroes as in the rest of the poem.[15] The events of *Iliad* 10 read like a morally sordid business, one hardly suited to the character of the gallant Diomedes. As we have seen in chapter 1, however, ambush is an integral part of Homeric warfare and is often done by its greatest heroes. Whereas combat in the *Iliad* takes place after the sun rises, an ambush like the one in the *Doloneia* takes place in the dark.[16] And while men such as Achilles are the heroes of the daytime action in the *Iliad*, Odysseus shows up his stealthy skills at night. He has been called by one scholar 'the protagonist par excellence of the shadows'.[17] It is in ambush that he shows himself most valuable in Book 10. While this distinction may seem to set the book apart from the rest of the poem, a recent book by Casey Due and Mary Ebbott shows that nocturnal attacks and ambush are part of a different genre, a parallel tradition, with its own traditional language, themes, conventions and poetics, but nonetheless part of the same poetry to which the entire *Iliad* belongs.[18]

The Night Operation

Book 10 begins on the plain before Troy, where for nine years the Greeks have been unsuccessfully besieging the city. Hector and the Trojans have driven the Greeks back to their ships. It is night and Agamemnon is despondent. He sees the countless fires of the Trojan bivouac. He cannot sleep. He must think of a plan to defend his people from destruction. The Trojans have not returned to the city and may be planning to rush the camp in a night attack.[19] Agamemnon gets up, puts on his tunic and boots, throws a lion skin over his shoulders, grabs his spear and goes down to his ship. There he meets his brother Menelaus, who also cannot sleep. Menelaus asks: Are you thinking of sending out a spy? 'Not a man in sight will take that mission on, I fear, and go against our enemies, scout them out alone . . . it will take a daring man to do the job.'[20]

Agamemnon then enlists the help of Old Nestor:

. . . sleeping is just as hard for you, it seems –
Come, let's go down to the sentry-line and see
if numb with exhaustion, lack of sleep, they've nodded off,
all duty wiped from their minds, the watch dissolved.
Our blood enemies camp hard by. How do we know
they're not about to attack us in the night?[21]

Agamemnon is correct to be disturbed. He is outnumbered and waiting to be attacked; he has no spies in the field, and his advisors are quite possibly asleep. Nestor and Agamemnon go out to meet other chiefs who have been summoned. Odysseus joins them. They find the men on the watch awake while they listened for the enemy coming. When everyone is assembled, Nestor addresses them about what a good spy might hope to find out:

My friends, isn't there one man among us here,
so sure of himself, his soldiers' nerve and pluck,
he'd infiltrate these overreaching Trojans?
Perhaps he'd seize a straggler among the foe
or catch some rumour floating along their lines.
What plans are they mapping, what manoeuvres next?
Are they bent on holding tight by the ships, exposed?
or heading home to Troy, now they've trounced our armies?
If a man could gather that, then make it back unharmed,
why, what glory he'd gain across the whole wide earth
in the eyes of every man – and what gifts he'd win![22]

This is an excellent assessment of what an intelligence operation might require. Courage, speed and power are as necessary here as on the battlefield. Nestor says there is *kleos* (glory) for undertaking a spying mission, making it parallel to fighting in battle. But success in this covert operation will also require special qualities of mind; wit (*noos*), craft (*metis*)[23] and an extraordinary sense of timing.[24] Spies must have an excellent sense of planning – the ability to lie in wait and spring an ambush. Like other ambushes in Homer, the *Doloneia* takes place on the third watch of night when the stars have turned their course.[25] The decision is that someone must venture across the plain and make certain, if he can, whether there is a night attack imminent. Diomedes immediately volunteers:

Nestor, the mission stirs my fighting blood.
I'll slip right into enemy lines at once –
these Trojans, camped at our flank.
If another comrade would escort me, though,
there'd be more comfort in it, confidence too.
When two work side-by-side, one or the other
spots the opening first if a kill's at hand.
When one looks out for himself, alert but alone,
his reach is shorter – his sly moves miss the mark.[26]

Many men are willing to accompany Diomedes but he chooses Odysseus as his partner for the qualities that make him a good ambusher, especially his ability to come back alive.[27] Brawn and brains make a perfect team: 'How could I overlook god-like Odysseus . . . With him accompanying me even from burning fire we could return home (*nostos*), since he is an expert at devising (*noos*).'[28]

The wily Odysseus does not wait to listen to the flattery heaped upon him by his comrades. He is ready to get underway immediately:

> Let's move out. The night is well on its way
> and daybreak is near. The stars go wheeling by
> the full of the dark is gone – two watches down
> but the third's still ours for action.[29]

The Greek scouts do not wish to be seen. They arm themselves with gear suitable for night work. They hide themselves in dark skins and leather helmets which are completely unlike what warriors wear at other times, e.g. Hector of the flashing helmet. They are dressed here for stealth.[30] Yet there are elements that link this episode to daytime combat. The arming of heroes is standard at the beginning of an *aristeia* – a scene in which a hero in battle has her or his finest moments.[31] An arming scene in the *Doloneia* links the mission of Odysseus and Diomedes with the combat scenes of the battle books. Arming is a ritualised form of preparation for combat, and in this case for the accomplishment of a deed of bravery, and it is another method of indicating the danger of the undertaking. This night mission is different, however, in its choice of night gear; uncommon valour requires a distinguishing dress. In the night-raid tradition, the dressing and arming of heroes has a poetic impact similar to the expanded arming scenes of conventional battle.[32] Like such scenes in the rest of the poem, they contribute both to the suspense by increasing the audience's anticipation of the coming ambush or raid. The details of each dressing or arming passage reveal important aspects of the heroes' character as a fighter.[33]

Odysseus is distinguished from Achilles in many ways. Other warriors are noted for their backs, muscles or swift feet. But Homer draws attention to the eyes of Odysseus.[34] The eyes indicate his foresight, provision and ability to size up a situation at a glance. Diomedes does all the killing in Book 10, but Odysseus is the first to see both Dolon and Rhesus. Spying is the perfect vehicle for expressing this practical sight, for it is, by definition, vision with a mission. As in a night ambush, almost anything goes.[35]

A good omen comes to them as they set out. A night heron, sent by Pallas Athena, can be heard on their right honking in the darkness although they cannot see it.[36] Odysseus is glad for the sign and prays to Athena:

Grant our return in glory back to the warships
once we've done some feat that brings the Trojans pain![37]

Homer describes graphically how they set off like a pair of lions through the black night.[38] They must crawl over dead bodies on the ground as they await their victim, picking their way among the corpses 'through piles of armour and black pools of blood'.[39]

Meanwhile, in the Trojan camp, Hector wants to know if his guards are awake and alert or if they are asleep on watch. The danger is so very real he has put boys, old men and women on guard. All the city must stay awake and watch for signs of enemy movement.[40] He also enlists volunteers to spy on the Greeks. Dolon, son of Eumedes the herald, speaks:

Hector, the mission stirs my fighting blood –
I'll reconnoitre the ships and gather all I can.
Come, raise that sceptre and swear you'll give me
the battle-team and the burnished brazen car
that carry great Achilles – I will be your spy.
And no mean scout, I'll never let you down.
I'll infiltrate their entire army, I will,
all the way till I reach the ship of Agamemnon!
That's where the captain's must be mapping tactics now,
whether they'll break and run or stand and fight.[41]

Dolon's enthusiasm is not matched by his qualifications. He is described as 'no feast for the eyes, but lightning on his feet'.[42] He lacks self-criticism, suggesting that he has been spoiled by his five sisters. He is arrogant to think that he, an insignificant person, will be rewarded with the chariot and horses of the great Achilles. In offering him this reward, Hector has not thought the matter out specifically. It is ironic that Dolon and Hector speak about getting the best horses and chariot of the Greeks, whereas the result of the night's event will be that Diomedes and Odysseus get the best horses of the Trojan camp.[43]

Dolon slings bow and arrows over his shoulder and wraps himself in a grey wolf skin, symbolic of the scout.[44] He puts on a cap of marten skin, takes a sharp spear and away he goes toward the ships. But Homer tells us he was never to come back from those ships with news for Hector.[45]

When Dolon gets clear of the crowds of men and horses, he sets out full of eagerness. Odysseus almost immediately sees him coming and says to Diomedes:

> . . . Who is this?
> A man heading out of the Trojan camp!
> Why? I can't be sure – to spy on our ships
> or loot the dead, one of the fighters' corpses?
> Let him get past us first, into the clear a bit,
> then rush him and overtake him double quick!
> If he outruns us, crowd him against the ships,
> cut him off from his lines, harry him with your spear
> and never stop – so he can't bolt back to Troy.[46]

They lay hidden just off the path, among the dead bodies, while Dolon runs quickly by without seeing them. When Dolon gets a furlong past them and into the clear, the two men run after him. Dolon stands still, hearing a noise. He thinks someone has come from the camp to fetch him back, perhaps Hector wants to retreat. But when they are only 'a spear-cast off'[47] he realises they are enemies.

Dolon runs as quickly as he can to escape, but they pursue him like a couple of savage dogs on the hunt, chasing a fawn or a hare through the woods, while Dolon runs whimpering before them. Odysseus and Diomedes cut him off from the Trojan line and chase him until he nearly reaches the watchmen beside the Greek ships.[48]

Diomedes charges with a spear, and calls out: 'Stop or I'll run you through! You'll never escape my spear!'[49] As he speaks he casts his spear, but he misses Dolon on purpose, as it passes over Dolon's right shoulder and sticks in the ground. This is the only place where a warrior purposely misses his enemy with his spear.[50] The goal here is not heroic conquest of a worthy opponent, but intelligence. They must keep him alive until they get the information they want.

The spear stops Dolon dead in his tracks. He is terrified, stammering, with teeth chattering in his mouth, and pale with fear.[51] The others come up panting and seize both his arms. He bursts into tears and pleads not very nobly:

> . . . Take me alive!
> I'll ransom myself! . . .
> father would give you anything,

19

gladly, priceless ransom –
if only he learns I'm still alive in the Argive Ships![52]

Odysseus tries to lull him into a false security:

> … Courage,
> Death is your last worry. Put your mind at rest.
> Come tell me the truth now, point by point.
> Why prowling among the ships, cut off from camp,
> alone in the dead of night when other men are sleeping?
> To loot the dead, one of the fighter's corpses?
> Or did Hector send you out to spy on our ships,
> reconnoitre them stem to stern?
> Or did your own itch for glory spur you on?[53]

There is something coldly efficient about this interrogation. Odysseus appears sympathetic, and later he even smiles at Dolon. It is, after all, Diomedes who will do the killing. Dolon admits to being a spy, lured on by the promise of Achilles' horses.

There is a great deal of attention paid to spatial orientation and geographical intelligence here.[54] Odysseus, smiling, continues his interrogation:

> Now out with it, point by point. Hector –
> where did you leave the captain when you came?
> Where's his war-gear lying? where's his chariot?
> How are the other Trojans posted – guards, sleepers?
> What plans are they mapping, what manoeuvres next?
> Are they bent on holding tight by the ships, exposed?
> Or heading home to Troy, now they've trounced our armies?[55]

Dolon does not think about how much damage the information can do, information he is so willing to give up in the hope of saving his own life. He is petrified with fear as he confesses:

> I'll tell you everything, down to the last detail!
> Hector's holding council with all his chiefs,
> mapping plans on old King Ilus' barrow,

clear of the crowds at camp. Guards my lord?
Nothing. No one's picked to defend the army.
Only our native Trojans hold their posts –
many as those with hearth fires back in Troy –
our men have no choice, shouting out to each other.
'Stay awake! Keep watch!' But our far-flung friends,
they're fast asleep, they leave the watch to us –
their wives and children are hardly camped nearby.[56]

Odysseus asks for details not only of the night watch, but also for detailed arrangements of the Trojan camp:[57]

Be precise.
Where are they sleeping? Mixed in with the Trojans?
Separate quarters? Tell me. I must know it all.[58]

Dolon identifies the troops and gives their exact positions:

To seaward, Carians, Paeonian men with bent bows,
Leleges and Cauconians, crack Pelasgians – inland,
towards Thymbra, camp the Lycians, swaggering Mysians,
Fighting Phrygian horsemen, Maeonian chariot-drivers –
but why interrogate me down to the last platoon?
You really want to raid some enemy units.[59]

Dolon's question is ingenuous. He can hardly think that Odysseus is seeking this information from idle curiosity. He continues:

There are Thracians, look, just arrived,
exposed on the flank, apart from all the rest
and right in their midst Eioneus' son, King Rhesus.
His are the best horses I ever saw, the biggest,
whiter than snow, and speed to match the wind!
His chariot's finished off with gold and silver,
the armour he brought with him, gold too.[60]

21

The fact that Rhesus and his men are separated from the others makes them a better target for an ambush. The detailed intelligence is necessary because of the difficulties of moving and fighting in the dark. The Greeks do not wait for verification. Once they have gotten what they need to know, Diomedes tells Dolon his fate:

> Escape? Take my advice and wipe it from your mind,
> good as your message is – you're in *my* hands now.
> What if we set you free or you should slip away?
> Back you'll slink to our fast ships tomorrow,
> playing the spy again or fighting face to face.
> But if I snuff your life out in my hands,
> you'll never annoy our Argive lines again.[61]

Dolon tries to put up his hand and caress his captor's chin. The attitude of a suppliant was to clasp the knees of the person appealed to with one hand and reach for his chin with the other and beg for mercy, but Diomedes gives him no time. He runs his sword through Dolon's neck and cuts through both sinews; while Dolon speaks his head is rolling in the dust.[62] Spies, when caught, can expect no protection or mercy.[63] They pull off his leather cap, wolf skin, bow and spear, and Odysseus holds them up high and gives thanks to Athena.[64]

Dolon is a living example of the coward described in 13.276–94 by Idomeneus. Ugly and arrogant, raised among sisters, he has only one of the virtues necessary for successful spying. But his speed was of no avail to him when he encountered a fleet-footed man with judgement and courage as well. Despite his name, he is devoid of cunning (*dolos*) and appropriately loses his head. By describing an inferior spy as a prelude to the successful foray which ends Book 10, Homer makes us accept night ambush as a part of military virtue, while showing us how this mode differs from heroic combat in broad daylight.[65]

The Greeks continue toward the Trojan camp. They come first upon the Thracians, three ranks of them, all dead tired and asleep. The lack of a night watch is perfect for an ambush. They are there exactly as Dolon has described them. Odysseus and Diomedes divide the tasks to be done and act as a team.[66] Odysseus offers his companion the choice, to get the horses or to kill the men. Diomedes chooses the killing. The 'combat' part of the mission is accomplished in complete silence. Diomedes begins the quiet carnage as Homer describes the impressionistic scene; his thirteenth victim is the Thracian King Rhesus. The Thracians never know who kills them. Rhesus' dream suggests the ordinary shame of dying unawares. The enemies do not exchange boasts or names as they do elsewhere in the *Iliad*. There is no chance of ransom or the discovery of a guest friendship.[67] They are not wringing victory from fully conscious individuals who recognise them as superior. They are killing silent bodies, already prone and on the ground. Except for Rhesus, none of them is identified.[68]

Odysseus shows his cool intelligence by dragging the corpses out of the way, so that their retreat may not be impeded. Diomedes and Odysseus ride on horseback out of the Trojan camp, leaving behind the magnificently ornamented chariot of Rhesus among the dead Thracians. Odysseus and Diomedes stop briefly to collect the spoils of Dolon that they had left on the way and ride toward the Greek ships.[69]

Some scholars still refuse to see ambushes, raids and spying as a respectable part of military operations. They identify these activities as dishonourable, the 'tactics of transgressors'.[70] Such people even question if the nighttime Odysseus is a hero to admire. Mera Flaumenhaft, for example, claims that darkness obscures the line between honourable and dishonourable. She compares the ambushers to animals that have no shame. She criticises Diomedes, who sparkles among men and gods on the battlefield in Book 5, but in Book 10 chases a lesser man in the dark, as a hound would pursue a hare or doe.[71] By treating the enemy as less than human, Flaumenhaft says the victor becomes less human, too. To her, the ambushers even look like beasts. She ignores the fact that Homer is using a lion here to describe Odysseus and Diomedes as a mark of their heroism. The lion simile is frequently used of warriors in combat elsewhere in the *Iliad* including Diomedes[72] and Achilles.[73] Flaumenhaft sees it rather as a human contest deteriorating into bestial predation. It is not surprising to her that Odysseus is the first warrior to threaten to feed his conscious victim's corpse to scavenger birds.[74] His threat suggests to her something other than the notion of combat as heroic duel.[75]

In response to this, we must think about the situation to which his deeds are appropriate. The *Doloneia* leaves us no illusions about the shamelessly grim and inhumane deeds war makes one commit. There are human virtues to be admired in the context of the conflict, for example, intelligence and foresight; Odysseus and Diomedes are, after all, intelligence operatives. They are sent forth as Achaeans against Trojans, and their glory is shared, with each other and their comrades whose morale is markedly raised by their success.[76] Darkness is appropriate to the work that spies or ambushers need to do. They have to move about undetected and remain unseen.[77]

While face-to-face combat may turn the tide of a battle and is an affair of glory, ambushes promise progress in the course of the war, too. They can bring honour and are eminently useful. Spying missions can often become ambushes, but this is not true of all of them. In this case, the expedition that began as a reconnaissance ends up as a raid for booty.[78] On an earlier visit to Troy, Diomedes killed many Trojans and returned bearing much news but no booty. In the spying and ambush in the *Iliad*, Odysseus never uses a weapon except in his last ambush, when he strings the great bow that will destroy the unsuspecting suitors. His use of poison arrows points more to efficacy than glory.[79]

Back in the Greek camp, the sound of the galloping horses announces their arrival. Diomedes takes the magnificent horses to his stable while Odysseus hangs the blood-stained spoils of Dolon on the stern of his own ship, until he can prepare a sacrifice for Athena. The horses, rather than any intelligence gathered, are the subject of conversation in the camp now. The booty provided more than enough reason for their little adventure; intelligence has turned out to be an incidental purpose. Better-trained scouts would have saluted Agamemnon and reported the story. But Diomedes and Odysseus, satisfied with themselves, just wash up, sit down to dinner and dip their cups into an overflowing bowl of wine. A couple of scouts had pulled off what a brigade of cavalry might have attempted in vain. The ill-fated Dolon, brash but not careful, had not only lost his own life but also provided the intelligence which resulted in the death of almost an entire contingent of allied soldiers. The game of espionage is not for amateurs.

The *Doloneia* as Ambush

Ambush in Book 10 is thus distinguished from heroic battle by its stealthy stratagems. Book 10 takes place at night, a unique time for military action in the *Iliad*. The action in this book has been criticised by some scholars as unheroic and even un-Greek. They have argued that Odysseus' killing of Dolon is inappropriate for the epic since the killing does not take place in combat and Diomedes lacks any anger that might justify ignoring supplication in battle. Diomedes' slaughter of the sleeping Rhesus has been viewed as non-heroic since there is no combat and the murder of a sleeping man requires no particular courage.[80]

They are right in that these are not daylight battles that follow the pattern of heroic combat set up elsewhere in the *Iliad*, but the changes in behaviour are quite appropriate. Book 10 consists of an account of two espionage missions – one ambushing the other. This is precisely the reason for the changes in behaviour, background, theme and tone in this book. Although they are partly reconnaissance missions, Odysseus and Diomedes gain much more information that they expected, which enables them to ambush Rhesus and carry off his horses for their own glory.

This mode of warfare is not to be scorned. Odysseus and Diomedes work in the dark in Book 10, but their deeds do not remain in the dark. Homer's scouts return triumphant to the acclaim of their comrades. They all know that the courage required by ambush is cold-blooded. This is silent bravery, not the kind shown in public confrontations. On the battlefield there is company, but in ambush, one is alone.[81] This is why Achilles taunts Agamemnon for never having the courage to go forth on ambush with the Achaean chiefs.[82] Menelaus worries that no one will be brave enough for the spying mission[83] and Idomeneus says that in ambush the coward will reveal himself.[84]

Nestor, the wise old warrior of the *Iliad*, knows best what qualifies as heroic. It is he who raises the question to the assembled Greeks about whether any one of them would dare go among the Trojans and discover their plans.[85] Nestor never abandons the heroic code and he would never encourage unheroic behaviour. Nestor declares that if anyone dared to spy on the Trojans and return unscathed, he would win 'great *kleos* (glory) to the heavens'[86] as well as many noble gifts[87] and invitations to feasts from all nobility who command ships.[88] Menelaus, too, says that scouting out the enemy during the night requires someone who is very bold at heart.[89] There is glory for both capturing or killing a spy and for being one.[90] Agamemnon says that such a mission is necessary in order to save the Greeks and their ships – the very outcome of the war depends upon it.[91]

Agamemnon selects Diomedes from among the many who are willing to volunteer[92] and Diomedes declares that his heart and manly *thumos* urge him to volunteer.[93] Diomedes, in turn, chooses Odysseus primarily for his courage, employing the same language that he uses to describe himself.[94] Diomedes is considered to be third, after Ajax among the eight greatest warriors in the *Iliad*.[95] The fact that many Greeks offer to undertake the task proposed by Nestor and that Diomedes cites his courage when he does are further indications that the mission of Book 10 was not considered to be either shameful or unheroic by the people who undertook it. Homer says that Agamemnon urges Diomedes to choose the 'best man' and not to leave behind a better man because of shame, but rather to be ashamed to pick a worse man. The use of the verbs of shame and honour are not random here. Agamemnon and the Greeks consider that whoever undertook the mission against the Trojans must be one of the best warriors and that it would be shameful if it were otherwise. It is a shame that requires and impels Homeric warriors in the *Iliad* to seek glory and to strive to become the best.[96] There is no shame attached to the mission, the activities therein, or the people who undertake it even though it involves espionage, an ambush, killing and action at night.[97] Even Athena is on the side of the Greek spies.[98] She signifies through her omen that she approves of the undertaking and she keeps them safe by warning Odysseus and Diomedes to get away from the Thracian camp.[99]

The consistent language, narrative and imagery preclude any suggestion that the expedition or characters of Diomedes and Odysseus are contrary to fundamental heroic values in the *Iliad*. The use of espionage and reconnaissance to stage an ambush are not in themselves unworthy actions for a Homeric warrior. The goal is simply different – in this case not heroic conquest, but information. Any distinction between the heroic and the shameful will lie in the character and aims of the warrior. This difference is highlighted by the poet's inclusion of the scene in which Hector asks for volunteers to spy on the Greek camps[100] and Dolon agrees to be a spy,[101] but only if he is well paid. Nestor focused on courage and glory; gifts for him are a sign of honour and are awarded after the attainment of glory. Nestor does not offer payment to his warriors so that they will volunteer, but rather asks for whoever is most brave and promises that such a man's excellence and success will be honoured. Dolon on the other hand (whom the poet describes as ugly) is more contemptible because he is motivated entirely by greed.[102] Dolon is not driven to help his community or eager to prove his valour. His only interest is in winning the rewards offered by Hector.[103]

The mission of Odysseus and Diomedes is one that is acceptable for heroes to undertake, and one that will enable them to win fame and glory because of the danger that is involved and the courage that is required to accomplish it. If they are successful, they will receive the standard form of recognition in conjunction with their glory: gifts and honours bestowed by the aristocracy of heroic warriors out of respect for their achievements on behalf of the community. This is appropriate because their effort will have been responsible for saving the Greek army. The *Iliad* consistently portrays individual human courage and effort that saves the community as deserving of honour and glory.

The intelligence provided by Dolon is of much greater importance than what a warrior captured in battle could give. Exactly because it is night, information on where the allies were sleeping and where the guards were posted made a deadly raid possible. The rules are obviously different than in the daytime, when everyone is awake and the guards are clearly visible. Even if such a raid is not depicted in the *Iliad* outside of Book 10, the night raid is not un-Homeric.[104] The danger of a night infiltration or night raid was very real. It was what kept the two kings up at night worrying. Nestor urged Agamemnon to set guards along the wall and trench because the enemy campfires were so close to the Greeks[105] and the guards do take their posts.[106] It is significant that Nestor declares that 'this night will destroy the army or save it'.[107] A night raid is expected even before the commencement of the *Doloneia*, and Nestor repeatedly refers to the pressing crisis.[108] Both sides are sleepless because of the proximity of the enemy. Agamemnon can see the Trojan fires and hear them.[109] He roams about because he must be sure the guards have not fallen asleep in view of the probability of a night attack by the enemy.[110] Nestor sleeps outside with his armour and weapons near,[111] as does Diomedes,[112] and Nestor is quick to rise in alarm when someone approaches at night.[113] The fear that the enemy might sneak up in the dark is not confined to Book 10. In Book 8, Hector ordered the Trojans to keep watch at night and to guard against a night raid by the Greeks. Even the women are brought in on the action:

> Now let heralds
> dear to Zeus cry out through the streets of Troy
> that boys in their prime and old grey-headed men
> must take up posts on the towers built by the gods,
> in bivouac round the city. And as for our wives,
> each in her own hall must set big fires burning.
> The night watch too, it must be kept unbroken,
> So no night raiders can slip inside the walls
> With our armies camped afield.[114]

The danger is so very real that Hector orders boys, old men and women to be on alert. The Greeks have the same worry. All of the city must stay awake and watch for signs of enemy movement. The anxiety on both sides and the very real possibility of a night ambush is palpable in Book 10. Night raiders and spies are both expected and feared. The death of Dolon is not unusual. He is treated no differently than others elsewhere in the epic, especially when one recalls the brutality typically shown towards captives on the battlefield.[115] Diomedes is hardly going to release Dolon to fight or spy again some other time.[116] A released Dolon could proceed to kill sleeping Greeks and the two heroes could hardly continue their mission with a prisoner hindering them. Homer's audience would have appreciated what the death of Dolon meant. Two brave men had saved the camp, and prevented a Trojan spy from returning to Hector with intelligence on the Greeks.[117] Dolon's death effectively stopped Hector's attempted night attack.[118]

The *Doloneia* illustrates that success in war is not always a matter of brute strength. It also takes stealth and intelligence to stage ambushes. Such spying tactics or ambushes are born of a situation where the enemy has not been or cannot be beaten in conventional battle.[119] The similarity between *Iliad* 10 and the *Odyssey* mentioned above is not the result having the same author or being composed at the same time but because they are both manifestations of the overarching theme of alternative warfare.[120]

If Hector had used a better man than Dolon (and had listened to Andromache), the outcome might have been different for the Trojans. Military intelligence gathering at night that is courageous, intelligent and favoured by the gods falls within the bounds of acceptable heroic behaviour. Neither night raids, nor espionage, nor ambush are despised in the *Iliad* nor are they considered cowardly. They involve great risk and require tremendous courage. The Greeks understood this. All else is modern commentary.

CHAPTER 3

Ambush in the Odyssey

THE MAIN PROTAGONISTS OF the *Iliad* and the *Odyssey* are often represented as two opposing archetypal warriors. Achilles is the quintessential daytime spearfighter in the *Iliad*, while Odysseus is portrayed in the *Odyssey* as the hero of the nighttime ambush.[1] This opposition is then carried over to strategy in warfare: the ambush is set up in opposition to heavy-infantry combat. Added to this polarisation is the value judgement that strength, force or power (*kratos* or *bie*) are the honourable characteristics of a warrior, while the ambush is just a variety of trickery and is demeaning to a Homeric hero.[2]

When proposing this ideology of Homeric warfare, scholars invariably quote the passage from *Odyssey* 9.408 where Polyphemus cries to his fellow Cyclopes: 'Nobody's killing me now by fraud and not by force!'[3] Polyphemus sets up the two contrasting possibilities: being killed by trickery or by strength.[4] It almost goes without saying that the situation Odysseus has got himself into in this episode requires trickery to overcome the strength of Polyphemus.[5] The Cyclops episode contains two other important features of ambush warfare, namely the use of disguise/concealment and the endurance of hardship over a long period of time, usually during the night. Odysseus will continued to display these characteristics throughout the poem.

The drastic polarisation of the use of force or trickery, Achilles vs. Odysseus, and spearfighting vs. ambush is completely artificial. Both modes of fighting are integral parts of Homeric battle tactics.[6] Scholars do us a disservice in suggesting that these categories are discreet or that they are embodied by one or another warrior. There are ambushes frequently attributed to Achilles, and Odysseus is portrayed as proud of his exploits as a spearfighter, so a single characterisation of them would never wholly suffice.[7] The contrast in fighting styles is not a constant feature of characterisation in Homer, and scholars have begun to see that the two concepts are actually complementary in many respects.[8] Norman Austin says this about Achilles and Odysseus:

> Differentiation is within a stock of traditional heroic virtues which are the common possession. All have the qualities necessary for a warrior, but an individual might show some superiority over his peers in one or another particular. Since it is precisely around these slender differences that the two poems have been constructed the effect is to render Achilles and Odysseus as polar opposites. Polar opposites they are, but only within the circumscribed confines of the Homeric aristocracy.[9]

The ambush and the spearfight are not essences of Odysseus and Achilles as ethical types, but rather they are a partial but concrete manifestation within a field of warfare of what is essential to each. The best description of Odysseus' ability to do both kinds of fighting comes in *Odyssey* 14.217–223 where he claims that Ares and Athena gave him 'courage and man-breaking power' but he is using it to choose comrades to set an ambush for his enemies.[10]

Ambush is certainly a more prominent theme in the *Odyssey* than it is in the *Iliad* because there are no set-piece battles in the story. The poem is organised around its central figure, Odysseus, who is presented as the master of the stratagem, of trickery in all its forms. His greatest fame, according to Quintus of Smyrna, is from the ambush that brought down Troy, and he consistently identifies himself with this strategy in the stories he constructs about himself.[11] Among his other traits, he has been compared to a spear-thrower, a hunter, an archer, a runner, a wrestler, a carpenter, a sail-maker, a lyre-stringer and a bard.[12] He is truly the 'man of many devices'. He often uses stratagems to defeat his enemies, but he can also display the ethos of a spearfighter. His strength and bravery can be used in either context.[13]

The Personality of Odysseus

The first reason that the fighting in the *Odyssey* differs from that in the *Iliad* is the character of its hero. Odysseus' personal traits are revealed in the stories he tells about himself. Posing in the *Odyssey* as a wanderer, he explains, above all, that he is an expert in night ambush.[14] He has all the physical and emotional characteristics suitable for the job. He is repeatedly singled out for his endurance, his capacity to last to the end, and his great daring.[15] Other useful characteristics are his patience and his ability to show restraint. Heroes such as Achilles are expected to show a willingness to overstep limits, i.e. to be shameless as well as unshameable in order to achieve their glory. On the other hand, Odysseus may be diverse and many sided, but he is never excessive. When he does overstep his boundaries and limits, he is successful because he does so by controlled calculation. Odysseus has internalised Athena's crafty quality. While someone such as Diomedes must be checked from without, Odysseus is self-regulated because of his ability to keep his eye on his goals.[16] We can see in this the characteristics of a man who can control himself in an ambush.

Odysseus seeks neither glory nor loot with uncontrolled abandon. He keeps his eye on the mission; what he wants to do is to finish the job. Odysseus captures personal equipment only once during a night ambush and that is in the *Doloneia*. He is thus distinguished from both the base and noble warriors in Book 10 of the *Iliad*. Dolon and Diomedes both want the valuable horses. When Odysseus stops to pick up Dolon's bloody spoils, however, his concern is at least partly connected with his intent to dedicate them and honour Athena.[17] Another military concern is not leaving a trail behind him to be discovered by any enemies who might follow him. Odysseus understands this better than Diomedes and Dolon. Although he is not averse to the idea of increasing his possessions, he is not acquisitive. Another characteristic he shares with ambushers is that he goes on foot. Odysseus does not battle from a chariot, nor is there any indication that Odysseus has horses. That is why the Thracian steeds he captures in the *Doloneia* are stabled with Diomedes.[18] He is no horse-tamer. When he finally triumphs at Troy, it is because the 'horse-taming' Trojans were unable to resist the temptation to take an enormous wooden horse within their walls. This is the only ambush in Homer which makes use of a horse.

Odysseus is the only warrior besides Menelaus who remembers the original purpose of the war. After the spying mission in *Iliad* 10, he claims no special credit for his success. His self-containment contrasts sharply with Achilles' continual need for visible and audible recognition of his excellence. Odysseus has qualities that set him apart from the spearfighters who crave public glory. It is interesting that in the *Odyssey* Menelaus is also portrayed as an ambusher. We see him inside the Trojan horse with Diomedes and Odysseus.[19] He is one of the leaders of the night mission Odysseus describes to Eumaeus[20] when he successfully ambushes Proteus.[21]

There is no question that Odysseus can be, at times, unethical. To realise the ends to which Odysseus would go to achieve his goals, one need only recall the story of how he tricked Palamedes, another crafty Greek hero of the Trojan war.[22]

The rivalry between Palamedes started at the time when Odysseus feigned insanity to avoid being 'drafted' into the army against Troy. It was Palamedes who revealed his malingering and Odysseus never forgave him. During the Trojan war, Odysseus compelled a Trojan prisoner to write a letter supposedly sent to Palamedes from the Trojan king, Priam, offering gold for information and action which would betray the Greeks.[23] He arranged for the letter to be dropped in the camp just after he had buried the exact amount of gold mentioned in the letter, under the tent of Palamedes. Odysseus claimed to have had a dream that warned him to have the Greek camp moved. He convinced Agamemnon to move the Achaean camp for one day. When the camp was moved, the Greeks found the gold where the tent of Palamedes had been. They took this as evidence of treachery and were furious. They ordered Palamedes to be stoned to death as a spy, in spite of his protestations of innocence.[24] This story of Palamedes is a study in the depths of deceit to which a man such as Odysseus might stoop. And what better way to destroy his rival than with a charge of espionage which, in the ancient world, was usually punished as a capital crime. So staging an ambush is the least of his moral qualms. Even Hermes, who has close ties with and is a helper to Odysseus in the poem, has a special affinity for ambush warfare.[25]

If Odysseus were really the polar opposite of Achilles in both his methods and his morals as portrayed in the *Iliad*, we would have to assume that the Greeks had lost all sense of morality by the time the *Odyssey* was composed. It is much more realistic to assume there had always been room for two kinds of activities in Greek warfare with different standards of behaviour. As we have seen in the first two chapters, ambush, espionage and intelligence gathering were known to Homer and are described many times in the *Iliad* along with direct combat. The same range of activities exists in the *Odyssey* where ambush is used as an effective means for the outnumbered, isolated hero to fight a just combat against scheming, unethical adversaries.

The Ambushes of the *Odyssey*

Ambushes can be found in the *Odyssey* in the same way they can be found in the *Iliad*. The noun *lochos* and the verb *lochao* appear twenty times in reference to eight individual ambushes. This compares with only nine occurrences in the *Iliad*.[26] We do not have to rely entirely on the appearance of the exact word 'ambush' (as a noun or verb) in the text in order to find an ambush in Homer. The ambush theme can be operative even if the word *lochos* is not explicitly used to describe it, and there are numerous examples of ambushes where the exact word is not used.[27] The *Doloneia* was one example in the *Iliad*, and many have suggested Book 22 of the *Odyssey* (the so-called *Mnesterophonia*) is another. Both books describe ambushes without exactly calling them such. There is a whole range of situations where this label can be used. When viewed in this way, the theme of the ambush takes a central role in the *Odyssey* where it is associated with its hero, Odysseus.

The most important ambush in the *Odyssey* is the use of the Trojan horse to cause the fall of Troy. In *Odyssey* 11.525ff. there is a reminiscence about the stratagem that (according to Quintus of Smyrna) made Odysseus famous. The Argives approach the Trojan horse where they will 'open and close the door of our stout-built ambush'.[28] No one criticises Odysseus or his morals here for the tricky manoeuvre that won the war for the Greeks. The *Odyssey* makes another reference to the fall of Troy in the part of the poem called Demodocus' first song (*Od.* 8.84–95) which tells of a quarrel between Achilles and Odysseus. Although scholarly opinion is sharply divided over the sources and implications of Demodocus' song, the explanation of the *Odyssey* scholia that the quarrel is over whether Troy will fall by force or trickery is generally accepted.[29] The contrast between Achilles and Odysseus in terms or force and trickery is cast in the form of an argument. The dispute over how Troy will fall appears as a dispute over modes of warfare, the spearfight or the ambush. In the end, however, the ambush won the war.[30]

The use of trickery rather than might also plays a role in the poem *The Little Iliad*.[31] A dispute arises between Odysseus and Ajax over who was the best of the Greeks after Achilles. The rivalry erupts into open conflict in the episode called the 'Hoplon crisis', a dispute over which of these two heroes will receive the armour of Achilles. The decision is ultimately entrusted to a Trojan prisoner of war who is asked whether Ajax or Odysseus has done his city greater harm. The Trojan chooses Odysseus, i.e. wisdom over force.[32] *The Little Iliad* includes several other ambush episodes: Odysseus ambushes Helenos; Diomedes and Odysseus steal the Palladion from Troy; and the wooden horse is built and filled with warriors who will ambush Troy. The whole poem seems to be a series of ambush themes connected to one another and culminating in the greatest ambush at Troy.

Similarly, much of the fighting in the *Odyssey* consists of ambushes and raids rather than set-piece battles. Odysseus' tales in the *Odyssey* often begin with attacks of this type. The sack of the 'sacred city of the Cicones', in Book 9, for example, is reminiscent of the 'sack of the sacred city of Troy'; only the glory is lacking.[33] There is no indication here, as in the *Iliad* catalogue, that the Cicones were Trojan allies, so the motive appears to be mere plunder. Later in the poem, the marauding suitors are compared to warriors attacking a city.[34] Interestingly, the first mention of Achilles in the *Odyssey* is in Nestor's recollection of a foray for booty.[35]

Fictional Ambushes

Odysseus is credited with three ambushes in the *Odyssey* that are presented in the poem as fictions, but they establish a firm link between the strategy of ambush and the character of Odysseus. Since Odysseus is the source of these tales, he is certainly conscious of them.[36] The most interesting of the three occurs in a lie he tells Athena when recounting the revenge he took on the son of Idomeneus:

> Ithaca ... yes, I seem to have heard of Ithaca,
> Even on Crete's broad island far across the sea,
> And now I've reached it myself, with all this loot,
> But I left behind an equal measure for my children.
> I'm a fugitive now, you see. I killed Idomeneus' son,
> Orsilochus, lightning on his legs, a man who beat
> All runners alive on that long island – what a racer!
> He tried to rob me of all the spoil I'd won at Troy,
> The plunder I sent to hell and back to capture, true,
> Cleaving my way through wars of men and waves at sea –
> And just because I refused to please his father,
> Serve under him at Troy. I led my own command.
> So now with a friend I lay in wait by the road,
> I killed him just loping in from the fields –
> With one quick stroke of my bronze spear
> In the dead of night, the heaven's pitch black ...
> No one could see us, spot me tearing out his life
> With a weapon honed for action. Once I'd cut him down
> I made for a ship and begged the Phoenician crew for mercy,
> Paying those decent hands a hearty share of plunder –
> Asked them to take me on and land me down in Pylos,
> There or lovely Elis, where Epeans rule in power.
> But a heavy gale wind blew them way off-course,
> Much against their will –
> They'd no desire to cheat me. Driven afar,

We reached this island here at the midnight hour,
Rowing for dear life, we made it into your harbour –
Not a thought of supper, much as we all craved food,
we dropped from the decks and lay down, just like that!
A welcome sleep came over my weary bones at once,
While the crew hoisted up my loot from the holds
And set it down on the sand near where I slept.
They re-embarked, now homeward bound for Sidon,
Their own noble city, leaving me here behind,
Homesick in my heart . . .[37]

Odysseus' enemy in this episode bears a significant name: Orsilochus 'the one who attacks the *ambush*'.[38] Another striking characteristic of Orsilochus is his epithet: 'the fleetest runner'.[39] Orsilochus is the fastest man in Crete, and the same is true of Achilles among his own people.[40] This epithet is used only for Achilles in Homer with the exception of this single instance. Here, at least, it suggests that Orsilochus is a hero of the same type as Achilles, a foremost man (*promos aner*) and a spearfighter. This passage has the same familiar theme: the lone hero has defeated many challengers and has overcome many attempts to kill him. An ambush is used as a last resort to exact revenge, and he is ambushed on his way home. Unlike the ambush of Tydeus in *Iliad* 4, or the ambush of Bellerophon in *Iliad* 6, Orsilochus is overcome by his assailant.[41] In this attack there is a reversal of the values normally assigned to ambusher and victim. In this story the sympathy lies with Odysseus (or at least his imaginary persona), not with the ambush victim. This illustrates my point that ambush is not bad in and of itself, but only in how it is used, who uses it or who is narrating the story.[42] In line with this, the parallel between this episode and the situation in which Odysseus actually finds himself at the time of the telling must not be missed. In this tale, Odysseus seeks revenge by means of an ambush against stronger opponents who unjustly deprive him of his property. Similarly in the latter part of the *Odyssey*, Odysseus confronts the challenge of overcoming the superior force of the suitors and regaining control of his possessions.

A second example of an ambush comes from an earlier tale told to Eumaeus in Book 14.[43] Odysseus describes how in his youth he excelled at warfare, and he emphasises his special expertise at the ambush. He associates himself once again with this tactic. As in the Orsilochus episode, the ambush is linked to the theme of powerful adversaries who deprive Odysseus of what is rightfully his.[44] Upon his return to Ithaca, Odysseus, posing as a stranger, tells Eumaeus, his former swineherd, about an ambush he led when the two of them were fighting together at Troy.[45] As the 'stranger' tells it, he made the mistake of leaving camp without his cloak. Later, when the weather turned cold, he would have frozen to death on that ambush had Odysseus not come up with a trick or stratagem: he sent Thoas back to the ships with a message, and when the latter threw off his woollen cloak, Odysseus passed it to his shivering friend. Within the framing narrative – Odysseus in disguise entertained by Eumaeus – this story of the old days at Troy wins Odysseus another cloak to protect him on this cold night. Thus Odysseus' tale of an ambush is itself a trap, a sort of verbal ambush, meant to test Eumaeus' character and the strength of his allegiance to his missing lord.[46]

The presentation of these ambushes set by Odysseus contrast sharply with the interpretation given this strategy in the Tydeus, Bellerophon or Diomedes episodes (see chapter 1). The fourth book of the *Odyssey* seems to be built on themes of ambush. There are the two stories about Odysseus involving ambushes, but the visit with Menelaus also includes the story of his ambush of Proteus,[47] from whom he learns of Aegisthus' ambush of Agamemnon. The book then ends with the suitors' plan to ambush Telemachus.[48]

The *Odyssey* develops the same positive view of the ambush evident in Idomeneus' speech, or on the shield of Achilles, where one is employed to defend a city from a besieging army.[49] Menelaus' ambush of Proteus is also represented in this same positive light.[50] Edwards, in his study of Achilles in the *Odyssey*, sees the contrast in the two poems' respective views of the ambush as a reflection of the contrast between Achilles and Odysseus as types within the epic tradition. He believes the difference between the two warriors reflects a profound difference in the ethical values of the poems.[51] According to Edwards, figures of strength/power are portrayed as villains in the *Odyssey*. He also believes the *Iliad* regards cunning and trickery as a last resort for those whose strength is unequal to open confrontation. As argued above, this polarisation should be questioned. Why should it only be used as a last resort? Ambush can certainly be the last resort of people who need a force multiplier, but it can also be used by people who need to achieve a military goal where force would be inappropriate and, in the end, less effective. We need not postulate an ethical difference. There are different types of military techniques appropriate at different times. Odysseus is a lone fighter placed in a situation where ambushes were appropriate. In the same way that Odysseus' strength is not hidden in the *Odyssey*, the wisdom of Nestor as a counsellor is certainly prized in the *Iliad*. Edwards feels that these qualities are marginalised in their positive aspect in the respective poems, but this can simply be a matter of focus; different qualities are being valued because the situation has changed. In the *Odyssey*'s ethical universe those who seek to prevail through force are posed as the disruptors of justice and the social order; those who resist and overcome them must rely upon their cunning to do so since they have no other means.

This positive attitude toward the ambush in Homer is evident also in two ambushes set by Heracles. Pindar recounts how he ambushes and slays the Moliones, the two brothers Eurytus and Cteatus, as they return home. He has had a struggle with their uncle, Augeas, who has refused to pay him for cleaning his stables.[52] Heracles was sent to steal the cattle of Geryon, a triple-bodied monster who ruled the island of Erytheia, and attacked him from an ambush as well.[53] Heracles' ambushes suggest other similarities between himself and Odysseus: the hardships imposed upon them by a divine antagonist, their wanderings or their enjoyment of physical pleasure – the feast, bath, sex. The use of the ambush by Heracles attests to its heroic quality.[54]

Other stories that show an ambush pattern include Demodocus' song, which tells of how Hephaestus ensnares Ares and Aphrodite. The tale of how Hephaestus overcame these gods exhibits the motifs and structure of an ambush as does Helen's account of Odysseus in disguise at Troy. The pattern is a close parallel to Odysseus' situation in the latter half of the poem.[55] The narrative resembles both Book 10 of the *Iliad* and Book 22 of the *Odyssey*.[56]

The Return as an Ambush

Edwards believes that the repeated association of this narrative pattern of ambush with Odysseus was very important within the *Odyssey*, but it was also a narrative feature of the epic tradition generally. The mode of engaging one's foe represented by these episodes clearly belongs to the stratagem of trickery and ambush. For an audience familiar with the conventions of epic poetry and Odysseus' association with the ambush, and who understood that ambush was an important aspect of warfare, Book 22 of the *Odyssey* would have been perceived as an ambush.

Book 22, in which Odysseus kills all the suitors, has been given the title *Mnesterophonia*, 'The Return'. Edwards argues convincingly that the entire *Mnesterophonia* is organised by a narrative pattern of the ambush.[57] Although the episode is narrated in Book 22, evidence for it being an ambush can already be seen in earlier books. The story of Agamemnon's return and death as it is presented in the *Odyssey* shows many correspondences to the return of Odysseus. Both return from their victories in Troy to a dangerous situation at home. In the *Odyssey*, ambushes are the special tactic of Aegisthus' twenty men who waited for Agamemnon to come back from the war in which they did not fight, and of the suitors – twenty of whom lie in wait for Telemachus day and night.[58] The suitors in Ithaca are paralleled by Aegisthus in Argos.

The ambush that the suitors set for Telemachus is mentioned no less than eight times in references scattered between Books 4 and 17. The suitors' plot against Telemachus is an attempt to prevent the power vacuum created by Odysseus' absence from being filled.[59] Leocritus predicts how the suitors would meet Odysseus should he return to reassert his lordship over his property. Foremost in his mind is that Odysseus would try to drive the suitors out of the house. Following the failed attempt to ambush Telemachus on his return from the Peloponnesus, Antinous fears that Telemachus will have the same intention when he returns from the countryside to his hall. Antinous argues that Telemachus will be able to turn the Ithacans against the suitors by revealing their attempt to murder him, and so succeed in driving them out. He suggests that they slay Telemachus before he can reach home, and divide his property among themselves.[60]

Following upon their first attempt at an ambush, Antinous proposes killing Telemachus in the fields or on his journey home, both locales associated with the ambush.[61] Thematically, the passage parallels the tale of the Pallantids' attempt to ambush Theseus when he arrives to assert his claim as heir to Aegeus. The inference that Antinous suggests an ambush here is supported by a later passage in which Telemachus refers to the possibility of the suitors secretly slaying him and dividing his property.[62] In view of the identity of Telemachus and Odysseus as lords of Odysseus' property, this episode ties in with the warning of Agamemnon, and the threat of Leocritus to strengthen the expectation that the suitors will try to ambush Odysseus if he returns.[63]

The ambushes set for Agamemnon and Telemachus serve as tokens of what Odysseus will confront when he at last reaches his home. The suitors will surely try to kill him, and the implication is that their strategy will be the ambush. The possibility of this ambush is acknowledged obliquely in a speech of Athena's. On the eve of his revenge, Odysseus confesses his fear about facing so many foes by himself. Athena rebukes him for having doubts, and boasts that, even if he were surrounded by fifty ambushes, with her help he would still emerge victorious.[64] Athena thus selects the theme of the ambush to reassure Odysseus.[65]

More recently, C. Dué and Mary Ebbott, in their book *Iliad 10 and the Poetics of Ambush*, have reinforced the idea that the theme of ambush overlaps with that of the journey and the winner of the ambush gets to return home. There are examples of this theme in both the *Iliad* and the *Odyssey*. Menelaus has to ambush Proteus in order to realise his homecoming. In the ambush of Tydeus by fifty Thebans he releases only one to return home,[66] and in the failed attempt to ambush Bellerophon the ambushers never return home.[67] In the last chapter we saw that certain scholars called the *Doloneia* 'Odyssean'. This is not because the word is late or non-Iliadic or even non-Homeric, but because it shares the same themes as the *Odyssey*, including both ambush, journeys, especially journeys home and those over a sea.[68]

The Value of Ambush

Very often ambushes are set by the villains who attack a lone figure with superior numbers, and thus the ambush is made out to be cowardly and an act of desperation. This is not, however, the only type of ambush that appears in the epics. By far, the largest group of ambushes in the *Odyssey* are those set by Odysseus himself. Not only does Odysseus set more ambushes than anyone else, but he also plans and carries through the one that tops them all. The foreshadowing of Odysseus' return, by means of the ambushes set for Agamemnon and Telemachus, sets the stage for a conflict of guile between Odysseus and his foes. For when it comes to ambushes, Odysseus is pre-eminent.[69]

The ambushes are indeed central to the theme of the *Odyssey*, but they are neither good nor bad, but rather useful. They can lead to glory or to doom, but that depends on the circumstances. The ambushes set for Agamemnon and Telemachus, for example, are posed as potential models for the course of Odysseus' return home (*nostos*). Through this paradigm, the *Odyssey* invests its hero with the ethos of the foremost men, such figures as Tydeus, Bellerophon and Diomedes, but also threatens him with the bad fate of Agamemnon. When it comes to ambushes, the *Odyssey* shows both possibilities. Odysseus can be both its perpetrator and its potential victim. In the grand finale of the poem, Odysseus anticipates the suitors' ambush with an ambush of his own.

Some have suggested that the *Iliad* and the *Odyssey* have separate perspectives on ambush, and that this reflects the essential differences between the *ethical systems* dominating the two poems.[70] On the contrary, the *Iliad* and the *Odyssey* agree upon the heroic quality of the ambush generally and upon its form and characteristic features as a narrative pattern. Yet each poem maintains its own perspective on this tactic. Whereas Edwards believes there was a sharp contrast between the ethical systems of the two poems, I suggest that tactics devolve from the situation and a hero may be either the perpetrator or the victim.

Ambush is central to the thematic development of the *Odyssey*. It serves as a structuring device, drawing together into an integrated whole such diverse characters, times and places as the return of Agamemnon and Menelaus, the journey of Telemachus, Odysseus' victory at Troy and the danger presented by the suitors at Ithaca. The effect of this series of ambushes is cumulative, exceeding the importance of any individual example.[71] An audience for whom the ambush was a familiar and important concept, and who was familiar with the narrative conventions of epic poetry, would have perceived the role of this theme in the poem.

The *Odyssey* does not conflict with the *Iliad*, but elaborates on it. Both poems can bestow glory for excellence in battle, but they can also value cunning and bravery in an ambush. The *Odyssey* shows the importance of giving hospitality to strangers (*xenia*), and combat for the purpose of revenge. Odysseus already has a claim to glory when he leaves Troy since, according to Quintus of Smyrna, he proposed the ultimate strategy of the wooden horse. His additional and final glory will be his revenge against the suitors who are trying to ambush him.[72]

Spying missions and ambushes take on the same overall structure of a journey. If spies, such as Dolon, do not return, they cannot share the critical information they have gathered. If warriors die in an ambush, they do not return home, their loved ones do not know where they are and they may not be able to recover the body for proper burial. The contrary is also true. Spies who are successful bring back the important intelligence, live to see their families again and are buried with appropriate honours. The failure of an ambush, even in very compressed versions of ambush narratives, is expressed in terms of a failed return home.[73]

The presentation of ambush in both the *Iliad* and the *Odyssey* relies upon a common tradition. Not only do the poems employ the same conventional form to narrate an ambush, but they both acknowledge as well its place in heroic warfare. Each poem presents a distinct perspective upon this stratagem, a perspective rooted in its priorities. The emphasis placed by the *Iliad* on the spearfighters winning a hero's death does not mean it necessarily portrays ambush as a stratagem of desperation, cowardice or deceit. Night attacks and ambushes simply come from a separate epic tradition, and not all the stories made it into the *Iliad*. In the

Odyssey, ambush is used to invest Odysseus with the heroic ethos of a Tydeus or a Bellerophon. The tradition recognises a very modern concept, that it is a stratagem by which the weak defend themselves against the injustice of a more powerful foe – in other words, intelligence is a force multiplier.

What we see here is not a diachronic development in which trickery is slowly introduced into the concept of warfare because morals have broken down, but the idea that both Homeric epics evince the existence of both qualities of a warrior: cunning and strength. This tradition continues throughout Greek history. In this sense, the *Iliad* and the *Odyssey* agree about the heroic quality of the ambush. As they are described in these two works, their form and characteristic features have the same narrative pattern. I suggest it is because there are two different types of fighting going on. One poem is about combat in war; the other is a travel narrative with no set-piece battles. This could just as easily be one of the reasons ambush serves as a theme of central importance in the *Odyssey* but not the *Iliad*.[74] Another is because Odysseus has been set up as the quintessential wily deceiver while Achilles is the quintessential spearfighter. And although the two characters seem like polar opposites in their methods, each has a role to play in Greek warfare. The ambush reveals how *metis* succeeds when the force used in a *polemos* does not.[75]

41

CHAPTER 4

The Archaic Age and the Problem of the Phalanx

WITH THE END OF the Bronze Age and the Homeric heroes came a dark age in Greece that lasted nearly half a millennium. Greek warfare was transformed when the community of the Dark Ages became the polis of the Classical city-state. By the eighth century warfare was in transition as the nobles of the *Iliad* disappeared and the common man began to emerge as a factor on the battlefield. The armies that defended the *poleis* of Classical Greece were markedly different from those described by Homer. Gone were the heroes who went to battle with their peers transported on chariots. With the birth of the polis, the warrior function expanded to all citizens capable of equipping themselves. When men from non-élite families became more important to the state economically as well as militarily, they asserted claims to an ever-increasing role in the political and military life of the polis over time. The enfranchisement of these individuals during the sixth and fifth centuries was the culmination and formalisation of a socio-economic, political and military process that had been taking place for nearly 300 years.[1] In other words, the development of a coherent community led to effective infantry tactics.[2] The arms in use then evolved to be more effective in the new style of fighting.[3]

These citizen-soldiers developed into an army of heavily armed foot-soldiers called hoplites who fought in closely packed, disciplined formations called phalanxes.[4] This is a rather unusual development in that 'no other society of primitive or peasant agriculturalists, as far as we know, ever saw the need to submit to any such thing'.[5] Many historians have made hoplites the central focus of Greek military history. These include especially those who adopt the approach of John Keegan, i.e. battle from the soldier's point of view. There are scholars who believe that hoplite battle represented the 'central and only truism in Greek warfare'.[6] As we shall see, however, there are many other types of Greek military experience.

Keegan opines that: 'Military history... must in the last resort be about battle.'[7] It does not, however, have to be about set-piece battles; military history may contain many other types of fighting. Since there is a great debate raging over when and how hoplites appeared, we cannot agree on exactly how the Greeks did or did not fight. What we should not do is discuss ambush as if it were only an exception to a hoplite 'rule'.

Rules of Conduct

It is a commonplace assertion that, before the large-scale use of peltasts, Greek warfare was limited to pitched battles, and these were more or less pre-arranged. Pierre Ducrey, among others, refers to the 'unwritten laws' that governed treaties, truces and the like.[8] H. Berve refers in a general way to 'Hoplitenpolitie' and notes that there were standards of warfare for conduct in inter-polis wars that were not observed in war against barbarians.[9] F. W. Walbank has a invaluable paragraph in which he notes that, although the concept of a code of conduct for war was one of importance from early times, the actual details are generally beyond our recovery, because of the incidental nature of the remarks.[10] More recently Hans van Wees has discussed the 'rituals, rules and strategies' of Greek warfare.[11] So how did the Greeks fight?

The distinguished military historian of the Persian wars, G. B. Grundy, wrote in 1911 that it seemed ironic that the Greeks could inhabit a country made up of mountains and broken terrain yet did not develop light infantry or have it play a greater part in Greek warfare.[12] A. W. Gomme also writes on the Greek failure to develop a mountain strategy in a country where almost every state had a mountain barrier defensible against hoplites.[13] These judgements would indeed be correct if they were only discussing the larger *poleis*, just fifth-century warfare, or only hoplites. With the total cultivable area of Greece at only twenty-two per cent of the whole, it would indeed be strange if a typical Greek army was composed of a type of force that could not possibly have been effective in four-fifths of the area of the country. When we look more closely at the evidence, however, and do not focus solely on the phalanx, we see that a good number of the Greeks fought in a manner totally compatible with their geographical surroundings. Unfortunately, these warriors have been ignored by ancient and modern historians alike. Much of this has to do with the social and political implications of the hoplite reform for light-armed warfare, which gave it a subordinate role in the fifth century.[14] The change to hoplite warfare brought on a corresponding change in attitudes towards bravery, and it reduced the importance of other combatants in the minds of historians both ancient and modern.[15]

When Did the Phalanx Appear?

The date of the appearance of true hoplites is still a hotly debated topic. Joachim Latacz introduced the idea that the phalanx was already in use in Homeric times and therefore the introduction of new armour did not 'revolutionise' warfare in any way in the Archaic Age.[16] He argues that massed formations engaged in the long-range exchange of missiles, and then joined the battle in mass hand-to-hand combat in close-order formation. This latter phase decided the outcome of each major engagement and this differed in no significant way from the warfare of the phalanx.[17]

Others have challenged this early emergence of the phalanx and have argued that the ideology of hoplite warfare as a ritualised contest developed only in the seventh century BCE. This view was popularised by Victor Davis Hanson in his *Western War of War*.[18] He believes that hoplite ideology dominated Archaic warfare as farmers agreed to decide disputes through pitched battles. After the creation of the hoplite panoply, for nearly two and a half centuries 'hoplite battle *was* Greek warfare.'[19]

Finally there is the group that sees the transition to the classic hoplite form of battle coming in the fifth century and stemming from victories over the Persians. This was accompanied by the idealisation of massed hand-to-hand combat by the historian of the war, Herodotus. For this group the ideology of hoplite warfare, as a ritualised contest, developed not in the seventh century but only after 480 when non-hoplite arms began to be excluded from the phalanx. Everett Wheeler, for example, argues that the infrequency of large wars between major *poleis* while the phalanx was developing on the mainland, and the apparent absence of major battles in the Archaic period, can discount the possibility that enough battles occurred to establish the kind of rules of conduct among forces that were necessary for hoplite battle. Most Greek city-states (except for the Spartans) had what he describes as essentially minutemen militias.[20]

Hoplite Phalanx or Mixed Contingents?

Another interpretation has emerged suggesting that the transition to the hoplite phalanx formation was a slow one, with mixed contingents being a common feature of Greek warfare.[21] Hans van Wees shows that, although heavily armoured infantry appeared in the seventh century, they continued to fight in a loose formation and to mingle in action with horsemen and light-armed troops.[22] He argues that the Archaic infantry in many ways was closer to Homer's heroic clashes than to the battles of the Classical period. Peter Krentz describes it as 'mass' fighting but not 'massed' fighting, i.e. they did not deploy in a tight formation massed together, but rather advanced and retreated and advanced again in a formation loose enough to allow horses, perhaps even chariots, to approach the killing zone and withdraw again. Brave men moved forward while tired men, frightened men or wounded men moved back. Evidence from vase paintings suggests that spearmen and bowmen stood side by side, and played a more prominent role than they would in later centuries.[23] The distinction between 'light-armed' and 'hoplite' was, quite simply, not always sharp. Stones, javelins and arrows flew, thrown and shot by some of the same men who then advanced to fight hand to hand.[24]

The first change came with the appearance of the bronze hoplite armour. According to van Wees, it was around 720–700 that a desire for greater protection in hand-to-hand fighting led to the introduction of the bronze panoply and the large, double-grip shield that created the hoplite. The shield was so heavy that it needed to rest on the bearer's left shoulder as well as his lower arm. Hoplites, therefore, adopted a sideways stance: left shoulder and shield turned towards the enemy, left foot forward, right foot placed well back for balance.[25] Van Wees cites poetic evidence for the stance of soldiers adapting to this new form of fighting.[26] Archaic poets speak of shields striking against one another with 'a terrible din' as the protruding lower rims of the shields clashed in accidental collisions and in deliberate shoving matches designed to expose an opponent or throw him off balance.[27]

According to this line of argument, the hoplite shield did not pre-suppose or dictate a dense formation, but could be used equally to good effect in open-order fighting.[28] For two generations after the introduction of the new shield, hoplites would have fought in a quite open formation because they continued to use their spears as missiles, which required a good deal of room for manoeuvre. Vase paintings show that a pair of spears continued to be standard hoplite equipment until at least 640. One or both of these weapons might be fitted with a throwing-loop – a string wound around the fingers so as to make the spear spin when thrown, giving it greater speed and force – which leaves no doubt that they were designed to be used as missiles.[29]

The next crucial step in the development of the hoplite phalanx came soon after 640 when, as countless images show, the majority of soldiers abandoned the use of throwing spears and fought exclusively hand to hand with a single thrusting spear and sword. The evidence comes from Tyrtaeus, the Greek elegiac poet who composed during Sparta's war of conquest in Messenia in the late seventh century BCE. For the first time, an explicit distinction was made by the poet between the light-armed and heavy-armed troops. Tyrtaeus encouraged the light-armed troops to use missiles, while he constantly appealed to the hoplites to fight the enemy face to face.[30]

By the late seventh century hoplites continued to fight in an order sufficiently open for light-armed men and mounted soldiers to mingle. The infantry was scattered here and there among the hoplites, 'squatting' for cover behind the latter's shields in the manner of archers as represented in Homer and Archaic art.[31] They did not have the separation of units one sees among the Persians where spearmen, archers and horsemen were in separate formations.[32] The Greeks continued to have heavy-infantry, light-armed and horsemen together in a motley crew.[33] In Athenian art, archers were an exceptionally popular subject which featured on some 750 surviving vases, most dating to between 525 and 500. These archers commonly stand, walk or run beside hoplites, and on about a hundred vases they take an active part in battle or ambush among heavy infantry. Sometimes hoplites fight over the body of a dead bowman.[34] Without maps, plans or precise pictorial evidence, it is difficult if not impossible to describe in detail how a battle in antiquity unfolded with hoplites, light-armed troops and even cavalry entering in turn, but there seems no doubt that light-armed troops participated.[35]

All we can say about the Archaic period is that the distinction between 'light-armed' and 'hoplite' was not always sharp. The mix of warriors and weapons continued until the fifth century when hoplites and light-armed troops were divided into separate units.[36] The strict separation of hoplites, light-armed and horsemen characteristic of the Classical phalanx, therefore, did not emerge until after the end of the Archaic period. Non-hoplite arms were excluded from the phalanx about the time of the Persian wars, when cavalry and light-armed troops started to fight in their own distinct units.[37] The experience of the Persian wars enabled the Greeks to see the physical and psychological power of a massed infantry charge, and from then on began to exclude non-hoplite forces from their phalanx. But they continued to appreciate the value of organised contingents of horsemen and archers. They soon established a larger cavalry force and started an archery contingent. This was used with some success at Plataea where an archer killed the Persian cavalry commander, Masistos.[38] By 431 they even had Persian-style mounted archers.[39]

True horsemen as opposed to mounted hoplites do not appear in Peloponnesian cities until the late fifth or early fourth century.[40] The Athenian contingent of infantry archers first appears at Plataea in 479.[41] Thucydides says that at the time of the Battle of Delium,[42] Athens had no organised light-armed troops. Little more than a dozen years later, Athens had its own light-armed men and did not have to rely on Thracians or allies.[43] At the Battle of Syracuse in 415, we see stone throwers, slingers and archers sent out as separate units, before the hoplite battle, to rout each other.

The impact of the Persian wars added two new ideological dimensions to hoplite claims of superiority: the notion that Greeks fought of their own free will, in obedience to the law, while barbarians only fought 'coerced by the whip', and the idea that a hoplite never gave ground but fought to the death, lunging with his spear until it broke, slashing with his sword until it snapped, then punching and biting until the end.[44] By the time Herodotus wrote Mardonius' speech about the Greek way of fighting, the hoplites had idealised their past into an 'archaic way of war' as a ritualised *agôn*, or contest.[45] As we have seen, however, the Archaic way of war was not a single head-on collision of hoplite phalanxes, excluding cavalry and projectile weapons. It was only in the mid-fifth-century that the Greeks had invented the *agôn*. It is in this context that we see the development of the massed phalanx and possibly the tactic of pushing *en masse* to punch through an enemy phalanx.[46]

Mixed Troops and Ambush

The traditional view, that early Greek battles were effectively won by a handful of outstanding aristocratic warriors and that in Classical Greece the only soldiers who mattered were hoplites, is simply the view from an élitist perspective. In reality, a much wider range of soldiers and social groups played an active role in defending the Greek city-states. There may have been a social dividing line between those who were obliged to serve (and enjoyed the political privileges that went with this status) and those whose services were voluntary and did not have full political rights. It is usually assumed that this dividing line coincided with the distinction between hoplites and light-armed, but in fact it cut across the body of hoplites.[47] We know very little about these social divisions because the historical accounts of the Classical period concentrated on the hoplites and ignored the light-armed. Although hoplites, cavalry, allied troops and mercenaries are often mentioned, the number of light-armed citizens is rarely specified, or sometimes their presence is ignored completely. It has been shown that hoplites were outnumbered by the light-armed whenever armies were mobilised by general levy.[48] General levies of the Spartan army, for example, included light-armed hoplites. At the Battle of Plataea these outnumbered the hoplites 7:1.[49] Although we are often told that light-armed troops participated in a battle, we are left in the dark about their exact part in the action because the narrator ignores them. In fact, most sources had an active dislike of light-armed infantry tactics and attitudes. Their hit-and-run charges, ambushes or quick fleeing on a battlefield was in direct opposition to the Classical hoplite ideal of standing one's ground in battle at any price.[50]

If each Greek city-state fought exclusively with hoplites in a phalanx then there would not be much use for the ambush. But, as we shall see in the following chapters, there is much evidence to suggest that the Greeks went right on ambushing each other throughout all periods of their history, and neither the Classical nor Archaic Ages are exceptions. There is more than enough evidence to show that the Classical Age is filled with examples of all kinds of deception.[51] The phalanx may have dominated the battlefield, but it was not the only form of fighting. Even hoplites themselves could be used for different types of fighting. The attention given to hoplite warfare is understandable, and for good reason. It was the dominant form of fighting in Greek armies and the type of fighting which brought most glory to the warrior. It was also the type of fighting that decided wars. The light-armed troops used in raids and ambushes did not decide major engagements. Therefore, when ancient historians gave detailed information about armed forces, they rarely acknowledged, let alone counted, the mass of ordinary light-armed citizens, ignoring the light-armed altogether along with the ambushes they may have performed.[52]

In spite of this blind spot about other troops caused by the admiration Greek historians had for the bravery of citizen hoplites, we can still glean enough information to say that great numbers of poor, light-armed citizens almost always fought alongside the heavy infantry and that cavalry, mercenaries, archers and other 'helpers' could have taken part in auxiliary operations.[53] The appearance of light-armed troops in the early Spartan army of Tyrtaeus' day shows that they had played the same role at least since the seventh century BCE.[54] In some cases their numbers were reduced for practical reasons. Far fewer light-armed troops went on overseas campaigns in the Archaic period, for example, when warships were small and commanders tried to fill them with as many hoplites as possible.

The Greeks had no squeamishness about slaughtering their enemies in any way possible, including during ambush and flight. In a fragmentary poem found on papyrus, Tyrtaeus imagines that Messenians 'will kill every Spartan that they catch fleeing the battle'.[55] In 510 the men of Croton routed the invading Sybarites and killed every single one they caught.[56] Fleeing from the Athenians after a defeat in 460, some Corinthians became trapped in a field surrounded by a ditch, with no exit. The Athenians blocked the front with hoplites, surrounded the Corinthians with light-armed troops, and stoned them to death.[57]

The Propaganda Factor

The reason there is so much debate over the nature and development of the hoplite phalanx is that only a handful of passages define our perceptions of Archaic and Classical battle. Besides the comments of Mardonius, the interpretation of the mechanics of a phalanx largely depend on Thucydides' account of Mantinea[58] and Polybius' well-known comparison of the phalanx and legion.[59] Polybius points out that the phalanx has only one time and one place in which it could perform its peculiar function.[60] If the enemy phalanx declined battle when one side offered it, the formation was quite useless. He goes on to explain that the Macedonian phalanx was not adapted to encounter unexpected attacks, unlike the Roman legion which could adapt itself to every place and time and could meet attack from every quarter.[61] Of course, Polybius had a subtlety concealed agenda of Roman propaganda behind his analysis – a comparison slanted to highlight Roman tactical superiority, which was aimed at discouraging further Greek resistance to Rome.[62] He also compares current Roman practices concerning deception with those of the Greeks: 'The ancients chose not to conquer their enemies by deception (*apaté*) regarding no success as brilliant or secure unless they crushed their adversaries' spirit in open battle . . . Therefore they declared wars and battles in advance, announcing when and where they were going to deploy. But now they say only a poor general does anything openly in war.'[63] Polybius condemns secrecy, surprise attacks and trickery in war, while upholding the Romans as paragons of virtue.[64]

We see the same attitude in Demosthenes when he wraps himself in a nostalgia about the 'Achilles ethos' and glorifies the 'good old days' when there was open warfare with citizen armies and conflicts were restricted to the spring and summer and without bribery.[65] His idealised vision of the past is in contrast to the revolutionising of warfare under Phillip II. They are both singing the same tune about 'the ancients' in contrast to the miserable present. Demosthenes' attitude comes from his series of outbursts against Philip and has no more historical validity that the supposed Archaic treaty banning missile weapons that belongs to the pan-Hellenic glorification of Archaic Greece as the golden age.[66] Ephorus, the fourth-century historian, is usually cited as the source for this pact, but, as Everett L. Wheeler has recently argued, the story was probably invented by Ephorus as part of a protest against the catapult, a frightening new distance weapon in his day.[67] Archaic battles included projectile weapons with light-armed men – javelin and stone throwers, slingers and archers fighting in the phalanx, not in separate units or behind the hoplites.[68] There was never a point when only hoplite fighters were used. Light-armed troops were able to fight in a more open formation than hoplites, with every man independent of his fellows. They existed throughout the Classical period. These light-armed troops could move rapidly from one threatened pass to another or stage an ambush.

Certainly fighting with hoplites caused the Greeks to be concerned about not merely the fact, but also the manner, of victory in battle. In Xenophon's *Cyropaedia*, a character urges an attack upon a small and vulnerable group of enemy soldiers. Cyrus says instead that it is better to wait for them all to assemble: 'If less than half of them are defeated, be sure they will say that we attacked a few because we feared the mass of them, and so they will not consider themselves defeated, and you will have to fight another battle.'[69] It is from this context of large battles that the Greek sense of 'fair play' in war may come, famously pointed out as characteristic of the Greeks by a Persian character in Herodotus.[70]

When Light-Armed, When Hoplite?

Some particularly poverty-stricken regions such as Aetolia had always used light-armed troops to stage ambushes, while larger *poleis* such as Athens had both hoplite forces and light-armed troops that are mentioned fighting side by side in a number of armed conflicts. At the Battle of Delium in Boeotia in 424, the Athenians found themselves with only hoplites and cavalry while their adversaries marshalled a force of 7,000 hoplites, 10,000 light-armed soldiers, 500 peltasts and 1,000 cavalrymen. The outcome is not surprising. The Athenians lost. Later in the Sicilian expedition, the Athenians imported peltasts from Thrace with the intention of transporting them by ship, together with other reinforcements. But the 1,300 mercenaries reached Athens too late and they were sent back to their homeland. They achieved an 'inglorious renown' through the carnage they inflicted on the little town of Mycalessus in Boeotia.[71]

References to light-armed troops become much more frequent in the course of the Peloponnesian war. The rules of engagement were changing. During an expedition to Aetolia, the Athenian general Demosthenes learned, to his cost, how effective these fighters and their type of combat could be against regular hoplites. The hoplites suffered constant harassment from projectiles and were unable to react with sufficient speed, for their opponents fled out of range as soon as they attempted to pursue them. It is true that, one year later, Demosthenes resorted to light-armed troops to overcome Spartan hoplites entrenched on the island of Sphacteria. The Spartans, too heavy and slow, were unable to catch up with their enemy over the undulating ground. They were also extremely vulnerable to the arrows, javelins and slingsmen's stones.[72]

While it is true that the Greeks of the Classical period deployed their hoplite troops on an open plain and did not sneak up on the enemy when attacking other hoplites, we actually have many examples of the Greeks attacking an enemy's camp or springing an ambush at night.[73] In spite of the image of the Spartans as the ultimate combat warriors, scholars have pointed out the irony of their having this image when they trained their warriors in stealth and deception.[74] On the one hand there is the idealised picture of their courage, valour and loyalty, often referred to as the 'Spartan mirage'.[75] On the other hand there is an image of them held by others who knew them, expressed by Pausanias,[76] that describes them as the most traitorous of the Greeks in war. It is true that they trained for battlefield combat but they also trained their soldiers in stealth, theft and other types of duplicity. Even the Spartans agreed that trickery could be heroic.[77] When a commander brought his hoplites out into a plain, he did so because he believed that his troops were a match for the enemy. Under these circumstances, there was no reason to try risky or deceptive manoeuvres. But we must also realise that a large hoplite battle was not always the venue of the action, and it was never the proper milieu for an ambush. The ambush is the preserve of lightly armed, mobile troops on broken terrain.

Ambush and Deception

Scholars have traditionally posited a period of decorous hoplite warfare, neatly contained in the Archaic period. Then, as the Peloponnesian war progressed, these conventions broke down and there suddenly appears, to everyone's horror, a gloves-off, no-holds-barred, realistic warfare. This change usually requires an explanation having to do with everyone's moral degeneration. But this is an artificial framework. Military trickery goes all the way back to the beginnings of Greek warfare.[78]

Big wars were never the whole story, not in the Archaic Age and not even in the great conflict between the Athenian Empire and the Peloponnesian League. Because of the prevalence of local conflict, the Peloponnesian war was not fought just by two 'blocks'. Hostility between neighbouring cities determined adherence to Sparta or Athens, in a quiltlike pattern.[79] Even within city-states themselves, a polis might just as easily be betrayed by a fifth column from within than an assault from without. Luis Losada writes: 'Developments in the use of light-armed troops and smaller fighting units, a natural result of the limitation of traditional hoplite battles, contributed to the tendency to attempt fifth-column captures.'[80] Indeed, the Athenian strategy during the Peloponnesian war was to avoid decisive land engagements and trust in their ships and walls. No battle of the traditional sort occurred until the eighth year of the war at Delium.[81] This is why light-armed troops, which were more manoeuvrable in smaller actions on different types of terrain, came into use to a greater degree than had previously been the case in Greek warfare.[82] Why would Greeks who would rather see their cities in the hands of a foreign enemy rather than in the hands of their domestic political enemies, have any moral qualms about sneaking up on their opponents?[83]

It is true that Greek city-states in the Classical period waged agonistic warfare against similar states, limiting it with agreed laws and conventions. At the same time Greek political rhetoric glorified the Archaic hoplite's love of honourable, pre-arranged pitched battles that were bloody but decisive.[84] But, as John Lendon correctly writes: 'Greek hoplite warfare existed in perennial tension between battle conducted according to understood rules and the crafty subversion of those rules.'[85] Classical warfare was full of deceptions and ambushes. Why the Greeks continued to apply the rules despite the fact that they were frequently broken, and despite the advantage that breaking them frequently yielded, has been discussed elsewhere, but one might ask whether the practical Greeks were simply choosing the tactics that were most appropriate for any given situation.[86] After all, the Greeks had to adapt to competition in the real world. My goal is limited to discussing the exceptions, and explaining why their tactics seemed appropriate at the time and whether or not they were successful. The examples are so numerous, I have divided them into three different categories: surprise attacks; night ambushes; and surprise attacks at sea. These will be the subject of the next three chapters. It seems a bit ironic, perhaps even surprising, that one can fill so many chapters with accounts on an activity that supposedly never happened in ancient Greek warfare.

CHAPTER 5

Surprise Attacks – Fifth Century

As illustrated in the last chapter, the Greeks of the Classical Age chose to fight in hoplite formations, which followed very specific rules of conduct when fighting. Scholars would agree that hoplite tactics were not based on surprise or speed.[1] Yet, although surprise attacks and ambushes were not tactics appropriate to the phalanx or the heavily armed soldier, there are dozens of examples in the Classical Age where operations were conducted at night or at dawn for the sole purpose of surprising the enemy. The statement that 'there is very seldom any attempt to take advantages or effect surprises' can only be true if it refers to attacking an enemy's phalanx before it was properly drawn up.[2] Surprise attack and ambush were certainly used in the Classical Age, and there is enough evidence to suggest that, when executed well, these were effective techniques, albeit difficult to stage. Surprise attack was a tactical possibility when the proper type of troops were available, and the right circumstances presented themselves.

While modern commentators insist that only infrequently do we find surprise attacks on Greek hoplite armies or their camps, nevertheless we see that a daring commander such as Pisistratus attacked an enemy during an afternoon siesta in 546,[3] and the Spartan king, Cleomenes, attacked an Argive camp during breakfast in 494.[4] The same Greeks who had no fear of fair fights were very afraid, according to Herodotus, of being 'worsted by guile' and often attacked first to avoid being unpleasantly surprised.[5] Even though the etiquette of Classical Greek hoplite warfare remained fixed, the ruse of attacking an army while it was off-guard never went out of style. Examples of surprise attack begin in the Archaic Age and continue non-stop into the next centuries.

When the Greeks told stories about their distant past, they always included clever ambushes: for example, Polyaenus reports an event concerning the Messenians in the eighth century that is a classic deception operation. The Spartans had been at war with the Messenians for twenty years, when the two kings, Polydorus and Theopompus, pretended to have a disagreement. A deserter was sent to leak the information that the kings were quarrelling and would separate their forces. The Messenians watched closely. Theopompus moved a little distance away with his army. When they saw his departure, the Messenians assumed Polydorus was by himself and advanced on him from the city with all their forces. When the scouts gave the signal, Theopompus came around unseen, captured the deserted city and attacked the Messenians from the rear, while Polydorus' men attacked from the front. Surrounded, the Messenians were defeated.[6] While the story comes from a much later date, and Polyaenus can be notoriously unreliable as a source, there is no reason why this operation could not have been staged in the eighth century. The Greeks loved to attribute clever stratagems to their ancestors, and seemed to have no moral qualms about using such techniques or attributing them to an earlier age where they might sully the supposed pristine reputation of their ancestors.

Surprise was a good principle in theory, but in practice it was hard to achieve.[7] Clausewitz himself warns that it would be a mistake to regard surprise as a key element of success in war. Surprise attack is not a magic bullet that works every time or in every situation. It must be used selectively. Two of the most common times to stage an ambush were at night or at dawn. For a night attack to succeed, for example, it is necessary to have a good knowledge of the layout of the defence as well as the enemy's dispositions during battle since the enemy knows the ground he occupies better than the attacker.[8] While night attacks can be especially effective against small forces, a larger force has enough resources to keep fighting until help arrives.[9] In planning a night attack, the projected cost can be tightly calculated, but the benefit is always a matter of speculation until the ambush is executed.[10] Clausewitz recommends that night operations stop at daybreak to enable the attacker to profit from the enemy's confusion.[11] Whatever the obvious difficulties, ambushes at night and dawn continued to occur throughout Greek history.

Thucydides, for example, uses the adverb *exapinaios* (all of a sudden, by surprise) to describe how during the winter of 429/8 the Thebans had entered the city of Plataea at night and both surprised and frightened the Plataeans who had posted no guards.[12] The fright was caused by the invasion being done by night when the Plataeans could not see, and also because they thought a far greater number had entered the city. Their fear caused the Plataeans to put up no fight and ask for terms. During the negotiations, they discovered how few Thebans there actually were, and only then did they counterattack. Their operation, too, was set up at night. The Plataeans dug through the common walls of their own houses and joined each other without being seen. They attacked while it was still night to create a panic among the enemy troops.[13] They also had the advantage of knowing the city better that the Thebans who were ignorant of the right way out. The only effective way out was the gate through which they had entered, and the Plataeans had that blocked. Even the women contributed to the effort as they pelted down roof tiles on the heads of the Thebans trying to escape.[14] However, it was also a Plataean woman who gave an axe to the Thebans so they could chop open the city gates and escape.[15]

One of the most famous events, and indeed a turning point of the Peloponnesian war, was an Athenian surprise attack in 425 on a hemmed-in force of Spartan hoplites on the island of Sphacteria (see map 2).[16] About 420 hoplites and an equal number of retainers occupied this cigar-shaped island. The Athenians had them blockaded, but they knew they could not maintain the blockade through the winter when the trapped men could escape. Each day of the truce allowed food to be smuggled to the Spartans on the island, and this meant they could hold out a little longer.[17] The Athenians did not want to lose this bargaining chip and were searching for a way to overcome the Spartans. Cleon saw this danger and committed an Athenian force to capturing the Spartans on Sphacteria.[18]

The Athenians were dubious about landing on an uninhabited island with pathless woods that would favour the enemy.[19] Even if they landed with larger force, they would suffer losses by being attacked from unseen positions (i.e. ambushed) because the Spartans knew the terrain better. Demosthenes is given the command[20] and the Athenians attempt a landing on both sides of the island (see map 2). They found themselves on the island in cramped conditions, which were then exacerbated by an accidental forest fire started by Athenian soldiers trying to cook a meal.[21] It was only after the woods were burned off that the Athenian commander, Demosthenes, could see how many Spartans they were up against.[22] He discerned that most of the enemy troops were concentrated near the centre of the island, guarding the water supply.[23] There was another force near the northern tip of the island opposite Pylos, meaning there were only thirty hoplites guarding the point of landing at the southern end.[24] The men in the Spartan outpost are described by Thucydides as being 'still in their beds and trying to snatch up their arms'.[25]

Cleon brought reinforcements,[26] in a second Athenian landing and they assaulted the island at dawn from two sides (see map 2).[27] According to Thucydides the Athenians landed 800 hoplites, 800 archers, 2,000 light-armed troops, Messenian reinforcements and 8,000 sailors from seventy ships hastily armed for the occasion.[28] Several thousand troops against 420 Spartan hoplites may seem like overkill, but the Athenians did not know what to expect. Demosthenes did not just rely on his overwhelming numbers. He divided his troops into companies of 200, which seized all the high places on the island so that whenever the Spartans fought they would find an enemy to the rear of their flanks.

First they attacked the small Spartan force at the southern end of the island, catching them while they were still in bed and swiftly wiped them out.[29] The main body of troops under Epitadas, seeing the southern outpost cut off, tried to close with the Athenian hoplites. The light-armed troops that they were up against, however, gave the Athenians advantage because, even when the Spartans lined up to fight the Athenian hoplites, the light-armed would attack them from the side and rear. If the Spartans in heavy armour fled, the light-armed pursued them; if they turned to fight them, the light-armed could fight at a distance with arrows, javelins, slings and stones.[30] The Spartans hoplites were not equipped for this type of fighting, although their helots may have been. Even Thucydides writes that the Spartans were 'not used to this kind of fighting' and they were thrown into disarray by the shouting and the dust clouds being caused by the melée and smoke from smouldering fires.[31] Deprived of visibility and with no means of fighting back, the Spartan hoplites retreated to the fort at the end of the island and hid behind a fortification to resist further attacks.[32] They held out for the rest of the day.[33]

This situation was still at a stand-off when the Messenian commander, Comon, came to Cleon and Demosthenes and said that, if they were willing to give him a portion of their bowmen and light-armed troops, he could find a path around the precipitous shore of the island and take the enemy by surprise in the rear.[34] He wanted these types of soldiers because they were more suited to a surprise attack on uneven terrain. With the light-armed troops, he picked his way as best he could along the steep cliffs of the island, and going by a route that the Spartans had left unguarded he managed to get behind them without being observed.[35] The Spartans, having relied on the nature of the terrain to protect them, now found themselves surrounded much in the way they had at Thermopylae, when a Persian had found a path behind them.[36] The Messenians suddenly appeared on high ground in their rear, striking panic into the Spartans – certainly no easy task. The Spartans had not wanted to waste troops guarding such an unlikely approach, so they were truly stunned by the appearance of Comon's men. The Spartans had been trained for face-to-face hoplite battle. They were unable to engage with their hoplites or reap the advantages of their own specialised training. They were held up instead by weapons shot at them from both flanks by light troops – a situation that had been set up by a night landing and a surprise attack.

Cleon and Demosthenes did not let their troops kill the Spartans, but rather took them alive as a bargaining chip.[37] A proclamation was made asking the Spartans to surrender[38] and the Spartans accepted.[39] This was a tremendous victory for the Athenians because 120 Spartan hoplites had been captured alive.[40] According to Thucydides it was the most unexpected event in the war.[41]

Sphacteria brought ambush to the attention of the hoplite world and, according to some, changed the nature of the war. The feat had been accomplished by good intelligence gathering, surprise tactics and it ended the stalemate in favour of the Athenians.[42] The Spartans complained about the manner of fighting being 'unworthy of a hoplite'. In reality, there was no way the Spartan hoplites could have 'won' in such a desperate situation, but this did not stop even their own side from suggesting that the Spartans at Sphacteria were no match for their own ancestors.[43] They should be given credit for fighting so well against a force of such great size. Modern commentators have joined in on the complaint against the Athenian tactics.[44] Stahl writes about the new tactics (*neue Taktik*) but sneers about 'der nicht gerade ehrenvolle Kampfesweise, deren die attische Seite sich bedient' ('the not entirely honourable tactics that the Attic side employed').[45] Contemptuous remarks such as these show how great the prejudice against anything that is not hoplite fighting can be. As Mao Tse Tung writes: 'Those who condemn these methods as being a combination of banditry and anarchism have not understood the essence of guerrilla warfare.' The efficiency of the operation and the success it brought the Athenians was its own justification. It effectively put a stop to further Peloponnesian invasions of Attica. Donald Kagan believes the outcome 'shook the Greek world'.[46]

The Athenian general Demosthenes had scored a victory because of his use of light-armed troops that were suited to pulling off this kind of attack.[47] He, perhaps, should have used the same tactics in 426 when the Messenians in Naupactus persuaded him to invade the territory of the Aetolians[48] (see map 3). It was assumed that the Aetolians were lightly armed and that this would ensure an Athenian victory. Things turned out differently. Rather than wait for Locrian reinforcements, who were trained in light-armed warfare, Demosthenes decided to penetrate deep into enemy territory with hoplites and stormed Aegitium. When the Aetolians took the offensive it became clear why this was a mistake. The light-armed enemy could move swiftly, attack and retreat. The hoplites were useless and found themselves driven into a forest that was set on fire. A combination of bad planning, poor intelligence and overambition led to disaster. Demosthenes has been criticised for being 'too fascinated' with the idea of surprise and, as we have argued, its use does not always guarantee success. For all his tactical wiles, he clearly had not absorbed the light-infantry lessons from the Battle of Spartolus in 429. Demosthenes escaped from this debacle, and he would go on to introduce ambush tactics again in the ensuing conflict.[49]

It was a much more prepared Demosthenes that Thucydides describes in his report on the Battle of Olpae in 426/5, where the general took advantage of the terrain to stage an ambush that acted as a force multiplier (see map 6). The Peloponnesian forces were larger than Demosthenes' Athenians. For this reason, Demosthenes laid an ambush of 400 hoplites and light-armed men in an overgrown hollow. When the enemy, exploiting their superiority, made their flanking movement, the soldiers in ambush emerged from behind them. They won the battle without much trouble. The surprise attack from ambush brought victory to the numerically weaker party.[50]

Many commentators have suggested that it was Demosthenes who introduced ambush as a tactic into Greek warfare at Olpae, but, as I have already argued, the technique had been around for a long time, just not used by hoplites.[51] Demosthenes was probably adopting Acarnanian tactics and advice at Olpae, since they had been successfully ambushing their enemies for centuries.[52] Plus, the Acarnanians knew the local terrain and were most likely to be able to find a site capable of hiding 400 men. The local intelligence provided by the allies, and their previous use of ambush, made the Acarnanians indispensable.

In 429 the Ambraciots invaded Acarnania (see map 6) together with allies and Peloponnesian troops. One of the invading forces, the Chaeonians, rushed forward to capture the city of Stratus. The Acarnanians of Stratus set an ambush for them around the city, and in a concerted attack charged the enemy from different directions. The result was similar to that at Olpae. The enemy was caught by surprise and retreated.[53]

After Olpae came a battle at Idomene in 426/25 (see map 6), which involved both a night attack and an ambush. When Demosthenes heard that the Ambraciots with all their troops were advancing his way, he decided to try an ambush again. Having successfully staged one and seen how effective it could be, and remembering

59

his disastrous experience with the Aetolians, he did not want to leave anything to chance. He sent part of his stronger troops ahead to hide in ambushes along the roads and to occupy certain strategic positions.[54] He then divided the rest of his forces, taking half by night towards Idomene, where the Ambraciots had encamped. The Ambraciots, suspecting nothing, had their camp on the smallest hill of Idomene while the largest hill was occupied by Demosthenes' men. He probably used Amphilocian troops, and indeed their light-armed javelin throwers would play a decisive part in the final stages of the battle.[55] That night he attacked the unsuspecting Ambraciots in their sleep after deceiving the guards by having Messenians address them in their own language. Those who managed to escape the ensuing massacre fled into the mountains. There, the heavily-armed Ambraciots were met by the Amphilochians' javelin throwers, who chased them to their death. Panic-stricken, some of the soldiers fled to the sea nearby, preferring to face the crews of the Athenian ships rather than be massacred by the hated Amphilochians. Only a few survived.[56] Idomene was Demosthenes' greatest triumph, and it was another success based on surprise and ambush.[57]

The contrasting outcomes of the Aetolian and Acarnanian campaigns can be explained by the intelligence collected on each. In Aetolia, Demosthenes relied on sources that were foreign to the country he invaded and was ignorant of the enemy's movements and the local terrain. In Acarnania and Amphilochia local allies provided better-quality intelligence, making the surprise attack possible. Many commentators consider Demosthenes ahead of his time in the use of light-armed troops, intelligence collecting and ambush tactics. What he was doing, rather, was incorporating tactics already known to other Greeks, but now used successfully by the Athenians and their allies in this campaign.[58]

Brasidas

Not only the Athenians used surprise and ambush. It has been suggested that Demosthenes influenced his contemporaries in their strategies. The Spartan Brasidas, like any good commander, Greek or not, was an opportunist. He preferred to take his enemies by surprise rather than to attack them when they were in a position of strength. The Battle of Amphipolis in 422, for which both Brasidas and Cleon recruited peltasts, provides an excellent opportunity to test this theory (see map 4). The importance of this battle lies in the fact that both opponents had been closely involved in the events at Pylos and had witnessed the success that Demosthenes had had with his light-armed troops.[59] If the Athenians could recapture Amphipolis, Brasidas' campaign in Thrace would lose most of its effect. He also believed Amphipolis had 'an embarrassment of potential traitors' to help the Spartans get through the gates.[60] Even with a strong edge in both light foot troops and cavalry, however, Brasidas relied on surprise.[61]

As soon as Brasidas saw the Athenians advancing, he withdrew his troops from the hill to the city of Amphipolis. He did not consider marching against the enemy with his entire army to fight a pitched battle, since he feared that the Athenians with their hoplites would win against his peltasts and cavalry. Instead, he decided to launch a surprise attack on the Athenians and fight a battle before the Athenian reinforcements arrived. He selected 150 hoplites and put the rest under the command of Clearidas. Brasidas wanted to charge with his men against the core of the unsuspecting Athenian forces that were stationed in front of Amphipolis. After that, all of Clearidas' troops would sally forth from another gate, and rush into the midst of the confused Athenians. This second, 'surprise' attack was meant to frighten the unsuspecting Athenians. The horsemen and peltasts, who could not be used to full advantage in a pitched battle, could undertake actions for which they were more eminently suited.[62]

The Athenians drew up in battle order on the road facing the city where they could watch for activity within the city and be ready to repel attackers. But when the scouts reported to Cleon that an enemy attack through the Thracian gates seemed imminent he decided on an immediate withdrawal to Eion (see map 4). He made the fatal mistake, however, of giving the orders simultaneously by trumpet signal and by verbal messages.[63] Some men moved on hearing the trumpet, while others stood waiting. This threw the whole line into confusion. The lack of cohesion exposed the entire Athenian army to attack on their unshielded right. As they moved past the southernmost gate, Brasidas sprang his trap.

The southern gate swung open and Brasidas himself rushed out at the head of 150 picked men. He charged at the double downhill to the road, probably only a few hundred yards. The Athenians would have had barely a minute to prepare before the enemy group struck the centre of the column like a projectile. Simultaneously, the rest of the Spartan army under Clearidas poured through the northern gate and attacked the Athenian right wing, throwing the whole line into confusion. The leading left wing bolted down the road towards Eion. The right wing put up more resistance, some of them rallying higher up on the hill, but they were finally surrounded and massacred by the Chalcidian cavalry and peltasts. Others got away over the mountains and, if not mopped up later, made their way to Eion. In all, the Athenians lost 600 hoplites, about one-seventh of their total strength. This would have been a total Spartan success except that Brasidas was fatally wounded early in the conflict; Cleon, too, was killed.[64] This is the only occasion where Brasidas was supreme commander in a major battle, and it was probably his greatest victory – a well-planned and well-executed surprise attack. Unfortunately, by staging a surprise attack and leading it himself, he had to bear the brunt of the fighting. Scholars have wondered whether he might have trapped even more Athenians, and incidentally saved his own life, if he had split his forces more evenly instead of handing over practically the whole army to his junior colleague and placing himself at the head of a small suicide group, but that consideration aside the surprise operation was a success.[65]

Demosthenes continued to fight the war, and he attached a great deal of importance to mobile troops. He recruited no less than 1,300 peltast mercenaries from the Thracian tribe of the Dii for the auxiliary expedition to Sicily in 413.[66] We see their use in a night attack in Thucydides[67] during the siege of Syracuse when Demosthenes decided on a surprise attack against Epipolae,[68] the ancient fortified plateau west of Syracuse (see chapter 6).

Dawn Attacks

A common way of achieving surprise was to attack at dawn while the enemy was asleep or at least unprepared. There are at least seventeen cases of dawn attack used in the fifth and early fourth centuries. There were seven cases of dawn attacks that involved naval assaults or descents on the coast, and six assaults on towns, forts or heavily fortified positions such as the wall at the Isthmus of Corinth in 369.[69] Xenophon offers the best rationale for dawn attacks on a fortified position: attacking just when the night watches are finishing and the rest of the men are either rising to go about their tasks or still sleeping. You can attack while in good order whereas your opponents are unprepared and in disorder.[70]

One classic example of this has already been discussed – the Athenian disembarkment on Sphacteria (see map 2).[71] The Athenians attacked the first guard post and killed all the hoplites in their sleep or while they were trying to arm themselves. There are many such examples already given by Herodotus dating back to the Persian wars.

Sailing at sea at night with a plan to attack at dawn was a common ploy. This stratagem was used already in 480 at Salamis.[72] At Sybota in 432 the Corinthians, taking provisions for three days, put off by night from Chimerium (see map 3) with the intention of engaging the enemy. At daybreak they came in sight of the Corcyraean ships already in the open sea and bearing down upon them. As soon as they saw each other, both sides took up their positions for battle. Evidently, neither side got the jump on the other.[73]

A dawn attack is related by Polyaenus in the story of an ambush set up by Nicias against the Corinthians at Solygeia in the summer of 425. The Athenians made an expedition into Corinthian territory with eighty ships and 2,000 Athenian hoplites, together with 200 cavalry on board horse transports; allied forces also went with them. The Corinthians had had previous intelligence from Argos that the Athenian expeditionary force was coming towards them, and they had accordingly occupied the isthmus with all their forces, except for those who dwelt north of the isthmus and the 500 Corinthians who were away doing garrison duty in Ambracia and Leucadia. All the rest were in full force, watching to see where the Athenians would land. The Athenian force set sail at night and put in to land between Chersonese and Rheitus at the beach in the country overlooked by the hill on which Solygeia sits (see maps 8 and 10). After landing 1,000 hoplites and stationing them in an ambush in various places, Nicias sailed away. At daybreak he sailed against Corinth again, this time openly. The Corinthians charged out quickly, intending to prevent him from disembarking. The men in ambush rose and killed most of them.[74]

In Sicily

The Sicilian expedition of 415–413 created many opportunities for surprise attack. There was no hope of taking the city of Syracuse by surprise, and it would have been difficult for the Athenians to land at Syracuse at all. So the Athenians, instead, tricked the Syracusans into leaving their city. They sent a man from Catana who was known well to the Syracusan generals. He told them that, on a date of their choice, his friends in Catana would shut the gates on the Athenians in the city and set fire to the Athenian ships. The Syracusans could then capture the Athenian camp by assault. The Syracusans took the bait and set out for Catana in full force, and camped for the night by the River Symaethus, in the territory of Leontini (see map 7). As soon as the Athenians learned of their approach, they took their entire force, including any Sicels and others who had joined them, put them all aboard their ships and boats, and sailed by night to Syracuse. At dawn, the Athenians landed opposite the Olympeium and fortified their camp unimpeded. The Syracusan cavalry, having ridden all the way to Catana and found that the

Athenian expedition had already put to sea, turned back and reported the news to the infantry. They were all forced to return to Syracuse to defend their city. In the time it took the Syracusans to march home, the Athenians had plenty of time to set up their forces in an excellent position where the Syracusan cavalry could do little damage to them.[75] This incident became famous and was picked up by many ancient historians including Plutarch, who declared it to be the best generalship Nicias showed in Sicily.[76] It certainly does not fit the agonistic model of Greek warfare. The Syracusans preferred a surprise attack, and the Athenians wanted to fight where obstacles protected their wings. Both sides wanted to gain what advantage they could.[77]

In the summer of 414, the second Syracusan counter wall was captured by the Athenians (see map 5). The Syracusans had built a stockade out from the city and through the marsh with a ditch alongside it, so as to make it impossible for the Athenians to carry their wall down to the sea. The Athenians, once they had finished their fortifications on the cliff, attacked the stockade and ditch. They then ordered the fleet to sail around from Thapsus into the Great Harbour of Syracuse and, at dawn, the army came down from Epipolae into the plain and made their way over the marsh by laying down doors and planks over the parts where the mud was thickest and the ground firmest. By daybreak, they had captured the ditch and the whole of the stockade except for a small section, which they captured later. The Athenians had won this confused battle, but their general Lamachus was killed.[78]

For the last decade of the Peloponnesian war we lose Thucydides, whose history stops in 411. Fortunately we have Xenophon whose work, *Hellenica*, is a continuation of Thucydides' history.[79] He reports a dawn attack that took place in the Hellespont in the winter of 411. Shortly after the Spartans had defeated the Athenians in a sea battle, Dorieus, son of Diagoras, sailed from Rhodes into the Hellespont at dawn with a Spartan flotilla of fourteen ships. They were spotted by the Athenian lookout on shore, who informed the generals of their presence. The generals then sailed out against Doreius with twenty ships, but he escaped from them. As he got away he attempted to beach his triremes in the area around Rhoeteum (see map 1). When the Athenians approached, they fought from both the ships and the land. When the Athenians realised they were accomplishing nothing, they sailed away to Madytus to join the rest of their forces.[80]

Sometimes the opportunity for a surprise attack arose spontaneously. In 406 Lysander's term as Spartan *nauarchos* (naval commander) came to an end, and he was replaced by Callicratidas. The new *nauarchos* learned that his relief fleet was already at Samos. He left fifty of his ships at Mytilene with Eteonikos as commander and sailed to meet the relief fleet with 120 ships. The Spartans stopped for their meal at Cape Malea on Lesbos on the same day the Athenians just happened to be taking their meal on the Arginousae islands. These sites were opposite one another – Cape Malea on Lesbos, across from Mytilene. Callicratidas saw the Athenian fires at night and tried to put to sea in the middle of the night with the intent of staging a surprise attack. However, heavy rain and lightning prevented the attempt. When the rain let up, he sailed again at dawn to the Arginousae islands. The battle eventually took place in better weather, but Callicratidas was killed when his ship rammed another and he fell overboard. The Spartans were defeated and the Athenians sailed back to the Arginousae islands.[81]

The Sicilian Greek cities that became tributary to Carthage after 405 are the context for a story related by Polyaenus at Acragas in 406. Himilco, the Carthaginian general, encamped near the wall at Agrigentum (see map 7). A large force advanced from the city. Himilco divided his army and attacked with one part, giving secret orders to flee voluntarily. They fled, and the Agrigentans who chased them were drawn far away from the city. Himilco set fire to wood in front of the wall and hid the rest of his men in an ambush. When the pursuers saw the smoke rising from the walls they thought the enemy was burning their city, so they turned around and retired to the city with those who were earlier fleeing from them, now attacking them from the rear. When they reached the ambush, Himilco's men rose up, killed some of them and captured others.[82]

Book 4 of Xenophon's *Hellenica* chronicles the campaigns of the Spartan king Agesilaus in Asia Minor in 395 and provides us with another attack on a camp. Based on intelligence supplied by Spithradates about the location of Pharnabazus' camp, Heridippas attacked the camp at dawn with cavalry and infantry, killing many Mysians who were Pharnabazus' advance guard. Pharnabazus and his men escaped, but the camp was captured along with many drinking cups and other possessions of the sort that Pharnabazus could be expected to have, as well as much baggage and many pack animals.[83]

The Fourth Century

The same kinds of tactics can be observed in the wars of the fourth century: the Corinthian war, the Theban war (378–372) and beyond. The Spartans showed their skill at deception in a daring, nighttime, amphibious raid aimed at Athen's harbour-fortress of Piraeus (see map 10). In 387, Teleutias, brother on the Spartan king Agesilaus II, decided to raid the harbour at Piraeus at dawn. When he was five or six stades* from the harbour he stopped and had his men rest, and when day dawned he led them on, and they followed. He commanded his men not to sink or incapacitate any merchant vessel with their own ships when the encounter came, but if they saw any trireme at anchor they were to try to damage it and render it unseaworthy. In addition, they were to tow any loaded merchant ships out of the harbour and to board the larger vessels whenever they could and capture the men on board. Some of his troops went so far as to leap on to the Deigma, an area in the middle of the quayside in the commercial quarter of the Piraeus where merchants displayed their wares. They captured some merchants and shipowners and carried them away.[84]

Even a Theban general such as Epaminondas, famous for his tactics in the open field, found night movements useful. When he wanted to invade Sparta, but knew the Spartan garrison held Oneium, he declared that he intended to take the army past at night. He slept at the foot of the mountain. The guards of the pass were worn out from staying awake the entire night under arms. When dawn began to appear, the Thebans launched a dawn attack on the Spartan camp and routed them from their position.

We actually have three different accounts of the incident. In Polyaenus' version Epaminondas attacked the guards, who had gone to sleep, defeating them easily, and went through the pass. The Spartan commander concluded a truce which was considered to be to the advantage of the Thebans and led his troops away. In Frontinus' version, Epaminondas, with the help of a few light-armed troops, harassed the enemy all night long. Then at daybreak, after he had recalled his own men and the Spartans had also retired, he suddenly moved forward the entire force, which he had kept at rest, and burst directly through the ramparts, which had been left without defenders. In Xenophon's *Hellenica*, in an episode from 369, Epaminondas had calculated perfectly, and fell upon the Spartans and Pelleneians just when the night watches were finishing and the rest of the men were rising, each one going about his task. Xenophon illustrates the perfect use of a surprise attack: the Thebans were prepared and in good order, while their opponents unaware and in disorder.[85]

The Greek tyrant, Dionysius of Syracuse, was famous for his use of mercenaries in surprise attacks.[86] He used such an attack on a siege wall in 357/6. First, he

---

* Half a mile, or one kilometre.

detained a group of emissaries from Syracuse, then towards morning plied his mercenaries with strong wine and sent them on a dash against the siege wall about the acropolis. The attack was unexpected, and mercenaries, with great boldness and loud tumult, began to tear down the cross-wall and attack the Syracusans, so that no one dared to stand on the defensive, except the mercenaries of Dio, who first noticed the disturbance and came to the rescue. Plutarch moralises that it was a 'treacherous pretence' on the part of the tyrant because he detained the deputation that came to him from Syracuse and then pulled a sneaky stunt to take the city. The attack was unsuccessful, giving fuel to the argument that surprise attacks are neither nice nor effective.[87]

Assaults on Cities

Various assaults on cities are reported as surprise attacks. Diodorus describes an assault on Athens in 408 from Decelea (see map 11). Agis, the king of Sparta, was in Decelea with his army, when he learned that the best Athenian troops were engaged in an expedition with Alcibiades. He led his army on a moonless night to Athens. He had 28,000 infantry, one-half of whom were picked hoplites and the other half light-armed troops. He also had some 1,200 cavalry, of whom the Boeotians furnished 900 and the rest had been sent with him by Peloponnesians. As Agis drew near the city, he came upon the Athenian outposts before they were aware of him and easily dispersed them because they were taken by surprise. He slew a few and pursued the rest within the walls. We should take notice of the mention of light-armed and cavalry troops; they become much more common later in the war, and will be the subject of the next chapter.[88]

Diodorus reports another attack on a city that occurred in Sicily in 405. Dionysius of Syracuse covered 400 stades at night in order to arrive at the Achradine gate of Syracuse in the middle of the night. He had a hundred cavalry and his 600 infantry bodyguard. Finding the gate closed, he piled reeds brought from the marshes up on the doors and set them on fire. While the gates were being burned down, he gathered his troops and made his way into the city. The staunchest soldiers in the city were gathered in the market place and killed by mercenaries. Dionysius himself ranged through the city killing anyone who came out to resist him.[89]

Polyaenus reports a series of Thracian nocturnal attacks in 402–401. After plundering Thrace, Clearchus did not return to Byzantium, but rather encamped near the mountains. When he detected the Thracians gathering, he knew that they would attack from the mountains drunk and rushing at them in the night. He ordered his men to remain in arms and to wake themselves up frequently. To be sure they were on guard, he took part of the army out in the dark then appeared, striking his arms in the Thracian manner to scare his men and be sure they were ready for a fight. Therefore, when the Thracians really did appear, intending to catch them asleep, they met the attackers, awake and armed, and killed most of them.[90]

Ambush in the Classical Age

The breakdown of military decorum during the Peloponnesian war, about which Thucydides writes, led to year-round fighting, unsuspecting cities being attacked at night, and atrocities against citizens. Much of this is the result of a thirty-year war, economic exhaustion and desperation. One might add, that a breakdown in the hoplite system also led to the use of more innovative tactics. When Griffith writes that Athens began to make use of 'foreign auxiliaries, who showed the way to the light infantry and guerrilla tactics of the fourth century' he was ignoring the fact that Demosthenes had already been applying these 'guerrilla tactics' with success in the fifth century during the Peloponnesian war.[91] Thucydides himself was conscious of the new developments in warfare taking place in the Peloponnesian war. The speech he puts in the mouth of Brasidas before Amphipolis emphasises the innovative nature of the actions. He had to explain to the men trained in hoplite battle the fighting advantage of the use of a small striking force separated from the whole army.[92]

As we have seen from all the above examples, surprise attacks occurred throughout the Classical Age. They are not entirely ignored by ancient writers, but they are certainly undervalued by modern ones. When the evidence for ambush and surprise attack was collected by W. Kendrick Pritchett, he found so many examples he had to divide them into several categories: night attacks, dawn attacks, daytime attacks occurring when the enemy was disorganised, sea assaults and ambushes.[93] These divisions are based on function, and they were all performed by Greek armies – mostly against each other. There is no division into 'good people' who do not ambush and 'immoral people' who do. Using ambush and surprise attack is a function of two variables: what kind of troops one has, and what kind of situation presents itself.

Some Greeks had always used ambush – mostly those who lived in mountainous country and were too poor to field a hoplite phalanx. Others, who had previously relied on hoplites, had to adapt to a new environment where ambush was now used against them. A commander such as Demosthenes, once ambushed by light-armed soldiers and defeated, would learn quickly to use the same tactics to his advantage. His calamitous defeat in Aetolia had taught him a lesson. His operations and those of other generals would now consist of laying ambushes behind the enemy along roads and in other suitable places, followed by surprise attacks, reconnaissance expeditions and the occupation of dominating positions to ensure the safety of the route taken by their own soldiers and as a precaution against surprise attacks by the enemy.[94] Demosthenes became famous for using innovative tactics that were both the cause of some of his successes and of his greatest failure. Joseph Roisman, in his study of Demosthenes' use of surprise, warns against an unwarranted faith in the effectiveness of military surprise. He argues that Demosthenes' choice of a night battle at Epipolae was an appalling risk and, in the end, an appalling fiasco.[95] It is true that Demosthenes' predilection for military surprise led him to plan, without adequate military intelligence, the catastrophic night attack on Epipolae, which set the stage for the ultimate defeat of the Athenian expeditionary force.[96] This can be attributed as much to overambition as it can to the choice to strategies. It is one of the great ironies that Demosthenes himself succumbed to the very tactics with which he had proved himself to be a strategist of exceptional quality.[97]

One of Mao Tse Tung's premises is that guerrilla activities should be, if possible, combined with those of regular troops. And that is exactly what Demosthenes did with his light infantry and peltasts. There is no absolute proof that Brasidas and Cleon were influenced by the strategy of Demosthenes, but once a commander has success with a certain strategy word spreads. Clinging to an old strategy that no longer works can be dangerous. In Gomme's discussion of the Battle of Amphipolis, he suggests that '. . . one cause of Athenian failure in the Archidamian war was too close adherence to old-fashioned hoplite tactics, in Aetolia, at Spartolus and Amphipolis'. Demosthenes had not carried enough weight.[98]

Even a conventional Spartan commander such as Brasidas, who was much more comfortable commanding hoplites and using conventional Spartan tactics, resorted to ambush for his greatest victory. This was not an aberration; he was learning from other commanders. He captured cities with the help of traitors and peltasts. He seemed to have a special talent for small operations – night attacks and surprises that required cunning, speed and daredevil courage. Had he lived in a later age when light-armed troops were more common, he might have become a great guerrilla leader.[99] Handicapped by his slender reserves of men and money, and not having the vast resources of the Athenians or command of the sea, he knew he had to avoid prolonged campaigns and sieges, and especially pitched battles.[100] It has been suggested that he lacked any larger strategic vision and that what he was even doing in Thrace is obscure. But whatever wider war aims were envisaged, Brasidas did a fine job on the ground with the few battles in which we see him fight, and his success was due to the very tactics scholars argue are so un-Greek.

In *The Greek State at War*, W. K. Pritchett remarks that the Greek language never developed a word for 'surprise attack', implying that the deed was a rarity.[101] Yet it was exactly this strict etiquette of behaviour that made ambushing so easy. The ruse of attacking during the midday siesta was never unsuccessful because no one expected it. The possibility of an ambush while on the march was so great that hostages were routinely taken as a preventative measure against the possibility: for example, Thucydides reports that in the Spartan operations in Ozolian Locris in 426 (see map 1) the Spartans sent an army of 3,000 men to help the Aetolians. Hostages were taken from the Amphissans, however, just to ensure that they would not ambush the Spartans along the way to Aetolia.[102]

Modern commentators have explained what they call 'the sparse use of surprise' by infantry in Classical Greece by postulating cultural inhibitions,[103] and yet the idea of a surprise attack when the enemy is off-guard, even during a celebration, is as old as the story of the fall of Troy itself. Aeneas Tacticus warned that a particularly dangerous time for a city was a festival.[104] On at least three occasions this idea was used by fifth columnists. Plataea (see map 3) was betrayed on a night during a festival period.[105] The oligarchic coup d'état at Argos was carried out during a festival and Aeneas Tacticus uses it as an example of the danger inherent in holding a festival outside the city.[106] Added to this is the Athenian plan to catch the population of Mytilene by surprise while they were celebrating a festival to Apollo outside the city.[107] Surprise attacks were used to cause panic and confusion, so attacking at night or during a festival would make the odds of this much greater. People roused from their beds at night could not mount any organised resistance. They would not know how many invaders there were, or even tell friend from foe in the dark. In the betrayals of Amphipolis,[108] Torone[109] and Plataea we see this kind of suspicion and confusion among the inhabitants.

The use of ambush became more frequent, but it was neither invented in the fifth century nor contrary to what the Greeks had been doing in previous ages. Despite being dismissed as being of no real military significance by Clausewitz and other modern commentators, ambushes and surprise attacks did yield some impressive results.[110] The Boeotian ambush of the Athenians at Coronea in 447 compelled the Athenians to evacuate Boeotia. The Phliasians' ambush of the invading Argives in 416 ended their campaign. Brasidas' surprise attack at Amphipolis in 422 earned him hero-worship,[111] while Lysander was worshipped as a god on Samos after his surprise attack at Aegospotami ended Athenian naval supremacy in 404.[112] Demosthenes' ambush of an army and subsequent surprise attack on its reinforcements in 426 inflicted what Thucydides called 'the greatest disaster that happened to any one Greek city in an equal number of days during the war'.[113]

Surprise attack is not meant to be ubiquitous or widespread. It must be used selectively. The Greeks were not getting 'sneakier', rather their armies were simply getting more specialised and professional. They were learning to operate overseas, and on varied terrain and to hire specialised troops as needed. It is along these lines that Greek commanders would develop in the coming centuries.

CHAPTER 6

Night Attack

THERE IS NO BETTER time to sneak up on the enemy than at night, and there are numerous and varied examples of night attacks, or night marches and dawn attacks being used by the Greeks.[1] Considering that night attacks are what the Greeks supposedly did not do, according to many scholars, there are more than enough examples to prove their assumptions false. Herodotus alone lists fifteen examples of night attacks, forty-four appear in Thucydides and another twenty-one in Diodorus, Plutarch and Xenophon.[2] This chapter will look at the fifth-century examples, i.e. those that occur in the Classical Age, when the majority of scholars discuss only hoplite battles. Certainly, large battles were customarily broken off at nightfall, but night attacks were used by all combatants in the fifth century, both Greek and foreign, Athenian and Spartan, and such operations could be highly successful when executed correctly in the proper situations.[3] This collection of examples suggests that moving troops at night to sneak up on a foe or to escape from an enemy was actually standard operating procedure during the Persian and Peloponnesian wars.

Herodotus

The eminent Greek scholar Henry Immerwahr noted in 1966 that battles occupied centre stage in Herodotus' *Histories*, but we should add that rarely were they major hoplite battles.[4] Many of the encounters that appear in Herodotus are ambushes involving non-Greek combatants or Asiatic Greeks drafted into the Persian army by Cyrus or Darius.[5] In 513, for example, in a classic tactic, the Scythians attacked the Persians who were out foraging for provisions. We are told the Scythians attacked in this manner by night as well as by day.[6] In the same campaign, Darius left the wounded and the donkeys behind in a camp while he proceeded to the Ister river to set up for a battle against the Scythians. When the animals found themselves deserted, they brayed loudly and the Scythians were convinced that the Persians were still in the camp. The deception was used to cover up Darius' night movement to get to the Ister river and set up for the battle. The next day, however, the Scythians discovered Darius had tricked them, and they made straight for the Ister.[7]

While we are told by modern commentators that, under normal conditions, large battles were broken off at nightfall, the war itself continued after sunset.[8] The Greeks were aware that they could be attacked at night, and they would have been foolish not to protect themselves against such ambushes. Plus, if they wished to be more proactive, they needed to ambush their enemies first. Not surprisingly, we see that the Greeks were not only successful in setting up night ambushes but that they also killed many important members of the Persian army this way. In 496, for example, the Carians learned that the Persians were marching against their cities, so they set themselves up on an ambush along the road in Pedasa, and a number of Persian generals were killed. We are told it was the Greek Heraclides of Mylassus who planned the ambush and led it himself.[9] In Mardonius' invasion of Macedonia in 492, he lost his fleet off Mt Athos and then the Byrgoi of Thrace attacked him in a night ambush on his camp and wounded him.[10] The wounding of an important general has serious effects upon a campaign.

Operating at night was not without its difficulty or dangers. Night, in general, was a scary time for any army. During Xerxes' march from Sardis to Abydos in 480 (see map 1), for example, he stopped at Troy to make a sacrifice to Athena of Ilion. His army was 'struck by fear' during the night, perhaps in a thunderstorm (as in Herodotus 7.42) and he did not resume his march until daylight. Polyaenus demonstrates how soldiers could be made resistant to night fears. He tells that when Clearchus was in Thrace the typical 'nocturnal fears' seized his army. He gave orders that if an uproar occurred during the night no one was to stand up. Whoever did stand up was to be killed as an enemy. This order taught the soldiers to feel contempt for nocturnal fear, and so they stopped jumping up and becoming agitated.[11]

Night operations were no more a magic bullet than daytime ambush. They were not easy to execute properly, and they could cause as much confusion as success. In 494, when the Chians landed at Mycale and entered the land of the Ephesians (see map 8), they marched by night and came upon women who were keeping the Thesmophoriae, a festival held in Greek cities in honour of the goddesses Demeter and her daughter Persephone. The Ephesians had not been given any advanced warning about the landing of the Chians and the city was lightly guarded during the festival. They thought the invading army consisted of robbers coming after their women, so they mustered all their forces and slaughtered the Chians.[12]

The great attack on Thermopylae in 480 by the Persians required a night march across the Asopus river (see map 3). The Persians took the path called Anopaia (of the same name as the mountains it runs through) that had been revealed to them by the spy Ephialtes. They reached the summit at dawn and surprised the 1,000 Phocian hoplites who knew nothing of their movements until they heard the noise of the enemy's approach because of the noise their feet made in the oak leaves.[13] That same night, the Persian fleet discovered the dangers of night manoeuvres when it tried to sail around Euboea and was caught in a storm on the open sea and destroyed.[14]

Even defensive military operations were carried out at night. After Thermopylae, when the Peloponnesians heard that Leonidas' men were dead, they came out from their cities and encamped on the isthmus, their general being the brother of Leonidas, Cleombrotus, son of Anaxandrides. They broke up the Scironian road for materials, and built a wall across the isthmus. They carried stones and bricks and logs and crates full of sand, and we are told that they worked both night and day.[15]

Night operations might consist of a simple departure of troops by night, as happened in 479 when the Spartans made a night march towards the isthmus. The ephors commanded that 5,000 hoplites, each attended by seven helots, should march under the command of Cleombrotus. They were sent north to assist the Athenians against the Persians. They did not even tell the envoys who had requested their help that they were leaving.[16]

Another tactic was making a change in the position of troops just before a dawn attack in order to surprise the enemy at sunrise. At Plataea in 479 the Spartans and Athenians decided to change positions and so switched places at the first signs of dawn. But the Boeotians detected the movement and reported it to Mardonius. He immediately shifted his Persian troops to the other wing, so that they would still be facing the Spartans. When Pausanias saw what the Persians were doing he realised that the enemy had discovered the change. He therefore marched his Spartans back to the right wing so that the Persians and Spartans were once again facing one another in their original positions.[17] In this case, the night movement did not work because operation security was lacking.

Mardonius did not miss the opportunity to berate the Greeks for their 'sneakiness', and sent a herald to the Spartan line telling them:

. . . everybody about here seems to think you are very brave. Everyone admires you for never retreating in battle and for never quitting your post: you stick to it, so they say, until death – either your enemy's or your own. But it turns out that all this is nonsense: for here you are, running away and deserting your post before the battle has even begun or a single blow been struck, and giving the place of danger to the Athenians, while you yourselves face men who are merely our slaves. This is by no means what brave men would do; indeed, we have been sadly mistaken about you. Your reputation led us to expect that you would send us a challenge, in your eagerness to match yourselves with none but Persian troops. We should have accepted the challenge, had you sent it; but you did not. We find you instead slinking away from us.[18]

This moralising speech, put in the mouth of Mardonius by Herodotus, does not accurately represent either the Persian or the Greek position, but merely sets up the familiar theme of blaming one's enemy for using a sneaky tactic, while continuing to use it yourself. From the examples we have seen, it is clear that both Greeks and Persians (and indeed everyone else) used night tactics to escape and save their men when they found themselves in sticky situations.

Herodotus records a night flight by the Persians during the siege of Sestos in 479 (see map 1). The Persians were blocked up in Sestos by the Athenians. They were not prepared for a siege and had not expected the arrival of the Greeks, which caught them unawares (another Greek surprise!). The people in the town were suffering and had been reduced to eating the leather straps off their beds. Artayctes and Oeobazus, the leading Persians, made their escape by night, letting themselves down from the wall at the back of the town where the enemy lines were weakest. On the following day the men of the Chersonese signalled to the Athenians from their towers to let them know what had happened; they also opened the gates. The greater part of the Athenian force went in pursuit of the fugitives while the remainder took possession of the town.[19]

Of all the notable night attacks in Herodotus, perhaps the most memorable is the one that used a technique that appears nowhere else in Greek history. Herodotus relates an incident that occurred just before the Battle of Thermopylae in 480. The Thessalians and their allies invaded Phocis. The Phocians had the diviner Tellias of Elis in their camp, who devised a stratagem involving a night attack on the Thessalian camp.[20] Six hundred of the bravest Phocian hoplites whitened themselves and their armour with chalk. Then they went out to attack the Thessalians at night, having been instructed to kill everyone who was not whitened. The Thessalian sentinels were the first to see them and fled, supposing they were seeing ghosts, then the rest of the army followed suit. The effect enabled the Phocians to discriminate between friend and foe in the mêlée, which was the difficult matter in night attacks. The incident gives us one of the most stark and vivid examples of what a night attack can achieve. Indeed, this is a technique that would not have worked at any other time except at night.

The Peloponnesian War

Thucydides gives an excellent example of the confusion that can happen during night fighting even when verbal signals are used for security.[21] The attack was set up by Demosthenes against the Syracusans on Epipolae in 413 (see map 5). Thucydides says this was the only such attack that took place in the Peloponnesian war between large armies.[22] Demosthenes had been using siege engines against the counter wall, but they were being continually set on fire by the defenders.[23] No matter where they attacked the wall in the daytime, they were turned back. Demosthenes realised that it would be impossible by day to avoid being seen both in the approach to and in the ascent of Epipolae, the ancient fortified plateau west of Syracuse. Thus he decided on a surprise night attack.[24]

He got the consent from his fellow commander, Nicias, to take enough provisions for five days, and assembled masons, carpenters and any military gear he considered necessary, like arrows. At first watch, about 10:00 p.m., he set out for Epipolae with the whole army, leaving Nicias in the lines.[25] They ascended the first hill of Euryelus unobserved by the enemy guards (see map 5). They took the first of three forts by surprise, putting to the sword part of the garrison.[26]

Escapees spread the word that the Athenians were on the plateau in force. The first to be informed of the Athenian attack were the 600 hoplites formed the year before to act as guards for Epipolae. The groups from the other forts advanced against the assailants, but when they encountered Demosthenes and the Athenians they put up a spirited defence; they were, however, routed.[27]

The Athenians now raced ahead to exploit their success, an initial corps cleared the way while a second force headed swiftly for the counter wall.[28] The Syracusans guarding it fled, allowing the Athenians to capture and tear down parts of it.[29] The Syracusans and their allies, including Gylippus and his men, came up to help from the outworks, but the night attack was unexpected and some men panicked and were initially forced back. In the dim light of the moon the advancing

2

Frontline Books
FREEPOST SF5
47 Church Street
BARNSLEY
South Yorkshire
S70 2BR

DISCOVER MORE ABOUT MILITARY HISTORY

Frontline Books is an imprint of Pen & Sword Books, which has more than 1500 titles in print covering all aspects of military history on land, sea and air. If you would like to receive more information and special offers on your preferred interests from time to time, along with our standard catalogue, please indicate your areas of interest below and return this card (no stamp required in the UK). Alternatively, register online at www.frontline-books.com. Thank you.

PLEASE NOTE: We do not sell data information to any third party companies

Mr/Mrs/Ms/Other.............. Name...

Address...

.... Postcode......................

Email address...

If you wish to receive our email newsletter, please tick here ☐

PLEASE SELECT YOUR AREAS OF INTEREST

Ancient History ☐	Medieval History ☐	English Civil War ☐	
Napoleonic ☐	Pre World War One ☐	World War One ☐	
World War Two ☐	Post World War Two ☐	Falklands ☐	
Aviation ☐	Maritime ☐	Battlefield Guides ☐	
Regimental History ☐	Military Reference ☐	Military Biography ☐	

Website: www.frontline-books.com • Email: info@frontline-books.com
Telephone: 01226 734555 • Fax: 01226 734438

Athenians could not tell whether the men running toward them were friends or foes, a problem that was compounded by the fact that the generals appear not to have placed anyone at the pass to direct traffic.[30] So as the different companies came onto the plateau, they found some Athenian forces advancing eastward unchecked, others running back towards Euryelus in retreat, and still others who had just come up through the pass and were not yet in motion. No one instructed the men newly arrived on the plateau which group they should join.[31]

With large numbers of similarly equipped hoplites milling about in a relatively confined space, it was impossible to tell which side anyone was on, even though there was a moon.[32] The leading Athenians were already in flight, but those coming up behind, including some still making the ascent, did not know what was happening and there was no one to direct them. Hearing a distinctive Dorian paean added to the panic.[33] The Argives and the Corcyreans on the Athenian side sounded just like the enemy.[34] They began to take anyone coming towards them as hostile, and their constant demands for the password soon gave it away to the enemy. The result was that they ended by fighting among themselves, and the rout was compounded by the narrowness of the escape route.[35]

All this disorder and panic ended in a general flight. As the Athenians were being pursued by the enemy many hurled themselves down from the bluffs and perished because the way down from Epipolae was narrow. Those familiar with the terrain made it back to their camp, but recent arrivals who did not know the lay of the land wandered around in the dark and were gathered up by the Syracusan cavalry the next morning and killed.[36] The result was the greatest disaster suffered by the Athenians in the war up to that point. Between 2,000 and 2,500 men were killed, and all hope of a quick victory at Syracuse abandoned.[37]

Thucydides admits that it was not easy to find out what happened from either side, even afterwards.[38] As he says, even in daylight those taking part in a battle know only what is going on in their immediate vicinity, but at night how could anyone clearly understand anything? His account is a classic illustration of the difficulties and dangers of fighting in the dark. A night attack is notoriously difficult to co-ordinate, even when those engaged know the terrain, have good maps and modern means of communication. Since no one on the Athenian side was as familiar with the plateau as the Syracusans, and the men who had just arrived with Demosthenes and Eurymedon had no knowledge of it at all, this ignorance was disastrous. In the darkness advance turned to retreat, and retreat to rout.

The difficulty of night operations should not be blamed entirely for the defeat. One feels the Athenians made mistakes that could have been avoided. There seems to have been some attempt to assign different objectives to different units, some directly attacking the Syracusan counter wall, while others dealt with the main body of enemy troops on the plateau.[39] But the latter seem to have had no clear objective and should have been made to halt and stand on the defensive once a certain point had been reached. This would have avoided much of the confusion, and it was not beyond the wit of even ancient commanders to devise some way of distinguishing their men from the enemy. Demosthenes, in particular, who had used his own Doric speakers to confuse the sentries at Idomene,[40] should have realised that the Doric speakers in the Athenian army in Sicily might cause confusion and should have told them to keep their mouths shut. Finally, although no one in the Athenian army could have been expected to know the terrain really well, it might have been a good idea at least to mix some of the older hands with the newcomers. Instead, it just ended in disaster.[41]

After this debacle, Thucydides reiterates his view of night attacks and says of the confusion that arose: 'Terrors and panics are apt to arise, especially at night and when they are marching through a hostile country.'[42] Thucydides may have been correct when describing the movements of large armies. We should not be convinced, however, that this is a general rule or the Greek view of night operations. We can see a clear pattern of using night attacks and many times, unlike this one, they worked. Surprise and night fighting are not a panacea; they are just one more tool in the toolbox of military possibilities.

In the winter of 432/1, Brasidas, a much more conservative commander than Demosthenes, attempted a surprise at Potidaea (see map 4):

> He reached the place by night and had planted a ladder against the wall before he was discovered. The ladder was planted just in those few moments when the guard on duty was passing on the bell and before he had time to return to his post. However, the alarm was given immediately afterwards, before his men were in position, and Brasidas quickly led his army back again, without waiting till it was day.[43]

Gomme writes of this being one of the 'rare attempts' at surprise attack by night on a defended town, and sneers that it was 'easily foiled'.[44] The incident itself even had an effect on military procedure. Because the ladder was placed at a point which the guard who was passing on the bell had just left, and before he had returned to his post. Sommerstein suggests that some time before 414 (the date of the play) the usual system was changed, as a result of this sort of incident.[45] After the change, the duty of the sentry and bellman was separated.[46]

At least ten other successful examples suggest that escaping at night was a common way to elude an enemy. In chapter 5 we related the story of Demosthenes' march from Olpae to Idomene with light-armed Amphilochians and Messenians in 426/5 (see map 6). The incident illustrates how verbal recognition could be used against a foe. After making a night march, Demosthenes reached the camp of the Ambraciots a little before daylight and took them by complete surprise. The Ambraciots were still in their beds. Demosthenes purposely put his Messenian soldiers in front to fool the sentinels. On hearing the Doric dialect, they supposed the troops to be their own men since they could not see them in the dark. Again, the factor that Thucydides stresses is that the enemy was indistinguishable to the sight.[47] This was an efficient, well-executed and deadly operation.

In 440 when the Athenians sailed to Samos with forty ships and set up a democracy, they took as hostages from the Samians fifty boys and fifty men who were deposited at Lemnos. The Athenians then withdrew from Samos, leaving a garrison behind. Some of the Samians escaped to the mainland and recruited 700 mercenaries. They crossed over by night to Samos. First they attacked the popular party and overpowered most of them. Then they secretly got their hostages out of Lemnos and revolted from Athens, handing over the Athenian officers and garrison that were on the island. The unit then prepared an expedition against Miletus.[48]

Withdrawing after a battle was often done at night. In 429 in Acarnania, Cnemus and the Peloponnesians retreated with their army to the Anapus river (see map 6), which was eighty stadia from Stratus at night. On the following day they took up their dead under truce and since they were helped by the Oeniadae, Cnemus withdrew to their country before the combined forces of the Acarnanians arrived.[49]

Another escape from a siege occurred at Plataea in 428. After the Plataeans had finished their preparations, they waited for a night that was stormy with rain and wind and at the same time moonless, and then set out. They were led by the men who were the authors of the enterprise. They crossed the ditch that ran around the city, then they reached the foot of the enemy's wall unobserved by the guards, who could not see ahead in the all-pervading darkness. The guards also could not hear because the clatter of the wind drowned the noise of the enemy's approach.

The invaders kept a good distance apart as they advanced and were lightly armed so that their weapons might not rattle against each other and cause detection. We are told they only had their left feet sandalled for security against slipping in the mud. They came up to the battlements at a space between two towers, knowing that this area would not be guarded. Those who carried the ladders went first. Next twelve light-armed soldiers with only a dagger and a breastplate; six went to each tower.[50] Then came another party of light troops armed with spears, but no shields so they could advance more quickly. Eventually, the invaders were discovered by the sentinels in the towers because of noise made by a tile knocked down by one of the Plataeans as he was laying hold of the battlements. The alarm was instantly given, and troops rushed to the wall, not knowing the nature of the danger owing to the dark night and stormy weather.

An interesting example of manipulating signals intelligence occurred during this same incident. Fire signals were raised to alert the Thebans of the attack and call for help, but agents in the city displayed a number of other signals at the same time to confuse the Thebans. It rendered the call for help unintelligible and prevented them from getting a clear idea of what was happening or coming to the aid of their comrades.[51]

A night march through Acarnania (see map 1) was executed by Eurylochus 426/5. He arrived at Mt Thyamus, which was located in the friendly territory of the Agraeans, and from there he passed into Argive territory after nightfall. He succeeded in passing unobserved between the city of Amphilochian Argos and the Acarnanian guard posts at Crenae. There he joined the Ambraciots at Olpae, where they united at daybreak[52] (see map 6). They halted at a place called Metropolis. The Athenians eluded them by making their landing by night and the Corinthians were notified by the raising of fire signals. Demosthenes had 200 Messenian hoplites and sixty Athenian archers, but realised he might be outnumbered, so he placed some of his troops in an ambush in a sunken road overgrown with bushes.[53] Demosthenes lost many men, but emerged victorious when the battle was completed later that day.

Brasidas staged a surprise attack with its objective being Amphipolis (see map 4). He set out in stormy weather in December 424 with snow in the air.[54] He began with an epic march, by day and night, from Arnae in the Chalcidice round the Strymonic Gulf to Amphipolis, fording a river en route and covering more than forty miles (sixty-five kilometres) in under twenty-four hours. He forced the lightly guarded bridge over the Strymon river below Amphipolis before dawn and appeared without warning before the city walls, taking a few prisoners and throwing the citizens into a panic.[55] Thucydides suggests that he could have captured the city then and there if he had attacked at once.[56] This suggestion is a bit hasty. A walled city protected on two sides by steep cliffs and a river 200 yards (200 metres) wide with a majority of its citizens against surrender would not have been stormed that easily.[57] Nor were the Spartans experts on siege works. Brasidas was, no doubt, expecting a betrayal; his allies the Argillians had already subverted some of the citizens. When, as at Megara, this did not happen, he camped outside to await events. According to Diodorus, the city surrendered on the day after Brasidas' arrival.[58] At least one modern commentator criticised the Athenians for not getting reinforcements there sooner and perhaps making 'a surprise attack on Brasidas' in return.[59]

To be successful, a night retreat must be orderly. When Arrhabaeus, a king of Lynkestis, revolted against his sovereign, King Perdiccas II of Macedon, in 424 Brasidas the Spartan helped Perdiccas against Arrhabaeus. In the summer of 423 the defection of the Illyrian allies to Arrhabaeus forced Perdiccas and Brasidas to retreat. When night came on, the Macedonians and the mass of the barbarians immediately took fright 'in one of those mysterious panics to which great armies are liable'.[60] They believed the advancing enemy was many times more numerous than they really were, and that they were surrounded. At daybreak, when Brasidas saw that the Macedonians had already decamped and that the Illyrians and Arrhabaeus were about to come against him, he formed his hoplites into a square. He put the light-armed troops in the centre. He instructed the youngest troops, who were certainly the fastest, to sally against the enemy in case they attacked at any point. Brasidas himself took 300 picked men to form a rearguard and repulse the enemy's attacks.[61] Brasidas addressed his troops, suggesting that the enemy's hit-and-run tactics were born of cowardice, but he knew how dangerous they were. Brasidas faced the same difficulties here that Demosthenes had faced in Aetolia, but he took the necessary measures to counteract them.[62]

Night operations were used for the purposes of security for secret negotiations. Scione, a city in Pallene, revolted from the Athenians and went over to Brasidas in 423. On their revolt, Brasidas crossed over by night to Scione, a friendly trireme sailing ahead and he himself following in a skiff at some distance behind. His idea was that, if he should meet with any boat larger than a skiff, the trireme would protect him, but if another trireme of equal strength should come along it would turn not against the smaller boat, but against the ship, and in the meantime he could get safely across. He succeeded in crossing and calling a meeting of the Scionaeans.[63]

A night escape from Mende occurred in the summer of 423 during the same operation. By that time both Mende and Scione on the Chalcidice had revolted against the Athenians. The Scionaeans and the Peloponnesians had come against the Athenians and taken position on a strong hill in front of the city of Scione. They hoped to capture it before the city was taken by the Athenians and invested with a wall. The Athenians made a furious assault upon the hill and dislodged the occupants. They encamped and, after raising a trophy, prepared for the work of circumvallation. While they were at work, the auxiliaries who had been previously besieged on the acropolis of Mende (see map 4) forced their way by night along the shore through the guard and reached Scione, and most of them made it through the besieging army and got into the city to help their fellow revolters.[64]

An example of a decampment by night to avoid battle occurred in 418. The Argives were tracking Spartan movements and made contact with them at Methydrium in Arcadia. Each party took position on a hill, and the Argives prepared to fight with the Spartans, thinking they were isolated, but King Agis III eluded them by breaking up his camp at night, and he marched to Phlius to join the rest of his allies. At dawn, the Argives discovered what had happened and marched first to Argos and then took the road to Nemea, where they expected the Spartans with their allies to pass by, but Agis had taken a different route.[65]

A night march and escape from a besieging army was carried out at Orneae in 416/5. The Athenians arrived with thirty ships and 600 hoplites, while the Argives joining them went out in full force and besieged the garrison at Orneae for a single day. Under cover of night, however, when the besieging army had bivouacked at a distance, the garrison at Orneae escaped. The next day, the Argives, on learning this, razed Orneae to the ground and withdrew and later the Athenians also went home with their ships.[66]

At Syracuse in the summer of 413 we see a stratagem designed to *prevent* the Athenians from marching at night. Hermocrates the Syracusan suspected that the Athenians intended to retreat by land at night to some other part of Sicily to regroup and renew the war. He pointed out to the authorities that they should not let the enemy get away by night. The Syracusans, he said, should march out at night, block the roads and seize and guard the passes.[67] The authorities agreed, but the problem was that people were celebrating their recent victory, which coincided with a festival to Heracles. Most of them would be too drunk to show up for night duty. What Hermocrates feared the most was that the Athenians would quietly get ahead of them by passing the most difficult places by a night march. Therefore, when dusk came, he took his friends to the Athenian camp with some horsemen. They yelled out at them as if they were well-wishers and said to tell Nicias not to lead the army off by night because the Athenians were guarding the roads. Instead, he should make his preparations at his leisure and to retreat by day. The Athenians who heard this informed the Athenian generals, who put off going out that night on the strength of this disinformation.[68] While the Athenians took an extra day to pack, the Syracusans used the time to occupy strategic points along the possible escape route and to tow off Athenian ships without opposition.[69]

Night Assaults

Night movements were not just used defensively to escape, but could also be adopted to stage offensive operations. A night landing of hoplites occurred in 426 along a night march to Tanagra. The Athenian fleet left Melos and sailed to Oropus in Graean territory. They landed at nightfall and the hoplites then proceeded by land to Tanagra in Boeotia. In answer to signals that had been arranged beforehand, they were met by the Athenian army from Athens itself, which had marched out in full force under the command of Hipponicus and Eurymedon. They made camp there, spent that day ravaging Tanagran territory and remained in their position for the night. The next day, after defeating those Tanagrans who sallied out against them and some Thebans who had come up to help the Tanagrans, they took some arms, set up a trophy and retired – one group back to Athens and the other back to their ships.[70]

We can see the planning stages of a surprise night attack at Embaton in 427 when a proposal was put forward to capture Mytilene (see map 9):

So that if we were to attack suddenly and by night, I think that, with the help of those inside the town who are still on our side, we ought to be able to gain control of the place. Let us not be afraid of the danger, but let us remember that this is an example of the unknown factor in warfare, and that the good general is one who guards against such unknown factors in his own case, but exploits them for attack in the case of the enemy.[71]

This certainly sounds like an endorsement of surprise attack in spite of the dangers of night operations.

A classic example of a night assault was carried out by the Melians in 416 against an Athenian position:

> ... the Melians made a night attack and captured the part of the Athenian lines opposite the marketplace. They killed some of the troops, and then, after bringing in corn and everything else useful that they could lay their hands on, retired again and made no further move, while the Athenians took measures to make their blockage more efficient in future.[72]

Attacking Towns, Escaping from Towns and Building Walls

The easiest way to capture a city was to have traitors within the walls, who would open a gate in the dead of night. We see this in action when Brasidas made his assault on Torone, the chief town of the Sithonian peninsula in Chalcidice, in 424/3 by a surprise night attack[73] (see map 4). Torone itself stood on a hill, but was also protected against naval attack by an outer wall on the seafront. This side was foolishly unmanned, and traitorous elements from the city were able to admit a small party of light-armed allied troops, armed with daggers, from Brasidas' force. These men stole uphill in the dark, killed the guards at the key watch-post below the city walls, and with the traitors' help broke open a gate on the south side and the main gates opening into the market square. Brasidas sent 100 peltasts out in front so that when the gate was opened they would rush in first. At a pre-arranged fire-signal, they entered. Brasidas and the main army formed up at the double into the square, all shouting to create confusion. This roused the fifty Athenians hoplites who had been sleeping in the square who now broke and ran, most of them to the nearby fort of Lechythos. Brasidas with the army continued up the hill to cover all possible escape routes, and by dawn the whole city was in his hands. The entire episode shows advanced planning, accurate intelligence gathering and superb execution.[74] Thucydides devotes more space than usual to this episode and rightly so. He thought it was worth reporting the taking of a fortified city with an Athenian garrison, done in only a few hours and with almost with no bloodshed, by means of a well-planned and skilfully executed surprise assault by night.[75]

At Plataea in 431 some 300 Thebans under the command of the Boeotarchs entered Plataea during the first watch of the night. They had been invited over by some of the Plataeans, Naucleides and his partisans, who opened the gates for them. The intention was to put power in the hands of the partisans, destroy the citizens of the opposite party and give the city over to Thebes. They found it easier to make entry unobserved because no watch had been set to guard the city.[76]

Defensive wall-building could be a night operation. In defence of Athens after the Spartan occupation of Decelea in 413, Thucydides says the Athenians were worn out trying to defend the walls during the day by turns, and then at night everybody except the cavalry was used.[77]

Another example of wall-building at night as a defensive strategy and a night attack on the wall comes at Epipolae in Syracuse in the summer of 414 (see map 5). Gylippus led forth his hoplites outside the walls and closed with the enemy. He had his cavalry and javelin men posted on the flank of the Athenians in open space where the work on both walls ended. In the battle, his cavalry attacked the left wing of the Athenians, which was opposed to them, and routed it. In consequence, the rest of the army was also beaten by the Syracusans and driven headlong within the fortifications. On the following night they succeeded in building their wall beyond the walls of the Athenians so that they themselves were no longer hampered by them and thus altogether deprived the Athenians, even if they should be victorious, of the possibility of ever investing the city in the future.[78]

In the winter of 412/11, the Spartan Hippocrates sailed from the Peloponnesus with ten Thurian ships commanded by Dorieus and two other commanders. He arrived at Cnidus, where a revolt had been organised by Tissaphernes. They were to use half their fleet to guard Cnidus and keep the rest at sea off Tropium. Hearing of this, the Athenians sailed out at night from Samos hoping to help the beleaguered city. They captured the six ships looking out at Tropium, although the crews escaped. After this they sailed to Cnidus and attacked the city, which was unfortified, almost capturing it. The next day they made a second assault, but with less effect because the inhabitants had strengthened their defences during the night and had been reinforced by the crews who had escaped from the ships at Triopium. The Athenians could not do so much damage as before, and so they withdrew and, after ravaging Cnidian territory, they sailed back to Samos.[79]

Night Operations: Common or Uncommon?

W. K. Pritchett was correct when he claimed that there was no example of a night assault on an encamped enemy by a Greek hoplite army previously drawn up in a plain in what Thucydides calls pitched-battle formation.[80] Hoplite armies were sometimes arrayed against each other for several days with only a short distance between them, but no effort was made at a surprise attack by night. This is, however, a very narrow definition of Greek warfare and the wrong place to look. As we see from the examples given in this chapter, both Greeks and their enemies used night operations and ambush, and these things were well known already by the time of Herodotus. Pritchett gives Epipolae as the only apparent exception to the rule since the Syracusans were on much higher ground and in part behind walls, but there were numerous operations in the fifth century, related by both Herodotus and Thucydides, when night operations were required and, when properly executed, were successful. In fact, the single most common motif in Herodotean military accounts is deception or trickery.[81]

The more we proceed through the fifth and into the early fourth century, the more common these tactics become, and we have the benefit of an experienced military writer to comment on the phenomenon. Aeneas Tacticus, writing two generations after the Peloponnesian war, specifically warns against the danger of betrayal at night.[82] If the Greeks thought the enemy might attack them at night, then they had to prepare for such eventualities, whether they were in a camp or behind the walls of a city. The Plataean fifth columnists admitted the Thebans at night;[83] the betrayal of the long walls at Megara took place before dawn;[84] the betrayal of Amphipolis began at night;[85] Brasidas' entrance into Torone was accomplished at night while Athenian hoplites were sleeping in the agora;[86] the betrayal of Selymbria occurred at night;[87] and Byzantium was betrayed at night.[88] On two occasions the weather also provided cover for the betrayals. If a preemptive strike on the enemy at night might give them an advantage, then they would be foolish not to use such an advantage. Night fighting, while difficult and risky, could pay off big time if applied at the right time and the right place. Brasidas pushed on to Amphipolis on a stormy, snowy night, trying to escape notice by everyone except the traitors inside the city.[89] The stormy weather was also a factor in his capture of the territory outside the walls.[90] The night Plataea was betrayed it was rainy.[91] The fact that it was rainy and no guards were posted helped cover the betrayal.[92]

To label these tactics as 'un-Greek' is simply wrong. The Greeks certainly had their military traditions, but they were also flexible enough to know that traditions may change even in the space of one war. Removing an army from a location and evading an enemy, escaping a walled city under siege, attacking the walls of a city, removing a fleet by sea were all tactics recognised and practised by the Greeks. In a case such as Brasidas' attack on Torone, we see the use of light-armed troops for infiltration, clandestine communications, killing a garrison at night and forcing entry into a city. The successful use of the cover of darkness for a surprise attack was not uncommon.

CHAPTER 7

Surprise Landings, and Assault by Sea

A TTACKS AND RETREATS BY night or surprise assaults in Greek warfare were not confined to the land. Navies as well as armies were moved into position at night in preparation for an attack at dawn. Setting out during the night by sea could be dangerous, and such manoeuvres were attempted when achieving surprise was absolutely necessary.[1] Triremes were both too fragile and too uncomfortable for long stays at sea. Trireme fleets did not mount blockades in the modern sense of the word. Rather, they moored in a harbour near the enemy and then ventured out to challenge the opposing fleet. In order to be ready, they used scouts both on land and sea to follow enemy movements and to signal information.[2] So, for example, when Themistocles planned the attack at Artemesium for the evening, we assume it was so that the engagement would be brief. One scholar refers to it as being 'less of a battle than a raid, and, indeed, an experiment'.[3] As we will see, however, this tactic was not as much of an oddity as modern commentators suggest. There are many examples of night sailings and at least five examples of assaults from the sea, all of which were successful.

Herodotus

Surprise landings are already documented by Thucydides as occurring during the Ionian Revolt. In 494, Histiaeus had been pushed to the island of Lesbos. Accepting eight triremes from the locals, he began raiding to make ends meet and descended upon Chios. He had a small force of 320 hoplites (forty per ship) plus some lightly armed rowers. He knew the Chian strength would be greater so he exploited the element of surprise and made a secret landing to set up a trap in the heavily wooded countryside at a place known as The Hollows. Having arranged the ambush, his men made their presence known by openly attacking nearby cropland. When the Chians raced towards the fields, they fell right into the waiting ambush.

The raiders butchered most of the defenders on the spot and captured the rest. Chios capitulated without further resistance.[4]

Some historians such as Barry Strauss believe the famous Battle of Salamis was set up as a surprise ambush.[5] At Salamis in 480 the Persians received a message carried by the slave named Sicinnus, who appeared in the Persian camp. He was probably sent by Themistocles as a provocation. The message he sent was that the Greeks had lost heart and were planning to flee. An intelligence bonanza of this magnitude should have seemed too good to be true; nevertheless, the Persians believed the message.[6] First they landed 400 of their men on the islet of Psyttaleia, which lies between Salamis and the mainland.[7] Then, at midnight, they advanced their western wing towards Salamis for encirclement (see map 11), and they also put out to sea the ships that were stationed off Ceos and Cynosura. They held all of the passage with their ships as far as Munychia. The purpose of their putting out to sea was so that the Greeks would not even have the liberty to flee, but would be hemmed in at Salamis and punished for their fighting off Artemesium. The purpose of their landing Persians on the islet of Psyttaleia was that, after a sea fight, the men and wrecks would be washed ashore there, since the island lay in the very path of the forthcoming battle. From here they could save their friends and slay their opponents. They did all of this in silence to keep it secret from the Greeks and, naturally, they made these preparations at night without resting.[8]

Once the battle was in full swing, the Greeks broke the Persian line and turned the Phoenicians and Ionians to flight. The battle should have effectively been over, except for the Greek pursuit, and yet the struggle went on for hours afterwards. The narrowness of the straits made it impossible for Persia's front lines to flee towards Phalerum without crashing into the ships that were still coming forward. By the evening of September 25 the Greeks had pushed the chaotic mass of Persians back. The action in the Battle of Salamis had returned to where the Persians had begun the night before, at the eastern end of the straits. While the Aeginetans lurked at the exit of the channel, the Athenians inside the straits drove the Persian ships into their hands. Meanwhile, a small Athenian unit had landed on the islet of Psyttaleia, which lay just to the south of the Aeginetan squadron.

For Aegina's ambush to succeed we may imagine that it was crucial first to remove the Persians from Psyttaleia. Had they remained there, they could have signalled to their ships about the ambush, which would have allowed some of the Persian triremes to escape by speeding up, hugging the coast or perhaps by steering a zigzag course. On top of that, if the Aeginetans had tried to hide their vessels in the shadow of Psyttaleia, the Persians might have threatened the men with arrows, so the Persians had to be removed. The mission was entrusted to a corps of Athenian infantrymen under Aristides' command. He did not have command of a ship during Athens' greatest naval battle. This is not surprising since he was a returned political exile. Instead, he had his great moment when the Greeks broke the Persian line and chaos reigned among the Great King's triremes. At this point it was safe to thin the ranks of the Athenian infantrymen lining the Salamis shore. Aristides gathered a large number of them – we do not know how many – and put them on small boats. They landed on Psyttaleia and slaughtered the Persians there down to the last man. Both the carnage on Psyttaleia and the Aeginetan ambush represent mopping-up operations because the Persian navy had been defeated.[9] But they were still important parts of the war and reliant on ambush as a tactic.

Not surprisingly, a night sail was used by the Persian admirals in retreat after Salamis in 480. By the king's command, they put out to sea from Phalerum and made for the Hellespont again with all speed, to guard the bridges for the king's passage.[10]

Thucydides

Sea landings, in and of themselves, could be dangerous. In 430 a fleet of forty ships sailed from Corinth to land 1,500 hoplites at Astacus and they quickly took the town. It was their last success because the fleet failed to take any other towns, although they struck numerous times along the coast of Acarnania. The fleet's commanders decided to make one last attempt and landed on Cephallenia to assault the town of Cranae. This final effort proved a worse failure because the landing party fell into an ambush by a defending force less than half its size. The survivors were chased back to their ships.[11]

As often happens when a superior force attacks, the defenders will use ambush as a force multiplier. In 426, the Athenian admiral Laches crossed from Italy to Sicily and set the Messenian colony of Mylae as his first target. He had forty ships, half of them Athenian and could land 1,600 hoplites, eighty archers and at least a few armed crewmen. This was enough to give him numerical superiority, since his opposition amounted to only two Messenian tribal *lochoi*, with perhaps 1,000–1,200 hoplites and 200–300 *psiloi* (light armed). Facing such an imbalance in manpower, the defenders decided to spring an ambush. The defence, however, did not work, probably because the scouts revealed the trap before it could be sprung. Exposed, the Messenians had to either run or fight. They chose to fight and took heavy losses.[12] Later in that same year Laches' Siculi reinforcements were set upon in a surprise attack by Syracusans.[13]

Demosthenes and Procles planned a surprise attack on a garrison responsible for the killing of their colleague Asopius two years earlier. In 426, the Athenians came ashore on the mainland territory of Leucas, where they made a feint towards the town of Ellomenus. As planned, the small group of marines fell back upon the approach of the local guard unit, whose 600 or so spearmen took the bait and pursued them right into the trap. The unit was decimated, and Demosthenes and Procles were able to cross over and invest the city of Leucas.[14]

Withdrawal of an army or fleet by night to avoid battle was not uncommon. There are eleven examples, of which only one was unsuccessful. The case that failed involved the Peloponnesian fleet at Rhium in 429, the third year of the Peloponnesian war. The Corinthian admirals Machaon and two colleagues were on their way to Acarnania to prevent the coastal Acarnanians from joining their countrymen in the interior.[15] As they sailed along out the Crisaean Gulf (see map 3), they realised they were being followed by Phormio and his twenty Athenian vessels that had put out from the mouth of the Euenos river and were hoping to attack them on the open sea.[16] The Corinthians, for their part, had no thought of engaging in a sea battle since their vessels were being used more like transports for carrying soldiers. Besides, they never thought the twenty Athenian vessels would dare attack their forty-seven ships.[17]

The Corinthians altered their plan of passage and returned to the Peloponnesian coast, putting in at some point near to Rhium, the narrowest part of the strait. Their bringing to was a feint intended to deceive Phormio and to induce him to return to his own camp.[18] The Peloponnesians then slipped from their moorings in the middle of the night hoping to get across the narrowest part of the Gulf and sneak away unobserved in the dark. But they were spotted and forced to fight the Athenians in mid-passage.

The Peloponnesians ranged their forty-seven vessels in as large a circle as possible without leaving an opening; the prows were outside and the sterns in. They placed within the circle all the small craft together with their five best sailors who could move out at a moment's notice and strengthen any point threatened by the enemy.[19] The twenty Athenian warships around them forced them to contract their circle, keeping them in mid-channel by continuously brushing past and feigning attacks. They had been warned by Phormio only to fake the attacks, but not attack for real until he gave a signal.[20] Phormio was hoping that the Peloponnesians would not retain their order like a force on shore, but that the ships would fall afoul of each other as well as the small craft in the centre and cause confusion. He was waiting for the wind, which usually rose towards morning and blew in from the Gulf. Phormio wanted to be the one to attack since he felt he had better sailors and that an attack timed to coincide with the wind was the best strategy.[21]

When the wind came up, the enemy's ships were in a narrow space, and with the wind and the small craft dashing against them, they at once fell into confusion. The ships fell afoul of each other while the crews tried pushing them off with poles. All their shouting, swearing and struggling with one another made captains' orders and boatswains' cries inaudible.[22] At this moment, Phormio gave the signal and the Athenians attacked. Sinking first one of the commander's ships, they then disabled as many of the rest as they could. Those who managed to escape fled for Patrae and Dyme in Achaea (see map 8). The Athenians gave chase, captured twelve ships and took most of the men out of them. They then sailed to Molycrium. After setting up a trophy on the promontory of Rhium and dedicating a ship to Poseidon, they returned to Naupactus.[23]

Assaults at sea certainly relied on the element of surprise. Thucydides tells of such an assault when the Peloponnesians attacked the Athenians and ravaged Salamis in the winter of 429/8, the third year of the Peloponnesian war. The Megarians persuaded the Spartan (Brasidas) and Cnemus (the Spartan admiral), plus the other Peloponnesian commanders, to make a daring surprise attack on Piraeus, the port of Athens. No one in Athens ever dreamed such an open attack would be tried, since they had such obvious superiority at sea. They had left Piraeus unguarded and open. According to the plan, each man was to take either an oar, a cushion or a rowlock thong,[24] and going overland from Corinth to the sea on the Athenian side, to get to Megara as quickly as they could. There they would hijack forty vessels that were in the docks at Nisaea and sail at once to Piraeus (see map 10). There was no Athenian fleet on the lookout in the harbour, and the Athenians had no idea that the enemy was going to spring a surprise attack. The Athenians assumed they would detect any open attack on Piraeus.[25]

Planning a surprise attack, however, is not the same thing as successfully executing one. The party arrived at Corinth at night, and launched the vessels from Nisaea, but rather than sailing to Piraeus as they had originally intended, they suddenly became afraid of the risk. Some of this was due to the weather having changed and the wind stopping, and partially because the forty ships had been in dry dock and might not have been watertight.[26] In any event, they decided to sail to Salamis, an island off the coast of Megara. There the Athenians had a fort and a squadron of three triremes to prevent any vessels from sailing in or out of Megara. The Spartans assaulted this fort, towed off the triremes empty and surprised the inhabitants by laying waste to the island. Although they did not reach their original target, they succeeded in panicking the Athenians when news of the raid was signalled from Salamis.[27]

Nighttime always provides an excellent opportunity to make an escape, especially when one is under siege. The famous uprising at Plataea in 427 had the population revolting against the Thebans. Even the women valiantly assisted the men by pelting the Thebans with tiles from the houses. Towards dusk, the oligarchs were in full rout and feared that the victorious commons might assault and carry the arsenal and put them all to the sword. The inhabitants set fire to the houses around the agora and the lodging houses, in order to bar their advance, sparing neither their own nor those of the neighbours. A great deal of commercial merchandise was destroyed, and the city risked total destruction if a wind fanned the flames. When hostilities ceased, both sides kept quiet, passing the night on guard against another attack. A Corinthian ship escaped from the island at night, and most of the mercenaries got away secretly to the mainland.[28]

Another night escape came when the Spartans not only sailed for home at night coasting along the shore, but also hauled their ships across the Leucadian isthmus in order to avoid being seen, as they would be if they sailed around, they got away.[29]

Cover of darkness could be used for provisioning troops by sea. During the siege of the Spartan hoplites on Sphacteria in 425, night operations were used to supply food and water to the embattled soldiers. The Spartans called for volunteers to convey to the island ground wheat, wine and cheese, and other food that might be serviceable in a siege. They were willing to pay a high price: they promised freedom to any helot who could get food in. Many took the risk, especially the helots, who put out from any and every point in the Peloponnese and came to shore during the night on the side of the island facing the sea. Divers also swam underwater from the harbour, dragging by a cord skins filled with poppy seed mixed with honey and bruised linseed. The Athenians had imagined it would take only a few days and were extremely frustrated by the unexpectedly long time it took to reduce a body of men shut up on a desert island with only brackish water to drink.[30]

The Athenians finally made their own landing on the island at night. While it was still dark, they embarked all their hoplites on a few vessels and put off, landing a little before dawn on both sides of the island, on the side towards the open sea and on that facing the harbour. They numbered about 800, all hoplites. Then they advanced at a run against the first guard post on the island[31] (see chapter 5).

Sneaking in troops by ship at night was a typical tactic. It was used at Solygeia in 425. The Athenians made an expedition into Corinthian territory with eighty ships and 2,000 Athenian hoplites together with 200 cavalry on board horse transports; allied forces also went with them. But the Corinthians, having previous intelligence from Argos that the Athenian army was coming, had long before occupied the isthmus with all their forces except those who dwelt north of the isthmus and 500 Corinthians who were away doing garrison duty in Ambracia and Leucas. All the rest, to a man, were now there watching to see where the Athenians would land.[32] How did the Corinthians get advanced news from Argos of the intended Athenian invasion? This is an interesting piece of lax security. Presumably, there had been free talk by people who had attended the relevant Assembly meeting and the news passed down to Piraeus. The generals of the Council of 500 should have been able to make military plans with reasonable expectation of confidentiality.[33]

In 424, the Athenian general Demosthenes was presented with an attractive offer to betray Megara to Athens.[34] Megara was close to Athens and controlled the land communication from the Peloponnesus to central Greece, where Sparta had important allies and friends. Taking Megara could block a Peloponnesian invasion at the isthmus and could provide Athens with easy access to Corinthian territory. The Athenians jumped at the opportunity.[35] Demosthenes planned an approach to Megara by land and by sea. The first phase of the plan called for a seizure of the long walls between the city of Megara and its harbour of Nisaea in order to prevent the Peloponnesian troops who guarded the walls and harbour from helping the Peloponnesian sympathisers in the city. It was a classic deception operation setting up the ambush. The Athenians sailed under cover of night to Minoa, the island situated opposite Megara, taking 600 hoplites under the command of Hippocrates, and took cover in a stone quarry not far from the town.[36] A second company consisting of light-armed Plataeans and frontier patrols (*peripoloi*) under the command of Demosthenes stationed themselves in the temple of Enyalius, just outside the city. Security was so good that all that night no one perceived what was going on except the men who were part of the plot. At the approach of dawn, their accomplices within the city began their work.[37] They succeeded in leaving their hiding place and entering the city gates. After they and their associates had gained the upper hand in the first skirmish with the alarmed Megarians, they handed over the gate to the Athenian hoplites, who had hurried to the scene. Immediately after this the walls were occupied. The vanguard of light infantry who had been hiding nearby captured the gate, after which the hoplites consolidated the occupied positions. The operation took place at night to ensure maximum panic among the Megarians, in which traitors and loyal citizens were indistinguishable. It goes without saying that light-armed men were the most suitable choice for a surprise attack because of their speed. The Peloponnesians deserted their watch and fled to Nisaea.[38]

We have already mentioned the escape at sea that occurred in the winter of 415/14. As the Syracusans approached Catana by land, the Athenians sailed off to Syracuse at night and put in unobserved at a place called Leon, which is six or seven stadia distant from Epipolae, disembarking the landing force there and anchoring their ships at Thapsus. They disembarked at daybreak at a point opposite the Olympeium, where they occupied a camping place. The Syracusan horsemen rode back from Catana to Syracuse to alert the infantry and help defend the city[39] (see map 7).

At Plemmyrium in 413, we have an example of both the army and navy being moved into position at night. Gylippus, the Spartan general, was fighting against the Athenians, and the naval battle was begun before dawn. When the fleet was ready, Gylippus led out his whole land force under cover of night, intending to make an assault by land upon the forts of Plemmyrium (see map 7). At the same time, on a pre-arranged signal, thirty-five Syracusan triremes would sail to the attack from the Great Harbour, and another forty-five would sail round from the lesser harbour, where their shipyard was. They would all join together with those inside the harbour and simultaneously attack Plemmyrium. The Athenians would find themselves under attack from both directions, and would be thrown into confusion. The Athenians hastily manned sixty ships to oppose them; twenty-five engaged with the thirty-five Syracusan ships that were in the Great Harbour, and with the other twenty-five went to meet the squadron that was sailing round from the shipyard. And so they all engaged at once in battle in front of the mouth of the Great Harbour, and for a long time held out against one another, one side wishing to force the entrance, the other trying to prevent this.[40] In the meantime, while the Athenians were down at the sea attending to the naval battle, Gylippus and his force made a sudden attack on the forts in the early morning. Once he had captured the biggest fort, the men in the other two smaller ones escaped to a merchant ship and to various small craft and those forts were captured too.[41]

Weather had a tremendous effect on what could be achieved at sea. The Peloponnesians attacked the Athenians on a sail from Cos to Syme in 412/11 (see map 8), the winter of the twentieth year of the war. There was great confusion because of the darkness, rain and fog.[42] From Cos, arriving by night in Cnidus, Astyochus, the Spartan admiral, was urged by the Cnidians not to disembark his sailors, but to sail immediately against twenty Athenian vessels out patrolling. These Athenian ships, along with Charminus, one of the commanders at Samos, were on the watch for the very twenty-seven ships from the Peloponnesus which Astyochus was himself sailing to join.[43] Astyochus, therefore, sailed directly to Syme before his arrival was reported on the chance that he might catch the Peloponnesian ships somewhere on the high seas. But rain and the foggy state of the weather caused his ships to lose their way in the darkness and become disoriented. At daybreak, when his fleet was still scattered, his left wing became visible to the Athenians while the rest of the ships were still wandering round the island. Charminus and the Athenians hastily put to sea against them with fewer than their twenty ships, thinking that these were the ships from Caunus they were watching for. Falling upon them at once, they sank three and damaged others and had the advantage in the action until, to their surprise, the main body of the fleet suddenly came into sight and they found themselves surrounded on all sides. Thereupon they took to flight, and after losing six ships the rest escaped to the island of Teutlussa and thence to Halicarnassus.[44]

Sailing before dawn and hugging the coast was a trick used many times over to escape detection. Night was the perfect time to make an escape, although, in some cases, not all the fleet got away safely. Thucydides tells of a night escape by sea from the Chersonese at Sestos in 411[45] (see map 4). The Athenians were at Sestos with eighteen ships, when they learned of the approach of the Spartan fleet. Their signallers alerted them and they observed the sudden blaze of numerous fires on the hostile shore, and so realised that the Peloponnesians were entering the straits. That same night, making what speed they could and hugging shore of the Chersonese, they sailed towards Elaeus, wishing to get by the enemy's ships and out into open water. They eluded the sixteen ships at Abydos (although they had been warned by their friends to be on the alert to prevent their sailing out). They sighted the fleet of Mindarus, which immediately gave chase. Not all ships had time to get away. The greater number escaped to Imbros and Lemnos, while four of those in the rear were overtaken off Elaeus (see map 9). One of these was stranded opposite the temple of Protesilaus and taken with its crew. Two others were captured without their crews and the fourth was abandoned on the shore of Imbros and burned by the enemy[46] (see map 9).

Fourth Century

Ambushes continued at sea well into the fourth century. One event concerned Conon, the Athenian admiral famous for his overwhelming victory over the Spartan fleet off Cnidus (the southwestern extremity of modern Turkey) in 394 and his restoration the following year of the long walls and fortifications of Athens' port, Piraeus. Conon and Arcsilaidas got their men to remain fighting by convincing them there was an enemy ambush. He writes:

> When the allies were deserting him, Conon sent a deserter to inform the enemy that they were about to run away and from where and when. The enemy set an ambush and waited. Conon then announced to the allies that it was safer to retreat because he had learned about the ambush. The retreating men, perceiving the ambush in advance, turned around and remained until they had fought the war through to a victory for him.[47]

In 387, Antalcidas in Abydos set up an ambush based on the tightest possible secrecy. His scouts had signalled to him that eight triremes were approaching. He embarked sailors on twelve of his fastest ships and gave orders that if anyone was lacking men he should fill up his crew from the ships left behind and lay in wait with the utmost possible concealment. Then, as the enemy was sailing past him, he pursued. When they saw him coming, the enemy fled. Antalcidas succeeded in overtaking the slowest of the Athenian ships with his fastest. By giving orders to the leaders of his own fleet not to attack the hindmost ships, he continued the pursuit of those who were ahead. And when he had captured them, those who were behind, upon seeing that the leaders of their fleet were being taken, out of discouragement were themselves taken even by the slower ships of Antalcidas, and the result was that all the ships were captured.[48]

Xenophon reports a night operation at Cape Zoster in 388. At Aegina, the Spartan ships under Gorgopas followed an Athenian flotilla at night as it returned to port and attacked the ships successfully as they landed near Cape Zoster in Attica. Eunomus waited for nightfall then hoisted his sail and with his ship led the way carrying a light, as was customary so that the rest of his ships, which were following, would not wander off-course. At that moment, Gorgopas immediately embarked his men and followed Eunomus, watching the light but keeping a bit behind so that Eunomus' men would not see or notice them – his boatswains kept time by clicking stones together instead of using their voices, and the men made a slicing motion with their oars.[49]

For those who argue that the Greeks do not fight at night, there is the continuation of this story on Cape Zoster. When Eunomus' ships approached the shore around Zoster in Attica, Gorgopas, by means of a trumpet, gave the command to attack. Now the men on some of Eunomus' ships were just disembarking, other ships were still coming to anchor, while yet other ships were making their way to shore. A sea battle by moonlight took place in which Gorgopas captured four ships that he put in tow and carried off with him to Aegina. The rest of the Athenian ships escaped.[50]

Some events combine a sea landing with a land ambush. Polyaenus tells of an event from 388, when Chabrias was sailing against an enemy city, and he landed the peltasts at night. At dawn he sailed towards the harbour that was farther from the city. The men from the city ran out to prevent the men from the ships disembarking. The peltasts from the ambush, appearing behind them, killed some, captured others alive, boarded the ships and put out to sea.[51]

Night assaults from sea continued in the fourth century. Another story about Chabrias from 388 sees him setting out on a voyage to Cyprus to aid Evagoras. He took 800 peltasts and ten triremes, to which he added more ships and a body of hoplites obtained from Athens. He and his peltasts landed at night on Aegina to set up an ambush in a hollow place a short distance beyond the Temple of Heracles. At daybreak, at the agreed signal, the Athenian hoplites came under the command of Demaenetus and ascended to a point about sixteen stadia beyond the Heracleium, where the so-called Tripyrgia is, an unknown location. When Gorgopas' vanguard passed the ambush spot, Chabrias and his peltasts rose up immediately and threw their javelins and stones at the enemy. The Athenian hoplites who had disembarked from the ships also advanced upon them. The enemy soldiers in the van, inasmuch as they were not a compact mass, were quickly killed. Gorgopas and the Spartans were among the dead. When they fell, the other troops took flight.[52] Chabrias' peltasts were particularly useful in the pursuit. There were 150 Aeginetans killed and 200 foreigners, i.e. resident aliens in Aegina.

A similar tactic of unknown date, but attributed by Polyaenus to Diognetus, had this Athenian trying to capture a certain city. He landed soldiers secretly at night, placed them in an ambush and at daybreak sailed in openly. The men from the city ran to their ships, and the men in ambush rushed to the city and captured it easily. After sailing in and anchoring, Diognetus disembarked the men from the ships and conquered those who had come out to defend their city.[53]

Polyaenus lists a number of strategies used by Diotimus, the fourth-century Athenian admiral.[54] In one adventure he has ten ships, which he disguises as five by pulling in the oars on one side, yoking them together, and only raising five sails. The Lacedaemonians were lured into an attack because of the small number of Athenian ships. Due to the Athenians' expertise, they sank six of the Laconian ships and captured the other four with their men. Such deception was considered both clever and fair, at least by the time Polyaenus was writing.[55]

In another adventure, Diotimus sailed at night into the enemy's territory. He landed many men from each ship and hid them in an ambush. At daybreak he held the ships at anchor near the men in ambush, and after ordering the men on deck to prepare to fight and the rowers to take up the Thalamians, Zeugite and Thranite oars, in turns, he tried to bring some of the ships to land.[56] The enemy ran up and tried to prevent the landing. But when he raised the pre-arranged signal, the men in ambush appeared, killed many of the enemy and routed the rest. Diotimus landed safely.[57]

Another ambush involving a combined, land and sea operation is related by Frontinus, Polyaenus and Diodorus. They tell the story of Alcibiades sailing in 409 to Byzantium in preparation for a siege of the city. Since Byzantium was a large city with many defenders, taking it would require having allies on the inside. The Athenian generals created the impression that they were going to raise the siege by sailing off in the afternoon with all their ships and withdrew their land army some distance. But they returned in the middle of the night and drew near to the city. They dispatched triremes with orders to drag off the Byzantine boats. They also raised a clamour to make it sound as if their entire force was there. They hid their land army near the walls and waited for the signal from their agents inside the city. The Byzantines in the city, unaware of the ambush, rushed out to help save their ships. The betrayers in the city raised the signal from the wall and admitted Alcibiades' troops by means of ladders in complete safety. In this way he took the city.[58]

Polyaenus mentions an ambush by one Archebius of Heraclea. When the enemy was constantly harassing the coast, Archebius dragged up fishing boats, made them difficult to move by tying ropes through the keel, and hid in ambush with some others. A trumpeter was up in a tree as a lookout (*skopos*). The lookout saw the enemy had anchored in one warship while two thirty-oared vessels disembarked. Some were looting while others tried to free the fishing boats from the ropes. It was then he blew his trumpet. Archebius, rousing his troops from ambush, fell upon the enemy and brought their thirty-oared vessels and the warships into the city's harbour.[59]

In a case involving not regular warfare but renegade mercenaries, we see how the element of surprise was used. In 413, the Athenians sent back a contingent of Thracian mercenaries so they would not have to pay them. Diitrephes the Athenian was appointed to command them on their return journey. They were to sail through the Euripus doing whatever damage they could to the enemy along the coast. Then they landed at Tanagra and did some looting. In the evening, he then sailed across the Euripus from Chalcis in Euboea, landed in Boeotia and led them against Mycalessus (see map 11). Diitrephes spent the night unobserved near the Temple of Hermes, which was two miles (three kilometres) from the town. At daybreak they assaulted the city and captured it because the population was off-guard and not expecting that *anyone would march so far inland from the sea and attack them* [italics, mine]. They sacked the houses and temples, butchered the inhabitants including women and children. Thucydides, once again, calls this *aprosdokeitos* – unexpected or unlooked for.[60]

Aeneas Tacticus warns against the use of diversionary tactics by invaders.[61] In the case of the betrayal of Byzantium, the Athenians used a seaborne raid, land troops and a diversion to gain entry to the city. After feigning a withdrawal from the area, they dispatched triremes for a night raid on the port. Meanwhile, the land army was brought up close to the walls. The raiders in the port made a great deal of noise and, consequently, the Peloponnesians and Byzantines rushed off to the scene of the disturbance. The fifth columnists them admitted Alcibiades and his troops.[62]

Land and Sea Operations

The Greeks considered it wholly acceptable to catch an enemy at a disadvantage in a sea battle. A common ploy was to attack when the enemy's crews had scattered for their midday meal.[63] The disastrous defeat at Syracuse happened in part because the Syracusans had established a market so close to their ships that their rowers could shop, eat and be prepared to fight again long before the Athenian crews were ready.[64] The disastrous defeat at Aegospotami happened because of a surprise attack that was made when the bulk of the crews were several miles away at market.[65]

What all these examples show is that the element of surprise was as important in naval operations as it was in land battles. The distinction between the two is artificial because the Greeks co-ordinated their land and sea attacks. In fact, as the Peloponnesian war progressed, there were fewer and fewer men who fought only at sea or only on land. Instead, there were men who were sometimes soldiers and sometimes sailors.[66] We often see Greeks carrying out night marches to meet a fleet arriving in port, or a night landing of the fleet disembarking hoplites for a land attack.

Outright deceptions also occurred, including several instances of disguised identity. Crews were put onboard captured ships, which then sailed towards or past the enemy, sometimes towing their own ships as if they had been captured. Decoys were used to create diversions.[67] The Greeks found nothing unusual in these operations. Nor do we see any moralising about such methods – quite the opposite. They are collected in handbooks by Greek writers and attributed to clever commanders. Individual leaders seem to have been free to choose the tactics they felt were appropriate and the only judgement made was whether the operation succeeded. If navies awaited the enemy in plain sight, it was not because they felt obliged to engage the enemy in plain sight but because they believed the place and time offered them the best chance of victory.[68]

CHAPTER 8

The Age of Light-Armed

THE PELOPONNESIAN WAR ENDED in 404 and closed out the fifth century with a surprise attack. Lysander, the Spartan, tricked the Athenians at Aegospotami, by attacking their vessels at a regular hour and then calling off his fleet. Once this had become an established procedure, the Athenians dropped their guard after the Spartans dispersed. Then, when most of the Athenians had scattered according to their usual pattern, he returned, attacked and slew the rest, and captured all their vessels.[1] The fourth century was thus ushered in with the defeat of the Athenian Empire and a Spartan hegemony that took its place and lasted until the Battle of Leuctra in 371. Sparta found itself engulfed in the so-called Corinthian war from 395 until 387 against a coalition of four allied states: Thebes, Athens, Corinth and Argos, which were initially backed by Persia. Then the Boeotian or Theban war broke out in 378 as the result of a revolt in Thebes against Sparta; the war would last six years.

There was obviously no shortage of warfare in the fourth century, and all sides continued to fight with hoplites, but the conditions of military life were slowly changing. Gone was the era of short military campaigns that took place only during the summer after the harvest. Cities were now attacked by night, fighting took place year-round, and atrocities were committed against civilians.[2] The prolongation of campaigns and a change in tactics set the stage for the professionalisation of Greek armies. Whereas hoplite warfare had not necessarily called for very elaborate training, the use of missiles and the tactics of staging ambushes required training at a higher technical level. When light-armed troops were utilised everything depended upon movement. Rapid changes of position, sudden strikes, speedy retreats and ambushes were all operations that needed to be carefully prepared with accurate intelligence. Because such operations had to be well directed and executed with speed and determination, it could mean training one's own troops or hiring well-trained mercenaries.[3]

The change from militiamen to paid fighters meant a change from amateurs to professional soldiers.[4] Foreign mercenaries were expensive and could not usually be hired in large numbers, but citizens could be recruited and trained to perform the same specialised functions provided by foreign, light-armed mercenaries. Athens' overseas expeditions in the fourth century were all carried out by mercenaries.[5]

Light-Armed Troops and Peltasts

An increasingly important role was played by light-armed troops in the fourth century, and they became a significant factor in the conduct and the outcome of battles.[6] Although hoplites mattered most in set battle on a large scale, war on land now had a place for other arms and other methods than those of the hoplite phalanx. Smaller tactical units gave a new manoeuvrability that had been impossible in traditional hoplite lines. These new troops became effective in gaining tactical advantage, usually through a sudden, surprise assault. Small striking forces became especially important in fifth-column operations.[7]

There were several types of light troops, the most common being archers, slingers and peltast-javelin men.[8] The peltasts became the most effective of the light-armed troops.[9] Peltasts were a sort of mean between the extremes of heavy- and light-armed men. They had all the mobility of light-armed troops, and yet sufficient offensive and defensive armour to cope, with a fair amount of success, with small bodies of hoplite troops (i.e. those not in set-piece battles). Using peltasts would increase the ability of Greek armies to stage surprise attacks and ambushes.[10] The name peltast comes from the fact that they were armed with a *pelte* (Thracian shield). In place of a dagger, they might also carry a kind of scimitar, a curved sabre known as a *machaira*, which could be used to deal slashing blows.[11] Peltasts were not much help in stopping a hoplite force head on; their main use was to protect the flanks of an advancing hoplite army against attacks from the light-armed troops of the enemy. The majority of Greek states had an organised body of light-armed troops. Athens was an exception until this was changed by commanders such as Iphicrates and Chabrias.[12]

Although their weapons might seem simple, these light troops were specialist soldiers. Their way of fighting entailed a higher degree of specialisation than the relatively straightforward, spear-and-shield techniques of hoplites fighting in formation. The accurate use of missile weapons was a skill acquired and maintained only by regular and constant practice. For this reason, light-armed troops tended to be professionals. At first, they were foreign mercenaries recruited in Thrace, Crete and Rhodes; later, they were natives recruited locally from city-states. Athens was the first to transform some of the poorer citizens into light troops.[13]

The Athenian general Iphicrates is credited by two ancient sources – Diodorus and Cornelius Nepos – with reforming the equipment of his hoplites. These military reforms have long been the subject of scholarly debate, but what is clear is that they were much better equipped to stage ambushes.[14] Iphicrates did away with the large hoplite shield – the *aspis* – and replaced it with the smaller *pelta*. He also lengthened the sword (*xiphous*) and the spear (*doratos*).[15] Of course, there were peltasts in use long before this time in other regions of Greece, but now the reform was coming to Athens.[16]

The defeat of the Athenian hoplites by light-armed cavalry and peltasts at Spartolus, the successful defence by Acarnanian slingers of Stratus against Peloponnesian hoplites, or the destruction of Ambraciot hoplites by Amphilochian light-armed, not only reinforced the lessons learned from the experience in Aetolia and Sphacteria but also carried them still further.[17] From the last phases of the Peloponnesian war and, continuing into the fourth century, armies began to contain significantly higher numbers of specialised troops than Classical ones had fielded.[18] This included the growth of a corps of archers, the addition of light-armed troops, the rise of mercenary troops recruited largely from abroad, and the development of cavalry.[19]

Generalisations about mercenary service can be misleading.[20] It is commonly assumed that mercenary soldiers did not become a significant factor of Greek social and political history before the fourth century. In fact, however, Greek mercenary soldiers had been serving in armies of southeast Mediterranean powers since the Archaic Age.[21] The reasons for soldiers becoming mercenaries and their terms of service vary. In Crete, for example, one would cite demographic developments and military traditions as well as socio-economic crisis.[22] Another accusation that dogged military operations was that the systematic use of mercenaries encouraged a selfish inertness at home, a dangerous licentiousness in the free companies abroad, and that it diverted the energies of the ablest citizens from patriotic objects to the baser pursuit of plunder and military fame. The fact is, however, that soldiers did not take up this line of work because it was so lucrative. Service in places such as Persia and Egypt might be lucrative, but service in Greece proper was not.[23]

Soldiers in the fourth century accepted military service knowing that there was no money in it for them unless they looted, stole or won booty.

Hoplite Armour and *Hamippoi*

Another military innovation that occurred in the fourth century was the lightening of the hoplite panoply. Some hoplites were still sporting extensive metal armour in the mid-fourth century, but the overall trend of the Classical period seems to have been a progressive lightening of hoplite armour. This made hoplites more mobile and thus better able to cope with the challenges of difficult terrain, enemy skirmishers and ambushes. Lighter panoplies were also cheaper. Konrad Kinzel suggests that this enabled more citizens to equip themselves as hoplites and enjoy the attendant political status that went with this type of fighting.[24] But were these troops really hoplites any more? Nick Sekunda also describes the shift in the use of armour plate in the late fifth century. He seems to think that armour all but disappeared as the Spartans were depicted wearing only a *pilos* helmet[25] and tunic, no cuirass, greaves, etc. and Boeotian hoplites were all but naked. Does this indicate a change in battlefield tactics? The availability of materials? And were these soldiers still considered 'hoplites', i.e. heavy infantry?[26] It certainly contributed to them being more mobile and able to counter attacks by light-armed soldiers.

Another military innovation of the fourth century was the introduction of *hamippoi*, a type of light-infantry corps that ran behind cavalrymen. The *hamippoi* were trained to fight alongside the cavalrymen. They would go into battle holding on to the tails and manes of the cavalry horses. *Hamippoi* were particularly useful in a straight cavalry fight, where they would hack at the enemy horsemen. One of their signature manoeuvres was to slip underneath the enemy horse and rip its belly open with a dagger. This certainly suggests that service in the *hamippoi* was not for the faint-hearted. In his pamphlet *On the Duties of the Hipparch*, Xenophon recommends that the Athenians raise a corps of such men from among the exiles and other foreigners in Athens, who had special reason to be bitter against the enemy.[27] Xenophon saw their value as being able to deliver a surprise as he points out that they could be hidden among and behind taller mounted troops.[28]

Hamippoi were first mentioned serving in the forces of the Syracusan tyrant Gelon, where his 2,000 cavalry were accompanied by an equal number of *hippodromoi psiloi* or *psiloi* who run alongside the cavalry.[29] *Hamippoi* are found in the Boeotian army during the Peloponnesian war. When the Spartan army was reorganised some time after the Battle of Mantinea in 418, the 600 *skiritai* were not folded into the ranks of the *morai* but were converted into the *hamippoi* and fought alongside the 600 cavalry.[30]

In short, as the fifth century progressed into the fourth, the trend was to lighten the armour of the hoplites and add soldiers from the lower classes, who could perform various new duties that required greater speed and manoeuvrability. This made ambushing more difficult and less likely if each side had mobile troops that could improvise.

The Generals in the Fourth Century

The need to develop specialised, light-armed troops encouraged the rise of professional generalship in the fourth century. The proper handling of such troops required something more than amateur leadership. Fourth-century generals had to recruit different types of soldiers, who used different types of weapons and tactics. W. K. Pritchett dedicates a chapter of the second volume of his comprehensive work, *The Greek State at War*, to this new breed of general.[31] Their careers were made possible by the changing political and military circumstances, and new operating conditions dictated some new fighting techniques.[32] The military commanders in the late fifth and early fourth centuries had to conduct military operations more and more independently, relying on their own skill and talent. They developed increasingly strong ties with their army rather than just their polis.[33] The independence of fourth-century commanders was a function of long-term service abroad and of operating independently of their home authorities. How much freedom they enjoyed in the field can probably never be precisely determined, but those who were elected or appointed to office by the larger city-states seem to have discharged their functions with as much loyalty as similar officials in the fifth century.[34]

Another motivation for the increased use of novel techniques and stratagems was that fourth-century military forces were sent out without being provided with money. The generals were expected to raise funds by plunder, by contributions from allies or even by foreign service. They and their troops seem to have had unlimited permission to plunder the enemy's country.[35] In the fifth century, mercenaries had been dismissed when the state lacked funds, but conditions had greatly changed in the fourth century. A great number of the stratagems that are collected in Polyaenus and assigned to Athenian generals of the fourth century have to do with the raising of money to pay their troops.[36] Six of the stratagems preserved in Polyaenus on Jason of Pherae, for example, deal with means for securing funds.[37]

Even with these new troops, staging an ambush was no easier to accomplish in the fourth century than it was in the fifth. Naturally, it was best done with soldiers who were trained by their leaders in the skills needed for such operations. This is where the light-armed troops, especially peltasts, excelled. Light-armed troops, unlike hoplites, were trained to be highly responsive and flexible. They had to be able to close with the enemy and kill quickly. Light infantrymen could be used to destroy the enemy on his own ground, make the best of initiative, stealth and surprise, infiltration, ambush and night operations.[38] Iphicrates trained his light-armed troops by staging fake ambushes, fake assaults, fake panics and fake desertions so his men would be ready if the real thing happened.[39] Light infantrymen were not tacticians; they could not respond mechanically to a set of conditions on a battlefield with a pre-determined action like a phalanx. Whoever led the ambush had to know how to use initiative, understand intent, take independent action, analyse the field of operations, collect intelligence and make rapid decisions. Initiative meant bold action and often involved risks. Initiative by the tactical leader may have been independent of what higher commanders wanted done to the enemy.[40] The men such leaders worked with were soldiers trained to fend for themselves through hardship and risk in hostile, uncompromising terrain. Such operations built a greater degree of teamwork and skill than other types of infantry formations as a result of the stress put on adaptability, close-combat skills and independent action.

Fourth-Century Ambush

Greek literature in the fourth century contains much more information on ambush than its fifth-century counterpart. Even didactic works such as Xenophon's *Cyropaedia*, while wholly removed from the context of real events, give lessons about commanding a Greek army.[41] The ambush against the forces of Gadatas[42] is a classic use of clandestine communications and the laying of an ambush among a cluster of small villages. We can also see a classic deception operation, where soldiers are arrayed along with the baggage train and the women to make their force seem larger than it is.[43] Any enemy attack would have to make a wider circuit around them and thereby thin out their own lines.

We cannot always be sure of the dates or even the historicity of certain stratagems, but they all seem to describe generic situations that crop up again and again. One of the most common ways to stage an ambush, for example, was to attack an army on the march. Polyaenus gives an undated example of the detection of such an ambush. While leading his army, Tissamenus saw many birds flying above a particular place, but not settling on the ground, and he concluded that they shrank from settling because they feared men lying in ambush. After investigating the spot, he attacked and cut down the Ionians who were waiting in ambush. This is a much repeated story, with several Roman commanders using the same tactic.[44]

Another piece of good advice was to be ready for an ambush whether you were expecting one or not. Polyaenus tells a story about Arxilaidas the Laconian who, around 370/69, was about to travel a suspicious road with his army. Pretending he had advance intelligence which he did not, he ordered them to advance prepared for battle because the enemy lay in ambush. But by chance a large ambush was discovered. He attacked first and easily killed all those in ambush, outsmarting them by his advance preparations.[45]

Playing on the known habits of barbarian tribes was another common practice. Polyaenus relates several stratagems used by Clerachus against the Thracians, which presumably date from a time just prior to his entering the service of Cyrus. All illustrate the frequency of Thracian nocturnal attacks.[46] This practice, according to Polyaenus, enabled Clearchus the Spartan to set an ambush for one of the local Thracian tribes, the Thrynians.[47] He withdrew a little distance with a number of soldiers, and ordered them to hit their shields, as was the Thracian habit, putting all the Greeks in camp on alert. When the Thracians attacked, they expected to find everything in camp peaceful and quiet, but the Greeks were ready for them and they were beaten off with severe losses.[48] When the Thracians sent envoys to negotiate a peace, Clearchus had the bodies of a few dead Thracians cut up and strung from trees. When the envoys asked about the meaning of the spectacle, they were told that a meal for Clearchus was being prepared! Such antics as these caused people to question the ethical aspects of Clearchus' conduct, but his military qualities are beyond dispute.[49] He displayed great military insight in critical situations and this meant using whatever tactics worked.[50]

The instances of surprise attacks, night marches and ambushes gathered in this chapter show how common ambushes had become in Greek warfare. This included not only light-armed troops but also hoplites being used for manoeuvres off the regular battlefield. Against hoplites, the function of peltasts was so often harassment, and the night was the most advantageous time. Isocrates equated peltasts with pirates.[51]

Pursuing a fleeing army was a tactic that also became more common because of the mobility of light-armed troops. Plutarch tells us that the Spartans thought it ignoble for the Greeks to kill men who were fleeing, and adds that this policy made enemies more inclined to run away than fight.[52] The practical reason for doing this, however, was not a lack of morality but rather a tactic to avoid the kind of thing that happened after the Battle of Haliartus in 395. The Thebans pursued the Spartans into the hills, where the Spartans immediately turned on them and attacked back with javelins and stones. They killed more than 200 Thebans.[53] Practicality played a bigger part in Greek military policy than moralising.

The shock over the effectiveness of these new soldiers and their new tactics became apparent when a detachment of peltasts won a brilliant victory over Spartan soldiers at Lechaeum in 394.[54] The commanders Callias and Iphicrates, looking down from the walls of Corinth, could see an approaching *mora* of Spartan soldiers. The Spartans were not numerous and were not accompanied by any light-armed or cavalry. The Athenans commanders determined that it would be safe to stage an ambush with their own peltasts.[55] They could aim their javelins at the Spartans' unshielded side when they passed. Callias stationed his hoplites in the ambush not far from the city walls, while Iphicrates led the peltasts in an attack, knowing if they lost they could retreat more quickly.[56] The Spartan commander ordered a group of the youngest soldiers to pursue the assailants, but when they did so they caught no one, since they were hoplites pursuing peltasts at a distance of a javelin's cast. Besides, Iphicrates had given orders to the peltasts to retire before the hoplites got near them. Then, when the Spartans were returning from their pursuit, out of formation because each man had pursued as swiftly as he could, Iphicrates' troops turned around and not only did those in front again hurl javelins at the Spartans but others on the flank also ran and attacked them on their unprotected side.[57]

Having lost many of their best men, with their returning cavalry's support, the Spartans again attempted to pursue the peltasts. Yet when the peltasts gave way, the cavalry bungled the attack by not pursuing the enemy at full speed but, rather, kept an even pace with the hoplites in both their attack and their retreat. Finally, not knowing what to do, the Spartans gathered together on a small hill about two stades distant from the sea and about sixteen or seventeen stades from Lechaeum. When the Spartans in Lechaeum realised what was happening, they got into boats and sailed alongside the shore until they were opposite the hill. The men on the hill were now at a loss as to what to do; they were suffering dreadfully, and dying, while unable to harm the enemy in any way, and in addition they now saw the Athenian hoplites coming at them. At this point they gave way and fled, some throwing themselves into the sea, while a few made it to safety to Lechaeum with the cavalry. The total dead from all the skirmishes and the flight was enormous; the Spartans had lost half their number in a skirmish with Iphicrates' peltasts.[58]

Iphicrates, the ambusher, had to beware of ambushes himself. Polyaenus reports that the Spartan harmost (military governor) set an ambush that caught Iphicrates off-guard while he was marching towards the city of Sicyon in 391. Iphicrates immediately retreated by a different, short, trackless route. He selected his strongest troops, fell on the ambushers suddenly and killed them all. He admitted that he made a mistake by not reconnoitring the area, but he exploited his prompt suspicion of an ambush well by quickly attacking the ambushers.[59]

Iphicrates won several successes in the Corinthian war, such as the recapture of Sidous, Krommyon and Oinoe from the Spartans.[60] Several scholars have seen the similarities in the tactics used by Iphicrates' peltasts and those that the Aetolians had used against Demosthenes, or that Demosthenes in turn used against the Spartans on Sphacteria.[61] The success of Iphicrates was a suggestive sign of the future which might be in store for the professional peltast. The fact that they could defeat the Spartans boosted their ego and was a blow against Spartan prestige. As Parke describes it:

> This success of the peltasts . . . was sufficient to make Iphicrates' name forever as a general. Moreover it conferred on this type of light-armed troops a reputation for deadliness in battle which they had never before enjoyed in popular estimation. To this new esteem may be attributed the frequent appearance of peltasts in all armies, especially in the Athenian, during the next half-century. Henceforth, they become the typical form of light-armed troops and superseded the less-clearly specified, earlier varieties.[62]

Ambushing, at what some commentators consider 'inappropriate times', now became a habit. Of course, what other time than 'inappropriate' could an ambush be? Several surprise attacks are attributed to Iphicrates by Frontinus. In one, Iphicrates attacked a Spartan camp at an hour when both armies were accustomed to forage for food and wood.[63]

Another ambush on which Xenophon provides fairly detailed information took place in 388 in the Hellespontine region. The Spartans sent Anaxibius to Abydos as harmost (military governor) to relieve Dercylidas.[64] He immediately took the offensive against the Athenians and their allies. The Athenians feared Anaxibius would find a way to weaken their position, and sent Iphicrates with eight ships and 1,200 peltasts to the Hellespont. First the two commanders just sent raiding parties against each other, using irregulars. Then Iphicrates crossed over by night to the most deserted portion of the territory of Abydos, and set an ambush in the mountains. He ordered his fleet to sail northwards along the Chersonese in order to deceive Anaxibius into believing they had left the area. Anaxibius suspected nothing and marched back to Abydos, but made his march in a rather careless fashion. Iphicrates' men in the ambush waited until the vanguard of hoplites from Abydos had reached the plain, and at the moment when the rearguard consisting of Anaxibius' Spartans started coming down from the mountains they sprang the ambush and rushed to attack the rearguard. Anaxibius' army formed a very long and narrow column and it was practically impossible for his other troops to hasten uphill to the aid of the rearguard. He stayed where he was and fought to the death with twelve other Spartans. The rest of the Spartans fell in flight. Only 150 hoplites from the vanguard still managed to get away but only because they had been in the front of the column and were nearer to Abydos. This makes the probable percentage of losses in the middle of the column somewhere between that of the totally destroyed rearguard and the twenty-five per cent of the vanguard. Iphicrates went back to the Chersonese with a successful operation behind him.[65] This carefully planned ambush, and indeed Iphicrates' victory, have been compared to a successful guerrilla operation.[66] With the defeat and death of Anaxibius, the danger for Athens of Sparta getting supremacy in the Hellespont was over. Iphicrates continued to operate against the Spartans in these parts until the Peace of Antalcidas, after which he entered the service of the Thracian kings.[67] When Iphicrates left for the Hellespont in 388, Chabrias succeeded him as commander of the peltasts in Corinth.[68] Because he had served under Thrasyboulus in the Hellespontine region, he was probably trained in the use of peltasts.[69]

Xenophon and the *Anabasis*

The Greeks also came to realise that hoplite warfare, although well adapted to the peculiar circumstances of fighting within their own country, was not capable by itself of facing circumstances of warfare outside Greece, or even in the lesser-known parts of Greece itself.[70] One of the few mercenary armies about whose composition we have exact information is Xenophon's Ten Thousand. Xenophon's

Anabasis provides an unparalleled wealth of information on Greek mercenary service overseas in the fourth century, and how mixed continents of Greek hoplites and peltasts worked together. The tactics and fighting methods of the peltasts in the service of Athens and Sparta differed in no way from those of the peltasts on the march of the Ten Thousand.[71]

The Peloponnesian war had produced large numbers of exiles who were forced to hire out as mercenaries, and ten thousand such soldiers found themselves recruited by Cyrus in his bid for the throne of his brother Artaxerxes. Many of Cyrus' troops had a background in non-traditional combat.[72] Non-hoplites including peltasts, archers, slingers and cavalry made up almost a fifth of Xenophon's army.[73] Xenophon's men developed a great proficiency at night marching, and the light-armed enabled them to set up ambushes and pursue a fleeing enemy.[74] On the defensive side, the use of light-armed and peltasts allowed Xenophon's army to safeguard its routes and protect against ambushes set for them.[75]

Because Xenophon and his men were travelling through unknown territory, one use of ambush was to capture intelligence assets: 'When the enemy was giving us trouble, we set an ambush. It allowed us for one thing to catch our breath, but besides, we killed a number of them, and we took special pains to get some prisoners for this very purpose – of being able to employ them as guides, men who knew the country.'[76]

We see the intelligence gathering structure of the Ten Thousand very clearly in Xenophon's *Anabasis*.[77] After having quartered their troops in local villages,[78] Democrates of Temnus was sent with a body of troops during the night to the mountains.[79] The Greeks had heard that late-arriving stragglers had seen fires, suggesting a Persian presence. Democrates was sent because he had the reputation of having made accurate reports in many similar situations.[80] Intelligence gatherers need to be brave, able to act alone without panicking and be accurate in their assessments. Indeed, Democrates is described as being able to discern what 'facts were facts' and what 'fictions were fictions'.[81]

When Democrates returned, he reported that he had not seen fires, but rather he had captured an intelligence asset – a man with a Persian bow and quiver, and a battle axe of the sort that Amazons carry.[82] When this man was interrogated about where he came from, he replied that he was a Persian and was on his way to the camp of Tiribazus to get provisions. They asked him for information about the size of Tiribazus' force and for what purpose it had been gathered.[83] The prisoner replied that Tiribazus had his own forces plus Chalybian and Taochian mercenaries, and that he himself had made his preparations with the idea of taking a position at the next mountain pass, which had the only road through which the Greeks could be attacked. Once the generals heard this information, they decided to bring their troops together in one camp.[84] They left a garrison behind under the command of Sophaenetus the Stymphalian and set out at once using the captured asset as a guide.[85] As soon as they crossed the mountains, the peltasts pushed ahead of the hoplites and charged the enemy camp. The Persians were taken by surprise and simply fled.[86] Some were killed, and twenty horsemen were captured as was Tiribazus' tent with its silver-footed couches, drinking cups and his staff. Once the hoplites heard what had happened, they thought it better to go back to their own camp before it could be set upon by the Persians. They sounded the recall trumpet and went home.[87]

We also see this type of operation when light troops set an ambush and captured 'some of the stealing rascals who are following us'.[88] From these fellows they learned about passages through the mountains. Knowing the geography was of crucial importance since attacking the Greeks in ravines or when crossing over bridges was a common Persian tactic.[89]

Xenophon planned an operation that depended on taking the enemy by surprise.[90] The mercenaries were faced with an enemy holding a mountain pass. Since the bulk of the mountain was apparently undefended, Xenophon suggested a night attack on an unoccupied section of it as a diversionary tactic. He goes on to say that in his opinion such a tactic would be perfectly feasible, since they would be neither overseen nor overheard.[91]

When faced again with the difficulty that a pass was occupied, this time by the Chalybians, the Greeks mounted a night operation.[92] Xenophon proposed that the mountain tops dominating the pass should be occupied by a separate detachment, which they did at night using hoplites and light-armed. The following day when the Chalybians marched up the road to the pass, the Greeks on the mountain top attacked them by surprise. Most of the Chalybians were blocking the road, but part of them turned to fight the Greeks higher up. The Greek hoplites and light-armed defeated their adversaries and gave chase. Meanwhile, the peltasts, who acted as shock troops, rushed towards the Chalybians in the pass. Normally in this type of ambush, hand-to-hand fighting would ensue, but when the Chalybians saw that their men in the mountains had been defeated they fled, leaving the pass free for the Greeks.[93]

Not only was setting ambushes useful, but the mere faking of an ambush could be effective. As the Greek army descended to Trapezus, a Greek city in Colchian territory on the Black Sea, they were afraid of being pursued by the tribe of the Drilai. They pretended to set an ambush. Ten Cretan archers, commanded by a Mysian, attracted the attention of the enemy by flashing bronze *peltai* in the sun. The Drilai, thinking this was an ambush, kept at a safe distance. When the Greek army had gotten far enough away, the Mysian received the signal to run with his men at full speed to join them. Although the Mysian himself was wounded running down the road, his companions, who had sought cover in the wood bordering the road, carried him with them. The Cretan archers kept shooting at the enemy from a safe distance and thus reached the safety of the Greek camp.[94]

After a voyage along the coast, the Greeks arrived at Heraclea, a Greek city on the border with Bithynia. Here the army split up. The Arcadians sailed straight to the Greek port of Calpe, disembarked at night and advanced against some Bithynian villages about thirty stadia inland. The Thracian Bithynians were completely taken by surprise and a large number of people were captured along with their cattle. It should be noted that these raids were done by hoplites with Thracian peltasts on the defensive.[95]

While the Greeks were crossing to Europe, they enlisted with Seuthes, king of the Odrysian Thracians.[96] Seuthes had been operating in the territory of the Thynians with a comparatively small army consisting of peltasts and horsemen. He feared a night attack from them, but with the Greek mercenaries he felt he could launch a surprise attack on them instead.[97] At Xenophon's request, the hoplites marched at the head during the night, followed by the peltasts. Seuthes brought up the rear with his horsemen, instead of riding in front. At daybreak, Seuthes and his horsemen rode out ahead to reconnoitre; he wanted to stop any wayfarers from warning the villagers. The rest of the Greeks waited, and followed the tracks of his horses. Since they found no footsteps in the snow on the mountains, they assumed they were not being tracked. Seuthes launched his surprise attack on the villages over the mountains. The initial surprise attack was successful.[98] The Thynians, however, after being driven from their village, returned at night and attacked the Greeks. They threw javelins inside the houses, tried to break off the points of the Greeks' spears with clubs, and set the wooden houses on fire. At dawn, the reassembled troops of Seuthes and Xenophon advanced back to the mountains. As the Thynians begged for mercy, it was left to Xenophon to decide whether or not he wished to take revenge on the Thynians for their night attack.[99]

On a number of occasions the decision was made to capture a position by craft rather than by a pitched battle. Xenophon records a jocular exchange where the Spartans are accused of being trained as thieves from childhood, and they in turn accused the Athenians of being thieves of public funds. If the comparison of military trickery to stealing reveals any moral qualms on the part of officers of the Ten Thousand about using such tactics, it never prevented them from using them.

Most of the rules of ambush and surprise remained the same in the fourth century. Weather could still thwart even the best night operation. Such was the case in a night operation planned by Thrasyboulus in 403. He set out with seventy followers from Thebes and occupied the fort at Phyle, a fortress with a commanding position. The Thirty Tyrants set out from Athens to retake the fort, bringing with them 3,000 hoplites and the cavalry. The weather was fine when they set out, but heavy snow fall fell during the night. Thrasyboulos saw it as a direct intervention of the gods on his behalf. The subsequent Athenian retreat was impeded by the snow, and descending from their rocky fortress the exiles inflicted further losses on their opponents, and they captured a large part of the baggage.[100]

Night Marches and Assaults

Night marches and surprise attacks continued to be common in the fourth century. Indeed, it was said that once the Arcadians decided to march somewhere, nothing could prevent them – not nightfall nor storms, nor distance nor even mountains.[101] In 390, an important military event occurred when Iphicrates invaded the territory of Phlius[102] (see map 11). He set an ambush while plundering the territory with a few followers. The men from the city came out against him in an unguarded way, but he killed so many of them that the Phliasians, who had previously rejected having Spartans within their walls, sent for the Spartans and put the city and the citadel under their protection.[103] Thus a previously democratic Phlius that had displayed both political and military dissidence towards Sparta in the late 390s now remained loyal to Sparta for the rest of the Corinthian war.

In 378, the Thebans, afraid that they would be the only ones at war with Sparta, hatched a plot.[104] Pelopidas set up an ambush as a deception in order to deceive the Spartans into attacking the Athenians. He and Gorgias chose Sphodrias, a Spartan, who was a good soldier but had weak judgement and was full of senseless ambition. They sent to him one of their friends who was a merchant with money, and planted the idea that he should seize Piraeus, attacking it unexpectedly when the Athenians were off their guard. It was set up as a night attack. Sphodrias was persuaded, took his soldiers and invaded Attica by night. Sphodrias underestimated the distance and by dawn found he was only at Eleusis (see map 11). There, the hearts of his soldiers failed them and his design was exposed. Plutarch says they saw light streaming from certain sanctuaries at Eleusis and were filled with 'shuddering fear'. Having lost the advantage of surprise, they turned back and abandoning the attack ravaged the countryside a little, then retired ingloriously to Thespiae. This once again illustrates the necessity of using brave men for night missions.[105]

Surprise can be deadly even when it is not planned. In 378, both the Athenians and the Spartans were operating with a contingent of peltasts in their service. The Spartan Cleombrotus marched with his troops to Plataea, taking a different route from the one through Eleutherae, which the Athenian Chabrias was guarding with his peltasts.[106] In the Cithaeron mountains, Cleombrotus' vanguard, made up of peltasts, came upon a contingent of 150 of Chabrias' peltasts. The latter were taken completely by surprise and nearly all of them were killed.

Using peltasts is not a silver bullet, nor does it give one a monopoly over the use of surprise. Once a surprise attack is used, your enemies copy your tactics. In the spring of 376, Cleombrotus marched again with an army to Boeotia.[107] Once again his peltasts went ahead to occupy the tops of the Cithaeron mountains overlooking the road. This time, however, the area had already been occupied by the Thebans and the Athenians, who were more alert than Chabrias' peltasts had been two years before. When Cleombrotus' peltasts reached the top of the mountains and were at close quarters with the enemy, the latter emerged from the ambush and killed about forty fleeing peltasts. Because of this disaster, Cleombrotus believed it was impossible to enter Boeotia, and therefore turned back without having effected his purpose.

Aeneas Tacticus reports a particularly deadly ambush in 376, in which failure to learn from one set of ambushes caused another set. The Triballi,[108] a tribe from the area of mid-Danubian Thrace, made an inroad into the country of the Abderites and set ambushes, then started raiding the country around the city. The Abderites held them in contempt because of previous successful operations against them and made a hasty attack from the city with great force and eagerness. But the Triballi drew them into the ambushes. On that particular occasion, it is said that more men perished in a shorter time than had ever been the case, at least from a single city of similar size. The others, not having learned of the destruction of their compatriots who went out first, rushed to the rescue, cheering each other on, but fell into the same ambushes until the city was bereft of men.[109]

Xenophon reports a night march with a double layer of secrecy in 371, during the truce brokered by Jason of Pherae after the Battle of Leuctra. When news had been brought of the truce between Sparta and Thebes, the polemarchs announced to their men that they should all be packed up after dinner because they intended to set out during the night in order to ascend Mt Cithaeron at dawn. Right after the men finished dinner, however, and before they could take any rest, the polemarch ordered them to set out, and as soon as it was dusk they led them away, taking the road through Creusis, because they were relying more on secrecy than on the truce. They proceeded with very great difficulty because they were withdrawing at night, in fear, and by a hard road, but arrived at Aegosthena in the territory of Megara.[110]

In 370, relations between Orchomenus and Mantineia were strained.[111] Sparta supported Orchomenus and dispatched Polytropus as general to Arcadia with 1,000 citizen hoplites and 500 Argive and Boeotian refugees.[112] Agesilaus waited for Polytropus to join him with his mercenaries. The Arcadians marched against them and Polytropus fought off the attackers but perished in the fight. Diodorus estimated the number dead at 200.[113] If horsemen from Phlius had not arrived just in time to stop the Mantineans from pursuing them, many of the mercenaries would also have been killed. Agesilaus thought the mercenaries would not join him now that they had been defeated, so he marched on Mantinea without them. Armies were sometimes easily surprised even by their own allies. A few days later, after a night movement, the horsemen from Phlius and the mercenaries who had slipped past Mantinea appeared in the Spartan camp early in the morning, causing great confusion at first because the Spartans thought they were the enemy.[114]

In 370, the Thebans invaded Laconia. They crossed the Eurotas river by Amyclae and after four days the Thebans and Eleians advanced in full force along with the cavalry from the Phocians, Thessalians and Locrians who were serving in this expedition. Although the Spartan cavalry formed against them, they were very few in number. To help counter this imbalance, however, the Spartans had set an ambush with about 300 of the younger hoplites, which they hid in the Temple of the Sons of Tyndareus (The Dioscuri).[115] When the Spartan cavalry charged, these men too sprang their attack and forced the enemy back. Eventually, the Thebans decided not to make another assault on the city, so departed on the road to Helos and then Gytheium, where the Spartans had their dockyards (see map

3). The ambush gave the Spartans enough of an edge to achieve their objective of saving the city.[116]

Night operations became a necessity in 366 during the Theban invasion of Phlius. The Phliasians survived by buying supplies from the Corinthians. But they had to provide a military escort for those who had to pass through enemy lines to get the supplies. While Chares was in Phlius, they asked him to convey their non-combatants (*proxenoi*) into Pellene.[117] Having left the men at Pellene, they then went to the market, made their purchases and loaded up as many of the animals as they could, and departed by night trying in this way to avoid ambush by the enemy. Xenophon praises their endurance and patience, and admires them for pulling off this dangerous night operation to bring supplies to their hard-pressed city.[118]

Another night attack in 362 is related by several ancient historians.[119] Two groups of Arcadians came to blows, each side sent for outside help. The Tegeans called in the Thebans under Epaminondas, and the Mantineans sought help from both Athens and Sparta. Epaminondas was advancing with his army not far from Mantinea when he learned from local inhabitants that the entire Spartan force was plundering the territory of Tegea. Supposing that Sparta was stripped of soldiers, Epaminondas planned a night attack and set out towards the city. He ordered his troops to take their supper at an early hour, and a little after nightfall led them out straight to Sparta.

The Spartan king Agesilaus, however, anticipating the cunning of Epaminondas (Diodorus) or being informed by a deserter (Polybius), made preparations for a defence.[120] He sent out some Cretan runners and got word to the men he had left behind that the Boeotians would shortly appear in Sparta to sack the city. They should not fear because he himself would come as quickly as possible with his army to bring aid to them. According to Diodorus, Epaminondas set out at night and took the city (Sparta) at daybreak.[121] Polybius says he took the city by surprise.[122] Epaminondas was disappointed in his hope, but after breakfasting on the banks of the Eurotas and refreshing his troops after their hard march he continued on to Mantinea, which would be left without defenders because the Spartans had run home to defend their city. He once again organised a night march and reached Mantinea about midday and found it undefended.

This is an interesting story because Diodorus and Polybius have Epaminondas shown attacking at night. This is in contrast to Polyaenus,[123] where Epaminondas is portrayed as cultivating a reputation for never attacking before sunrise.[124] It is thus difficult to appraise the historical value of the stratagem, because the only attested example in the historians of Epaminondas' activity by night in the Peloponnesus is his march to Sparta.

Assaults and Escapes from Walled Cities

Assaults and escapes from walled cities were already an important part of warfare at the end of the Peloponnesian war. There are numerous examples of deceptions and tricks, in particular in the assaults on cities, where peltasts were used to great advantage.[125] Much activity, therefore, was expended in the fourth century assaulting cities, or gaining access by stealth.[126]

Storming towns at night was often a successful tactic. In 408, King Agis of Sparta was in Decelea with his army when he learned that the best Athenian troops were engaged in an expedition with Alcibiades. He led his army on a moonless night to Athens with 28,000 infantry, one-half of whom were picked hoplites and the rest were light-armed troops. There were also attached to his army some 1,200 cavalry, of whom the Boeotians furnished 900 and the rest had been sent with him by the Peloponnesians. As he drew near the city, he came upon the outposts before they were aware of him and easily dispersed them because they were taken by surprise. He slew a few and pursued the rest within the walls.[127]

In 405, Diodorus claims Dionysius of Syracuse covered a distance of 400 stades and arrived at the gates of Achradine in the middle of the night with 100 cavalry and 600 infantry. Finding the gate closed, he piled upon it reeds brought from the marshes and burned the gates. His troops entered the town and captured the cavalry trying to defend the city. They were gathered in the marketplace, surrounded and cut down. Then Dionysius rode through the city slaughtering anyone who resisted.[128]

Later in 404, Dionysius of Syracuse treated with humanity the exiles who returned, wishing to encourage the rest to return to their native land too. To the Campanians, he awarded the gifts that were due and then dispatched them from the city, having regard to their fickleness. These made their way to Entella and persuaded the men of the city to receive them as fellow inhabitants, then they fell upon them at night, slew the men of military age, married the wives of the men with whom they had broken faith and possessed themselves of the city.[129]

From the same book of Diodorus we have an example of gates being opened by treachery in 395 at Heraclea. Medius, the lord of Larissa in Thessaly, was at war with Lycophron, tyrant of Pherae. After getting reinforcements of Boeotians and Argives, Medius seized Pharsalus where there was a garrison of Spartans; he sold the inhabitants as booty. After this, the Boeotians and Argives parted company with Medius. They seized Heraclea in Trachis, and on being let in at night within the walls by sympathisers they put to the sword the Spartans whom they seized, but they allowed the other Peloponnesian allies to leave with their possessions, no doubt in an attempt to weaken the Spartan alliance.[130]

Plutarch, in his *Life of Pelopidas*, reports a plot from 379 when Thebes was garrisoned by the Spartans, to open city gates and stage a surprise attack.[131] The Theban exiles took twelve men disguised as hunters, in short cloaks and leading hunting dogs. They entered the city at different points during the day. The weather changed to wind and snow. They made their way to the house of Charon, where they were changing into their armour when a messenger came from the polemarchs summoning Charon. At first, they thought they had been discovered. While the storm continued, a messenger from the Athenians brought a letter with details of the plot to Archias (the polemarch?). Instead of reading it, Archias, who was drunk, put it under his pillow and went to sleep.[132] When the time came for the attack, the exiles went out in two bands, one under Pelopidas and one under Charon. They broke into various houses and killed leaders, raided shops for arms and at the break of day had control of the city without ever having engaged the 1,500-man garrison. Even Plutarch says that it was not easy to name a case where such a small number of men, so destitute, have overcome enemies so numerous and powerful. The subsequent political change was momentous. This is a clear of example of ambush as a force multiplier.[133]

Mercenary service in Sicily found its high point under tyrants such as Dionysius of Syracuse.[134] We see him using them during the siege of the Siceli at Tauromenium. Dionysius took advantage of the winter storms when the area about the acropolis was filled with snow. He discovered that the Siceli were careless in their guard of the acropolis because of its strength and the unusual height of the wall, so he advanced on a moonless and stormy night against the highest sectors. After many difficulties, both because of the obstacles offered by the crags and because of the great depth of the snow, he occupied one peak, although his face was frosted and his vision impaired by the cold. Still he was able to break through to the other side and lead his army into the city. The attempt, however, still did not work. The Siceli stormed out against him and pushed out the troops of Dionysius. Dionysius himself was struck on the corselet in the flight, sent scrambling and barely escaped being taken alive. Since the Siceli pressed upon them from superior ground, more than 600 of Dionysius' troops were slain and most of them lost their complete armour, while Dionysius himself saved only his corselet. After this disorder, the Acragantini and Messenians banished the partisans of Dionysius, asserted their freedom and renounced their alliance with the tyrant.[135]

Diodorus reports that in 397, when Dionysius was besieging the Motyans, he made it a practice to sound the trumpet towards evening for the recall of his troops and break off the siege.[136] So once he had accustomed the Motyans to this practice, the combatants on both sides retired as usual. He dispatched Archylus of Thurii with the élite troops, who waited until nightfall then placed ladders against the fallen houses. Using these to mount the walls, they seized an advantageous spot, where they admitted Dionysius' troops. When the Motyans realised what was taking place, they rushed with all eagerness to the rescue, but they were too late. They fought fiercely but, in the end, the Sicilian Greeks wore down their opponents by the weight of their numbers.[137]

In Rhegium in 393 (see map 7), the Carthaginians fled into the city after a loss of more than 800 men, while Dionysius withdrew for the time being to Syracuse; but after a few days he manned 100 triremes and set out against the Rhegians. Arriving unexpectedly by night before the city, he put fire to the gates and set ladders against the walls.[138]

At Corinth in 392, Praxitas, the commander of a Spartan *mora* garrisoned at Sicyon, entered the long walls that connected Corinth to its port at Lechaeum, through a gate opened by the two Corinthian defectors, and he established a palisaded camp as they waited for reinforcements. On the second day, the Argives arrived in full strength along with the mercenaries under Iphicrates. Although outnumbered, the Spartans fought bravely, and then followed their victory with the taking of Lechaeum.[139]

From Egypt in 362/1 we have the story of a night escape from a city. Having lost many men in their attack on the walls, the Egyptians then began to surround the city with a wall and a ditch, shutting in Agesilaus and his men. As the work was rapidly nearing completion by reason of the large number of workers, and the provisions in the city were exhausted, Tachos despaired of his safety, but Agesilaus, encouraging the men and attacking the enemy at night, unexpectedly succeeded in bringing all the men out safely.[140]

Similarly, Diodorus reports an attack on the walls of Syracuse in 356/5 (see map 7). Nypsius, the commander of the mercenaries, wishing to renew the battle and retrieve the defeat with his army, which had been marshalled, during the night unexpectedly attacked the wall that had been constructed. And, finding that the guards had fallen asleep in a drunken stupor, he placed the ladders that had been constructed in case they were needed against the wall. The bravest of the mercenaries climbed on the wall with these, slaughtered the guards and opened the gates.[141]

Another unsuccessful assault on a siege wall occurred in 357/6. Dionysius plied his mercenaries with strong wine and sent them on a dash against the siege wall around the acropolis. The attack was unexpected, and the barbarians, with great boldness and loud tumult, began to tear down the cross-wall and attack the Syracusans, so that no one dared to stand on the defensive, except the mercenaries of Dion, who first noticed the disturbance and came to the rescue.[142]

Warfare in the Fourth Century

Despite the anecdotal form of many of our sources, we can see that warfare had changed in the fourth century. As G. T. Griffith pointed out many decades ago, it is not easy to imagine a time when soldiers were not a special class of men who made fighting their profession. The Greeks of the fifth century had no need for professional soldiers. The payment of a wage to fighting men ran contrary to the ideology of the citizen-soldier, i.e. hoplites. They were recruited from a class of men who could arm themselves and fight at their own expense.[143] When Greek cities went to war, every man did what he could.[144] As wars increased in number and intensity, however, the professionalisation of warfare followed. Thucydides writes that before the Peloponnesian war the Athenians devoted their bodies to their country.[145] Later, patriotic enthusiasm would decrease and fighting was left to professional soldiers who received wages.[146]

The use of public finance to pay soldiers transformed warfare by making it possible to mobilise more manpower for longer periods of time and so wage war on land and at sea with an intensity and persistence that had not been feasible in earlier generations. Military service became less and less remunerative especially because of the steep increase in the cost of living in the fourth century. From then on, wages had to be complemented with booty.[147]

Athens had used mercenaries during the greater part of the fourth century and used them more freely than any other Greek city-state. Yet the Greeks were conscious of the incompatibility of their autonomy and the presence of foreign troops in a polis.[148]

The rise of Hellenistic monarchies, combined with a large supply of mercenary soldiers available, meant that professionals and the techniques of war that they could bring with them would be many and varied. Battle became much more costly as the spirit of competition gave way to the desire for complete destruction. Wars were now made up of raids, commando attacks and guerrilla warfare whose heroes were peltasts and these techniques came to rival open combat.[149]

There were always those who waxed poetic about the 'fair and open battle' of the past. Xenophon, in the *Cyropaedia*, has a character urge an attack upon a small and vulnerable group of enemy soldiers. Cyrus overruled him and said it would be better to wait for them all to assemble. If less than half of them are defeated, they will say the Greeks attacked because they feared to face the great mass of the enemy. If they do not feel defeated, there will be another battle.[150] But is this really the Greek attitude towards fair play in war or a just nostalgic remembrance of times past when hoplite armies gathered their full forces on a plain, almost as if by appointment?[151] Or, one might ask, what happened when the Greeks were faced with opponents who did not recognise the 'rules of the game'? As the Athenians expanded their empire overseas, they found themselves fighting more frequently, in unfamiliar terrain as longer conflicts replaced seasonal and occasional clashes. Professionalism spurred on by the increase in scale, occurrence and duration of conflicts rendered operations more technical. Diversity of terrain favoured a new emphasis on cavalry and light infantry. It became necessary to co-ordinate different types of armed contingents and this made battles more complex than the head-on collisions of phalanxes. Mercenaries with professional skills, often recruited from non-Greeks, supplemented or replaced citizen levies. Generals did not just lead a charge; they had to out-think as well as out-fight the enemy.

Using light-armed troops and mercenaries for ambush was one of the strategies the Greeks adopted. As Griffith points out: 'The mercenaries of the fourth century became standardised to a type, the type evolved by Iphicrates, i.e. the Iphicratean peltast.'[152] He believed they became so widespread that actual Thracians were driven from the market. There appears to be no mention by ancient authors of Thracian peltasts in the seventy years before Alexander.[153] Griffith suggests that their disappearance was due to the improved Greek peltast.

Thus, when new circumstances arose, they demanded new experiments from the inventiveness of the Greeks. The Greeks had learned to make an efficient army suitable for service in other lands. Hoplites had to be supported by good light-armed troops and, if possible, by cavalry. The first half of the fourth century developed the military art along these lines, and the Greek hoplite force, in conjunction with these new groups using the tactics of surprise, speed and ambush, became one of the most effective military forces.

Fourth-century authors speak of deception, surprise and ambush constantly. It is clear from the works of Aeneas Tacticus that ambush was always considered a dangerous possibility. Aeneas assumes that ambushes will be a danger,[154] and he recommends that defenders set their own ambushes.[155] He tells a cautionary tale about how some officials used the citizens' desire to ambush the enemy to bring in mercenaries and take over the city.[156] He even recommends that defenders attack the invaders when they are drunk[157] or when they are preparing dinner. He gives examples of disinformation leaked successfully to the enemy[158] and anecdotes about tricks used to capture cities.[159] He gives detailed instructions on how an army should sally from a town when enemy troops were in the surrounding area.[160] He instructs that hoplites should leave town in separate formations in marching order since, if unordered groups leave in succession, there was a danger that each group would fall into an enemy ambush. Aeneas recommends that to avoid ambushes the available horsemen and light-armed precede the hoplites in order to reconnoitre and occupy the dominating positions in the area, so that the hoplites can be informed of the enemy's movements in good time and hence avoid unexpected disasters.

Xenophon gives exactly the same advice about troop order.[161] Both Aeneas and Xenophon were generals with extensive field experience. They were basing their advice on practice. It is not difficult to find examples. We see this when Agesilaus' horsemen, during his campaign in Asia Minor, were riding to a hill in order to survey the terrain and they unexpectedly came upon Persian horsemen.[162] With the order by which the horsemen and peltasts marched ahead followed by the hoplites, it is obvious that the peltasts and horsemen were always the first to engage with the enemy. Another example of this marching order can be seen in Xenophon's *Anabasis*. His troops are in the territory of the Thracian enemies; in front of them are the Bithynians. He sends horsemen ahead and orders the peltasts to the hill tops and ridges.[163] The practice at the end of the fifth century seems to have been the same as the fourth century, when Aeneas Tacticus was writing (c.360–350). Xenophon and Aeneas Tacticus have so much in common that classicist David Whitehead plausibly suggests that the two men knew each other and spoke together.[164] The Greeks in Xenophon's day considered deceiving enemies normal behaviour. Certainly, surprise attacks and ambush came under this heading. The Greeks were still using animal metaphors for ambush as they had in the *Iliad*. When Xenophon talks about men who deceive the enemy, he compares it to using decoy birds to lure birds into an ambush.[165]

Fourth-century commanders such as Agesilaus became admired by later writers. Most of Frontinus' examples are Roman, but among the Greeks he mentions one Spartan figure prominently. Of the twenty-one stratagems he cites, nine are attributed to Agesilaus.[166] Polyaenus goes even further. For him Agesilaus was the central character and his thirty-three exempla extend over his entire career as a general.[167]

Scholars like to point out that light-armed troops did not play a decisive part in any battle on Greek soil, except in two cases during the Peloponnesian war where hoplites were caught on ground unsuited to their formation and their tactics.[168] This misses the point, however, that having light-armed troops made it easier to set up ambushes, spring surprise attacks at night or dawn and fall upon hoplites when they least expected it and were ill-prepared. The fact that hoplites themselves were lightening their armour (see above) suggests that they saw the changing conditions of warfare as the fifth century progressed.

Whatever sneering may have been done against light-armed troops before or during the Peloponnesian war, it soon became clear to commanders of Greek armies serving abroad in the fourth century that they could not reply solely upon heavily armed hoplite troops. Hoplites need the support of effective bodies of men whose armour rendered them more mobile.[169] The demand for various types of light-armed soldiers had become greater as the Peloponnesian war progressed, and in the fourth century this need got greater as Greeks fought overseas against native troops skilled in these ways of fighting. Archers, javelin men, slingers and, above all, peltasts were found to be necessary. The predominance of a solely hoplite army was gone. The fourth-century Greek army had been remade as a co-operative effort by trained hoplites, peltasts and cavalry, many of them mercenaries and all obedient to a general.[170]

G. B. Grundy was correct when he warned against reading into the fourth century a wholescale racial decay, physical and intellectual, and perhaps we might add moral because of the types of warfare used.[171] Many writers believe the fourth century saw a 'change in the ethos of warfare', i.e. a moral decay.[172] What we are seeing rather are military changes that reflect the reality of warfare in an age of overseas warfare, increased professionalism in the armies, the development of new fighting techniques, the development of a new leadership and the ability of the Greeks to divorce themselves from the hoplite paradigm. These were all brought changes to Greek warfare, but we can discuss them without suggesting that their world had become degenerate.[173]

The idea that cleverness in warfare is 'a luxury' may be an opinion held by armchair historians, but not by generals in the field. Such attitudes are often attributed to great commanders such as Agesilaus and Alexander, but the fact remains that these commanders were expert military tricksters.[174] Moralisers could continue to claim that victory by guile was no victory at all, but when an ambush killed all its targets the dead were very much defeated. A pass taken, information gained, an enemy surprised and defeated were all good things for both the general and the men in the field.[175]

CHAPTER 9

The Successor States and into the Hellenistic Age

FOR TWENTY YEARS ALEXANDER'S generals and governors fought over his sprawling empire. Even after the Battle of Ipsus in 301 when the major successor states emerged, these kingdoms continued to fight each other in the internal wars of succession. They fought rebellious Greeks and natives, they attacked lesser powers who struggled to exist between them, and they repelled invaders from the outside world. A Hellenistic Greek might define 'peace' as merely the short break between wars.[1] War became an endemic part of life in the Hellenistic world as the populations of Greece, Asia Minor and Syria had to endure the campaigns of competing rulers. Kings, such as the Seleucids, owed their royal status to victory in war. They had to be active military leaders just to maintain their thrones.[2]

The great irony of the Hellenistic Age, at least for this study, is that although warfare is endemic, and the use of ambush was at its peak, our sources suddenly dry up. We have no Herodotus, no Thucydides and no Xenophon to supply our evidence. If the history of Hieronymus of Cardia had survived, we would have had an eyewitness account of the wars of Alexander's successors. At least we have Diodorus and Plutarch who used his works, and with Polybius, Polyaenus and Frontinus added we can catch an occasional glimpse of what was going on militarily.[3] What we can say, generally speaking, is that the tendency towards specialisation and professionalisation that had begun in the fourth century was enhanced during the Hellenistic period by the new needs of kings, and the requirements of cities and leagues.[4]

The actual forms of conflict in the Hellenistic Age were varied, and corresponded to the different goals of warfare. Disputes might lead to raiding, seizing cattle and other moveable goods, or the burning of farms and the kidnapping of farmers, women or agricultural slaves.[5] Polis warfare, too, could take on a whole spectrum of variations including different modes of local warfare. In this atmosphere, cities and their citizens needed versatility in their choice of military options. Hellenistic war was not just made up of large battles such as Raphia, where 140,000 men fought, but also ambushes and surprise attacks. Indeed, the majority of the Hellenistic male population experienced warfare not in great tactical battles, but in the form of temporary raids, incursions into the territory of the enemy, surprise attacks against cities and occasional street fights.[6] The professionalisation of military units did not diminish the importance of citizen militias; it simply added a whole new array of soldiers with varied skills that could be drawn up.

Training

Because warfare in the Hellenistic Age became more specialised, it required more training of troops. The contrast between the training of a citizen and that of a mercenary is brought out by the speech of Polydamos at Sparta in 374. He was quoting Jason of Pherae when he said: '. . . there are only a few men in each city who train their bodies rigorously. But in my forces there is not a single man who cannot match me in the capacity for hard work.'[7] In some Hellenistic cities they dispensed with the mercenary peltast of the late Classical Age and replaced him with trained citizenry, who could play a similar role, but without any of the social and political problems the use of hired peltasts posed.[8]

Angelos Chaniotis, in his study of Hellenistic warfare, gives an overview that suggests that military training had a more or less uniform structure in most areas, 'the result of mutual interest rather than common origins'.[9] Chaniotis points out that a clear indicator of the specialisation of troops is the use of more technical terminology. A wide range of specific military terms can be seen in Hellenistic literature; some of these go back to the fourth century but they culminate in the Hellenistic period.[10] The specific designations for troops beyond the generic designations for the cavalry, the phalanx of hoplites, light-armed and the fleet reflect the existence of specific weapons, special training and specialised skills.[11] This specialisation was not limited to professional armies, but extended also to citizen armies. Their special skills were sometimes a matter of local tradition. The Cretans, for example, were famous as archers, the Achaians were slingers and the Thessalians were cavalrymen.[12] Improvements could be made on these traditional weapons: for example, a particular type of sling, the *kestros*, was invented during the Third Macedonian war.[13]

For many boys, military training started earlier than their registration as ephebes; it began in the gymnasium, where exercise and physical conditioning were thought be good training for warfare.[14] The gymnasium was one of the best-documented institutions of the Hellenistic city.[15] Their training gives us a hint about what weapons would be used. In a small place such as Samos (see map 8), the programme in the gymnasium included prizes for use of the catapult, use of the *lithobolos* (an engine used for hurling stones), use of the javelin, archery and fighting with shield and lance (hoplite battle or *hoplomachia*) as well as with small shields of the Galatian type (*thyreomachia*). The same selection of disciplines is found in Sestos in Thrace[16] (see map 1).

After their military training, young men were assigned to both military and paramilitary duties. We have evidence from Crete that they performed policing duties, especially in the countryside and they controlled the frontier of the city.[17] In other cities, we see young men manning the forts on the frontiers.[18] Similar troops are known from Athens and Asia Minor.[19] In Athens, the *kryptoi* ('the secret ones') protected the fertile countryside.[20] There is evidence from Caria of groups of young men serving as mounted 'patrol of the mountains' (*orophylakesantes*),[21] and as mounted guards assigned to patrol the borders of Boeotia.[22] These young troops operated on the periphery of the city and have been defined by some as 'liminal groups', not unlike foreign mercenaries and, therefore, operating outside of the rules of hoplite battle.[23]

We are particularly well informed regarding the Cretan soldiers who, from the fourth century on, are to be found in almost all armies of the Mediterranean, often on opposite sides.[24] Even Rome enrolled Cretans. Examples of ethnic stereotyping occurred because of this specialised training. Polybius brands the Cretans with the label 'brigands and pirates' because of their raiding abilities.[25] This kind of moralising demonstrates Polybius' prejudice, but says nothing meaningful about how effective or useful such troops were, nor how proud they were of their local traditions. We, know for example, how proud the Arcadians were of their mercenary tradition. Lycomedes, the Arcadian statesmen, said that the Arcadians were chosen for service overseas because they were the best fighters with the sturdiest bodies among the Greek peoples.[26] With the emergence of the widespread use of mercenaries, a number of peoples achieved their moment of renown thanks to their specialisation in the use of particular arms: the bow for the Scythians and Cretans; the sling for the Rhodians; and the javelin for the Aetolians, Acarnanians and Thracians.

Mercenaries

As we saw in the last chapter, from the beginning of the fourth century armies already contained significantly higher numbers of light infantry and cavalry than classical ones had fielded.[27] Peltasts and light-armed troops remained important throughout the Hellenistic period, but of all the military developments of the Hellenistic Age the one that has drawn the most attention is the use of mercenary troops.[28] Although mercenaries are documented from the earliest period of Greek warfare, the Hellenistic period saw a huge increase in the number of regions that supplied mercenary soldiers.[29] Greek males had always been able to travel and seek their fortunes a long way from home.[30] Mercenaries were initially drawn from remote, poor or mountainous regions – Crete, Achaea, Thrace, etc. – which is why they were often looked down upon. They were expected to depend for their keep on the success of the campaigns for which they had been enlisted.[31] They took part in various battles in the Peloponnesian war and continued to fight in the service of outside powers such as Egypt or Persia.

With the campaigns of Alexander, thousands more Greeks had the opportunity to serve as mercenaries, and this demand only grew under Alexander's successors.[32] In fact, mercenaries came not merely to supplement but, in many areas, to displace the citizen hoplites. Hellenistic kings mobilised large numbers of these troops in their wars for the division of Alexander's empire. The supply of Greek soldiers needing employment thus coincided with this new intra-Hellenic demand. These same men could later be settled as veterans in new cities and military colonies.[33] The job of *xenologos*, or recruiter of mercenaries, became a lucrative position.[34] The kingdoms that emerged from this process needed trained military manpower in order to man garrisons, avert barbarian invasions, control native populations and fight against other kingdoms.[35]

The mercenary did not become popular among Greek citizens. The profession was usually portrayed as a miserable one, especially by writers of Greek comedy who wrote for a settled, urban population. The average citizen not only scorned the man who had to earn his keep by fighting, but also feared him since the mercenary was a potential threat to his own existence.[36] Gangs of mercenaries threatened the Greek *poleis* in the fourth century. Aeneas Tacticus reflects the political instability of the times when he warns city authorities of the danger of arms being smuggled inside the city, which could then be used by mercenaries and hostile groups of citizens to overthrow the existing order.[37]

This changeover to mercenary troops was deplored by people such as the Athenian orator Isocrates, who mourned the replacement of a citizen militia by mercenaries in much the same terms as Machiavelli would later write about Florence.[38] Aristotle drew an explicit moral contrast between the citizen hoplite's preference for death in battle over the disgrace of flight and the professional mercenary's preference, despite superior fighting skills, for saving his skin.[39] On the other hand, in the defence speeches of the fourth century from Athenian courtrooms, speakers who had served as mercenaries under Iphicrates in Thrace emphasised how honourable their period of service had been.[40]

Moralising aside, as long as Hellenistic states continued to engage in the pursuit of power by force at each other's expense, they would increasingly turn to mercenary soldiers who would not only pay for themselves but also enrich, even temporarily, their employers.[41] True, such soldiers would not find themselves commemorated for patriotic self-sacrifice if they died in battle the way that citizen-soldiers had been by the Classical Greek *poleis*. Neither would the panoplies of armour taken from the enemy dead be displayed in the temples of the victors or at a pan-Hellenic sanctuary site in the same way or in the same spirit as before. Their reputation was not helped by soldiers sacrilegiously looting religious shrines such as Delphi, or by plays that held the *miles gloriosus* up as a stock comic figure.[42]

In one way, Aristotle's charge was unfair. These new mercenaries were no more or less ready to risk their lives in battle than citizens called away from their peacetime occupations. These men were professional, not only in being full-time soldiers, but also in being more innovative in military technique than citizen hoplites. Demosthenes' complaint against Philip of Macedon that he campaigned all year round using mercenaries and cavalry, archers, light-armed infantry and siege engines simply reflects his nostalgia for a past model that was simply gone.[43] The short campaign culminating in the pitched battle becomes increasingly replaced by ambushes, stratagems and sieges of the kind that had existed in the earlier period, but now they came to the fore.[44]

The important feature of these new mercenaries was that they were adept at the new mode of fighting. Griffith believes it was this fighting for which the mercenary was best adapted, especially as the reformed peltast of Iphicrates had become probably the model for mercenaries in general.[45] Mercenaries were not merely auxiliaries now, but the exemplary practitioners of a new mode of fighting. It was not that heavy-armed infantry had become useless, or that Greek morals had declined, but rather that there were more options for the kinds of techniques that could be used in warfare, and a rise in the number of situations where ambush would be appropriate.

Warfare was still regarded as a normal feature of interstate relations, and risking death in battle was still seen by the young Greek male as the supreme manifestation of virtue. A young man could still be brought up to admire the exploits of warriors from the past, but the norms, values and beliefs that had motivated a citizen-soldier were increasingly unlikely to be replicated in an environment where military prowess might require different skills. Greek culture had always accepted lethal violence against fellow Greeks as normal behaviour. As long as assassinations, civil strife, proscriptions and executions were commonplace, and the recurrent themes of murder, revenge, blood-guilt, retribution and even human sacrifice appear as dramatic themes, why would an ambush be so shocking?[46]

Yet, the moralising continued. Polybius rails against the Cretans. He accuses them of specialising in ambushes and treachery:

> The Cretans both by land and sea were irresistible in ambuscades, forays, tricks played on the enemy, night attacks, and all petty operations which require fraud, but they are cowardly and down-hearted in the massed face-to-face charge of an open battle. It is just the reverse with the Achaeans and Macedonians. I say this in order that my readers may not refuse to trust my judgement, because in some cases I make contrary pronouncements regarding the conduct of the same men even when engaged in pursuits of a like nature.[47]

All these activities were the regular ones of light-armed soldiers.[48] Ambush was exactly what these soldiers were solicited for and everyone was buying their services. The Cretan cities were the objects of frantic solicitations on the part of the Hellenistic sovereigns and many other cities, in particular Rhodes. Rhodes sent ambassadors to the island of Crete to conclude treaties of alliance with individual cities or groups of them.[49] The treaties were aimed principally at ensuring stable supplies of troops for the powers of the Hellenistic world.[50]

Hellenistic Ambush

With only meagre sources at our disposal, we can still document numerous cases of ambush, and they take the usual forms. Even the era of Philip and Alexander, so heavily based on the new Macedonian phalanx, has yielded examples of surprise and deception: for example, Polyaenus tells us about Philip when he was besieging the Thessalian city of Pharcedon in 356. The Pharcedonians surrendered, but as Philip's mercenaries entered the city they fell into an ambush as many of the inhabitants threw stones and javelins at them from the roofs and towers. Philip, however, had already planned an ambush of his own. He ordered his Macedonians to make an assault on the rear part of the city, which was deserted because all the citizens were participating in ambush at the front. The Macedonians placed ladders against the wall and, when they reached the top, the Pharcedonians stopped hurling things at the mercenaries and ran hurriedly to ward off the men who had seized the wall. Before they could close in hand-to-hand combat, the Macedonians already had control of the city.[51]

The Third Sacred war (356–346), fought between the Delphic Amphictyonic League (represented by Thebes) and Philip II of Macedon with the Phocians, set up the context for a story about diversionary tactics at sea used to set up an ambush. Polyaenus reports that, after ravaging the territory of Abdera and Maroneia in 352, Philip was returning with many ships and a land army. Chares, the Athenian, set an ambush with twenty triremes near Neapolis, a city on the east coast of the isthmus of Pallene (see map 4), in the Chalcidice between Aphytis and Aegae. After selecting the four fastest ships, Philip manned them with his best rowers in terms of age, skill and strength, and gave orders to put out to sea before the rest of the fleet, and to sail past Neapolis, keeping close to the shore. They sailed past. Chares put out to sea with his twenty triremes in order to capture the four ships. Since the four were light and had the best rowers, however, they quickly gained the high sea. While Chares' ships pursued vigorously, Philip sailed safely past Neapolis without being noticed, and Chares did not catch the four ships.[52]

Even a clever commander such as Philip could find himself lured into an ambush. Onomarchus, the Phocian general in the Third Sacred war, set up such an operation against a Macedonian phalanx.[53] He put a crescent-shape mountain in his rear, concealing men on the peaks at both ends with rocks and rock-throwing engines, and led his forces forward into the plain below. When the Macedonians came out against them and threw their javelins, the Phocians pretended to flee into the hollow middle of the mountain. As the Macedonians pursued with an eager rush after them, the men on the peaks threw rocks and crushed the Macedonian phalanx. Then Onomarchus signalled the Phocians to turn and attack the enemy. The Macedonians under attack from behind, and being pelted with rocks from above, retreated rapidly in great distress. During this flight Philip, no doubt covering his own reputation, said: 'I do not flee, but retreat like rams do, in order to attack again more violently.'[54]

There is a dispute among historians over whether Alexander the Great would actually use deception or whether he was above such tactics. A pair of passages in Arrian's *Anabasis* provide a good illustration of a double standard concerning surprise and ambush. On the eve of Gaugamela, Arrian presents the story of Parmenion suggesting to Alexander that a surprise attack by night should be considered.[55] Alexander replied that it was a dishonourable to steal the victory, and that he had to win his victories openly and without stratagem.[56] The entire scene was probably invented to show that Parmenion was not as confident of a victory on the battlefield as Alexander.[57] In 326, in contrast, during the campaign against Porus on the Hydaspes river, Alexander had to come up with a way to bypass Porus and his elephants, which were blocking his passage. Alexander used a feinting tactic to induce Porus to stand his ground and then he successfully crossed, under cover of night, some seventeen miles (twenty-seven kilometres) upstream.[58] No one has suggested that this successful night operation was sneaky or morally dubious.

A similar example is told about Alexander when he took Thebes in 335 by hiding a sufficient force, and appointing Antipater to command it. He himself led a diversionary force against the city's strong points. The Thebans went out and fought nobly against the force they saw. At the critical moment of the battle, Antipater led his force out of hiding, circled around to where the wall was unsound and unguarded, captured the city there and raised a signal. When Alexander saw it, he shouted out that he already had Thebes. The Thebans, who were fighting fiercely, fled when they turned around and saw the city captured.[59] Both Philip and Alexander pioneered the successful use of the Macedonian phalanx and mixed contingents, yet both of them understood the use of deception and ambush when the situation called for it.

Surprises, ambushes and deception continued in Greece proper during the era before the complete Macedonian take over. Diodorus complains about the wars in the 350s being characterised by all forms of knavery including false truces.[60] He reports a night attack on a camp in Greece by the Boeotians in 352/1. The Phocians were assaulted by night near Abai, where many were slain.[61] In the same year, the Phocians made a night attack upon the Boeotians and slew 200.[62]

From 323 to 301 we follow the struggle for power between the successors of Alexander.[63] Cassander, king of Macedonia from 305 to 297, provides an example of a stratagem designed to take a city by stealth. When returning from Illyria in

314, being a day's march from Epidamnus, he hid a force in ambush. He then sent horsemen and infantry to burn villages high in the mountains of Illyria and Atintanis that were clearly visible to the Epidamnians. The Epidamnians assumed Cassander had left after the destruction, and came out of their city to tend their farms. Cassander sprang the ambush and captured 2,000 of the men outside the city. Finding the city gates open, he entered and occupied Epidamnus.[64]

Rather than just appearing on the battlefield expecting a fair fight, it was now common for each general to try and out-trick the other.[65] The Greek general Eumenes of Cardia, who participated in the wars of the *Diadochi* as a supporter of the Macedonian Argead royal house, staged a surprise in the autumn of 317 at the Battle of Paraetacene.[66] Eumenes and Antigonus met in a battle in Asia at an unknown site in the province of Paraetacene. The armies were camped close together, but a deep riverbed separated them. Supplies were short on both sides. Antigonus sent messengers to tamper with the loyalty of Eumenes' army. The deserters came from Antigonus' side with the intelligence that he was going to march his army away by night into the unplundered province of Gabiene. The cunning Eumenes, however, sent pretended deserters the other way: Eumenes would attack his camp during the night, they lied to Antigonus, to confine him to his camp so that Eumenes could reach Gabiene first. Sending his baggage on ahead, Eumenes had a lead of two watches before Antigonus detected the ruse and set out in pursuit. Leaving his infantry to make their slow way, Antigonus led on his cavalry. At dawn, Eumenes saw the horsemen on the ridge behind him and thought that all of Antigonus' army was there. He ordered his forces into battle formation and so wasted his lead.

In 290, the Aetolians took possession of Delphi, a position of prestige that was enormously enhanced when they defended it against an attack by the Galatians, referred to in the sources as Gauls, in the winter of 279/8.[67] It did not hurt the Greek cause that night operations seemed to have spooked the Gauls much in the same way that it occasionally spooked the Greeks. They encamped where night overtook them, and during the night they fell into a panic. They imagined they heard the trampling of horses riding against them and the attack of enemies, and after a little time the panic spread through the camp. Taking their weapons, they divided into two parties, killing and being killed, neither recognising their mother tongue nor one another's forms or the shape of their shields.[68] The victory over the Gauls established the Aetolians firmly in north central Greece.

Cleomenes III, king of Sparta, waged a war against the Achaean League led by Aratus of Sicyon from 229 to 222. This is the context of the story told in Polybius.[69] When Aristoteles of Argos revolted against Cleomenes' supporters, Cleomenes sent a force under the command of his general Timoxenus to help him. We are told that these troops made a 'surprise attack' and succeeded in entering and capturing the city. We are not told how Cleomenes took Argos back in spite of a gallant Achaean resistance or whether it involved subterfuge. Cleomenes eventually defeated Aratus in a battle by Mt Lycaeum in 227.

The third century produced a number of examples of ambush and complaints about them. The raids and plundering of the Aetolians, and their predatory habits, kept them constantly embroiled with Macedon. In 219, Philip V called the deputies from the allied cities to assemble at Corinth, and held a council to deliberate on the measures to be taken with regard to the Aetolians. Polybius says that, in addition to such charges as plundering a sacred temple in time of peace, the Arcadians entered a complaint that the Aetolians had attacked one of their cities under cover of night. The deputies of the allies, after hearing all these complaints, decided unanimously to make war on Aetolia.[70]

Polybius reports the ambush of a force attacking a rearguard during a march near Thermon in 218 during the hostilities with Philip. The Aetolians had gathered to defend their country and numbered about 3,000. As long as Philip was on the heights, they did not approach him but remained hidden in strongholds under the command of Alexander of Trichonium. As soon as the rearguard had moved out of Thermus, they entered the town at once and attacked the last ranks. With the rearguard thrown into some confusion, the Aetolians fell on them with more determination and did some execution, emboldened by the nature of the ground and this opportunity. But Philip, having foreseen this, had concealed under a hill on the descent a picked force of peltasts. When they sprang up from this ambush and charged those of the enemy who had advanced farthest in the pursuit of the rearguard, the whole Aetolian force fled in complete rout across the country with a loss of 130 killed and about as many taken prisoner.[71] It was a serious defeat at the hands of the Macedonians in 219 that finally drove the Aetolians into the arms of the Romans, who eventually stripped them of their powers and let the League die a quiet death.[72]

Taking a city by stealth and trickery continued to be a major activity in the Hellenistic period. For a city, a foreign attack and a long siege were costly. It not only meant the temporary loss of its countryside with all its resources, but also the substantial destruction of the urban centre, especially as artillery devices became increasingly effective at punching through walls.[73]

We are told of an ambush in 219 when Philip V besieged the Aetolian city of Phoetia and it surrendered. During the following night, a force of 500 Aetolians arrived to help, under the impression that the city still held out. The king got word of their approach and placed an ambush in a favourite spot, then killed all the captured troops except for a very few.[74]

Polybius describes the destruction of a marauding army of Eleans under Euripidas in January–February 218. Euripidas, whom the Aetolians had sent to the Eleans to command their forces, made an attack on the territories of Dyme, Pharae and Tritaea and had collected a considerable amount of booty. He was on his way back to Elis when Miccus of Dyme, substrategus of the Achaeans, taking with him the complete levies of Dyme, Pharae and Tritaea, marched out and attacked Euripidas and his men as they were retiring. Pressing on too vigorously, however, Miccus fell into an ambush and was defeated with considerable loss: forty of his infantry and about 200 taken prisoners.[75] A year later in 217, Polybius reports an almost identical situation where Lycus and Demodocus were the commanders of the Achaean cavalry. On hearing of the advance of the Aetolians from Elis, they collected the levies of Dyme, Patrae and Pharae and with these troops and the mercenaries invaded Elis. Reaching the place called Phyxium, they sent out their light-armed infantry and their cavalry to overrun the country, placing their heavily armed troops in ambush near this place. When the Eleans with their whole force arrived to defend the country from pillage and followed up the retreating marauders, Lycus issued from his ambush and fell upon the foremost of them. The Eleans did not wait to charge but turned and ran at once on the appearance of the enemy, who killed about 200 of them and captured eighty, bringing in all the booty they had collected in safety.[76]

Another report from 218 has the Ptolemaic forces defending the city of Atabyrium in the Jezreel valley. Antiochus III and his Seleucid army lured them to their death by means of an ambush. The city lay on a conical hill, the ascent of which was more than fifteen stades. First he hid a force in ambush, then on the ascent he provoked the garrison into sallying out and skirmishing. He feigned fear and began to retreat, enticing the advanced guard to follow his own retreating troops for a considerable distance downhill. Finally, he turned his own troops around and advanced on them, while those concealed in the ambush issued forth.

He attacked the enemy and killed many of them, and throwing them into panic took the city by assault.[77]

Aratus of Sicyon [d. 213 BCE], a third-century Greek statesman who brought his city-state into the Achaean League and led the League forces, has an ambush attributed to him by Polybius where the besiegers of a town failed because of a mistake in signalling. Aratus was plotting with elements in the city of Elea to exit the city quietly. One of the men was meant to act as a signaller. He was to reach a certain tomb on a hill outside the city and take a position there wearing a mantle. The others were to attack the officers who kept the gate at midday when they were sleeping. Once they received the signal that this was done, the Achaeans were to spring from their ambush position and make for the city gate at full speed. The arrangements were all made and when the day came Aratus arrived and hid in the riverbed waiting for the signal. But at the fifth hour of the day, the owner of some sheep, who was in the habit of grazing them near town, had some urgent private business with his shepherd and came out of the gate dressed in a mantle and went and stood on the identical tomb looking round for the shepherd. Aratus and his troops, thinking that the signal had been given them, made a rush for the town, but the gate was immediately closed in their faces by its keepers. Their friends inside the town had as yet taken no action, and the consequence was that Aratus' coup failed. This debacle brought destruction on those of the citizens who were acting with him too, because once they were detected the citizens put them on trial and had them executed. This incident illustrates, once again, that even a well-planned ambush can end in disaster if something goes wrong with the execution. In this case, Polybius was of the opinion that the flaw in the plan was the use of a single signal by the commander who, he claims, was still young and ignorant of the accuracy secured by a double signal and countersignals.[78]

An ambush story comes from Philip V's taking of the city of Lissus in Illyria in 213. The arrival of Philip was no secret; considerable forces from neighbouring parts of Illyria had collected at Lissus to confront him. But the Acrolissus stronghold had such natural strength that they stationed only a small garrison to hold it. At first, the battle seemed even, but eventually Philip withdrew his forces. Seeing Philip slowly withdrawing his divisions one after another, the Illyrians mistakenly thought that he was abandoning the field. They let themselves be enticed out of the city owing to their confidence in the strength of the place. They abandoned Acrolissus in small groups and poured down using by-paths to the level ground, thinking there would be a thorough rout of the enemy and a chance at capturing some booty. Instead, the troops Philip had placed in ambush rose unobserved and delivered a brisk attack. At the same time, his peltasts turned and fell on the enemy. The force from Lissus was thrown into disorder and retreated in scattered groups running for the shelter of the city, while those who had abandoned Acrolissus were cut off from it by the troops that had issued from the ambush. In this way both Acrolissus was taken without striking a blow, and Lissus surrendered the next day after a desperate struggle.[79]

The same kind of story is told about the mercenaries of Pellene in 200. Their scouts reported the invasion of the enemy, and at once they advanced and attacked the invading Achaeans. The Achaeans, however, had been ordered to retreat and lure them into an ambush. When the pursuit took them to the place where the ambush had been set up, the Achaeans rose up and cut some of them to pieces (*katakopeisan*); others were made prisoners.[80]

Conclusion

The heyday of mercenaries seems to have been the last thirty years of the fourth century and perhaps the first thirty years of the third. Our principal literary sources end with the Battle of Ipsus in 301. After Ipsus the Hellenistic world slowed down, not to peace but to warfare under a new and more settled system.[81] During this generation, mercenaries were for a short time the most important soldiers in the service of the great army commanders. We would know a lot more about ambushing in this period if we had biographies of some of the great commanders, or even the diary of a common soldier, but nothing of this sort has survived.[82] Men such as Leosthenes the Athenian, the 'mystery man' of Hellenistic history,[83] or the Aetolians Theodotus and Scopas[84] could have told us something about their activities in the field. These were generals who lived by their wits and died in the field. They were stars of their profession, but they have vanished from the historical scene.

Ambush took the same forms in the Hellenistic Age as it did in the fifth and fourth centuries. The Hellenistic army was one of professionals, with its many specialised troops. Most of the non-phalangite Greek mercenaries from the Hellenistic period were peltasts. Specialist contingents such as the Cretan archers fought in their own native style. Commanders had a vast array of professional fighters to choose from. The use of these diverse troops is exemplified under the command of Eumenes II at Magnesia, where he broke up the charge of Antiochus' war chariots with his Cretan archers, slingers and mounted javelin men.[85]

When men ranked commanders in the Hellenistic Age they thought in terms of personal prowess as well as intellectual quality. Cleverness and courage were the qualities that described a good commander.[86] A general's ability to think quickly and capitalise on the speed and flexibility of his troops to stage an ambush was considered a great asset. And while high social status was never given to peltasts, skirmishers or mercenaries of any kind, no Hellenistic army operated without them. Warfare had become endemic and too complicated to rely on simply the phalanx. The terrain on which an army might have to fight was far-ranging and required the flexibility of highly mobile, light-armed troops. The ever-present possibility of an ambush meant one had to be on guard for the safety of one's army, one's city and one's life. Sometimes, the only way to secure this safety was to ambush the enemy first. Polybius might mourn the loss of a kinder, gentler age, but what he could not conjure up was a past that did not have ambush as part of its military repertoire.

CHAPTER 10

Why the Greeks Used Ambush

NEITHER THE GREEKS NOR anyone else set up an ambush because of anything genetic, as a cultural imperative or from a lack of morality. Ambush is a tactical choice; it is a method used for its military practicality. It is appropriate only in certain times and places. It cannot be used ubiquitously, or done by every type of soldier. Army or navy units set up ambushes for the following reasons.

As a Force Multiplier When One Is Outnumbered
An ambush is used when advanced intelligence is needed to attack a powerful, more formidable enemy. An ambush takes advantage of them before they can arrange themselves in their customary battle formations. Ambush can also be used when one's forces are less heavily armed than the opponents, i.e. skirmishers attacking heavily-armed hoplites.[1]

When It Is the Only Mode of Attack Available
Ambush is not the choice of a power that can put a large force on a battlefield with heavy armour and shock force. Ambush is the choice of a group that must work with smaller forces, and lightly-armed troops.[2] For example, ambush and guerrilla warfare are the classic choices for a people occupied by an imperial power and whose native armies have been disbanded. Since they have been disallowed weapons or a formal military, they are forced to become guerrilla fighters. Indeed, under those very conditions it is the optimum choice if one is fighting with lightly armed forces not trained in the tactics of set-piece battles. Light infantry can destroy the enemy on his own ground, make the best of initiative, stealth, surprise, infiltration, ambush and night operations.[3] The ultimate insult comes when the occupying power uses the pejorative terms 'assassin' and 'terrorist' against those

people they have disarmed and forced into this mode of fighting in the first place. To their own people these combatants are, of course, called freedom fighters.

To Establish the Element of Surprise

Ambush is used against armies on the march, temporarily halted or otherwise out of formation. One achieves surprise by striking the enemy at a time or place or in a manner for which he is unprepared. Surprise delays enemy reactions, overloads and confuses his command and control structure, reduces his effectiveness and induces psychological shock in soldiers and leaders.[4] This shock enables attackers to succeed with fewer forces than they might otherwise have required. If surprise and shock are achieved, a unit can attack an enemy two or three times its size. If surprise is lost, if the enemy is well protected, or if it has other advantages the attacker will need at least three times as many troops as the enemy they are attacking.[5]

When the Terrain Dictates It

If one is fighting on rocky, mountainous, forested or broken terrain, ambush is more practical than a set-piece battle. Weather conditions can also play a role in the choice of ambush spots. Terrain is the ally of light infantrymen; they do not avoid difficult or close terrain – they seek it out. Mountains, ravines, forests, jungles, stream beds or even folds in the ground may be used to hide friendly forces until they close with the enemy.[6] Greece has more of this sort of terrain than large, empty plains. The helplessness of Greek heavy infantry when attacked by light-armed troops on broken ground has often been remarked upon.[7]

When the Opportunity Presents Itself

Sometimes there is a need for immediate action. If one receives information that the enemy is approaching, one may have to attack before being caught oneself. Ambushing can keep the enemy from knowing or countering your own movements and tactical operations. Speed and surprise give more security to your own unit.[8] Night, rain, snow, smoke, dust and fog all help to mask attacking forces.

An Ambush Can Be Used As a Diversion

Evidently, even the threat of an ambush could be a deception. In Polyaenus a deserter is sent to tell Nicias that, if the Athenians try to escape at night, they will be ambushed by the Syracusans.[9] They stay put rather than attack, and this gives the Syracusans time to take the river crossings and bridges in advance and then attack the next day and slaughter the Athenians.

Ambush is Used to Capture Intelligence Assets
This is one of the most common tactics used by the Greeks overseas. In Xenophon, *Anabasis* we see natives captured so they might be used as guides.[10]

As Part of a Deception Plan
Ambushes can be used actively to mislead the enemy, to make them think you are after something you are not, to make them think your army is somewhere it is not or to find out what their intelligence resources are.[11]

Ambush to Demoralise the Enemy
Large numbers of casualties can demoralise the enemy.[12]

Because Your Intelligence Assets Are Better Than the Enemy's
If you can anticipate enemy locations and movements, you can use that intelligence to neutralise them.[13]

Greeks Using Ambushes

Not only did the Greeks use ambush for the above reasons, commanders such as Demosthenes or Iphicrates became famous for it.[14] Right from the beginning of their written literature, the Greeks ambushed their enemies. In Xenophon's *Hellenica* we see the stages of planning: selection of the right place; concealment; delay till the right moment; surprise and panic of the victims; and hand-to-hand combat clearly laid out.[15]

There is nothing cowardly about ambushing. Indeed, ambush is one of the deadliest forms of fighting. Tactically, it is a very murderous form of battle that exploits surprise to its maximum.[16] Modern field manuals define area ambushes as operations used to 'interdict enemy movements and *inflict maximum casualties on enemy forces* [italics mine]'.[17] It is not the polar opposite of killing in battle, it *is* killing in battle, but on a smaller scale. Mardonius says the Greeks preferred battle where they face their enemy at arm's reach to kill and be killed, and this is what ambush is – hand-to-hand combat, close up and deadly. Tyrtaeus states: 'No man ever proves himself a good man in war unless he endures to face the blood and slaughter.'[18] Well, ambush is blood and slaughter. Ambush by small forces can rack up the carnage quite quickly. There are passages in Greek literature that condescend to light-armed troops such as bowmen, slingers and other troops who hurl weapons from a distance, but ambushers are not in this category. They fight close up and dirty – face to face. Thanks to John Keegan, there has been much interest in recent years in the 'what it was like for them?' approach to ancient military operations. We should be asking: 'What was it like for an ancient soldier to spring an ambush on the enemy?' It is easy to dismiss ambushers as cowards, but quite something else to examine the physical aspects of wielding an ancient weapon, waiting for the enemy to approach and then killing them at close range. The psychological question of who was equipped for such duty and what place this activity had in Greek warfare is a valid one.

In many of the examples we have seen, ambushes caused carnage.[19] Casualties were very high and often the attacked force was wiped out. Indeed, casualties increase in direct proportion to the amount of time the soldiers are exposed to enemy attack. The most effective way to suppress the enemy is to kill him. This is done with violent, close-combat action once a unit has closed with the enemy.[20] The area in which the enemy finds himself is not called a 'kill zone' for nothing. The high casualty rate is stressed even in the ancient sources. Thucydides talks about the dawn operation of Demosthenes using the Messenians against the Ambraciots.[21] He comments about how many of them were killed on the spot. Those who escaped the first onslaught fled into neighbouring ravines where ambushes had been sent up and the Ambraciot troops were *slaughtered*. In many of the passages below we encounter the verb *diaphtheiro* which means to destroy utterly.[22]

In Herodotus, the Persians are attacked during a night march and cut to pieces.[23] In Thucydides, an attack by the Amphilochians by the Ambraciots produced a 'slaughter'.[24] Also in Thucydides, the Sicels ambush a force that is off-guard, and destroy 800 of the enemy; only one Corinthian envoy escaped and led the remaining 1,500 to Syracuse.[25] In Polyaenus, all the Corinthians who are ambushed are killed.[26] In Polybius, the mercenaries of Pellene ambush the Achaeans and cut them to pieces.[27] In Xenophon's *Hellenica*, Iphicrates sets an ambush in the territory of Phlius that killed so many of them that the city, while previously anti-Spartan, called backs its pro-Spartan exiles and put the city and the citadel in the hands of the Spartans to guard.[28] Also in *Hellenica*, Anaxibius and 200 of his Spartans were killed in a mountain pass in Abydos.[29]

Of course, there is no guarantee of success with an ambush and the tables can be turned. Polyaenus relates how, when Iphicrates was attacking Sicyon, an ambush was set for him.[30] He admits he made a mistake not by reconnoitring the area. Yet he recovered, attacked the ambushers and killed them all. In Thucydides, Aristius killed a large number of Sermylians by ambush near their own city.[31] In Xenophon, *Hellenica*, Chabrias landed in Aegina, set up an ambush in a hollow and quickly killed 150 Aeginetans and 200 resident aliens.[32] In Polyaenus, Arxilaidas the Laconian is shown attacking ambushers and 'out-generalling' them because of his advance intelligence and preparations.[33]

Aeneas Tacticus proves that some people never learn the lesson.[34] The Triballi laid waste to the country of the Abderites and set ambushes.[35] The Abderites resented being tricked and victimised, so they made a hasty attack with great eagerness, and the Triballi drew them into another ambush. The rest of the people in the city, not hearing of what had happened (bad intelligence gathering), rushed out to the rescue of their comrades and fell into a third ambush. It is said that more men perished in a shorter time than had ever been the case, at least from a single city of similar size. In Polyaenus, Cassander ambushed the Epidamnians and killed no fewer than 2,000 men outside the city and then got into the city gates to do more damage.[36] Polybius has Lycus kill 200, capture 800 and a large amount of war booty from the Eleans.[37] By ambushing some and putting others to flight, one causes panic in those watching the action.[38]

Light-armed troops are best suited to springing an ambush, but hoplites were used also. In Thucydides, Demosthenes sets up an ambush with 200 Messenians hoplites;[39] Xenophon's *Hellenica* has the Spartans using younger hoplites,[40] and in *Anabasis* he has his rearguard ambush natives who are following him.[41] Xenophon's *Hellenica* also mentions Chabrias using peltasts.[42] Polybius describes an ambush where Lycus overruns the countryside with light-armed infantry, but puts his *heavily-armed* troops in ambush then springs it on the Eleans.[43]

Ambushers need not even be soldiers, although soldiers are obviously the preferred choice. Civilians, even women, as we have seen, could set up an ambush. Polyaenus tells of Philip accepting the surrender of the Pharcedonians in Thessaly and as his troops entered the town people threw stones and javelins down upon him from the roofs.[44] Also in Polyaenus, Onomarchus lures Macedonians into the hollow of a crescent-shaped mountain and crushes their phalanx with rocks.[45] Native tribesmen can set an ambush as well as the Greeks.[46]

In short, ambushes are lethal and quick. As soon as the enemy is hit, the ambushers only have a few seconds to kill the enemy before he recovers from his initial shock and fights back or leaves the area. Such forces must pre-plan their escape to be sure they are not ambushed by reinforcements. When authors talk about the 'madness that is close combat' the only difference between a hoplite battle and an ambush is scale.[47] The famous military strategist Ardant du Picq writes: 'A man surprised needs an instant to collect his thoughts and defend himself, during this instant, he is killed if he does not run away.'[48]

The Skills

Staging an ambush is not something easy to accomplish. It is best done with soldiers who are trained by their leaders in the skills needed for such operations. Troops must be trained to be highly responsive and flexible. They must be able to close with the enemy and kill him. Light infantrymen can be used to destroy the enemy on his own ground, make the best of initiative, stealth and surprise, infiltration, ambush and night operations.[49] Iphicrates trained his light-armed troops by staging fake ambushes, fake assaults, fake panics and fake desertions so his men would be ready if the real thing happened.[50] Light infantrymen are not tacticians. They cannot respond mechanically to a set of conditions on a battlefield with a pre-determined action like a phalanx. Whoever leads the ambush must know how to use initiative, understand intent, take independent action, analyse the field of operations, collect intelligence and make rapid decisions. Initiative means bold action and often involves risks. Initiative by a tactical leader may be independent of what higher commanders want done to the enemy.[51] The men such leaders work with are soldiers trained to fend for themselves through hardship and risk in hostile, uncompromising terrain. Such operations build a greater degree of teamwork and skill than other types of infantry formations as a result of the stress put on adaptability, close-combat skills and independent action.

The troops developed in the fourth century needed a more prolonged and thorough training than the Greek states in the fifth century. The exception was Sparta. The Spartans had to be almost a professional army, and there had to be at least a cadre of professional officers to train them. Without a standing army of full-time soldiers, strong positions could not be permanently garrisoned.[52] An officer class, corresponding to our commissioned and non-commissioned officers, was a thing no Greek state (except Sparta in its own way) wanted or thought of.[53] The hoplite system had been a democratic one. Every man supplied his own armour and weapons. It was not like a modern army where the government owns the tanks, the jeeps, the guns, the bullets. A citizen contributed to the needs of the state when called upon.[54] Institutionalised naval warfare or the permanent garrisoning of passes and frontiers would have been beyond the economic capacity of most early Greek states. It was something more suitable for Hellenistic kings.

The weapons of ambush were the sword, the spear, the knife and the garrotte, or even bare hands if necessary. Each soldier had to be an aggressive and skilled fighter in hand-to-hand combat. Training in skills such as navigation, camouflage, foraging, tracking and stalking, and using weather and terrain as an ally were all useful.[55] Such soldiers operated under dangerous and stressful conditions. They had to carry only the equipment and supplies needed for the mission to assure mobility, but also enough to be able to defend themselves. They had to maintain operational security to keep the enemy from finding out their location. Surprise is achieved by operations that make good use of speed of action and secrecy.[56] Reconnaissance is a constant process. Physical security keeps the unit from being surprised itself. This includes rear and flank observation during the offence and defence, the use of covered and concealed routes during movement, and making sure that silence is maintained. Good discipline is a must. Just springing the ambush is not enough. As soon as the enemy is hit, he reacts. Ambush members have one or two seconds to kill the enemy in the kill zone before he recovers from the initial shock and either attacks you or leaves the area.[57] There must be a withdrawal route secured if one is operating in enemy territory; the unit withdraws from the area as soon as it can. One must be alert for other forces in the vicinity and cover any tracks out of the ambush area to keep from being followed.

Nature of the Ground Chosen for the Ambush

The most common types of ambush among the Greeks were: those made along the line of march; and those made by an attacking force decoying the defenders of a walled city from the safety of their position. There are fifteen examples of ambush along the line of march or sail.[58] There are seventeen examples of ambush of defenders of city by besieger.[59] Pritchett finds five examples of ambush of a force assaulting a city,[60] three of ambushes during battle,[61] three examples of ambush by marauders from land,[62] and four of ambush by marauders at sea.[63] There are also numerous cavalry ambushes.[64] In addition to the Greek authors, the Roman military writer Frontinus has a section *On Ambushes (De insidiis)* that lists fifty-seven examples, of which six are Greek.[65]

The frequency of ambushes in siege warfare is illustrated by the attention that Aeneas Tacticus devotes to the subject in his highly regarded treatise on military science. In his work there are numerous occurrences of the words *enedra* (seven) and *enedreo* (seven), as well as one of *enedreutikos.*[66] The references occur in sections that recommend measures to be taken in regulating forays outside the city walls (fifteen to sixteen) and the secret sallies by night (twenty-three). Bands within a besieged city were to be organised to avoid enemy ambushes,[67] when the former sallied forth to prevent devastation to their fields. Special measures were also to be taken when the defenders set ambushes outside the city walls at night to prevent revolutionary factions from seizing the city from within.[68] All these measures are concerned with defence against aggression.

Ambushes became so much a part of warfare by the time of Polybius that he goes into great detail about the ground best suited for ambushes. He feels that flat and treeless plains are better than woods. The ambushers could hide in any watercourse with a slight bank that had reeds or bracken. Thorny plants could be made use of to conceal not only infantry but even the dismounted horsemen at times. This allowed the attackers a good view of the surrounding area, while they remained concealed themselves.

Cavalry Scouts

As ambushes become more frequent and dangerous, so the Greeks realised the importance of cavalry scouts to prevent against them.[69] The use of advance mounted guards minimised the ambush of large armies on the march, and a number of passages testify to the use of cavalry scouts to prevent ambush. The earliest examples are the *skiritai* used by the Spartans.[70]

Advance contingents of any kind are referred to first as *prodromoi* by Herodotus, such as the force sent to Thermopylae under the command of Leonidas.[71] These are not all scouts, but later the term *prodromoi* is used to describe units created during the reforms of Iphicrates.[72] Kromayer and Veith write that their chief purpose was for intelligence gathering, especially trained skirmishers.[73]

In *The Cavalry General* Xenophon recommends the use of *proodoi* in advance of the army primarily to show the men what paths they should follow, but also to discover an enemy. His advice could hardly be more succinct:

> . . . a prudent general can hardly show his wisdom better than by sending out advanced patrols in front of the ordinary exploring parties to reconnoitre every inch of ground minutely. So to be apprised of the enemy's position in advance, and at as great a distance off as possible, cannot fail to be useful, whether for purposes of attack or defence.[74]

His recommendations for reconnaissance are equally useful:

> It is the business of the hipparch to take infinite precautions . . . to make himself
> acquainted with the details, not only of his own, but of the hostile territory . . .
> should he personally lack the knowledge, he should invite the aid of others – those
> best versed in the topography of any district. Since there is all the difference in the
> world between a leader acquainted with his roads and one who is not; and when it
> comes to actual designs upon the enemy, the difference between knowing and not
> knowing the locality can hardly be exaggerated.[75]

For Athens, Aristotle mentions mounted *prodromoi*.[76] They appear to be a selected
body of light cavalry used for scouting, who were successors to the horse archers
of the fifth and early fourth centuries.[77] The *hamippoi* existed among the Boeotians
as light infantry who were stationed with and fought alongside the cavalry. The
Athenians may have copied this practice.[78]

By the first century, Onasander in his *Strategikos* writes with regard to military
formations: 'He [the general] must send ahead cavalry as scouts to search the roads,
especially when advancing through a wooded country, or a wilderness broken up
by ridges. For ambushes are frequently set by the enemy . . . in a level and treeless
country, a general survey is sufficient.'[79]

Although the Greek military organisation did not advance to a state of highly
specialised functions, these passages mentioning *skiritai, proodoi* and *prodromoi*
suggest that marching armies and their commanders realised the need for
protection on the march against ambush. The vanguard of an army should be made
up of men, including horsemen, whose function it was to establish the route and
prevent ambushes. By the Hellenistic period such forces became prolific. Arrian
has Alexander taking the lightest armed troops and archers to march along a rough
and difficult road, leaving troops behind to guard the roads where he thought they
might be ambushed.[80]

In short, the use of ambush is a type of warfare best described by Mao Tse Tung
in his masterpiece *Guerrilla Warfare*:

> What is basic guerrilla strategy? Guerrilla strategy must be based primarily on
> alertness, mobility, and attack . . . In guerrilla warfare, select the tactic of seeming
> to come from the east and attacking from the west; avoid the solid, attack the
> hollow; attack; withdraw; deliver a lightning blow, seek a lightning decision.

When guerrillas engage a stronger enemy, they withdraw when he advances; harass him when he stops; strike him when he is weary; pursue him when he withdraws. In guerrilla strategy the enemy's rear flanks, and other vulnerable spots are his vital points and there he must be harassed, attacked, dispersed, exhausted and annihilated.[81]

The tactics followed by Demosthenes' light infantry operated basically along these lines.[82] E. C. Woodcock notices this and observes that: 'There is only one way by which an inferior power can win battles against an enemy who has superior numbers, and Demosthenes discovered it . . .'[83] He believes it was done by concentrating forces at a given time and in a given place where the enemy would be, for the moment, inferior. We should add, however, that it can be done by surprise attack.

Communications

Good communications between the ambushers was necessary for a successful attack. Similarly, communications between fifth columnists and the enemy were necessary for the success of a betrayal.[84] All such communications had to be kept secret. In the case of attacking a city at night with the use of conspirators within, the fewer people who knew about the plot the better. Thucydides notes the secrecy involved in the betrayal of the long walls at Megara.[85] There are only a few cases where numbers are mentioned. At Torone and Mende, the conspirators were few[86] and at Byzantium apparently five men arranged the betrayal.[87] These were all successful. The planned ambush on the gates of Megara, however, was known to many[88] and was betrayed.[89] The plot to betray Siphae and Chaeronea involved a number of conspirators[90] and was also betrayed[91] because the ambush was planned a considerable time before it was actually executed. There was, therefore, more time for the information to leak out.[92] This was also true in the betrayal of cities when diplomatic channels and spies had to be used to communicate with the conspirators. One had to be very careful about signalling, especially using lights, lamps or torches at night. They could be seen by the enemy and tip off the target that an attack was imminent.[93]

Counterintelligence

Since the primary aim of an ambush or a betrayal was surprise, the best defence against it was to know about it ahead of time. Some would say foreknowledge was, in fact, the only effective defence.[94] Walls and harbours could be fortified and guarded to thwart a surprise attack. Festivals could be cancelled if it was suspected they would be used as a cover for a surprise attack.[95] At Megara, when the oligarchs found out about a suspected plot, they argued that it was not in the best interests of the city to march out to battle. They did not let on what they knew about the planned ambush, but they were careful to guard the gates against any fifth columnists.[96] Apart from basic defensive measure, a city could call in allied forces to secure the walls. Spartolus appealed to Olynthus for a garrison to prevent its betrayal to the Athenians.[97] One of the ways to prevent a betrayal was to detect the fifth columnists and have them executed before they could do any harm.[98] Informers were often used to reveal the conspiracies. Sometimes the informers were people actually involved in the plots.[99] Their motives are not always clear, but certainly rewards were offered by cities for such valuable intelligence. In fact, Aeneas Tacticus recommends that rewards be offered for information leading to the arrest of anyone plotting against a city.[100] Informers were encouraged at Athens from Solon's time on.[101]

In short, the increase in the use of light-armed troops and smaller tactical units contributed to the active solicitation of fifth columns by attacking forces. The techniques required for these types of surprise operations included the clandestine exchange of information between traitors and the enemy, timing of attacks at night or during festivals, the strategic deployment of forces in commando-type strikes, and surprise attacks. Except for Losada's study on fifth columns, these techniques have been largely ignored in the study of Greek military history. The basic strategic aim of such techniques was surprise, and yet this seems to go unnoticed by historians. Gomme, when discussing sieges in the fifth century, says that it was 'a matter of wonder . . . that surprise was not more often attempted'.[102] Frank Adcock writes:

> . . . surprise is highly valued by all good judges of war, and the power to achieve it is one criterion of military and naval resourcefulness. Yet surprises are not common in Greek or Macedonian war by land or sea. It is on the whole true that the art of reconnaissance and the gathering of intelligence was not a strong point of fleets or armies in antiquity. To achieve surprise usually needs good intelligence, just as does the capacity to guard against it.[103]

These kinds of attitudes need to be discarded. Surprises were not rare during the fifth century, and were much in evidence during the Peloponnesian war. The offensive and defensive techniques employed, and the number of fifth columns used to subvert cities, make it clear that the use of surprise and the capacity to guard against it were common.[104] The use of intelligence to both plan surprise attacks and to detect them was present even if we do not have a huge amount of information about it.[105] The numerous examples of surprise attacks – at night, at dawn, at sea, etc. – and the number of subversive plots, both successful and unsuccessful, support this conclusion. The cultural and intellectual history of the generation that lived through the Peloponnesian war was affected by this constant danger of surprise and subversion. Their reactions to the betrayals, their attitudes towards treason and internal security, and their fortress mentality may have been a result of these events. There were cultural implications for subsequent Greek military, political and cultural history.[106]

CONCLUSION

The Complexity of Greek Warfare

CONSIDER THE IRONY THAT the Greeks never developed a word, a true generic term, for surprise attack – something they did so frequently that one can fill ten chapters with examples. And yet scholars assert that this is something the Greeks rarely, if ever, did.[1] If the material collected here proves anything, it is that ambush and the use of surprise had always been a part of ancient Greek warfare. The Greeks were very good at sneaking up on their enemies – even other Greeks. Concomitantly, they also had ambivalent attitudes towards the appropriate and inappropriate routes to military success and to admirable and despicable human qualities or behaviours.

As Hans van Wees writes: 'It is the nature of nostalgia to project ideals onto the past, to make believe that the highest standards and noblest achievements used to be everyday realities. For Demosthenes and Polybius, pitched infantry battle clearly was such an ideal: a form of combat more prestigious than any other.'[2]

From Homer onwards we hear warriors quoted by ancient writers expressing disdain towards ambushes, surprise attacks or any form of what they consider 'unfair advantage'. Some even denounced the use of fortifications and siege engines as cowardly. A brave man kills his enemy face to face.[3]

Ancient historians had already done some editing of their own record. They eliminated a discussion of ambush for the same reason they eliminated women's participation in war – they considered it beneath them.[4] This élitist attitude left little for modern historians to work with. It did, however, obligate the modern historian to explain the absence of the use of surprise by giving reasons ranging from poor source material, cultural inhibitions or the impracticality of mounting such operations because of insufficient intelligence gathering.[5]

Many historians have found the realities of ambush distasteful, and they have dealt with them in several different ways. First, there are those who postulate

153

that there was little use of ambush by infantry in Classical Greece, and thus edit it out of the narrative. Pritchett plays down the important of ambush, and says that the Greeks were ambivalent about ambushing.[6] Whitehead reached a similar conclusion when he says that ancient sensibilities about deception and theft were 'manifestly different' from our 'modern, cynical sensibilities'.[7] While we certainly recognise that pitched infantry battle was always important to the Greeks, both as a military practice and a military ideal, we must never be led to think that it was the only significant form of warfare in Greece.

The Ubiquity of Ambush

The argument that ambush was a rarity in Greek warfare simply will not hold because there are too many examples of it in the historical record. Even in periods when we have poor, fragmented sources, the Greeks still wrote about ambush and surprise attacks. The Homeric, Archaic, Classical and Hellenistic Greeks all ambushed and, furthermore, they spoke and acted similarly with regard to ambush and surprise attack. Warfare, in all its diversity, took on many different forms, but the warrior mentality remained much the same from Homer to Xenophon, or at least was much more uniform than previous writers have believed. One did what one had to do to win, minimising one's own casualties while maximising those of the enemy.

That the Greeks understood the concept of ambush is displayed in their earliest writings on warfare. In the *Iliad* and *Odyssey*, ambushing an enemy was no different than trapping a lion on a hunt. There was no disapproval except from the person who was caught in the ambush.[8] While a man might declare his disdain for being ambushed, deceived or shot from a distance, this would not mean he would hesitate to use such a tactic against his own enemies if the possibility arose. To set an ambush was to act as a person at war would normally act.

The problem here is one of focus. If historians only focus on large battles, then they will only see hoplites fighting them. The practice of raiding, as opposed to agricultural ravaging as a challenge preliminary to pitched battle, existed in all periods of Greek history. Hoplite battle was only part of the repertoire of intra-communal violence. Freebooting raids and *petites guerres* were frequent.[9] The polis was a military organism, and its capacity for self-defence, violent interaction with neighbouring communities over disputes, and aggression meant there would always be local military activity.[10] Historians and poets tend to fasten on the big 'agonal' or ritually competitive pitched battles, but much fighting would have been what the Germans called *kleinkrieg* – guerrilla warfare, attacks on cities or villages, impromptu raiding and response to raiding (the Greek for impromptu is *ex epidromes*). The *Iliad* tells us about this sort of thing as well as the big battles and the great main siege. In these informal, non-ritualised fighting types of warfare there was not as much room for Achillean heroism.

Those who focus on the big battles tend to see the use of other types of troops as a breakdown of the hoplite system and of Greek morality in general. Such historians see a change in the 'unwritten hoplite code'. For Josiah Ober it was the Peloponnesian war, especially Pericles' strategy of avoiding a decisive battle, that changed Greek warfare for ever.[11] For Victor Davis Hanson, the change came earlier during the Persian wars with the growth of the Athenian navy, and the increasing wealth of Athens, which allowed new kinds of fighting in the decades before the Peloponnesian war.[12] No matter how far back one goes in time, however, there are always accounts of deception, guile and surprise. Whatever the hoplites are doing, there is always a parallel story happening with other troops.

Certainly warfare changed over time as more mercenaries and light-armed troops entered the fray and the Greeks found themselves fighting overseas. As the reformed peltast of Iphicrates became the model for mercenaries in general, the more we see ambush, forays and retreats in place of the decisive battle. The poorest citizens could equip themselves for service as light-armed and such troops were highly effective.[13] They proved tactically superior to the cavalry and the hoplites. Mercenaries provided specialists and a more fluid style of warfare.[14] They had never been totally absent from Greek warfare.

Another argument used to diminish the importance of ambush is that it never decides battles or wars. But this is to expect a result that ambush can never be expected to deliver. Ambush has never been the main way of fighting a war. The use of surprise has always been situational. As Clausewitz notes, the weaker the forces a commander had the more appealing boldness and deception or surprise attack became.[15] When a commander feels he is unable to defeat the enemy in an open battle, then the idea of an ambush becomes more appealing. Since the best opportunities for ambush do not come during a pitched battle, it is hardly surprising to find ambushes taking place most frequently against armies on the march.[16]

Another major objection that historians, both ancient and modern, have had to the technique ambush is that surprise attack is a form of deception. They do not like having such 'sneaky' techniques attributed to the Greeks or Westerners in general. As we have seen, however, deception has always been a part of Greek warfare. Peter Krentz collected over 120 examples of deception used by the Greeks. As long as 'the habit and discipline of war' existed, there would be ambush as well as set-piece battles. There is a long list of Greek commanders who used deceptive tactics and were admired for it. The list starts with legendary figures and continues on to historical deceivers.[17] Xenophon writes: 'For there is really nothing more profitable in war than deception . . . On thinking over the successes gained in war, you will find that most of them, and the greatest ones, have been won with the aid of deception.'[18] This is not an isolated quotation taken out of context. Deception seems to have fascinated Xenophon and he mentions it in eleven different works.[19] He insisted that a good general must not only learn deceptions from others but must also invent his own, i.e. new devices to deceive his opponents. Furthermore, a good commander should expect others to try and outwit him and guard against being deceived.

Surprise was considered an essential element of victory by almost all ancient military writers. Aeneas Tacticus, Frontinus and Polyaenus wrote entire collections of the ways and means of surprise – textbooks for victory. These books, especially Frontinus, were well known in late antiquity and throughout the Middle Ages.[20] The use of surprise, deception and originality reflected well upon the quality of a general both then and now. Again, I am not suggesting that surprise and ambush were the basis of military planning, nor as the condition *sine qua non* of victory. Rather, ambush was considered a welcomed technique that could complete or facilitate a victory.

Ancient Attitudes

Part of the blame for ambiguous attitudes towards ambush must be laid at the door of the ancient Greeks themselves. It is certainly not difficult to find statements made by ancient authors disparaging ambushes, surprise and deception. But it is important to consider the context of the quotation, the bias of the author, and the audience to whom the comment is aimed. The Spartan Brasidas mocked barbarians who avoided set-piece battles[21] and told the Acanthians that it was more disgraceful to gain an advantage by deception than by open force,[22] but then at Amphipolis he told his own men that the most successful soldiers do not attack openly but take advantage of the opportunities offered, and that such tactics have the 'most brilliant reputation in war'.[23] Pausanias says there was a tradition disparaging the Athenians for their victory at Sphacteria because it was 'stolen' by a surprise attack.[24] On the other hand, Plutarch quotes Archidamus as saying after defeating the Arcadians that 'it would have been better to have defeated them by intelligence than by strength'.[25] Even the oft-quoted passage of Polybius, which characterises ambushes as violations of the 'ancient sense of military honour', can be balanced against his own statement[26] that a rash general is susceptible to plots, ambushes and deceptions, and in the following section he says that the commander who perceives and takes advantage of the weakness of an enemy's leader will most quickly win a decisive victory. He implies that a good commander will use deception when he can.

The later Greeks romanticised their earlier history and tried to believe that there was a time when a uniform code of ethics existed that had somehow later been lost. We can see such romanticising in Demosthenes' rhetoric in his *Third Phillipic*, where he argues that Philip was a more dangerous enemy than the Spartans, who always played by the 'old-fashioned rules'. We see the same rhetoric in Herodotus[27] and Polybius.[28] That is not to say that the contrast with the past had no validity. Demosthenes was contrasting the days gone by, when war was seasonal and 'principled', whereas contemporary war was permanent and waged by any means.[29] True, war had changed, but the reality of war had always been brutal and had always included an element of surprise and deception.

So when Polybius, comparing the practices of his own day to those of an earlier era, writes: 'The ancients would not even consent to get the better of their enemies by fraud, regarding no success as brilliant or secure unless they crushed the spirit of their adversaries in open battle,' he was engaging in a nostalgia over a lost time that may have never existed.[30] As we have seen, Homeric warriors happily deceived their enemies. The Homeric term *metis* (cunning intelligence) could encompass many characteristics that included flair, wisdom, forethought, subtlety of mind, deception, resourcefulness, vigilance and opportunism with various other skills.[31] These are the sorts of mental skills displayed by any general worth his salt. Deception, trickery and foresight imply that one has collected intelligence properly. The success of an ambush or a surprise attack depends to a great extent upon foreseeing the result of a particular situation and knowing the exact time to employ the proper means.[32]

Herodotus, Thucydides and Polybius all included speeches against deception and made their speech-makers claim that the Greeks' ancestors waged strictly non-devious warfare. Patrick Porter labels this phenomenon 'exaggerated self-celebration'.[33] Commanders used ruses, night ambushes and raids when they believed they would work. Duplicitous moves included pretending to be friendly, pretending to be done for the day, sending false information, feigning flight, making a misleading agreement and seizing undefended cities. They were all a part of the Greek toolbox. Sparta trained boys to steal food, stay awake at night, lay ambushes and prepare spies.[34] A number of scholars have tried to argue away these references by saying the 'stealing' was actually a ritual activity, or that ambush and living off the land were training to hunt down escaped helots, but the fact remains that when Brasidas made his speech he was talking to Spartan hoplites about how to attack Cleon's hoplites.[35] Xenophon believes that *apaté* produced the greatest success in war. Cassius Dio echoes this view when he praises the generalship of P. Martius Verus and praises him for his ability, like Odysseus, to outwit the enemy by *apaté*, which is the 'true strength of generals'.[36] In Xenophon's *Anabasis*, Cyrus takes the Armenian king by surprise, capturing both him and his family.[37] The moral argument in the passage is about the king acting unjustly by refusing troops and the tribute, not the surprise attack.[38]

The military ethics of Odysseus, i.e. avoiding pitched battle and embracing indirect means, always competed with the 'Achilles ethos' of open battle, for the mind of Greek commanders. Both Athenians and Spartans denounced their enemy's stratagems, but carried out their own. Greek strategic culture could also sustain conflicting ideas about grand strategy. Greek culture contained both Achillean traditionalists who saw the world as an anarchic place where only power could ensure security, and Odyssean 'modernists' who stressed multilateralism and co-operation.[39] This is not too different from our modern debate between unilateralism, power and the role of force in international affairs.[40]

Military Hierarchies

We have encountered many stereotypes used by ancient Greek writers that held up certain modes of fighting for praise while ignoring or degrading others. Mocking Paris for being a bowman is the best example. The figure of Odysseus, however, clearly shows that the virtues of the spearfighter and the bowman could be easily combined. Alexander historians certainly knew the value of auxiliary troops such as archers. It is ridiculous to suppose that archers, who in pre-artillery days before 400 held off many city-besiegers, were held in universal contempt. To refer to a bowman as nothing more than a 'savage tribalist' is as incorrect as it is condescending.[41] Even in Athens, where foreigners and citizens were categorised separately, the official casualty lists show barbarian archers who were honourably recorded alongside the citizen dead. Simon Hornblower, in his article 'Warfare in ancient literature', points out that many things about ancient warfare were left out, including the participation of women and slaves. He goes on to say that not all warfare was regular warfare and that what is left out is due to the 'bias of ancient historians'. Less organised, non-ritualistic fighting occurred at a level below which poets and historians had no interest. They concentrated on groups and individuals from the élite. They did so to 'uphold an essentially male ideology . . .'[42] Graham Shipley says the same thing when he notes that: 'The selection of war as the paramount activity can be regarded as an attempt to direct energy towards maintaining a particular social structure, one in which citizen was dominated by aristocrat, non-citizen by citizen, female by male, and barbarian by Greek.'[43]

The reason some warriors disparage other warriors is a certain snobbery that gives a higher social status to one type of fighting over another. Complex societies have been establishing such hierarchies since time immemorial. Some ways of fighting mark the participants as brave and estimable while others do not. The status of a type of military force depends more on the power of the people who serve in it than upon the difficulty of the skills involved, its demands on participant's courage or their military effectiveness. Whenever we talk about status and prestige we must add 'prestige with whom?'[44] With the Greeks we find the most status is attached to hoplite warfare. But Greek warfare had more aspects to it than this and should not be reduced to hoplite snobbery.[45] The Greeks used many types of fighting, and some of the techniques they used, like ambush, were controversial – then as now.

In Greece, the relative status of military forces could vary geographically as well as between different classes. Thessalian nobles, for example, secure in their formidable reputation as the best cavalry in Greece, were unlikely to have esteemed the peasant levies that composed their infantry. Mercenaries were, by definition, outsiders so their professionalism and military contributions did not prevent Athenians from considering them impoverished, thieving, brutish semi-barbarians. Yet mercenaries were manifestly effective troops – or they would have been quickly out of work. The types of forces in which mercenaries typically served suffered by association. Peltasts, archers and slingers were often mercenary outsiders and less esteemed as a result.[46]

Despite the usefulness that major city-states found in hiring slingers, their status remained low. Xenophon calls slingers 'the most slavish' of soldiers since no number of slingers alone could stand up against even a few hoplites.[47] Slingers were no more dependent on other forces than were hoplites or cavalry, but their status was low because they were often mercenaries from outside the world of the city-states. Also, slings were cheap to make and carried by poorer men. Slings also lacked the Homeric cachet that may have counterbalanced some of the contempt for the peltast or archers.[48] Nor were there important military states that depended primarily on the sling, as horsemen and archers were among the most important troops of the Persians and Scythians. Yet even here prestige is in the eye of the beholder: the city of Aspendus, which was probably a source of these specialised troops, put a slinger on some of its coins to advertise its proudest export.[49]

War and Morality

The morality of ambush is the sticking point of this entire discussion. Is it merely sour grapes when the Spartans complain about Sphacteria, or narcissism when Alexander brags at Gaugamela about never using surprise attacks? Were ancient sensibilities manifestly different than ours, or were they capable of the same stereotypes that we make today?[50] People such as Xenophon, who not only saw nothing wrong in breaking the rules, but also positively recommended it, are accused of not being 'gentlemen'. This label may work on the cricket field, but it has nothing to do with battlefield realities either ancient or modern. Expecting people to act like gentlemen on the battlefield is nothing more than a utopian ideal. The notion of hoplite warfare being a contest to be won in a properly chivalrous way and crowned with a fair victory really does not hold up to close scrutiny. Much of wartime activity was taken up by ambushes and surprise attacks. Nor will the argument stand that such behaviour was considered bad by Homeric and pre-Classical standards and pragmatic when warfare became more brutal. Warriors throughout Greek history knew the reality of warfare; only the armchair historians or those with an ideological axe to grind moralise about it.[51] There is no precedent in earlier Greek literature for the Plutarch–Curtius–Arrian view of Alexander with its 'heroic disavowal of ambush and surprise'. The Greeks felt that *dolos* (trickery) was a perfectly fair way to win a duel, and both *polemos* (war) and *lochos* (ambush) were equivalent fields of a warrior's endeavour.[52] Indeed, ambush was the best test of a soldier's bravery.[53] The assertions of the moral superiority of open fighting on a battlefield as opposed to ambush is, as one scholar labels it, the 'retrospective, artificial analogue in Latin Literature'.[54] The Roman condemnation of the 'Odysseus syndrome' has been identified by more than one author for the hypocrisy it represents.[55]

That is not to say that pejorative terms were not used for such behaviour, but one must always ask through what lens such value judgements are being made.[56]

The only generalisation that seems to hold is that trickery used against you is base, but trickery against your enemy is prudent.[57] Everett Wheeler's study of the Greek and Latin vocabulary of trickery shows that the tone of the various words used to describe such stratagems is usually positive or at least neutral. But as he points out, in war losers seek excuses for defeat: 'Victims of deception or even an opponent's superior skill can always cry "foul" with or without just cause. Often the attitude of a writer toward the respective parties or a particular even determines whether a stratagem is praised as genius, defended as necessity, or condemned as a war crime.'[58]

The old chestnut about hoplites vs. light-armed troops is repeated over and over: that hoplites despised light troops because they disapproved of what they considered to be the 'dishonourable fighting methods' employed by the peltasts, and they 'disdained weapons that killed indiscriminately at a distance'. Peltasts were only capable of closing in and cutting down dispirited and panic-stricken individuals or small groups of hoplites who had become separated from the main phalanx, but no army of light-armed troops could stand and fight shoulder-to-shoulder against an array of armoured hoplites with levelled spears.[59] But why should they? To foist the hoplite ideal into ages where it may not have existed, and onto troops that were never meant to fight by those rules, is as bad as inserting our own 'disdain' into ancient contexts.

Many of the things listed as 'military protocols' followed by the Greeks turn out to be chimeras when more closely examined. Peter Krentz writes eloquently on the subject of practices such as limiting the pursuit of retreating opponents, restrained punishment of captured opponents, returning enemy dead and the use of non-hoplite arms. He concludes that most practices turn out to be a matter of tactical necessity rather than formal conventions designed to ameliorate warfare.[60] The notion of *klope* in warfare evidently contains no intrinsic moral element. If any implication is detectable at all, it is that a sensible commander is doing a sensible thing.[61]

Orientalism

Our attitudes towards how Greeks and non-Greeks fought can degenerate into a form of Orientalism. This type of historical distortion, caused by our misperceptions of the East, has been debated in a rich body of scholarship concerning the way Westerners define themselves in relationship to 'the other'.[62] And nowhere has there been a more potent site for this Orientalism than in the discussion of warfare.[63] Crude generalisations based on the idea of 'national character' and how

161

it manifests itself in 'fighting abilities' have caused some of the biggest mistakes in military history.[64] Yet, this stereotype about Western warfare continues to exist in the military, the Academy and the public mind. It is dangerous because it distorts our understanding of ourselves and our enemies. The stereotype distorts our perceptions of the data and the histories we write about our past.

Patrick Porter has written a book on what he calls 'Military Orientalism'. Military historians in the West have used war to formulate what it means to be 'Western' or 'non-Western'. The battlefield has been particularly heated in the discussion of the Greeks, who are seen as the avatars of Western culture. This cultural debate is thus not new; it is not even modern. The clash between East and West had already begun with Homer's *Iliad* and the battle between Achaeans and Trojans. Even later, Greek historians would cast this as a struggle between Europe and Asia.[65] Herodotus sets up the war with Persia as a battle of East against West, and an argument over what constitutes 'Greekness' in warfare. His description of the Persian wars only hardened this division. His battle narratives contrast Greek hoplites with Persian bowmen, and citizen-soldiers with heavy shield and spear juxtaposed against Eastern archers.[66] Persia's armies revealed its culture as being 'fierce, opulent and servile' while the Greek hoplites came to symbolise the clash of freedom against autocracy.[67] Hoplite warfare became an extension of the culture that produced it and thus there was now a 'Western Way of War'. The problem with this picture is that it is a stereotype.

One of the ways this 'Orientalism' has been expressed is in the nineteenth-century fascination with the 'decisive battle'. Works such as Edward Creasy's 1851 classic, *The Fifteen Decisive Battles from Marathon to Waterloo*, featured clashes between the bearers of Western civilisation against the 'Orientals'. Heroes of Western warfare such as Alexander the Great and Scipio Africanus defeated the 'Eastern peril' and kept the world safe for democracy.[68] These discussions were not just about simple battle descriptions and tactics, but also about the morality of the tactics used.[69] This same discussion has been interjected into Greek military history and has resulted in the hijacking of the Greeks wholesale for modern political purposes. Victor Davis Hanson's books *The Western Way of War* and *Carnage and Culture*[70] have become among the best-known examples of this stance. His books on Greek warfare, the American family farm and the greatness of military leaders use Greek models to create the vision of a neo-conservative rural utopianism that follows Classical models. He stresses the importance of the agrarian heartland for the defence of the state, a kind of ancient Greek 'homeland security' before the term became popular in America.[71] Here statements about Greece's (or America's) way of war are not so much ethnographic insights as an assertion of power.[72]

These ideas had a huge effect on the Bush administration and other historians.[73] War's power to express and reproduce cultural identity has never been more evident than at the beginning of the twenty-first century. The current conflict between America and al-Qaeda has been endlessly described as a 'culture war'. This defence of empire, however, is not new. Before Hanson, Basil Liddell Hart and Russell Weigley had already identified British and American 'ways of war'.[74] As recently as 2005 *The Cambridge History of Warfare* had a 'Western Way of War' as its organising principle.[75] What these books all have in common is their underlying theme, the triumph of the West; indeed, it is the subtitle of the Cambridge history. Historians wish to see ambush as 'primitive warfare' characteristic of tribes but not city-states. Rational, civilised men such as the Greeks did not need to stoop to such tactics.

John Lynn argues against this idea of a continuous 'Western military tradition',[76] and I would argue against there being even a continuous Greek military tradition. He is certainly correct that the entire Western military tradition is never free from deception and indirect warfare.[77] Jeremy Black also comes down decisively against Hanson's thesis when he writes:

> ... modern doctrine in the US army – presumably, a Western Force – stresses not face-to-face mass charges, as in Greek phalanx warfare, but indirection, weak spots, and mobility, the very strategies and tactics that Hanson characterise as inferior, non-Western ways of war. It is hard to see what, other than politically motivated polemic, can be salvaged from Hanson's thesis – certainly nothing of value for serious military history.[78]

Deception and overwhelming force are not mutually exclusive absolutes but relative parts of a spectrum. The fact that the Greeks took hostages as security against deception is a clear indication that this was a common occurrence. In 479, before the Battle of Mycale, for example, the Samians sent a delegation secretly to the commander of the allied Greek fleet then stationed at Delos, and proposed their help in the forthcoming attack on the Persians in Asia Minor. According to Herodotus, they offered themselves as hostages and to sail with them 'if you suspect us of treachery'.[79] A similar proposition of hostages to be held as security against deception is reported by Herodotus in the story about the behaviour of the

Corinthians during the Battle of Salamis.[80] It seems to have been the custom of the Greeks to propose themselves as security for the truth of an important diplomatic or military offer.[81]

Historians create this picture of the Greeks as the avatars of a 'Western Way of War' so that they can contrast it with the sneaky Eastern way of war. This Orientalist view has been used against the Chinese, Japanese, Vietnamese, al-Qaeda or whatever foreign power we happen to be opposing at the time.[82] Perhaps one of the most famous recent examples of this is John Keegan who, after 11 September 2001 wrote that the war launched on that day (generally referred to as 9/11) was part of an older conflict between 'settled, creative and productive Westerners and predatory, destructive Orientals'. Hence the portrayal of 'Oriental cunning' evasion or subtlety against Western 'openness' or desire for decisive battle with 'rules of honour'. Orientals like ambush, treachery and deceit. He reduces military history to a morality play that showcases Western virtues and Oriental vices.[83] This is a nostalgia shared by British, American and Israeli military writers yearning for a time when their enemies shared their preference for a fair fight.[84] Norman Dixon in his book *On the Psychology of Military Incompetence* writes: 'One cannot know one's enemy by stereotyping him.'[85] Neither can we know our friends the Greeks by that means.

There is nothing wrong with seeing the Greeks as avatars of Western culture, but to see them as stereotypical beings, completely cut off from anything Eastern, fossilises them and denies the Greeks the ability to change, to learn or to adapt. Too many Classical scholars like to keep their Greeks free from the vices of the modern world and free from mongrelisation. We still see references to 'the difference between the Greek and the Oriental mind'.[86] Their Greeks are brave, honourable but ultimately static. Cultures at war can certainly create a distinct and lasting set of beliefs and values based on the prevailing attitudes, habits and values of their military. They can have preferences regarding the use of force and its role and effectiveness in political affairs. But cultures at war can also contain rival and clashing narratives, taboos that can be enforced or ignored, and 'porous borders across which new ideas and practices are smuggled'.[87] This is particularly true of the Greeks. At any given time, competing views of warfare and tactics were in play. Players were free to choose which methods they thought were most appropriate. Indeed, they found themselves in situations where they were forced to change their culture. The Greeks were capable of changing their tactics, compromising or violating taboos. For reasons of utility, they might find themselves acting in spite of tradition, not because of it. The Greeks were far too competitive to give up the edge because of some traditional practice.

Seeing the Greeks as multifaceted and adaptable is much better than the 'primordialist' idea that their behaviour was a clear, semi-permanent tradition rather than the acts of its subjects.[88] This is even more true of our view of the enemies of the Greeks. The unbalanced preoccupation with difference and separation, or with the exotic nature of non-Western war, can be a poor basis for understanding how people behave. By depicting culture as a unitary force that drives behaviour, we are oversimplifying the relationship between culture and action, and damage our ability to watch people acting strategically. Amartya Sen points out that culture becomes an impoverished concept when it is treated as homogenous and insular. The Greeks were not a hermetically sealed people with no outside influences. To treat them that way ignores the multiple identities that people are capable of choosing from. To think this way creates a dangerously self-fulfilling notion that the two camps are bound to be separate and hostile.

Hoplite warfare was not the only means of Greek warfare and those who overemphasise it distort the historical picture. Even Victor Davis Hanson, who has written more about the hoplite phalanx than most historians, states that: 'To suggest that all disagreements between even adjacent Greek *poleis* would over centuries always follow the same rituals of formal infantry battle is untenable, as many states additionally resolved their quarrels through arbitration, with sneak attacks, at sea, behind walls or simply by capitulation rather than set battle.'[89] Greek warfare was like warfare any place else. The Greeks used wars to change the enemy's position. Like all societies, they used available weapons and methods of warfare to achieve their ends. And their wars reflected the society of which they were a part.[90]

Cultural determinism, where people are almost prisoners of their own culture, and where strategy and war are bound only by culturally specific norms is too restrictive a picture. The Greeks had all the tools they needed for changing their culture. They had the time necessary because we are observing them over a period of half a millennium. They had the motive to change because of the political situations in which they found themselves (polis to empire). They had the capacity to change, and in the cases where they had skilful leadership their generals recognised how to make the change.[91]

Warfare evolved because practical people solved specific problems related to their fights against their neighbours and foreign enemies. Often the foreign enemies were much more powerful than the Greeks. Whenever faced with an enemy they could not possibly beat by using conventional tactics, they sought a different path. Each generation added its own refinement, and the cumulative result can be seen in the warfare of the Hellenistic Age.

Fighting the Stereotypes

Western warfare has never been free of deception and surprise. Sun Tzu is often quoted as an example of Easterners stressing intelligence and deception, praising the ideal of the bloodless victory and stressing the economical logic of finding non-military ways to prevail. But he is not alone. Machiavelli stressed the same things when he wrote that: 'Man is equally lauded who overcomes the enemy by deceit, as is he who overcomes them by force.'[92] Machiavelli, like Sun Tzu and the Greeks, lived in a 'fragile, multipolar and predatory political environment of competing city-states, ever-shifting alliances and meddling foreign powers.'[93] In the late twentieth century, the literature on surprise becomes enormous.[94] Modern historians are much more likely to appreciate what the Greeks were doing when they incorporated surprise into their repertoire. Historians such as B. W. Liddell Hart who championed the indirect approach and psychologically confounding the opponent would understand immediately what the Greeks were up to. But even he warns that a commander must know what can and cannot be done. For a surprise to succeed it was necessary to take the line least expected by the enemy or attack the place where it offered the least resistance. Clausewitz thought it a mistake to regard surprise as a key element of success in war. It is an attractive principle in theory, but hard to accomplish in reality.

Examples selectively taken from the Greeks are used not just to tell us anything meaningful about the Greeks but use them to justify current policy.[95] As Porter writes: 'For politicians and decision-makers, history is both ambivalent and politically potent as a way to legitimise policy.' Historians will choose the historical examples that align with their policy preferences. Such selective appeals to tradition distort the historical picture by leaving out examples that do not fit their stereotype. This book has endeavoured to include all those 'embarrassing exceptions'. The problem is that Greek culture offers no clear grid for policy, but throws up clashing lessons and analogies from the past. The ancient Greek hoplites, with their open and frontal combat between phalanxes in broad daylight, are regarded by some as the epitome of direct battle. But the fact is that the Greeks practised deception as well.

The democratic West, born in ancient Athens and later revived, depended on cunning military devices. But the issue is so tied to a quest for the elusive 'Western cultural identity' that the overreaching thesis of a Western Way of War becomes selective and ahistorical. It bypasses the history of Western strategies of deception, evasion and indirectness, in its desire to present strategic culture as symptomatic of core societal values or societal pathologies. All sorts of societies have adopted these techniques when coming up against a heavily-armed opponent. Furthermore, ethnocentrism leads to a tendency to reject or ignore information.[96] At worst it degenerates into dismissive racism.

The problem with the idea of cultural essentialism is that it often fails to highlight the many complexities of people's wartime behaviour. Both sides are capable of being wily, pragmatic or suicidal if they have to win. This conceptual framework allows people to see only what they want to see in history, making facts fit a theory to confirm its urgent contemporary agenda, which is to advise today's decision-makers and military leaders. However well intentioned, the theory, traditions and legacies are only part of the context in which strategic decisions are made – one variable in a matrix of negotiated interests along with material circumstances, power imbalances and individuals.[97] Cultural legacies are certainly part of the process of decision-making and behaviour, but they are neither exhaustive nor static elements within it.[98]

Ethnocentrism is a dangerously faulty methodology. It can seriously interfere with historical thinking and strategic thinking. Ethnocentrism makes us incurious about the enemy or even evade reality about them. It creates feel-good history but not a particularly accurate historical picture. It is an important source of mistakes in historical analysis. The original meaning included a strong identification with one's own group and its culture, the tendency to see one's own group as the centre of the universe, the tendency to perceive events in terms of one's own interests, the tendency to prefer one's own way of life (culture) over all others (seeing it as involving the best and right ways of acting, with an associated bias against other groups and their ways of acting), and a general suspicion of foreigners, their modes of thought, action and motives.[99]

Surprise is not the whole of war, but it remains one of the means in war. The best means even today:[100] 'Man does not enter battle to fight, but for victory. He does everything that he can to avoid the first and obtain the second.'[101] 'When the arms are similar on both sides, the only way of giving the advantage to one side is by surprise.'[102]

This pragmatic approach to the use of surprise sums up the reality of warfare both ancient and modern. Certainly, the Greeks debated the justness of certain kinds of warfare. Indeed, they debated the justness of war itself. The Greek philosophers Plato and Aristotle wrote on the subject in the fourth century.[103] But the possibility of treachery in warfare was also always present.[104] War was a grim business, and in war the force of cultural influence is limited at every turn by harsh reality. No soldier would be happy to fight in a fashion they thought placed them at a disadvantage relative to their enemies.[105]

The 'sheer devilry' of some of the tricks recorded by Greek and later Roman historians is a tribute to the practicality of commanders who understood that flexibility in the field could keep their men alive and hopefully help them score a victory.[106] Historians who concentrate solely on strategy and great battles tend to ignore surprise and characterise it merely as the product of luck. They are robbing the Greeks, and indeed the entire West, of one of its most important military skills. Ancient warfare was a much more subtle and varied phenomenon than the ideal suggested by those historians wanting to view it through the lens of a single ethos. As we get more archaeological evidence from regions such as Thessaly, which were outside the confines of the polis, combined with the growing recognition of the need to consider Greece within its wider Mediterranean context, we find a more complex picture of the military history of ancient Greece.[107] And like every civilisation before and after, the Greeks realised that more than courage and endurance alone were needed to win. With the skills, guile and stealth of an Odysseus, they might overcome the most amazing odds.

Notes

Preface

1 P. Sabin, H. van Wees and M. Whitby, *Cambridge History of Greek and Roman Warfare* (Cambridge: Cambridge University Press, 2007). The authors are, of course, aware of the literature on the subject; Hans van Wees has written on ambush in his book *Greek Warfare. Myths and Realities* (London: Duckworth, 2004), pp. 131–50. Another recent publication, L. L. Brice and J. T. Roberts (eds), *Recent Directions in the Military History of the Ancient World* (Claremont, CA: Regina Books, 2011) suffers from the same lacuna.

2 Chester Starr, *Political Intelligence in Classical Greece* (Leiden: Brill, 1974).

3 Frank Santi Russell, *Information Gathering in Classical Greece* (Ann Arbor: University of Michigan Press, 1999).

4 See R. M. Sheldon, *Intelligence Activities in Ancient Rome: Trust in the Gods But Verify* (New York and London: Frank Cass, 2005); N. J. E. Austin and B. Rankov, *Exploratio: Military and Political Intelligence in the Roman World from the Second Punic War to the Battle of Adrianople* (New York and London: Routledge, 1995).

5 W. K. Pritchett, *The Greek State at War* (Berkeley: University of California Press, 1974), vol. 2, pp. 177, 330.

6 Pritchett, vol. 2, p. 177 citing J. Kromayer and G. Veith, *Heerwesen und Kriegführung der Griechen und Römer* (Munich: C. H. Beck, 1928); H. Droysen, *Heerwesen und Kriegführung der Griechen* (Freiburg: Mohr, 1889); Hans Delbrück, *History of the Art of War*, trans. by Walter J. Renfroe, Jr (Lincoln, NE and London: University of Nebraska Press, 1990), vol. 1, *Warfare in Antiquity*. The same *lacuna* is found in P. Ducrey, *Warfare in Ancient Greece* (New York: Schocken, 1986).

7 E. L. Wheeler, *Stratagem and the Vocabulary of Military Trickery* (Leiden: Brill, 1988), pp. 26, 44 for *lochos*, pp. 26, 44, 86 for *enedra*, p. 26 for *enedreuo*.

8 A. Pauly and G. Wissowa, *Real-Encyclopädie der Klassischen Altertumswissenschaft* (Stuttgart: J. B. Metzler, 1957) or C. Daremberg and E. Saglio, *Dictionnaire des Antiquités Grecques et Romaines* (Paris, 1877–1919; available at: http://dagr.univ-tlse2.fr/sdx/dagr/index.xsp; accessed February 2012). There are no such headings

in Simon Hornblower and Anthony Spawforth, *The Oxford Classical Dictionary* (New York: Oxford University Press, 1996), 3rd edn.

9   J. Roisman, *The General Demosthenes and His Use of Military Surprise* (Stuttgart: Steiner, 1993); E. Heza, 'Ruse de guerre – trait caracteristique d'une tactique nouvelle dans l'oeuvre de Thucydide', *Eos* 62 (1974), pp. 235ff.

10   Van Wees, *Greek Warfare,* ch. 10.

11   O. Lippelt, *Die Griechischen Leichtbewaffneten bis auf Alexander den Grossen* (Weida in Thuringia: Thomas and Hubert, 1910).

12   E. L. Wheeler, 'Land battles', in *CHGRW*, vol. 1, p. 190.

13   Wheeler, 'Land battles', in *CHGRW*, vol. 1, p. 190.

14   Wheeler, 'Land battles', in *CHGRW*, vol. 1, p. 190.

15   Thucydides, *The Peloponnesian War*, trans. by Walter Blanco, ed. by Walter Blanco and Jennifer Tolbert Roberts (New York: W. W. Norton, 1998), 6.69.2.

16   See M. Whitby, 'Reconstructing ancient warfare' in *CHGRW*, vol. 1, pp. 54–81.

17   Wheeler, 'Land battles', in *CHGRW*, vol. 1, p. 190.

18   Wheeler, 'Land battles', in *CHGRW*, vol. 1. p. 187.

19   Wheeler, 'Land battles', in *CHGRW*, vol. 1. p. 188.

20   Thucydides 6.17.5; 68.2, 69.1, 98.3, 7.3.3.

21   J. G. P. Best, *Thracian Peltasts and Their Influence on Greek Warfare* (Groningen: Wolters-Noordhoff, 1969).

22   Lippelt, *Die Griechischen Leichtbewaffneten bis auf Alexander den Grossen*.

23   On Demosthenes see especially Roisman, *The General Demosthenes*; and G. Wylie, 'Demosthenes the general – protagonist in a Greek tragedy', *G&R* 40, 1 (April 1993), pp. 20–30. On Brasidas, see G. Wylie, 'Brasidas – great commander or whiz kid?' in E. L. Wheeler (ed.), *The Armies of Classical Greece* (Aldershot, Hants and Burlington, VT: Ashgate, 2007), pp. 423–43.

Introduction: The Odysseus Syndrome

1   Homer, *The Odyssey*, trans. by Robert Fagles (New York: Viking, 1996), line 77. Geddes even advanced a theory that the books of the Homeric poems should actually be divided into two groups. The Achillean and the Odyssean. The *Achillead* is the work of one age and one poet, and the non-Achillean books of the *Iliad* and the entire *Odyssey* are the work of another poet.

2   These are, of course, only very general stereotypes. See the comments of S. Hornblower, 'Warfare in ancient literature: The paradox of war', in *CHGRW*, vol. 1, p. 42.

3   Wheeler, 'Land battles', in *CHGRW*, vol. 1, p. 188. See Wheeler, *Stratagem*, pp. xiii–xiv, 92–110.

4   Peter Krentz, 'Fighting by the rules: The invention of the hoplite *agôn*', in E. L. Wheeler, *The Armies of Classical Greece* (Aldershot, Hants and Burlington,

VT: Ashgate, 2007), pp. 23–39 argues that such agonal conventions developed only after the Persian wars.

5   See J. L. Myers, 'Akhruktos Polemos' (Herodotus V.81), *CR* 57 (1943), pp. 66–7; V. Ilari, *Guerra e Diritto Nel Mondo Antico*, vol, I: *Guerra e Diritto Nel Mondo Greco-Ellenistico Fino All III Secolo* (Milan: A. Giuffrè, 1980), pp. 103–8; Xenophon, *Anabasis*, trans. by Carleton L. Brownson (Cambridge, MA: Harvard University Press, 1961, 2 vols), 3.2.8 for a *polemos akeryktos* with the Persians after Tissaphernes' murder of the Greek generals. Wheeler, 'Land battles', in *CHGRW*, vol. 1, p. 190.

6   F. E. Adcock and D. J. Mosley, *Diplomacy in Ancient Greece* (New York: St Martin's Press, 1975), p. 202.

7   Thucydides 4.126.5.

8   Herodotus 7.9.2.

9   Herodotus 6.115.

10 Thucydides 3.98.4.

11 Thucydides 4.40.2.

12 On the literature, see J. E. Lendon, *Soldiers and Ghosts. A History of Battle in Classical Antiquity* (New Haven: Yale University Press, 2005), pp. 401–2, 410–11.

13 'Fair and open', Xenophon, *Hellenica* 6.5.16; cf. Andocides 3.18; Isocrates 15.118. Defeat by strategy not regarded as real defeat: Herodotus 1.212; Demosthenes, 60.21; Plutarch, *Pelopidas*, 15.4–5; Polybius 13.3.3; Arrian, *Anabasis* 3.10.3.

14 Herodian 4.14.8 in a speech by Macrinus to his troops when facing the Parthians.

15 Quintus Curtius Rufus, *History of Alexander*, trans. J. C. Rolfe (Cambridge, MA: Harvard University Press, 1985), 4.13.

16 Quintus Curtius Rufus, 4.13, Loeb trans.

17 P. Porter, *Military Orientalism. Eastern War Through Western Eyes* (New York: Columbia University Press, 2009).

18 M. R. Davie, *Evolution of War* (New Haven, Yale University Press, 1929), p. 176.

19 J. J. Ardant du Picq, *Battle Studies; Ancient and Modern Battle* (Harrisburg, PA: The Military Service Publishing Co., 1947), p. 43.

20 Ardant du Picq, p. 112.

21 C. Oman, *A History of the Art of War in the Middle Ages* I (New York: Franklin, 1959), p. 205.

22 J. F. Cooper, *The Deerslayer* (New York: President Pub. Co., 1940), p. 36. The British criticised Francis Marion's guerrilla unit as 'criminal' and blamed him for his 'ungentlemen-like' methods of fighting. Best, p. 26.

23 http://memory.loc.gov/cgi-bin/ampage?collId=lljc&fileName=005/lljc005. db&recNum=94 (accessed 6 February 2012); Porter, p. 3.

24 See especially Col. C. E. Callwell, *Small Wars. Their Principles and Practice* (Wakefield: E. P. Publishing, 1976), pp. 49–50 and *passim*.

25   LTC Alfred Ditte, *Observations sur les Guerres dans les Colonies* (Paris: Henri Charles-LaVauzelle, 1905).

26   V. D. Hanson, *The Western Way of War: Infantry Battle in Classical Greece* (New York: Knopf, 1989), p. 1.

27   Hanson, *Western Way of War*, p. xv.

28   See E. Said, *Orientalism* (New York: Vintage Books, 1978), p. 328.

29   J. H. Poole, *Tactics of the Crescent Moon* (Emerald Isle, NC: Posterity Press, 2004), p. xxvi. This simply does not hold up. For set-piece battles east of Constantinople, see 100,000 Ottomans facing off against 40,000 Safavids, at the Battle of Chaldiran in 1514, or the Battle of Khanwa in 1527, one campaign in Mughal Babur's bid to lay claim to northern India.

30   John Keegan, *A History of Warfare* (New York: Knopf, 1993), p. 387.

31   C. Coker, *Waging War Without Warriors? The Changing Culture of Military Conflict* (Boulder, CO: Lynne Rienner, 2002), pp. 147–8.

32   P. Bracken, *Fire in the East: The Rise of Asian Military Power and the Second Nuclear Age* (New York: Harper Collins, 1999), p. 130.

33   R. M. Cassidy, *Counterinsurgency and the Global War on Terror; Military Culture and the Irregular War* (Stanford, CA: Stanford Security Studies, 2008), p. 3.

34   Poole, *Tactics*, pp. xxviii, 5.

35   William Lind in his Foreword to H. John Poole, *Phantom Soldier: The Enemy's Answer to US Firepower* (Emerald Isle, NC: Posterity Press, 2001), pp. xiii–xiv.

36   US Marine Corps, *Small Wars Manual* (Washington, DC: 1940), pp. 13, 18, 28; available at www.au.af.mil/au/awc/awcgate/swm/full.pdf (accessed 6 February 2012).

37   Porter, p. 12 poetically describes the span as 'from Themistocles to Schwarzkopf', but this author will argue it begins with Homer.

38   W. E. Kaegi, 'The crisis in military historiography', *Armed Forces and Society* 7 (1981), p. 311; Wheeler, *Stratagem* was the first study of the vocabulary of military trickery.

39   Among the questions asked are: is culture a constant? Is it an ethnocentric error to speak of universal principles of strategy? The poles of this debate are represented by Michael Handel who sees strategy as having a global objective logic and Ken Booth who argues that strategy is heavily dependent on cultural context. See Porter, p. 3.

40   Porter, p. 1.

41   Keegan, *A History of Warfare*, p. 387.

42   Porter, p. 1.

43   Porter, p. 18.

44   Pritchett, vol. 2, p. 179 citing Polybius 13.3.2–7.

45   Polybius 13.3.2–7. Pritchett, vol. 2, p. 179; Wylie, 'Demosthenes the general', p. 28 following Hanson, *The Western Way of War*, p. 11. For the corrective, see Wheeler, *Stratagem*, pp. 1–24.

46   For examples of this attitude see Sallust, *The War with Jugurtha*, trans. by J. C.
      Rolfe (Cambridge, MA: Harvard University Press, 1920), 81.1; Livy 42.47.4–9.
      Cf. Diodorus 30.7.1; Polybius 13.3 and other sources listed in Sheldon, *Intelligence
      Activities in Ancient Rome*, p. 35. Hoplite fighting is immortalised in the work of
      Tyrtaeus, *The War-elegies of Tyrtæus, Imitated and Addressed to the People of Great
      Britain, with Some Observations on the Life and Poems of Tyrtæus*, trans. by Henry
      James Pye (London: printed for T. Cadell, jun. and W. Davies, successors to
      Mr Cadell, 1795), 10.11–24.

47   For examples of Roman moralising, see Julius Caesar, *The Gallic War* 1.13 : 'The
      Helvetii had learnt from their parents and ancestors to fight their battles with
      courage, not cunning nor rely upon stratagem' (Loeb translation). For modern
      examples see Poole, *Tactics*, p. xxvi; G. Brizzi, *I Sistemi Informativi dei Romani.
      Principi e Realtà Nell' Età Delle Conquista Oltremare (218–168 a.C.)*, Historia
      Einzelschriften 39 (Wiesbaden: Steiner, 1982), pp. 8–37, 56–77, 87, 269–73.

48   On the need for a more multifaceted, variegated and ultimately accurate picture
      of the Greeks, see P. du Bois, *Trojan Horses. Saving the Classics from Conservatives*
      (New York: New York University Press, 2001), p. 19.

Chapter 1: Ambush in the *Iliad*

1   The nature of Greek combat is still a hotly debated topic. Joachim Latacz
     published a monograph in 1977 arguing that Homeric warriors fought in hoplite
     phalanx resembling those of the Archaic Age. See J. Latacz, *Kampfparänese,
     Kampfdarsteelung und Kampswirklichkeit in der Ilias, bei Kallinos und Tyrtaios*,
     Zetemata 66 (Munich: Beck, 1977). He is followed by V. D. Hanson (ed.),
     Hoplites: The Classical Greek Battle Experience (London and New York: Routledge,
     1991), pp. 80–1, nn. 11–12. Pritchett, vol. 4, pp. 25–6 even went so far as to suggest
     there were distinct 'companies' or 'battalions'. Although Latacz' argument quickly
     became popular, see now the argument against it in H. van Wees, 'The Homeric way
     of war: the *Iliad* and the hoplite phalanx', *G&R* 41 (1994), pp. 1–18.

2   B. Fenik, *Typical Battle Scenes in the Iliad: Studies in the Narrative Techniques of
     Homeric Battle Description* (Wiesbaden: Steiner, 1968), found a remarkable series
     of formulaic patterns in the battle books of the *Iliad*. All of these involved single
     combat or warriors fighting in pairs.

3   M. F. Williams, 'Crossing into enemy lines: Military intelligence in *Iliad* 10 and
     24', *Electronic Antiquity* 5, 3 (Nov. 2000), p. 1–2. On the societal duty to show
     one's courage publicly, see A. W. H. Adkins, *Merit and Responsibility; A Study in
     Greek Values* (Oxford: The Clarendon Press, 1960), pp. 30–60 on 'Homer: Mistake
     and moral error' (critiqued by A. A. Long, 'Morals and values in Homer', *JHS* 90
     [1970], pp. 121–39) and James M. Redfield, *Nature and Culture in the Iliad: The
     Tragedy of Hector* (Chicago: University of Chicago Press, 1975), p. 99.

4   See M. Mueller, *The Iliad* (London and Boston: Allen & Unwin, 1984), pp. 77–8 on the ethos of Homeric fighting. He says there is not room for strategy or cunning in Homeric Greek warfare, with the exception of Book 10 which he sees as a 'later addition'. He is followed by M. F. Williams, p. 3. The question of the historicity of Homeric society, in general, is still a thorny one. See K. A. Raaflaub, 'A historian's headache. How to read "Homeric society"', in N. Fisher and H. van Wees (eds), *Archaic Greece: New Approaches and New Evidence* (London: Duckworth and The Classical Press of Wales, 1998), pp. 169–93.

5   One of the first people to comment on this was Heza, p. 227 who writes: 'Il y a beaucoup d'embuscades dans L'*Iliade*', Krentz, 'Fighting by the rules', p. 116 and P. Krentz, 'Deception in Archaic and Classical Greek warfare', in H. van Wees (ed.), *War and Violence in Ancient Greece* (London: Duckworth, 2000), pp. 167–200. E. L. Wheeler points out that sneaky behaviour pre-dated the vocabulary describing it: Wheeler, *Stratagem*, p. 1.

6   M. F. Williams, p. 4.

7   M. F. Williams, p. 4. It is hazardous trying to date individual elements in the *Iliad*. On possible anachronisms concerning weapons see G. S. Kirk, *The Songs of Homer* (Cambridge: Cambridge University Press, 1962), pp. 183–4 and G. S. Kirk, 'War and the warrior in the Homeric poems', in J. P. Vernant, *Problèmes de la guerre en Grèce Ancienne* (Paris: La Haye, Mouton, 1969), pp. 94–95, 111–113.

8   Raaflaub, pp. 169–93 argues that the poem does not represent the Mycenaean Age when the war supposedly happened. Kirk, 'War and the warrior in the Homeric poems', p. 93 also points out how hard it is to resist the temptation of viewing the 'Homeric world' as a real one when the truth is, of course, that the epic is, to an important extent, fictional.

9   Anthony Edwards argues that the ambush (*lochos*) was generally categorised as a form of trickery (*dolos*). Anything that led to a victory except through strength or might (*kratos*) was deemed unworthy of a Homeric warrior: A. T. Edwards, *Achilles in the Odyssey* (Königstein: Anton Hain, 1985), p. 19. M. Flaumenhaft, 'The undercover hero; Odysseus from dark to daylight', *Interpretation* 10, 1 (Jan. 1982), p. 14 claims that ambushes are dishonourable, the tactics of transgressors. She believes that ambushers, like animals, have no shame (ibid. p. 15).

10 See Heza, p. 228 who points out that it is the word *dolos* that Nestor uses to describe the military activities of the Greeks during the nine years of the Trojan war in Homer, *Iliad* 3.118–119. Edwards, *Achilles in the Odyssey*, p. 20. See also P. Vidal-Naquet, 'The black hunter and the origin of the Athenian Ephebia', *Proceedings of the Cambridge Philological Society* 14 (1968), pp. 49–64 who outlines the mythic, ritual and historical foundations for a contrast between heavy-armed, disciplined infantry combat and attack through trickery, often by light-armed warriors.

11 C. Dué and Mary Ebbott, *Iliad 10 and the Poetics of Ambush* (Washington, DC: Harvard University Press, 2010), p. 313. Mera Flaumenhaft disagrees and makes

a distinction between the lion who attacks a farm at night and who acts on his own behalf, as opposed to human warriors who are supposed to fight for their communities. In wartime, ambushes are generally community affairs: Flaumenhaft, p. 15. For examples of the hunting metaphor, see Homer, *Iliad* 4.107: Pandarus breaks the truce using a bow which Homer says he made from the horn of an unsuspecting ibex he killed while lying out of sight. The ambush in 18.510 goes after sheep and sleek cattle. The unsuspecting herdsmen, 'with no foreknowledge of the guile' being used against them, lose their life.

12 Homer, *Iliad* 20.89–90; 188–90. Achilles as ambusher of Lycaon in Homer, *Iliad* 21.34–39 and the commentary by Dué and Ebbott, p. 68. See also A. H. Jackson, 'War and raids for war booty in the World of Odysseus', in J. Rich and G. Shipley (eds), *War and Society in the Greek World* (London and New York: Routledge, 1993), pp. 64–75 who discusses raiding and warfare in the Dark Age.

13 Homer, *Iliad* 1.154, 11.670ff.; Flaumenhaft, p. 16.

14 Homer, *Iliad* 3.443–46.

15 Cattle raids by Nestor, Homer, *Iliad* 11.670–81; by Achilles, Homer, *Iliad* 20.89–90, 188–90. Kirk, 'War and warrior in the Homeric poems', p. 116 who points out that such raids, while not in keeping with the heroic world ascribed to Agamemnon and his companions, are perfectly consistent with what we know about Bronze Age warfare.

16 Dué and Ebbott, pp. 80, 82–4, 352, 362, 373 on cattle raids and horse stealing. They point out that S. I. Johnston, 'Myth, festival, and poet: The Homeric hymn to Hermes in its performance context', *CP* 97 (2002), pp. 109–32 shows that the cattle raid tradition is, in fact, the central theme of the Homeric hymn to Hermes whose diction resembles that of *Iliad* 10 in many places.

17 Homer, *Iliad* 1.227. Dué and Elliott trans. Stanley Lombardo translates this passage as: 'You've never had the guts to buckle on armour in battle or come out with the best fighting Greeks.' He leaves out any reference to ambush entirely. For the importance of a daring or enduring heart for spying missions or ambush, see Homer, *Iliad* 10.231, 10.244 and 10.248 and Dué and Ebbott, p. 275.

18 Edwards, p. 18 where he lists fighters in this formation as *laos*, *promachoi* and *promos aner*, various forms of front-line fighters.

19 See G. S. Kirk, *The Iliad: A Commentary* (Cambridge: Cambridge University Press, 1985–93), vol. 1, p. 77. The ambush is composed of 'the best Achaeans'.

20 Edwards, p. 18. Xenophon, *Cyropaedia* 1.6.39–41; Polyaenus, *Stratagemata* 1, proem 3–5.

21 Homer, *Iliad* 13.275–86. A. T. Murray trans., Loeb Classical Library edn.

22 This claim is also made in Homer, *Iliad* 1.227; 6.188, 13.270; Homer, *Odyssey* 4.277, 4.778, 8.512.

23 Homer, *Iliad* 1.227, 6.188, 13.276, Homer, *Odyssey* 4.272, 8.4.409512–13, 11.523–24, 14.217–218. See Dué and Ebbott, p. 283, 375; Edwards, pp. 18–24.

24　Homer, *Iliad* 13.280. Ambushers are imagined as *pukhinos* – closely packed because of the density of the men hiding together in a cramped space. The *Odyssey* used the term in 4.277 and 8.515 for the wooden horse which involves many men enclosed in a small space. In the ambush of Tydeus in Homer, *Iliad* 4.391–398 fifty-two men lay in wait for him.

25　Edwards, p. 21; Flaumenhaft, pp. 13, 17.

26　See Edwards, p. 19 who considers it just another example of *dolos*; R. G. A. Buxton, *Persuasion in Greek Tragedy; A Study of Peitho* (Cambridge: Cambridge University Press, 1982), pp. 63–6; G. Nagy, *The Best of the Achaeans* (Baltimore: Johns Hopkins University Press, 1979), pp. 1–24; M. Detienne and J. P. Vernant, *Cunning Intelligence in Greek Culture and Society*, trans. from the French by Janet Lloyd (Hassocks, Sussex: Harvester Press; Atlantic Highlands, NJ: Humanities Press, 1978), pp. 12–13.

27　Dué and Ebbott, p. 86.

28　Homer, *Iliad* 11.379.

29　Edwards, p. 24.

30　The story of Pandarus attempting to shoot Menelaus (Homer, *Iliad* 4.112–115) is used as a parallel by Dué and Ebbott, pp. 59–60. They discuss the overlap in the descriptions of archery and ambush. Pandarus is not chosen for the job because he is lacking in moral character (and thus willing to sneak up on someone) but because he is an excellent archer. See also ibid. p. 252 on the ways archery and ambush are conceptually and even visually linked and how Paris' wearing a leopard skin is iconographic sign of his archer status.

31　See R. Edgeworth, 'Ajax and Teucer in the *Iliad*', *Rivista di Filologia e di Instruzione Classica*, 113 (1985), pp. 27–31 for his discussion of this fighting method; Dué and Ebbott, p. 60.

32　In Homer, *Odyssey* 8.215–222 Odysseus boasts of his pre-eminence at military archery. See Hornblower, 'Warfare in ancient literature', p. 41, and Dué and Ebbott, p. 294.

33　S. Farron, 'Attitudes to military archery in the *Iliad*', in A. F. Basson and W. J. Dominik (eds), *Literature, Art, History: Studies on Classical Antiquity and Tradition in Honour of W. J. Henderson* (Frankfurt am Main: Peter Lang, 2003), p. 169. W. McLeod, 'The bow at night: An inappropriate weapon?', *Phoenix* 42 (1988), pp. 121–5 on the bow as a particularly appropriate weapon for night attacks.

34　Farron, pp. 171–5 highlights the passages in which Teucer's success with the bow in battle is actually praised or desired by his comrades. He is followed by Dué and Ebbott, p. 61. Cf. B. L. Hijmans, Jr. 'Archers in the *Iliad*', in J. S. Boersma (ed.), *Festoen; Opgedragen aan A. N. Zadoks-Josephus Jitta bij Haar Zeventigste Verjaardag*, Scripta Archaeologica Groningana 6 (Groningen: H. D. Tjeenk Willink, 1976), pp. 343–52.

35　The controversial scene featuring a debate about archery in Euripides, *Hercules*, trans. by Tom Sleigh, with introduction and notes by Christian Wolff (Oxford and

New York: Oxford University Press, 2001), pp. 140–235 illustrates how complex and even conflicting the ancient attitudes could be. Dué and Ebbott, p. 61. J. E. Lendon, *Soldiers and Ghosts*, p. 34 writes: 'Despite the contempt in which using the bow is held by some heroes, it is heroic arête just like fighting with a spear.' This is in complete contrast to V. D. Hanson, *The Wars of the Ancient Greeks* (London: Cassell, 1999), p. 158 who calls bowmen nothing more than 'savage tribalists'.

36 J. E. Lendon, *Soldiers and Ghosts*, p. 34.

37 Homer, *Iliad* 13.227. See Dué and Ebbott, p. 311 on Tydeus and ambush as a theme in Theban epic tradition.

38 Homer, *Iliad* 6. 191.

39 Edwards, p. 25.

40 Edwards, p. 23.

41 Following Edwards, pp. 22–3. See also Dué and Ebbott who also discuss the subthemes that constitute an ambush.

42 Dué and Ebbott, p. 244.

43 Dué and Ebbott, pp. 73–5; also pp. 274, 289 on the difficulties of a night watch.

44 Edwards, p. 23 points out that the exchange of taunts by which heroes usually identify themselves in a Homeric battle and count coups prior to the fighting are missing in the ambush. Also missing are the exchange of spears, the anger of a hero at the death of a friend or comrade, and the attempt at revenge. Cf. Fenik, *Typical Battle Scenes in the Iliad, passim*. E. Vermeule, *Aspects of Death in Early Greek Art and Poetry*, The Sather Classical Lectures 46 (Berkeley: University of California Press, 1979), pp. 83–6.

45 See the discussion of the battlefield by M. Detienne 'La phalange: Problèmes et controverses', in J. P. Vernant, *Problèmes de la Guerre en Grèce Ancienne* (Paris: La Haye: Mouton, 1968), pp. 123–4; J. Latacz, pp. 76–171 who believes that the battle tactics portrayed by Homer are essentially the same as those of hoplite and phalanx familiar from Tyrtaeus and Callinus. See however van Wees, 'The Homeric way of war', pp. 1–18.

46 On *dolos* see Dué and Ebbott, pp. 71–2.

47 In a discussion of the trials and exploits which are typically encountered by the youthful hero in Greek myth, Francis Vian includes: 'to emerge unscathed and victorious from an ambush'. Vian lists the ambushes set for Tydeus and Bellerophon discussed above, but also the ambush set for Theseus by the Pallantids as he returned to Athens. F. Vian 'La function guerrière dans la mythologie grecque', in J.-P. Vernant (ed.), *Problèmes de la Guerre en Grèce Ancienne* (Paris: La Haye, Mouton), p. 67.

48 'Ambushes were regarded by Homer as the best test of a man's courage.' H. van Wees, *War and Violence in Ancient Greece* (London: Duckworth, 2000), p. 132.

49 Homer, *Iliad* 11.369.

50 Homer, *Odyssey* 14.217.

51 Commentators have taken the example of the night raid in Book 10 and then generalised to the rest of the poem. They claim ambush denies the humanity of one's opponent. To some, an ambusher can never aspire to a code of honour. An ambush is the complete antithesis of honourable battle. See Flaumenhaft, pp. 9–41.

52 For the Trojan horse, one must turn to Apollodorus's *Epitome* which gives a grand summary of traditional Greek mythology and heroic legends in three books. *The Little Iliad* is a lost epic of ancient Greek literature. It was one of the Epic Cycle, that is, the 'Trojan Cycle', which told the entire history of the Trojan war in epic verse. About thirty lines of the poem survive. Quintus of Smyrna, *Posthomerica* (*Fall of Troy*), trans. by A. S. Way (Cambridge, MA: Harvard University Press, 1913), pp. 314–35 gives the names of the thirty Greeks inside the horse. John Tzetzes, *Antehomerica et Posthomerica* (Charleston, SC: Nabu Press, 2010), Book 12, pp. 315–30, gives a figure of twenty-three, in late tradition it seems it was standardised at forty.

53 Homer, *Odyssey* 4.266–289, 8.492–520; 11.523–53.

54 See O. Andersen, 'Odysseus and the Wooden Horse', *Symbolae Osloenses* 52 (1977), pp. 6–7. Euripides refers to the Wooden Horse as an ambush twice: Euripides, *Trojan Women, Iphigenia among the Taurians, Ion*, trans. by David Kovacs (Cambridge, MA: Harvard University Press, 1999), lines 534–5, 560–1. A rather interesting parallel to the stratagem of the Wooden Horse appears in an ambush narrated by Thucydides 4.67.1–4. See also F. Frontisi-Ducroux, *Dédale: Mythologie de l'Artisan en Grèce Ancienne* (Paris: Maspero, 1975), pp. 140–1.

55 Lesches, *The Little Iliad*, 1. trans. by H. G. Evelyn-White, Loeb edition of *Hesiod, the Homeric Hymns and Homerica* (Cambridge, MA: Harvard University Press, 1914).

56 The *Aeneid* also devotes a book to its own night raid, that of Nisus and Euryalus in *Aeneid* 9. See Dué and Ebbott, p. 136.

57 Translation from Andersen, p. 6.

58 Flaumenhaft, p. 16 says this victory 'raises a subordinate military manoeuvre to the means of final victory'.

59 Homer, *Iliad* 7.232, 242–3.

60 Van Wees, *Greek Warfare*, p. 160.

61 For examples of the single shot, four of the five men in the opening scene of the first battle are hit by a spear thrown at them without warning. See the discussion in van Wees, *Greek Warfare*, p. 161 with the following examples: those killed while dismounting Homer, *Iliad* 11.151–2; the archer's use of surprise 8.266–79; 11.369–79; killed by a third party 15.539–41; 16.319–25; killed while body-snatching 4.467–9, 15.524–9; 17.288–94; stabbed in the back during flight 5.38–41; killed while in shock 13.434–44; 16:401–10, 806–21.

62 Homer, *Iliad* 16.745.

63 Homer, *Iliad* 14.456–7.

64   Deluded hopes Homer, *Iliad* 13.374–84; 16.830–42; 21.184–99; 22.331–3.
      Savaging of corpses 11.452–5; 16.836; 21.122–7; 22.335.6.

65   J. E. Lendon, *Soldiers and Ghosts*, p. 25.

66   Flaumenhaft, p. 16. Even the great Achilles is killed in an ambush by Paris and
      Apollo; see Dué and Ebbott, p. 351.

67   See Dale Sinos' review of Anthony T. Edwards, *Achilles in the Odyssey: Ideologies of
      Heroism in the Homeric Epic*, in *AJPh* 109, 1 (Spring, 1988), pp. 133–5.

68   Dué and Ebbott, pp. 70, 77.

69   Edwards, p. 26.

70   Edwards lists as evidence of post-Homeric negative comments on the ambush:
      Hesiod, *Works and Days* 702–705; Simonides 136 (in Diehl); Euripides, *Rhesus*
      507, 560–61: 'no brave man deigns to kill the enemy by stealth, but fights face to
      face' (trans. by David Kovacs); Xenophon, *Agesilaus* 11.5 (cf. 2 12); Xenophon,
      Hiero 6.3 (cf. Xenophon, *Memorabilia* 2.1.4–5). Herodotus 6.37.1; Herodotus
      6.103.3; Euripides, *Andromache* 1114–5.

71   J. E. Lendon, *Soldiers and Ghosts*, p. 158.

72   This has not stopped commentators from criticising the night raid of *Iliad* 10 for
      being 'ineffective'. See D. B. George, 'Euripides' *Heracles* 140–235: Staging and the
      stage iconography of Herakles' bow', *GRBS* 35 (1994), pp. 145–57 for a detailed
      study of the debate on Euripides' *Herakles*; Dué and Ebbott, p. 61. They argue
      this in spite of the fact that the Achaeans themselves rejoice at the victory when
      Odysseus and Diomedes return.

Chapter 2: The Ill-fated Trojan Spy

1   This is a much expanded version of the article published as R. M. Sheldon, 'The
      ill-fated Trojan spy', *Studies in Intelligence* 31, 1 (1987), pp. 35–9, reprinted in
      American Intelligence Journal 9, 3 (Fall 1988), pp. 18–22. This same episode is
      discussed in Greek tragedy, namely the *Rhesus*, attributed, by some, to Euripides.
      Regardless of authorship, the *Rhesus* has always been understood as an Athenian
      tragedy produced in either the fifth or fourth centuries BCE. Several previous studies
      have examined how the myth of Dolon/Rhesus is treated in both genres. B. Fenik,
      Iliad X and the Rhesus, Collection Latomus vol. 73 (Brussels: Bercham, 1964), and
      Dué and Ebbott, pp. 28, 122 both believe the narrative traditions about Rhesus
      predate our *Iliad*.

2   Edwards does not even discuss the ambush; M. Nagler, *Spontaneity and Tradition:
      A Study in the Oral Art of Homer* (Berkeley: University of California Press, 1974),
      p. 136 calls it '. . . a disaster stylistically' – heroically because of the disgraceful
      conduct exhibited by Odysseus and Diomedes, and thematically because it takes
      place in the dead night . . .' Alexander Shewan wrote a spirited defence in his
      monograph *The Lay of Dolon* (London: Macmillan, 1911) in which he said: 'There

is hardly a textbook of Greek literature or handbook to Homer but regards it with disfavour, tempered only occasionally by a word of tolerant pity or faint praise' (ibid. p. viii). R. M. Henry called it 'one of the most worthless books of the *Iliad* from a poetical point of view': R. M. Henry, 'The place of the *Doloneia* in epic poetry', *CR* 19 (1905), p. 192. See Agathe Thornton's defence in *Homer's Iliad: Its Composition and the Motif of Supplication* (Göttingen: Vandenhoeck and Ruprecht, 1983), pp. 164–9.

3   See Dué and Ebbott, pp. 7–9. The most recent and often-cited commentary on *Iliad* 10, B. Hainsworth, *The Iliad: A Commentary*, vol. 3 (Cambridge: Cambridge University Press, 1993), p. 154, as part of the six-volume Cambridge University Press commentary edited by G. S. Kirk, asserts that the book 'does not belong in our *Iliad*'. Leaf's *Commentary on the Iliad* (London: Macmillan, 1883) reserves his harshest criticism for Book 10. He refers to it as 'turgid and tasteless' (10.5), 'strange' (10.7), 'unsuitable' (10.8), 'burlesque' (10.84); Martin West's *Iliad* treated Book 10 in its entirety as an interpolation that did not belong in the poem; see Dué and Ebbott, pp. 23–4, 237–8, 290.

4   The recent study is Dué and Ebbott. The quotation comes from Shewan, p. viii.

5   The T. Scholion on the first line of *Iliad* 10 asserts the separate composition, claiming that it was added to the *Iliad* by Pisistratus. See Dué and Ebbott, p. 5. F. Eichhorn, *Die Dolonie* (Garmisch-Partenkirchen: Moser, 1973) wrote on the unity of Book 10 with the *Iliad*, in rebuttal to F. Ranke's *Homerische Untersuchungen I: Die Dolonie* (Leipzig: Teubner, 1881) and Friedrich Klingner, 'Über die Dolonie', *Hermes* 75 (1940), pp. 337–68. See James P. Holoka's review of Eichhorn, *Die Dolonie*, in *The Classical World* 69, 1 (Sept 1975), pp. 72–3.

6   As for the question of whether both the *Iliad* and the *Doloneia* were written by the same person, see G. Danek, *Studien zur Dolonie*, Wiener Studien Beiheft 12 (Vienna: Österreichische Akademie der Wissenschaften, 1988), *passim*. See M. M. Willcock's review Danek, *Studien zur Dolonie*, in *Classical Review* 39, 2 (1989), pp. 178–80, and W. C. Scott's review of Danek, *Studien zur Dolonie*, in *AJPh* 112, 4 (Winter 1991), pp. 549–52. Most recently Dué and Ebbott, pp. 3–13 put this question in focus as it relates to *Iliad* 10.

7   Fenik, *Iliad X and the Rhesus*.

8   Dué and Ebbott, pp. x, 12.

9   Dué and Ebbott, pp. 9, 86.

10   Shewan, p. 34; Dué and Ebbott, p. 10.

11   A. Shewan's defence of *Iliad* 10 was a reaction to the excesses of the scholarship of his time against single authorship. See Dué and Ebbott, pp. 10–11 for a discussion of his Unitarian position. Shewan, p.10 thinks the primary reason to accept the *Doloneia* as part of the *Iliad* was because it was, according to him, good poetry.

12   Dué and Ebbott, p. 13.

13 A. Lord, *The Singer of Tales* (Cambridge: Cambridge University Press, 1960, 2nd edn 2000), p. 194 suggests that *Iliad* 10 may be a legitimate multiform of *Iliad* 9, i.e. both books orally composed with the same traditional poetic system, and both equally 'Homeric.' See Dué and Ebbott, pp. 13, 28.

14 Dué and Ebbott, p. 29.

15 Dué and Ebbott, pp. 284–5.

16 Dué and Ebbott, pp. 128, 263 discuss the effect darkness has on the character's senses and how it confuses friend and enemy. Heza, p. 227 points out that night usually stops combat, but at night, surprise attacks begin. Flaumenhaft, p. 9. The word 'night' occurs more frequently in Book 10 than in any other book of the *Iliad* – sixteen times. See N. Austin, *Archery at the Dark of the Moon: Poetic Problems in Homer's Odyssey* (Berkeley: University of California Press, 1975), p. 72.

17 Flaumenhaft, p. 9. Since sight is limited at night, hearing becomes a more important sense, and what one hears is less certain and in need of interpretation. In fact, the interpretation of sounds becomes a key element in the capture of Dolon. On the role of visual and auditory perception, see Dué and Ebbott, pp. 63–5.

18 Dué and Ebbott, pp. 10, 13, 31–3.

19 Homer, *Iliad* 10.35–41. On the idea that the Trojans may be planning an attack and that the Achaeans face destruction, see Dué and Ebbott, pp. 265, 272.

20 All quotations in this chapter are from the Robert Fagles translation and use the line numbers from that edition.

21 Homer, *Iliad* 10.112–117.

22 Homer, *Iliad* 10.241–251.

23 Homer, *Iliad* 10.226.

24 Dué and Ebbott, p. 280; Flaumenhaft, p. 13; M. F. Williams, p. 11.

25 Flaumenhaft, p. 13. In the Homer, *Odyssey* 14.480 Odysseus says that this is prime time for wily schemes.

26 Homer, *Iliad* 10.258–266.

27 On returning as part of the poetics of ambush, see Dué and Ebbott, pp. 77–8, 125, 287, 321, 375; Edwards, p. 22 identifies two leaders as a common feature of the Homeric ambush. R. Rabel, 'The theme of need in *Iliad* 9–11', *Phoenix* 45 (1991), pp. 288–91 sees the emphasis in *Iliad* 10 on co-operation among heroes to succeed in contrast to Achilles' behaviour in *Iliad* 9. In Diomedes' description of the ideal night raid team, *noos* and *noeo* are cited three times in three lines together with *metis* (Homer, *Iliad* 23.590). It is no surprise, therefore, that he chooses Odysseus whose associations with *metis* and *noos* are clear in Homer, *Iliad* 10.137 and 10.247.

28 In their commentary on these lines, Dué and Elliott, p.79 discuss how the qualities of a willing heart and audacious spirit are appropriate to ambush.

29 Homer, *Iliad* 10.293–296.

30 The armour they wore is in many ways atypical. Most distinctive is what they wore on their heads. Diomedes and Odysseus wore leather skull caps. The Greek word

πιλοσ (low helmet or skull cap) is of unknown derivation; Liddell, Henry George and Robert Scott, *A Greek-English Lexicon* (Oxford: Clarendon Press, 1968), s.v. *kataitux*. Dué and Ebbott, pp. 146, 252, 291–2 discuss Menelaus wearing a helmet that is bronze and unsuited for a spying mission. In contrast, Menelaus is portrayed as an ambusher in Homer, *Odyssey* 4.280, 14.470–471, 4.388–463.

31　Thornton, *Homer's Iliad*, p. 75. In a well-known 1958 article, James Armstrong shows how formulaic arming scenes are employed at climactic moments in the poem with great effect. J. Armstrong, 'The arming motif in the *Iliad*', *AJPh* 79 (1958), pp. 337–54; Dué and Ebbott, pp. 54, 357. M. F. Williams, p. 13.

32　On the associations of wearing animals skins and ambush, see Dué and Ebbott, pp. 250–2; Cf. K. Reinhardt, *Die Ilias und ihr Dichter* (Göttingen: Vandenhoeck und Ruprecht, 1961), pp. 247–8.

33　Dué and Ebbott, pp. 290–1.

34　The eyes his grandmother kissed when, as a child, he visited Autolycus (Homer, *Odyssey* 19.417). See Flaumenhaft, p. 20 for other eye references.

35　Flaumenhaft, p. 23. On the difference in the powers of observation between Diomedes and Dolon, see Dué and Ebbott, p. 331; and ibid. p. 372 on the reliance on senses other than sight.

36　Homer, *Iliad* 10.322–323. Dué and Ebbott, p. 297 point out that night herons exhibit ambush-like behaviour in their hunting. A heron waits while standing still for its prey to come into range at night. It also plunders the nests of other birds. The heron is the messenger of Athena, and this goddess most resembles Odysseus in that she embodies *metis*, *dolos* and *noos*, the skills that are the hallmark of ambush warfare (ibid. p. 364).

37　Homer, *Iliad* 10.330–331.

38　Homer, *Iliad* 10.348.

39　Homer, *Iliad* 10.350.

40　Homer, *Iliad* 8.557–562.

41　Homer, *Iliad* 10.372–380. For the anxiety about the night watch falling asleep, see ibid. 10.98. Dué and Ebbott, pp. 261, 264, 324 on Dolon finding his way beyond the wall and ditch of the Greek encampment.

42　Homer, *Iliad* 10.370. Dué and Ebbott, p. 321 on Dolon's swiftness.

43　Dué and Ebbott, pp. 315–17 defend Dolon against the condemnation of doing 'work for pay'. Nestor says the spy will get kudos and gifts (*doron*). This is true of both sides. On the condemnations, see A. Schnapp-Goubeillon, 'Le lion et le loup. Diomédie et Dolonie dans l'Iliade', *Quaderni di Storia* 8 (1982), p. 58; J. Holoka, 'Looking darkly: Reflections of status and decorum in Homer', *TAPA* 113 (1983), pp. 8–9; and N. Coffee, *The Commerce of War: Exchange and Social Order in Latin Epic* (Chicago: University of Chicago Press, 2009), p. 62.

44　In later times, scouts who rode reconnaissance ahead of the main war party were 'wolves'. Often these scouts wore a wolf skin, partly for camouflage but more importantly for symbolism, drawing to themselves the cunning and hunting ability of the wolf. This is common, for example, in Plains Indian mythology. Dué and Ebbott, p. 56 say only that cloaks and animal skins are significant elements in the night dressing scenes of *Iliad* 10. It may also be that in the epic tradition the bow was so closely associated with ambush warfare that a poet would naturally include it as part of a spy's equipment (ibid. p. 62). L. Gernet, 'Dolon le loup', *Mélanges Franz Cumont* 4 (1936), pp. 196–7 suggests there was an initiation ritual involving the wearing of a wolf skin, and thus there is a religious and ritual background to Dolon's attire. M. Davies, 'Dolon and Rhesus', *Prometheus* 31(2005), pp. 31–2 sees Dolon as the 'ambivalent helper'.

45   Homer, *Iliad* 10.390–394. Dué and Ebbott, pp. 328–30 discuss the marten skin and any associations with weasels and 'weasily' behaviour, or the ambushing behaviour of the marten. Davies, p. 32; Gernet, pp. 190–191, O. M. Davidson, 'Dolon and Rhesus in the *Iliad*', *Quaderni Urbinati di Cultura Classica* 30 (1979); and P. Wathelet, 'Rhésos ou la Quête de l'immortalité', *Kernos* 2 (1989), pp. 220–1 all discuss the significance of the wolf skin.

46   Homer, *Iliad* 10.398–406.

47   Homer, *Iliad* 418.

48   Homer, *Iliad* 10.421–423. Dué and Ebbott, p. 334.

49   Homer, *Iliad* 10.370–371.

50   Homer, *Iliad* 10.372.

51   Dolon's fear is explicit here and the chattering of his teeth and paleness are the evidence. In Homer, the coward is exposed by his skin changing colours from his fear, as well as his inability to sit still and his pounding heart, whereas the brave man's skin does not change colour. Cf. Homer, *Iliad* 13.276–286 with Homer, *Odyssey* 22.42 where the suitors are similarly described when they realise the stranger is Odysseus. Dué and Ebbott, p. 337.

52   Homer, *Iliad* 10.442–446.

53   Homer, *Iliad* 10.447–455.

54   Dué and Ebbott, p. 66.

55   Homer, *Iliad* 10.471–477.

56   Homer, *Iliad* 10.479–489.

57   In the *Rhesus* 573 they ask Dolon for the password to the Trojan camp. See Dué and Ebbott, pp. 128–9 on the need to tell the difference between friend and foe in the dark and the use of passwords in the Trojan camp.

58   Homer, *Iliad* 10.90–492.

59   Homer, *Iliad* 10.495–500.

60   Homer, *Iliad* 10.501–508.

61   Homer, *Iliad* 10.516–522.

62   See Dué and Ebbott, p. 355; on the supplication gesture, see K. Crotty, *The Poetics of Supplication: Homer's Iliad and Odyssey* (Ithaca, NY: Cornell University

Press, 1994) and D. Wilson, *Ransom, Revenge and Heroic Identity in the Iliad* (Cambridge: Cambridge University Press, 2002). Beheading an enemy occurs several times in Homeric epics, either as a killing or as an act carried out after a killing. Homer, *Iliad* 11.261, 13.201–205, 14.493–507, 17.126, 20.481–483,
•   Homer, *Odyssey* 22.310–329. On mutilation and revenge in Homer, see J. E. Lendon, 'Homeric vengeance and the outbreak of Greek wars', in H. van Wees (ed.), *War and Violence in Ancient Greece* (London: Duckworth, 2000), esp. pp. 3–11.

63   Dué and Ebbott, p. 319.

64   Gernet, pp. 192–6 and Davidson, p. 64 discuss the hanging of the wolf skin in a tree and connect it to initiation rituals. Dué and Ebbott, pp. 358, 359 on the need to mark the spot where the spoils have been stored. G. Stagakis, 'Athena and Dolon's spoils', *Archaiognosia* 5 (1987–8), pp. 55–71 argues that the spoils were not dedicated to Athena.

65   See Dué and Ebbott, p. 124 who discuss Dolon's name and the connection between the word *dolos* and the ambush theme, including spying missions.

66   Dué and Ebbott, p. 66; p. 349 on the lack of a night watch; p. 350 on the need for spatial information in an ambush.

67   Flaumenhaft, p. 14. The characters of Rhesus and Dolon are received and reworked in subsequent literature, namely the tragedy Rhesus and Virgil's *Aeneid*. He seems to have had a much expanded role compared to the one we see in *Iliad* 10 and he was a much greater threat to the Greeks, on which see Dué and Ebbott, pp. 89–151. Virgilian scholars have considered the points of comparison between the *Doloneia* and the night episode in *Aeneid* 9. For a recent discussion, see Dué and Ebbott, pp 136–51.

68   Flaumenhaft, p. 14; B. Fenik discusses sources in *Iliad X and the Rhesus*; Dué and Ebbott, pp. 28, 96 discuss the elements of the spying mission, the ambush and the prophecy. Cf. H. Heusinger, *Stilistische Untersuchungen zur Dolonie* (Leipzig: Druck von C. and E. Vogel. 1939), pp. 74–90.

69   On the question of who exactly took the horses of Rhesus, Odysseus or Diomedes, see G. Stagakis, 'The hippoi of Rhesus', *Hellenika* 37 (1986), pp. 231–41. He also discusses whether *hippoi* meant just the horses or the horses and the chariot too.

70   For example Flaumenhaft, p. 14. In an interlinear scholion on this line in the Venetus A manuscript, Aristarchus understood this 'great deed' to mean murdering Hector. Fenik, *Iliad X and the Rhesus*, p. 20 asserts that the *Doloneia* could portray night missions as an assassination attempt on Hector since an assassination attempt would be unacceptable portrayal of Odysseus and Diomedes. See Dué and Ebbott, pp. 103, n. 20, 254–5, 299 for the opposite view. which compares the courage needed for night operations in Books 10 and 24. Cf. M. F. Williams, pp. 17–20, and p. 22 on Hermes pretending to be on a reconnoitring expedition in Book 24.

71   Homer, *Iliad* 10.360–64.

72   Homer, *Iliad* 5.161.

73   The simile is always used of great warriors in combat (with the exception of Book 10) e.g. Hector in Homer, *Iliad* 15.275; 630; Hector 18.161; Patroclus and Hector 16.752, 756; Achilles 20.164; 24.572.

74   Homer, *Iliad* 11.450–55.

75   Flaumenhaft, p. 15.

76   Notice the political motives here – the Greek sentinels protect their own (Homer, *Iliad* 10.180–189). Dolon distinguishes between the Trojans who keep night watch, and their allies who sleep. The allies' children and wives do not need to be protected (ibid. 10.418–22). The Trojans defend themselves out of necessity; the allies have come to win glory.

77   Dué and Ebbott, p. 62 point out that even the normal weapons carried in daylight may be a liability at night. Metal can reflect in the moonlight or campfire light and betray the presence of the ambushers. Darkness enables hiding, the surprise nature of the attack and the escape.

78   Flaumenhaft, p. 20. D. M. Gaunt, 'The change of plan in the "Doloneia", *G&R* 18, 2 (1971), p. 197 argues that the theme changes from a spying mission to a direct attack because there were two traditional stories upon which the poet could draw. One focused on reconnaissance and the other on an assassination attempt on Hector or some great hero.

79   Dué and Ebbott, pp. 54, 57; McLeod, pp. 121–5 discusses the effectiveness of the bow in night ambushes and demonstrates how archers can find their targets in the dark. Of course, the bows that Dolon and Odysseus take on their respective missions are not, in fact, used as weapons in this episode (ibid. p. 61).

80   Ranke, pp. 48–9 believes that Diomedes' character was tarnished by Book 10 because the night raid was unheroic. Fenik, *Iliad X and the Rhesus*, p. 20, n. 3 disagrees, saying that Diomedes' portrayal was consistent with his portrait in the Epic Cycle. Shewan, p. 155 also finds no departure from heroic ideal in the killing of Dolon. Cf. M. F. Williams, p. 11. See Dué and Ebbott, pp. 104–5 who discuss alternative (local) versions of the story where Rhesus is killed during an *aristeia*. They show that in *Rhesus* the eponymous hero rejects ambush and states that courage can only be found in the *polemos* (ibid. pp. 126–7); this is in contrast to the Homeric epics, which ascribe courage to ambush. They identify Diomedes as a warrior who excels at both *polemos* and *lochos* (ibid. p. 305).

81   Homer, *Iliad* 10.37–41.

82   Homer, *Iliad* 1.223–28.

83   Homer, *Iliad* 10.37–41.

84   Homer, *Iliad* 13.276–94.

85   Homer, *Iliad* 10.204–217.

86   Homer, *Iliad* 10.212.

87   Homer, *Iliad* 10.213.

88   Homer, *Iliad* 10–214–217.

89 Homer, *Iliad* 10.37–41. Kirk, *The Songs of Homer*, p. 350; G. S. Kirk, *Homer and the Epic: A Shortened Version of the Songs of Homer* (London: Cambridge University Press, 1965), pp. 218–19, 222; M. F. Williams, p. 12.

90 Dué and Ebbott, p. 336.

91 Homer, *Iliad* 10.41–45. Cf. Nestor at 10.118, 144–45, 172–74, 192–93.

92 Homer, *Iliad* 10.227.

93 Homer, *Iliad* 10.22.

94 Homer, *Iliad* 10.244.

95 M. F. Williams, p. 12. Diomedes is notable for his fighting skills. He is the one who exhorts the Greeks to continue the war without Achilles (Homer, *Iliad* 9.31–49; 9.696–709) and is one of the nine warriors who volunteered to fight Hector in single combat in order to decide the war (ibid. 7.161–169). He even dared to fight the gods and lived (ibid. 5.327ff.). O. Taplin, *Homeric Soundings. The Shaping of the Iliad* (Oxford: The Clarendon Press, 1992), p. 135 calls him Achilles 'without the complications'.

96 L. Collins, *Studies in Characterization in the Iliad*, Beiträge zur klassischen Philologie, 189 (Frankfurt am Main: Athenaeum, 1988), pp. 21–6 on the ethics of the *Iliad*; D. L. Cairns, *Aidos: The Psychology and Ethics of Honour and Shame in Ancient Greek Literature* (Oxford: The Clarendon Press, 1993), pp. 59, 68–71; J. B. Hainsworth, *The Iliad: A Commentary*, at 10.237–9; M. F. Williams, p. 12.

97 M. F. Williams, p. 12.

98 Athena provides a favourable sign when the heroes depart from the Greek camp (Homer, *Iliad* 10.273–276) and is prayed to by both Odysseus and Diomedes at their departure (ibid. 10.277–282, 283–295). They also pray to her on their return (ibid. 10.578–579). Odysseus dedicates his spoils to her (ibid. 10.462–468, 571). On the other hand, the gods play no role in assisting Dolon who does not pray to them. Fenik, *Iliad X and the Rhesus*, p. 23 describes her involvement as 'typically Homeric' in that she does not infringe upon the initiative and credit of Odysseus or Diomedes.

99 Homer, *Iliad* 10.507–511.

100 Homer, *Iliad* 19.299–331.

101 Homer, *Iliad* 10.324.

102 Homer, *Iliad* 10.321–323. J. S. Clay, *The Wrath of Athena* (Lanham, MD: Rowman and Littlefield, 1997), pp. 75–6; Cairns, pp. 54–60 notes that the words of physical disfigurement or ugliness are linked to shame. M. F. Williams, p. 14.

103 Homer generally portrays the Trojans as weaker, less courageous and more interested in prizes than the Greeks. See Hainsworth on 10.13–14.

104 On the charge of Book 10 being un-Homeric, see Dué and Ebbott, pp. x, 3.

105 Homer, *Iliad* 9.66–68, 76–77.

106 Homer, *Iliad* 9.79–88.

107 Homer, *Iliad* 9.78.

108 See Homer, *Iliad* 10.118, 144–45, 172–74, 192–193. Some scholars believe this passage indicates that Book 10 was carefully inserted into our version of the *Iliad*. Shewan, however, does not think that Hector really fears a night raid but rather that this passage was inserted to foreshadow the *Doloneia*.

109 Homer, *Iliad* 10.12–15.

110 Homer, *Iliad* 10.97–101.

111 Homer, *Iliad* 10.73–79.

112 Homer, *Iliad* 10.150–156.

113 M. F. Williams, p. 15 points out that the anxiety that is present in both books indicates that Book 10 follows naturally upon Book 9 and ties the two books together.

114 Homer, *Iliad* 8.517–529 Fagles trans.; 8.517–529 Greek text.

115 C. W. MacLeod, *Homer: Iliad, Book XXIV* (Cambridge: Cambridge University Press, 1982), p. 16 says '. . . mercilessness is a feature of war which Homer deliberately stresses' as he does war's brutality. Shewan, p. 155 says that there is no departure from the heroic ideal in killing Dolon: 'The heroic ideal can be, and often is, rated too high.' Homeric warriors are often brutal and so is the aftermath of their wars.

116 Homer, *Iliad* 10.446–453.

117 Homer, *Iliad* 10.336–337.

118 Hainsworth, on 10.544–553, strangely remarks that Odysseus and Diomedes exceeded their orders, yet learned nothing about the Trojan intentions for the morning. Shewan, p. 156 believes that the capture of Rhesus' horses also countered Hector's threat by answering his promise of the horses of Achilles for Dolon. There was a tradition that if Rhesus' horses ate food and drank Trojan water, Troy would not fall.

119 Dué and Ebbott, pp. 70, 243.

120 Dué and Ebbott, p. 86.

Chapter 3: Ambush in the *Odyssey*

1 See, for example, M. F. Williams, p. 2.

2 M. F. Williams, p. 3; Vidal-Naquet, 'The black hunter and the origin of the Athenian Ephebia', pp. 49–64 outlines the mythic, ritual and historical foundations for a contrast between heavy-armed, disciplined infantry combat and attack by light-armed warriors, often characterised as 'trickery'. See also P. Vidal-Naquet, *The Black Hunter, Forms of Thought and Forms of Society in the Greek World* (Baltimore and London: The Johns Hopkins University Press, 1986); Nagy, pp. 45–8.

3 Homer, *Odyssey* 9.408; Fables trans. p. 455.

4 Dué and Ebbott, pp. 84–5, 254 who show how the blinding of the Cyclops displays the traditional features of an ambush. On the contrast between strength and stealth,

see D. Wilson, 'Demodocus' *Iliad* and Homer's', in R. Rabel (ed.), *Approaches to Homer: Ancient and Modern* (Swansea: The Classical Press of Wales, 2005), pp. 1–20; Edwards, p. 19; Buxton, pp. 58–63; Frontisi-Ducroux, pp. 182–5; Detienne and Vernant, pp. 19–20; K. Rüter, *Odysseeinterpretationen: Untersuchungen zum ersten Buchund zur Phaiakis* (Göttingen: Vandenhoeck, 1969), pp. 247–54; E. Howald, *Der Mythos als Dichtung* (Zürich and Leipzig: Niehans, 1937), pp. 14–50 who argues that the myth underlying the Troy Cycle is organised around a 'Heldenpaar' contrasting cunning with force. Polyaenus, *Strat. Proem*, 305 discusses Homer, *Odyssey* 9.409 in these terms.

5 Homer, *Odyssey* 9.476. There is the *metis* of getting the Cyclops drunk, using the sheep as a disguise and getting out of the cave. See Dué and Ebbott, p. 85.

6 Edwards, p. 19. Edwards argues that the *Iliad* and the *Odyssey* offer the Greek audience two distinctly different views of heroism. I am arguing that the contrast also includes different forms of warfare. See Sinos, pp. 133–5, for a review of Edwards.

7 Edwards, pp. 38–9. For Odysseus as a spearman see Homer, *Odyssey* 11.401–410, 5.306–312, 16.241–42 and 18.376–80.

8 D. Wilson, *Ransom, Revenge, and Heroic Identity in the Iliad*, pp. 45–8; D. Wilson, 'Demodocus' *'Iliad'* and Homer's', p. 1; Edwards, p. 39; J. H. Finley, *Homer's Odyssey* (Cambridge, MA: Harvard University Press, 1978), pp. 25–30, 41, 209–10; N. Austin, pp. 81–129.

9 N. Austin, p. 109.

10 However Flaumenhaft, p. 18 argues that Odysseus holds back from battle, is reluctant to join the expedition to Troy and was even the last to volunteer to join Diomedes in the night expedition in the *Doloneia*. A. Heubeck, *Der Odyssee, Dichter und die Ilias* (Erlange: Palm and Enke, 1954), notes that the word for ambush, *lochos*, would later come to mean a 'troops of soldiers'. He believes it as used in Homer, *Odyssey* 20.49 in this sense.

11 Hector comments on this in the *Rhesus* line 507. Odysseus is also said in the *Little Iliad*, 1 to have ambushed Helenus.

12 Flaumenhaft, p. 18.

13 Edwards, p. 21.

14 Homer, *Odyssey* 13.260ff,, 468ff., 14.216–21. On his associations with *metis* – craft, see Dué and Ebbott, pp. 271–2.

15 He is called at various times enduring, much enduring, or enduring and suffering in mind. The Greek words used are all derived from *tlao*. They suggest his suffering, both the afflictions of war and the insults of his homecoming: Flaumenhaft, p. 18.

16 Flaumenhaft, pp. 18–19.

17 *Iliad* 10.462–64; 529, 571.

18 Homer, *Odyssey* 9.49–50.

19 Homer, *Odyssey* 4.280.

20 Homer, *Odyssey* 14.470–71.

21 Homer, *Odyssey* 4.388–463; Dué and Ebbott, pp. 78–9, 253.

22 Hyginus, *Fabulae: The Myths of Hyginus*, trans. by Mary Grant (Lawrence: University of Kansas Publications, 1960), 105.

23 Hyginus, 105.

24 There are other versions of the story that say there was no such plot, and that Palamedes was drowned by Odysseus and Diomedes when he put out to catch fish. See Ovid, *The Metamorphoses of Ovid*, trans. and with an introduction by Mary M. Innes (Harmondsworth, Middlesex: Penguin Books, 1955), 13.56; Vergil, *The Aeneid*, trans. by Stanley Lombardo, introduction by W. R. Johnson (Indianapolis, IN: Hackett, 2005), 2.82. See Edwards, p. 27 on the two being geographical opposite.

25 Dué and Ebbott, p. 86 point out the similarities in formulaic diction between various ambush narratives in *Iliad* 10 and the *Homeric Hymn to Hermes*.

26 Eight references to the ambush of Telemachus: 4.670, 4.847, 13.425, 14.181, 15.28, 16.369, 16.463, 22. 53; other ambushes: 4.388, 4.395, 4.441, 4.463, 4.531, 13.268, 14.217, 14.469, 20.48; the wooden horse: 4.277, 8.515, 11.525.

27 See Dué and Ebbott, p. 70 where they break down the subthemes that constitute an ambush.

28 Murray translation: Homer, *Odyssey* (Cambridge, MA: Harvard University Press, 1931), 2 vols.

29 For a discussion of the three songs, see A. Thornton, *People and Themes in Homer's Odyssey* (London and Dunedin: Methuen, 1970), pp. 43–5. Edwards, p. 40. The scholium preserves the opinion of Aristarchus: K. Lehrs, *De Aristarchi Studiis Homeriicis* (Leipzig: Teubner, 1882), p. 147. See Aeschylus, *Prometheus Bound* 209–15 for a parallel to this dispute over force and trickery.

30 D. Wilson, 'Demodocus' *Iliad* and Homer's', pp. 1–20

31 The *Little Iliad* is a lost epic of ancient Greek literature. It is one of the better-attested epics in the Epic Cycle, i.e. that told the entire history of the Trojan War in epic verse. Nearly thirty lines of the original text survive.

32 This contrast is supported by Hector's comment at *Rhesus* 497–507 where he states that Odysseus had done the Trojans more harm than any other Greek. He then goes on to list some of Odysseus' trickier exploits with the conclusion that he is always found in ambushes.

33 Homer, *Odyssey* 9.39–42. See Jackson, 'War and raids for war booty in the world of Odysseus', pp. 64–76.

34 Homer, *Odyssey* 14.85–88.

35 Homer, *Odyssey* 3.103–06; Flaumenhaft, p. 16.

36 Edwards, p. 32.

37 Homer, *Odyssey* 13.256–284; Fagles trans, lines 13.289–323.

38 K. F. Ameis and C. Hentze, *Homer's Odyssey* (Leipzig: Teubner, 1879) regarded this name as an invention for the immediate context. E. Risch, *Wortbildung der*

Homerischen Sprache (Berlin: de Gruyter, 1974), pp. 191–2 asserts the meaning
of the name was 'the one who attacks the *lochos*' or the one who urges the *lochos* to
attack. Edwards, p. 33 prefers the former.

39 Homer, *Odyssey* 13.260.

40 Homer, *Odyssey* 13. 321–25; 790–92. Edwards, pp. 15–16 and 16, n. 3 for the
pattern of swift, forceful figures overcome through trickery.

41 See chap. 1 on these two ambushes: Tydeus in *Iliad* 4.385–398 and Bellerophon
in Homer, *Iliad* 6.178–190.

42 Edwards, p. 33.

43 Homer, *Odyssey* 14.214–22.

44 Homer, *Odyssey* 22.199–210; Edwards, p. 33.

45 Homer, *Odyssey* 14.468–506.

46 Edwards, pp. 33–4. See the discussions of this tale by Heubeck, pp. 26–7; P. Walcot,
'Odysseus and the art of lying', *Ancient Society* 8 (1977), pp. 15–16; and Nagy,
pp. 235–8. On Odysseus' speech generally, see Detienne and Vernant, pp. 30–1.

47 Homer, *Odyssey* 4.384–480.

48 Dué and Ebbott, p. 82 compares *Odyssey* 4 to the *Doloneia* and the *Little Iliad*
because each has connected themes that build on one another and create a larger
song. They discuss the connections between prophecies and ambushes (ibid. p. 97).

49 Edwards, p. 34. A similar contradictory evaluation of the word *metis* is also
apparent. See Detienne and Vernant, pp. 30–1.

50 This is significant in view of the close parallels between the *nostoi* (returns) of
Odysseus and Menelaus. See Howald, pp. 51–6, 63–73 and W. F. Hansen, *The
Conference Sequence, Patterned Narrative and Narrative Inconsistency in the Odyssey*,
Classical Studies 8 (Berkeley and Los Angeles, CA: University of California, 1972),
pp. 8–19.

51 Edwards, *passim*.

52 Homer, *Odyssey* 22.26–34.

53 D. L. Page 'Stesichorus: the Geroneis', *JHS* 93 (1973), pp. 138–54 argues this
interpretation from a fragment of Stesichorus' lost *Geryoneis*. Cf. Edwards, p. 34.

54 Edwards, p. 35. On the relationship between Odysseus and Heracles, see Howald,
pp. 39–43; and 617–26 with the comments of K. Galinsky, *The Herakles Theme*
(Oxford: Blackwell, 1972), pp. 12–14. For post-Homeric texts expressing a positive
view of the ambush, see Vidal-Naquet, 'The black hunter and the origin of the
Athenian Ephebia', pp. 49–64 and compare Hesiod, *Theogony* 154–82 for an
interesting parallel.

55 Homer, *Odyssey*. 8.266–366. This pattern has been noticed by W. Burkert, 'Das
Lied von Ares und Aphrodite, Zum Verhältnis von Odyssee und Ilias', *RhM* 103
(1960), pp. 140–2 and Thornton, *People and Themes in Homer's Odyssey*, pp. 44–5.

56 Homer, *Odyssey* 4.240–64.

57 Edwards, p. 35.

58 Homer, *Odyssey* 4.529ff.

59 Edwards, p. 29.

60 Edwards, p. 29.

61 Edwards, pp. 29, 32 and verses 267–8.

62 Homer, *Odyssey* 17.80.

63 Edwards, p. 30.

64 Homer, *Odyssey* 20.49–51.

65 Note that the meaning of *lochoi* in 49 is disputed. Some take it to mean ambush while others interpret it as 'infantry formations'. Edwards, p. 30, n. 27 for references.

66 Homer, *Iliad* 4.397.

67 Homer, *Iliad* 6.188–190.

68 Dué and Ebbott, pp. 103, 276–8.

69 Edwards, p. 31.

70 Edwards, p. 18.

71 For other studies that have explored the manner in which the *Odyssey* employs repetitions of narrative patterns and themes to tie together the diverse strands of its plot, see S. Said, 'Les crimes des prétendents la maison d'Ulyse et les festin de l'Odysée', *Études de la Litterature Ancienne* (1979); F. Bader, 'L'art de la fugue sand l'Odyssée', *REG* 89 (1976), pp. 18–39; and Fenik, *Iliad X and the Rhesus*, pp. 91–138. Edwards, p. 40.

72 See Sinos for review of A. T. Edwards' book.

73 See, for example, Homer, *Odyssey* 1.234–243 where Telemachus says that, if his father had died at Troy, he would have had a proper burial and the *kleos* of a warrior but since he apparently died before reaching home he is without *kleos*. See the ambush of Tydeus by fifty Thebans, where he released 'only one to return home' (Homer, *Iliad* 4.397). Similarly, in the ambush of Bellerophon, the ambushers never return home (Homer, *Iliad* 6.188–190). Dué and Ebbott, pp. 78, 287–8.

74 Edwards, p. 18.

75 Dué and Ebbott, p. 103.

Chapter 4: The Archaic Age and the Problem of the Phalanx

1 On the historical origins of hoplite warfare, see H. van Wees, 'The development of the hoplite phalanx. Iconography and reality in the seventh century', in H. van Wees (ed.), *War and Violence in Ancient Greece* (London: Duckworth, 2000), pp. 125–66. P. Cartledge, 'Hoplites and heroes: Sparta's contribution to the techniques of ancient warfare', *JHS* 97 (1977), pp. 11–27; I. Morris, *Burial and Ancient Society: The Rise of the Greek City-State* (Cambridge: Cambridge University Press, 1987); A. Snodgrass, 'The hoplite reform revisited', *DHA* 19, 1 (1993), pp. 47–61; Van Wees, 'The Homeric way of war', pp. 1–18. On the arms, armour and social class of these citizen-armies, see H. van Wees, 'Tyrants, oligarchs and

citizen militias', in Angelos Chaniotis and Pierre Ducrey, *Army and Power in the Ancient World* (Stuttgart: Steiner, 2002), pp. 61–82; see also Van Wees, *Greek Warfare*, Part II, 'Citizens and soldiers'; and H. van Wees, 'The myth of the middle-class army: Military and social status in ancient Athens', in T. Bekker-Nielsen and L. Hannestad, *War as a Cultural and Social Force. Essays on Warfare in Antiquity* (Copenhagen: Det Kongelige Danske Videnskabernes Selskab, 2001), pp. 45–71.

2   Hanson, *The Western Way of War* argues for homogeneity among the so-called middle class in part due to their relationship to and with each other on the hoplite battlefield. J. Salmon, 'Political hoplites', *JHS* 97 (1977), pp. 84–101 makes the case for the subconscious community formed by hoplite warfare in the late Archaic Period and the political effects which this may have created.

3   Some scholars have argued that the *hoplon* shield was introduced and the style of fighting followed. This model is problematic, however, for both political and military reasons. The introduction of new military equipment without a pre-existing doctrine on how to use it, especially in a pre-modern economy where doing so would be a risky economic venture, seems highly unlikely. See S. Morillo, J. Black and P. Lococo, *War in World History. Society, Technology and War from Ancient Times to the Present* (New York: McGraw Hill, 2009), vol. 1, p. 40. On the significance of the heavy shield as a defining characteristic of the hoplite, and a debunking the notion that the hoplite was actually named for his shield see J. Lazenby and D. Whitehead, 'The myth of the hoplite's *hoplon*', *CQ* 46,1 (1996) pp. 27–33; Wheeler, 'Land battles', in *CHGRW*, vol. 1, pp. 186–7.

4   It was French scholars who wrote about Greek warfare as an *agon*, a contest, conceived like a tournament with ceremonies and rules. See, for example, Vernant, *Problèmes*, p. 21; Detienne, p. 211. The idea was picked up by Y. Garlan, *Recherches de Poliorcetique Grecque* (Paris: Boccard, 1974) and Y. Garlan, *War in the Ancient World*, trans. by Janet Lloyd (London: Chatto and Windus, 1975); R. Lonis, *Guerre et Religion en Grèce à l'Époque Classique* (Paris: Les Belles Lettres, 1979). On agonal warfare, see also van Wees, *Greek Warfare*, pp. 115–117, 126–8, 131–2, 223–6.

5   D. Dawson, *The Origins of Western Warfare: Militarism and Morality in the Ancient World* (Boulder, CO: Westview Press, 1996), p. 50; V. D. Hanson, 'The ideology of hoplite battle: Ancient and modern', in Hanson, *Hoplites*, p. 6 calls it a 'wonderful, absurd conspiracy' that was seldom accompanied by sieges, ambushes, strategems, etc.

6   J. Keegan's *The Face of Battle* (New York: Viking Press, 1976) began the trend. The quotations is from Hanson, *Hoplites*, p. 253. See the remarks of John W. I. Lee, *A Greek Army on the March, Soldiers and Survival in Xenophon's Anabasis* (Cambridge: Cambridge University Press, 2007); F. E. Ray, *Land Battles in 5th Century BC Greece* (Jefferson, NC: McFarland, 2009), p. 14.

7   Keegan, *The Face of Battle*, p. 29.

8   P. Ducrey, *Le Traitement des Prisoniers de Guerre dans la Grèce Antique* (Paris:

Editions E. de Boccard, 1999), pp. 1–8, 289–311 and *passim*. Josiah Ober has made the most explicit attempt to get out the unwritten conventions of hoplite warfare. In J. Ober, 'The rules of war in Classical Greece', in *The Athenian Revolution: Essays on Ancient Greek Democracy and Political Theory* (Princeton: Princeton University Press, 1996), pp. 53–71, he lists a dozen common customs that were developed after the Homeric epics were put in writing and which did not break down until around 450 during the Peloponnesian war. See also Krentz, 'Fighting by the rules', pp. 23–9.

9   H. Berve, 'Staat und Staatsgesinnung der Griechen', *Neue Jahrbücher für Antike und Deutsche Bildung* 1 (1938), pp. 6–7. Cf. Lonis, pp. 90–109.

10   F. W. Walbank, *A Historical Commentary on Polybius* (Oxford: The Clarendon Press, 1957), vol. I, 264. It is a commonplace to refer to Strabo's report (10.1.12) that rules of war were agreed upon by Chalkis and Eretria at the time of the Lelantine war. Strabo quotes an inscription in the sanctuary of Artemis at Eretria, prohibiting missiles (*telebola*). The Argives and probably Thucydides believed as an historical fact that the Spartans and Argives agreed to decide the possession of Thyrea by means of a combat between groups of 300 men each chosen from the two armies. M. Ostwald, *Nomos and the Beginnings of the Athenian Democracy* (Oxford: The Clarendon Press, 1969), p. 42 concludes that religious customs began to be undermined in the last third of the fifth century. Ober, 'The rules of war in Classical Greece', pp. 53–71 tries listing the rules, but this theory has recently been attacked by Krentz, 'Fighting by the rules', pp. 23–39.

11   Van Wees, *Greek Warfare*, p. 118.

12   G. B. Grundy, *Thucydides and the History of His Age* (Oxford: Blackwell, 1948), vol. I, p. 244.

13   A. W. Gomme, *A Historical Commentary on Thucydides* (Oxford: Clarendon Press, 1970), vol. 1, pp. 12–15.

14   A. M. Snodgrass, *Arms and Armour of the Greeks* (Ithaca, NY: Cornell University Press, 1967), p. 85; Cartledge, 'Hoplites and Heroes', p. 24; M. T. Trundle, 'Identity and community among Greek mercenaries in the Classical World 700–322 BCE', in E. L. Wheeler, *The Armies of Classical Greece* (Aldershot, Hants and Burlington, VT: Ashgate, 2007), p. 486; van Wees, *Greek Warfare*, pp. 45–9.

15   Cartledge, 'Hoplites and heroes', p. 24. As Aristotle put it: 'in a *politeia*, the class that does the fighting wields the supreme power' (*Politics* 1279b3); and, we might add, writes the history. On the opposition of ruses de guerre and hoplite fighting, see Heza, pp. 235–44.

16   Latacz, pp. 154ff. Cf. P. Greenhalgh, *Early Greek Warfare* (Cambridge: Cambridge University Press, 1973), p. 73; Cartledge, 'Hoplites and heroes', p. 20 and V. D. Hanson, 'Hoplite technology in phalanx battle', in V. D. Hanson (ed.), *Hoplites*, pp. 67–8 and n. 14 have developed and refined this view arguing that the hoplite shield did not dictate a dense formation but pre-supposed an existing practice of close-order fighting.

17 See the discussion of Latacz' theory by A. M. Snodgrass, 'The hoplite reform revisited', in E. L. Wheeler, *The Armies of Classical Greece* (Aldershot, Hants and Burlington, VT: Ashgate, 2007), pp. 3–61, and van Wees, 'The Homeric way of war', pp. 1–18; 131–55.

18 H. van Wees summarises this view and lists the adherents in 'The development of the hoplite phalanx', p. 125, n. 1; Hanson, *The Western Way of War*, p. 241. On the so-called 'Hoplite revolution' and military revolutions in general, including the legacy of Michael Roberts, see Wheeler, 'Land battles', in *CHGRW*, vol. 1, pp. 186–7; Krentz, 'Fighting by the rules', p. 112; Ducrey, pp. 56–64. W. G. Runciman, 'Greek hoplites, warrior culture, and indirect bias', *Journal of the Royal Anthropological Institute* 4, 4 (Dec. 1998), p. 731.

19 Hanson, *The Western Way of War*, p. 241. Van Wees, 'The development of the hoplite phalanx', pp. 155–6 disagrees with this interpretation and suggests that the hoplite phalanx did not reach its Classical form until after the Persian wars.

20 Van Wees, 'The development of the hoplite phalanx', pp. 125–66; Wheeler, 'Land battles', in *CHGRW*, vol. 1, p. 190.

21 The evidence for the view that the hoplite phalanx was fully developed by either 700 or 650 BCE is listed by van Wees, *War and Violence in Ancient Greece*, p. 152, nn. 5 and 6. Morris, esp. pp. 196–200.

22 Van Wees, *Greek Warfare*, pp. 166–95; Krentz, 'Fighting by the rules', p. 23.

23 Krentz, 'Fighting by the rules', pp. 35–6; J. K. Anderson says that when you see the combination of armoured spearmen and light-armed missile throwers on a vase it more likely reflects guerrilla warfare in the mountains of Messenia: J. K. Anderson, 'Hoplite weapons and offensive arms', in V. D. Hanson (ed.), *Hoplites: The Classical Greek Battle Experience* (London and New York: Routledge, 1991), p. 16. Van Wees would argue that this is simply the mixed fighters of the archaic period.

24 R. D. Luginbill, 'Othismos: The importance of the mass-shove in hoplite warfare', *Phoenix* 48, 1 (1994), pp. 651–61 criticises the notion that hoplites had either the discipline or the training to change from an open formation engaged in individual combat to the close order necessary for a push. His argument, however, is predicated on the fact that we accept the *othismos* as a fact. For the contrary argument, see van Wees, *Greek Warfare*, pp. 166–77, esp. 173.

25 Van Wees, *Greek Warfare*, p. 167.

26 Poets talk about soldiers 'leaning their shields against their shoulders' and exhorting men to stand up 'legs well apart, both feet planted firmly on the ground, biting your lip'. Hoplites squat and run with their left shoulder twisted forward: van Wees, *Greek Warfare*, pp. 167–8 with illustrations.

27 Van Wees, *Greek Warfare*, p. 168.

28 On the stance of the hoplite, the protection afforded by the hoplite shield and its use as an offensive weapon see van Wees, *Greek Warfare*, pp. 168–70.

29 For the evidence of hoplites with javelins, see van Wees, 'The development of the hoplite phalanx', pp. 125–66, esp. 134ff. on 'battle scenes: what they do and do not show'; see also van Wees, *Greek Warfare*, pp. 169–71, 173–4, esp. p. 170 on the throwing loop.

30 Van Wees, *Greek Warfare*, pp. 172–4.

31 As evidence for this interpretation, van Wees points out that archers made up about one-third of all warriors and they stood in the front-line as the equals of spearmen: see van Wees, *Greek Warfare*, p. 167, figure 13. Bowmen also carried swords and helmets and sometimes a shield. In vase paintings they are always shown face to face with an opponent and they kill with a shot to the head or neck. Archers continued to fight alongside spearmen, but from the early seventh century onwards they were represented in art not as independent fighters but as unarmoured men kneeling or squatting behind hoplites: van Wees, *Greek Warfare*, p. 170. The *Iliad* vividly describes how this works. The archer stands 'under a shield' of a heavy-armed soldier, but every so often jumps out, looks around to see if he can shoot someone in the crowd, fires a shot and quickly returns to the cover of the shield (Homer, *Iliad* 8.266–72; 4.112–115, 15.440–4). Thus close co-operation between spearmen and bowmen, unattested in earlier art, must have been a new tactic, made possible by the large, new shields and encouraged by the greater emphasis on close combat. Crouching for safety at a distance from the enemy only makes sense if there is a danger of being hit by missiles. See van Wees, *Greek Warfare*, p. 168, figure 14, p. 171, figure 18 for Greek pictorial examples of such crouching archers.

32 Herodotus 1.103.1 reports that Greek mercenaries at the Lydian court during the reign of Cyaxares in the late seventh century were surprised by the separation of fighting men in the Median army. The story grew up that Cyaxares had been the first to do this.

33 Van Wees, *Greek Warfare*, p. 173.

34 Van Wees, *Greek Warfare*, p. 175 and figures 19, 20. Nine out of ten archers are in Scythian dress, and their exotic appearance helps explain why they were popular with artists when ordinary archers were much more rarely portrayed: painters like the contrast between 'barbarian' bowmen and Greek heavy infantry. Scythian archers had no precedent in epic poetry, nor is the idea of putting them among hoplites likely to have been an artistic fiction designed purely for symbolic effect – Thracian peltasts, equally exotic and also often represented in Athenian art, were not shown mingling with hoplites in this way. In all probability, Athens did employ Scythian mercenaries at the time, and these did operate as shown, mixed in with a loose hoplite formation rather than as a separate, independent force.

35 Ducrey, p. 74.

36 Krentz, 'Fighting by the rules', p. 29. For a list of armed archers on Athenian vases, see F. Lissarague, *L'autre Guerrier: Archers, Peltastes, Cavaliers dans l'Imagerie Attique* (Paris: Découverte; Rome: Ecole française de Rome, 1990), p. 129.

37 Although there may have been a small cavalry force at Athens in the sixth century, it is only after 479 that the Athenians establish what I. G. Spence calls a 'proper cavalry corps': I. G. Spence, *The Cavalry of Classical Greece: A Social and Military History with Particular Reference to Athens* (Oxford: The Clarendon Press, 1993), pp. 9–19; G. Bugh, *The Horsemen of Athens* (Princeton: Princeton University Press, 1988), p. 39; J. E. Lendon, *Soldiers and Ghosts*, p. 44.

38 Herodotus 9.22.1.

39 This is an interesting example of cultural borrowing. See Krentz, 'Fighting by the rules', p. 124 and M.C. Miller, *Athens and Persia in the Fifth Century* BC: *A Study in Cultural Receptivity* (Cambridge: Cambridge University Press, 1997) for a study of how profoundly Persian culture influenced the Greeks. Herodotus says that the Persian cavalry were armed like their infantry (i.e. some combination of spear, long knife [*akinakes*], bow, helmet and body armour). Although many used javelins instead, he mentions horse archers at Plataea in 479. In the western empire the bow became less popular than the spear by 400 BCE. The 10,000 survivors of Cyrus' mercenaries were harassed by Artaxerxes' horse archers until they organised a force of slingers to shoot back.

40 Spence, pp. 1–9.

41 Herodotus 9.22.60. Archers on ships appear at the Battle of Salamis a year earlier. See Aeschylus, *Persians*, English trans. by Herbert Weir Smyth (Cambridge, MA: Harvard University Press; London: Heinemann, 1922), 454–464; A. Plassart, 'Les archers d'Athènes', *REG* 26 (1913), pp. 151–213.

42 Thucydides 424.

43 Thucydides 8.71.2; Xenophon, *Hellenica*, 1.1.33–34.

44 Free will Herodotus 7.104.4; barbarians 'coerced by the whip', Herodotus 7.103.4; 223.3; hoplites fighting to the end 7.225.3.

45 Mardonius' speech in Herodotus 7.9.2.

46 For attacks on the so-called *othismos*, or massed push, see G. L. Cawkwell in 'Orthodoxy and hoplites', *CQ* 39 (1989), pp. 375–89; A. D. Fraser, 'The myth of the phalanx-scrimmage', *CW* 36 (1942), pp. 15–16; P. Krentz, 'The nature of hoplite battle', *ClAnt* 16 (1985), pp. 50–61 who sees *othismos* as little more than a metaphor. For those taking a more traditional approach, see J. Lazenby, 'The killing zone', in V. Hanson, *Hoplites*, pp. 87–109; Hanson, *The Western Way of War*; Pritchett, vol. 1, p. 175, vol. 4, pp. 66–73; J. Buckler, 'Epameinondas and the Embolon', *Phoenix* 39 (1985), pp. 134–43; J. K. Anderson, 'Hoplites and heresies: A note', *JHS* 104 (1984), p. 152; A. J. Holladay, 'Hoplites and heresies', *JHS* 102 (1982), pp. 94–103; and a return to the traditional view in Luginbill, pp. 323–33 who lists the earlier bibliography.

47 Van Wees, 'Tyrants, oligarchs and citizen militias', p. 65; van Wees, 'Men of bronze: The myth of the middle class militia', in van Wees, *Greek Warfare*, pp. 47–57. See Konrad Kinzl, *A Companion to the Classical Greek World* (Malden, MA:

Blackwell, 2006), p. 483 on the diversity of hoplites in Argos, Boeotia, Corinth, Megara, etc.

48 Van Wees, 'Tyrants, oligarchs and citizen militias', p. 65 who gives the example of the Athenians invading Boeotia in 424 BCE, where the proportion of light- to heavy-armed in the Boeotian forces was about 3:2; in the Athenian army the proportion was 2:1. See Thucydides 4.93.3–94.1.

49 Van Wees, 'Tyrants, oligarchs and citizen militias', p. 65. Thucydides 5.64.2. Plataea: Herodotus 9.28–29.

50 The high mobility and fluidity of light infantry meant their encounters rarely produced a clear winner, unlike hoplite confrontations which were decided the minute one side left the field. This led Thucydides to comment on the performance of the light-armed troops in the initial stages of the confrontation between the Athenians and the Syracusans in 415 BCE. He felt they fought with fluctuating fortunes 'as is usual with these troops': Thucydides 6.69; van Wees, *Greek Warfare*, pp. 61–5.

51 Krentz, 'Deception in Archaic and Classical Greek warfare', pp. 167–200.

52 Thucydides knew the precise number of Athenian heavy infantry invading Megara, but waved away the light-armed as 'a not inconsiderable crowd': Thucydides 2.31.1. Xenophon, when describing the military potential of Thessaly notes that the region could field 6,000 horsemen and 10,000 hoplites but only describes its light-armed troops as 'large enough to take on the whole of mankind': Xenophon, *Hellenica* 6.1.8, 19. N. Whatley, 'On the possibility of reconstructing Marathon and other ancient battles', in E. L. Wheeler (ed.), *The Armies of Classical Greece* (Aldershot, Hants and Burlington, VT: Ashgate, 2007), p. 316 (p. 134 in original *JHS* article) points out the absence of information about Greek formations and the stationing of light-armed troops and attendants who would have been present. See also L. Trittle, 'Warfare in Herodotus', in Carolyn Dewald and John Marincola (eds), *The Cambridge Companion to Herodotus* (Cambridge University Press, 2006), p. 212; van Wees, *Greek Warfare*. pp. 61–5.

53 Van Wees, *Greek Warfare*, p. 61.

54 Van Wees, *Greek Warfare*, p. 62, pp. 154–8 (Homer), pp. 173–4 (Tyrtaeus). Tyrtaeus F 19.19–20; cf. 19.2 for rock throwing. See Tyrtaeus F 23a.10–14 for hurling javelins, and light-armed fighters.

55 Tyrtaeus fr. 23a-20–22 (West trans.). See Krentz, 'Fighting by the rules', p. 39.

56 Diodorus Siculus 12.10.1; Krentz, 'Fighting by the rules', p. 31.

57 Thucydides 1.106.1–2; Krentz, 'Fighting by the rules', p. 31.

58 Thucydides 418.

59 In the famous passage of Herodotus (Herodotus 7.9b.1–2), Mardonius in a fictional conversation relates to Xerxes I how the Greek art of war was absolutely silly. He says they fight for trivial reasons and limit battle to a level playing field where the victors take casualties and the losers are annihilated. This puts into the mouth of the

Persians a view that the Greeks were strategically limited and tactically ritualistic in conducting war. This excludes Xenophon and *Tactica* and the artistic evidence: Thucydides 5/70–71.1; Polybius 18.28–32. Cf. E. L. Wheeler, 'The legion as phalanx in the Late Empire', pt 1, in Y. Le Bohec and C. Woolf (eds), *L'Armée Romaine de Diocletian à Valentinian*, 1ère Actes du Congrès de Lyon, 12–14 Sept 2002 (Paris: CERGR, 2004), pp. 327, 331–2, 336–9; and Wheeler, 'Land battles', in *CHGRW*, vol. 1, p. 191. On the view that there were very few large battles in the Archaic Period at all, see W. R. Connor, 'Early Greek land warfare as symbolic expression', in E. L. Wheeler, *The Armies of Classical Greece* (Aldershot, Hants and Burlington, VT: Ashgate, 2007), pp. 83–109.

60   Polybius 18.31.2.

61   Polybius 18.31.2; Polybius 18.32.7.

62   Wheeler, 'Land battles', in *CHGRW*, vol. 1, p. 191.

63   Polybius 13.3.2–6.

64   Wheeler, 'Land battles', in *CHGRW*, vol. 1, p. 191.

65   Demosthenes, *Third Philippic*, 9.47–52.

66   Polybius 10.1.12; Polybius 13.3.2–4; Strabo, *The Geography of Strabo*, trans. by Horace Leonard Jones (Cambridge, MA: Harvard University Press, 1982–9), 10.1.12; E. L. Wheeler, 'Ephorus and the prohibition of missiles', *TAPA* 117 (1987), pp. 157–82. As an example of someone who accepted the treaty as historical see J. K. Anderson, *Military Theory and Practice in the Age of Xenophon* (Berkeley: University of California Press, 1970), p. 1; and Wheeler 'Land battles', in *CHGRW*, vol. 1, p. 191. Despite Polybius' claim that the ancient's agreed not to use unseen missiles or missiles shot from a distance, the only such agreement we know of appears in Strabo. He claims it was inscribed on a column in the sanctuary of Artemis Amarynthia, prohibiting missiles in the Lelantine war.

67   Wheeler, 'Ephorus and the prohibition of missiles', pp. 157–82; Krentz, 'Fighting by the rules', p. 29.

68   Van Wees, 'The development of the hoplite phalanx', pp. 146–56; van Wees, *Greek Warfare*, pp. 166–77. On slingers, see E. C. Echols, 'The ancient slinger', *CW* 43 (1950), pp. 227–30; and M. Korfmann, 'The sling as a weapon', *Scientific American* 229, 4 (1973), pp. 34–42. On javelin men, see Ray, pp. 14–15.

69   Xenophon, *Cyropaedia* 3.3.47 (based on the Loeb trans.); cf. Thucydides 6.11.6.

70   Already by the time of the Ionian revolt Aristagoras of Miletus tried to draw both the Spartans and the Athenians into the conflict with Persia by speculating on the Greeks' contempt for the 'inferior' fighting methods of the Persians' light-armed: Herodotus 5.49.3; 97.1. On Persian armaments, cf. Herodotus 7.61.1. For statements on the formality of Greek warfare, see Herodotus 7.9; Demosthenes, *Orations* 9.4; Polybius 13.3.2–6. For the Greek dichotomy between fighting 'openly' and trickery, see Heza, pp. 227–44.

71   Thucydides 7.29.3; 7.30.4. On this incident, see chap. 7.

72 Ducrey, *Warfare in Ancient Greece*, p. 112.

73 On the lack of hoplite-on-hoplite ambush, see Pritchett, vol. 2, pp. 156ff.; and Connor, pp. 83–109.

74 Heza, p. 229.

75 On the 'Spartan mirage', see F. Ollier, *Le Mirage Spartiate* (Paris: de Boccard, 1933). Paul Cartledge, 'The politics of Spartan pederasty', *Proceedings of the Cambridge Philological Society* 27 (1981), p. 18 describes this Spartan mirage as the partly distorted, partly imaginary picture of Sparta that its non-Spartan admirers needed and wanted to believe represented the reality. See also Heza, p. 229.

76 Pausanias 4.17.3.

77 J. E. Lendon, *Soldiers and Ghosts*, pp. 86–7.

78 See the comments of J. E. Lendon, *Soldiers and Ghosts*, p. 82. 'It is not difficult to build up a dossier of military tricks practised by a variety of Greek states before the outbreak of the Peloponnesian war' (ibid. p. 83).

79 See the comments of John Ma, 'Fighting *poleis* of the Hellenistic world', in H. van Wees, *War and Violence in Ancient Greece* (London: Duckworth, 2000), p. 355.

80 L. A. Losada, *The Fifth Column in the Peloponnesian war* (Leiden: Brill, 1972), p. 41.

81 F. E. Adcock, *The Greek and Macedonian Art of War* (Berkeley: University of California Press, 1957), pp. 16–17; Losada, p. 42.

82 Kromayer and Veith, p. 88; Adcock, pp. 16–17; Losada, p. 42.

83 Losada, pp. 2–3.

84 Porter, p. 77.

85 J. E. Lendon, *Soldiers and Ghosts*, p. 83. See also Krentz, 'Fighting by the rules', p. 28.

86 Certainly every hoplite battle of which we have a detailed account shows some ritual elements. See J. E. Lendon, *Soldiers and Ghosts*, p. 83

Chapter 5: Surprise Attacks – Fifth Century

1 Pritchett, vol. 2, p. 156.

2 Whatley, p. 304 (p. 122 in the original *JHS* text).

3 Herodotus 1.63.

4 On this incident at Sepeia, see Herodotus 6.79; Plutarch, *Cleomenes* 17 has the attack take place at night. Ray, p. 49 tries to reconcile the two versions. Cf. the section entitled 'De tempore ad pugnam eligendo' in Frontinus, *Stratagems*, Book 2. Three of the stratagems used by Roman generals (nos 1, 2, 15) were devised because the enemy drew up in battle array early before breakfast.

5 Herodotus 6.77–78. Godley trans.

6 Polyaenus 1.15. Krentz and Wheeler trans.

7 Carl von Clausewitz, *On War*, ed. and trans. by Michael Howard and Peter Paret (Princeton, NJ: Princeton University Press, 1976), p. 198.

8   Clausewitz, p. 198. Thucydides also comments on the attacker's difficulties resulting from their poor vision and intelligence (Thucydides 7.44).

9   Clausewitz, pp. 273–5. Cf. Hannibal at the *Iugum Calliculae*: Livy 22.15–17; Plutarch, *Fabius Maximus* 6; Polybius 3.93–94; Walbank, vol. 1, pp. 429–30; Silius Italicus, *Punica* 7.311ff.

10   E. Luttwak, *Strategy: The Logic of Peace and War* (Cambridge: Cambridge University Press, 1987), p. 10.

11   Clausewitz, p. 275.

12   Thucydides 2.3–4.

13   Thucydides 2.3.1–4.

14   On the topography of Plataea and its strategic value, see Grundy, *Thucydides and the History of His Age*, vol. 2, pp. 336ff. On the military value of women throwing roof tiles, see D. Schaps, 'The women of Greece in wartime', *CP* 77, 3 (July 1982), pp. 195 and W. D. Barry, 'Roof tiles and urban violence in the ancient world', *GRBS* 37, 1 (1996), pp. 55–74. Women could add to the discomfort of a hard-pressed enemy as Thucydides says they did at Plataea (and also Corcyra). As far as we know, however, no one lured the enemy into a city specifically to expose him to the women on the rooftops.

15   See Thucydides 2.4 on Plataea, and the fateful hit of the Argive woman who laid Pyrrhus low in 272 BCE: Plutarch, *Pyrrhus* 34; Pausanias 1.13.8; Polyaenus 8.68; Diodorus Siculus 15.83. See Schaps, p. 195; Barry, pp. 55–74. Plutarch tells the tale of women smuggling weapons in for otherwise unarmed men to use in a surprise attack. Plutarch, *Moralia* 246D-247A, 248E-249B (the latter are Iberian, not Greek women).

16   For a detailed discussion of this campaign, see most recently J. E. Lendon, *Song of Wrath. The Peloponnesian War Begins* (New York: Basic Books, 2010), chap. 7.

17   Thucydides 4.26.1–8.

18   Thucydides 4.28.4.; D. Kagan, *The Peloponnesian War* (New York: Viking, 2003), pp. 147–150; J. F. Lazenby, *The Peloponnesian War. A Military Study* (London and New York: Routledge, 2004), p. 77.

19   Thucydides 4.29.3.

20   Thucydides 4.29.1.

21   Thucydides 4.30.2.

22   Thucydides 4.30.3.

23   Thucydides 4.31.2.

24   Thucydides 4.31.2.

25   Thucydides 4.32.1. For a different reading of the text, see Gomme, *HCT* 3, 474. J. F. Lazenby, *The Spartan Army* (Warminster, Wilts: Aris and Philips, 1985), p. 119 notes how difficult it is to keep soldiers on alert for an invasion and gives an example from the Falklands war.

26   Thucydides 4.30.4.

27   Thucydides 4.30.4.

28   Thucydides 4.32.2. Kagan, *The Peloponnesian War*, p. 151; van Wees, *Greek Warfare*, pp. 62, 65; Lazenby, *The Peloponnesian War*, p. 76 who writes there could hardly have been fewer than 10,000 Athenian troops.

29   Thucydides 4.32.1.

30   Thucydides 4.32.4.

31   Thucydides 4.30.

32   See Thucydides 4.32.4; Kagan, *The Peloponnesian War*, p. 151.

33   Thucydides 4.35.3–4.

34   Thucydides 4.36.1.

35   Thucydides 4.36.2–3.

36   Thucydides 4.36.2. For *adokeitos* used of surprise attacks see Pritchett, vol. 2 (1974), p. 156 and S. Hornblower, *Commentary on Thucydides* (Oxford: The Clarendon Press, 1991), at 5.10.7, vol. 2, p. 448.

37   Thucydides 4.37.1.

38   Thucydides 4.37.2.

39   Thucydides 4.38.1.

40   Lazenby, *The Peloponnesian War*, p. 75.

41   Thucydides 4.40.

42   It has been argued, of course, that since the victory had been won by a *klope polemou*, i.e. a theft or cheat in war, it was therefore not a victory. See D. Whitehead, 'Klope Polemou. "Theft" in ancient Greek warfare', in E. L. Wheeler, *The Armies of Classical Greece* (Aldershot, Hants and Burlington, VT: Ashgate, 2007), p. 291. See also Roisman, *The General Demosthenes*, p. 40 who believes Demosthenes' contribution to the Athenian victory was overrated.

43   Thucydides 4.40.2 has one of the Spartans remark that it would be a very valuable arrow that could pick out the brave men. See the remarks of Lazenby, *The Peloponnesian War*, pp. 9, 78.

44   Von Wilamowitz, in his evaluation of the Battle of Sphacteria, shows the same Spartan mentality when he writes: 'Ist es nicht so recht ein Kampf von Soldaten höchsten Ranges mit einem Haufen Miliz? Für spartanische Manneszucht und Mannestugend ist Sphakteria kein geringeres Zeugnis als Thermopylae': U. von Wilamowitz-Moellendorf, 'Sphakteria', *Sitzungber. Der Preuss. Akad der Wiss* 17 (1921), p. 310. Euripides seems to be the exception in his time: see Euripides, *Hercules* 188–203 (420–421 BCE).

45   P. Stahl, *Thukydides, die Stellung des Menschen im geschichtlichen Prozess*, Zetemata 40 (Munich: Beck, 1966), pp. 152, 153 and n. 80. Quoted in Best, p. 26.

46   Kagan, *The Peloponnesian War*, p. 152. Roisman, *The General Demosthenes*, pp. 33–41; D. Leebaert, *To Dare to Conquer* (New York: Little, Brown, 2006), p. 56.

47   Best, p. 21 credits Demosthenes with having picked the type of troops used on Sphacteria.

48 Thucydides 3.94.3. For a more thorough treatment of this campaign, see Roisman, *The General Demosthenes*, pp. 25–6.

49 The criticism comes from Roisman, *The General Demosthenes*, p. 26, but see Best, p. 18. Cf. Ray, pp. 166–7.

50 Thucydides 3.107–108; Polyaenus 3.1.2 reports 300 men; Best, p. 19. On the topography, see N. G. L. Hammond, 'The campaigns in Amphilochia during the Archidamian war', *BSA* 37 (1936–7), pp. 128–40; J. E. Lendon, *Song of Wrath*, pp. 240–2. Ray, pp. 168–72, especially the diagram of the battle on p. 170.

51 Best, p. 18; Gomme, *HCT 2*, 420; Roisman, *The General Demosthenes*, pp. 29–30. J. F. Lazenby, *The Peloponnesian War*, p. 64 compares Demosthenes' ambush to Hannibal's at Trebbia.

52 See Roisman, *The General Demosthenes*, p. 29 who finds it no accident that the troops who lay in ambush were Acarnanians.

53 Thucydides 2.81.4–6. For another Acarnanian ambush in 426/5, see Thucydides 3.108.1; Roisman, *The General Demosthenes*, p. 29. On Stratus see Ray, pp. 157–9.

54 Thucydides 3.110.

55 Thucydides 3.107.2.

56 Thucydides 3.112; Roisman, *The General Demosthenes*, p. 29.

57 Thucydides 3.112; Roisman, *The General Demosthenes*, pp. 30–3. E.C. Woodcock, 'Demosthenes, son of Alcisthenes', *HSCPh* 39 (1928), pp. 93–108 also notices his use of surprise, ambush, reconnaissance, scouts and informants who knew the terrain.

58 Hammond, 'The campaigns in Amphilochia during the Archidamian war', p. 139; D. Kagan, *The Archidamian War* (Ithaca, NY: Cornell University Press, 1974), p. 214; Best, pp. 19ff; Heza, p. 236; but Roisman, *The General Demosthenes*, pp. 30–1 suggests that there is little in this story to suggest Demosthenes, as a general, was ahead of his time.

59 Thucydides 5.10 and see Wylie, 'Brasidas – great commander or whiz kid?', pp. 91–2. Best, p. 29. On Bradisas' role, see Thucydides 4.11.4–12; Diodorus Siculus 12.62.1–5.

60 J. E. Lendon, *Song of Wrath*, pp. 33.

61 Brasidas had 1,500 hired Thracians, 1,000 from Myrcinus and Chalcidice and others from Amphipolis and neighbouring tribes for a total of 4,000–5,000 in all. All Cleon had was some poorly armed retainers and 120 archers for light support although he had sent to Macedonia and Thrace for more skirmishers. See Ray, pp. 193–5 for the dispositions on each side.

62 Best, p. 33; see Losada, pp. 40–1.

63 Or so argues J. K. Anderson, 'Cleon's orders at Amphipolis', *JHS* 85 (1965), pp. 1–4; see also Wylie, 'Brasidas – great commander or whiz kid?', p. 439.

64 Thucydides sneers at 5.10.9. Cleon's lack of field experience in commanding hoplites may be responsible for the disaster to his army. In 'Cleon's orders at Amphipolis', Anderson suggests that his manoeuvre might have succeeded if it had been carried

out more quickly and he had programmed his senior officers beforehand.
D. Cartwright, *A Historical Commentary on Thucydides* (Ann Arbor: University of Michigan Press, 1997), p. 201 believes that being killed by a Myrcinian peltast highlighted the ignominy of Cleon's death because he was brought down by a 'light-armed soldier'.

65 As it was the entire Athenian left wing escaped almost unscathed. See Wylie, 'Brasidas – great commander or whiz kid?', p. 440.

66 Thucydides 7.27.1. H. W. Parke, *Greek Mercenary Soldiers from the Earliest Times to the Battle of Ipsus* (Chicago: Ares, 1981), p. 18.

67 Thucydides 7.43.6.

68 Epipolae was enclosed with walls some twelve miles (nineteen kilometres) long by the tyrant Dionysius I (c. 430–367 BCE). The southern wall, of which considerable remains exist, was probably often restored. Epipolae narrows to a ridge about 180 feet (55 m) wide at one point. Here are the ruins of the most imposing fortress to survive from the Greek period. On the attack, see Roisman, *The General Demosthenes*, pp. 52–70.

69 Examples are presented by Pritchett, vol. 2, p. 161, in table 3. Excluded are examples (Thucydides 2.90; 3.76) where the opposing fleets put out to sea at dawn, but in which the naval battle proper did not take place until somewhat later. Similarly, the Athenian disembarkment on Sphacteria (Thucydides 4.31) is not listed. See J. S. Morrison and J. F. Coates, *The Athenian Trireme: The History and Reconstruction of an Ancient Greek Warship* (Cambridge: Cambridge University Press, 1986), p. 75.

70 Xenophon, *Hellenica* 7.1.15–16 offers a reason for dawn attacks on fortified positions. It was the hour when the night guards were retiring but before the general body had risen and gotten under arms.

71 Thucydides 4.31.

72 Herodotus 8.85.

73 Thucydides 1.48.2.

74 Thucydides 4.42–44 relates the same story as Polyaenus 1.39.1 but without the double landing. On the Battle of Solygeia see J. B. Salmon, *Wealthy Corinth* (Oxford: The Clarendon Press 1984), pp. 318ff; J. Wiseman, *The Land of the Ancient Corinthians* (Goteborg: Paul Åstrom, 1978), pp. 56ff. The description of the battle is so vivid, it has been suggested that Thucydides himself participated in it (Gomme, *HCT* 3.494) but see R. S. Stroud, 'Thucydides and Corinth', *Chiron* 24 (1994), p. 286. Ray, pp. 177–9.

75 Thucydides 6.64–66. Diodorus Siculus 13.6.2–5 picks up the story as did Frontinus 3.6.6 and Polyaenus 1.40.5 who get the facts wrong and attribute it to Alcibiades. See Krentz, 'Deception in Archaic and Classical Greek warfare', pp. 167–8; Losada, pp. 116–17.

76 Plutarch, *Nicias* 16.3.

77 Thucydides 6.64.3 415/14. Krentz, 'Deception in Archaic and Classical Greek warfare', p. 168.

78 Thucydides 6.101.3 Syracuse 414 BCE.

79 Actually there is a gap between the last events in Thucydides and the beginning of Xenophon. See R. B. Strassler (ed.), *The Landmark Xenophon's Hellenika*, trans. by John Marincola, introduction by David Thomas (New York: Pantheon, 2009), p. 3.

80 Xenophon, *Hellenica* 1.1.2–3 Hellespont 411 BCE. According to Strassler, p. 3 scholars are still not exactly sure where this battle took place.

81 Xenophon, *Hellenica* 1.6.28–33. For more on Callicratidas, see J. Roisman, 'Kallikratidas. A Greek patriot?', *CJ* 83, 1 (Oct.–Nov. 1987), pp. 21–33.

82 Polyaenus 5.10.4. Krentz and Wheeler trans.

83 Xenophon, *Hellenica* 4.1.24 395. Paphlagonia.

84 Xenophon, *Hellenica* 5.1.21 Piraeus 387. John Marincola trans.

85 Frontinus 2.5.26; Cf. Diodorus Siculus 15.68; Polyaenus 2.3.9; Xenophon, *Hellenica* 7.1.16 (369 BCE).

86 G. T. Griffith, *Mercenaries in the Hellenistic World* (New York: AMS Press, 1977), pp. 194–6.

87 Plutarch, *Dion* 30, Syracuse 357/6.

88 Diodorus Siculus 13.72.2–4. Neither Xenophon nor any other ancient writer mentions this attack. Since it failed and had no material effect on the course of the war, its omission is not surprising. See D. Kagan, *The Fall of the Athenian Empire* (Ithaca, NY: Cornell University Press, 1987), p. 321. Jean Hatzfeld, *Alcibiade: Étude sur l'Histoire d'Athènes à la Fin du Ve Siècle* (Paris: Presses Universitaires de France, 1951), p. 316, n. 1 says this large undertaking should not be confused with the small raid Agis undertook in 410 mentioned by Xenophon 1.1.33–34. Numbers given by Diodorus Siculus often tend to be inflated.

89 Diodorus Siculus 13.113.1. On Dionysius' takeover of Syracuse, see M. I. Finley, *Ancient Sicily* (New York: Viking Press, 1969), vol. 1, pp. 74–87. On the reliability of Diodorus Siculus see L. J. Sanders, *Dionysius I of Syracuse and Greek Tyranny* (NY: Methuen, 1987), pp. 110–57 and L. Pearson, *The Greek Historians of the West* (Atlanta, GA: Scholars Press, 1987), pp. 157–91.

90 Polyaenus 2.2.6. On Clearchus and his use of peltasts, see Best, p. 52; Parke, *Greek Mercenary Soldiers*, p. 19.

91 Griffith, p. 4.

92 Losada, p. 43. In his comments on Brasidas' speech, Gomme, *HCT* 3, 644 notes: 'The Spartans were the chief upholders of the conventional hoplite battle.'

93 Pritchett, vol. 2, p. 156.

94 Best, p. 20.

95 Roisman, *The General Demosthenes*. See also the review of Roisman, *The General Demosthenes* by Simon Hornblower, in *CR* 44, 2 (1994), pp. 336–7.

96 Roisman, *The General Demosthenes*, pp. 52–70; see the review of Roisman, *The General Demosthenes* by Stewart Flory, in *JMH* 57, 4 (Oct. 1993), pp. 716–17.

97 When the attack on Epipolae failed, Demosthenes strongly advocated the siege to be relinquished immediately and for the Athenians to return home (Thucydides 7.47.3). Nicias ignored this advice and retreated overland. The tactics which the Syracusan cavalry and infantry used when pursuing the Athenians were similar to those Demosthenes had encountered at the start of his career and which he himself had learned to use so advantageously. He had no more chance than the Spartans on Sphacteria. Both Demosthenes and Nicias were killed (Thucydides 7.83.3–84).

98 Gomme, vol. 3, p. 654; cf. Best, pp. 34–5.

99 Wylie suggests he might have become another Sertorius: Wylie, 'Brasidas – great commander or whiz kid?', p. 441.

100 Sparta lacked the allied contributions available to Athens and was chronically short of money as well as manpower.

101 Pritchett, vol. 2, p. 156.

102 Thucydides 3.101.2. There were differences in how each community gave up hostages. Some joined the expedition and the hostages were a guarantee that they would not change sides and would remain faithful to the Spartans. Some communities were willing to allow safe passage of foreign troops without taking an active part in the war. This latter option was a regular feature of Greek warfare. For other examples: Herodotus 6.73, 85ff., 6.99; Thucydides 3.102.1; Diodorus Siculus 11.36.5ff. where the Ionians attacked the Persians without regard to the hostages. See M. Amit, 'Hostages in ancient Greece', in *Rivista di Filologia e di Istruzione Classica* 98 (1970), p. 135.

103 Adcock, 40ff; Gomme, *HCT* 1, 17ff; Pritchett, vol. 2, pp. 156, 174ff.; Losada, p. 114; Roisman, *The General Demosthenes*, p. 71; and Krentz, 'Deception in Archaic and Classical Greek warfare', pp. 201–32 have been the exceptions.

104 Aeneas Tacticus 22.16–18.

105 Thucydides 3.56.2, 65.1.

106 Aeneas Tacticus 17.2.

107 Thucydides 3.3.3.

108 Thucydides 4.104.1.

109 Thucydides 4.111.2, 112.1 and 113.1.

110 Clausewitz, p. 202 claims that craft, cleverness and cunning 'do not figure prominently in the history of war. Rarely do they stand out amid the welter of events and circumstances'.

111 Thucydides 5.11.1.

112 Plutarch, *Lysander* 18.

113 Thucydides 3.113.6.

Chapter 6: Night Attack

1 Pritchett, vol. 2, pp. 164–9 lists seventy-seven examples of night attacks, retreats or movements in the dark. He does not include night attacks recorded by Polybius because they are so numerous. Starting with the First Punic War, armies, particularly the Carthaginians, frequently marched and attacked by night. Why does Pritchett think this statistic is 'meaningless'? He considers the year 362 as a logical terminus because the Sacred Wars of the 350s transformed the whole aspect of the Greek world, including the military. See A. W. Pikard-Cambridge, in *CAH*, vol. 6 (1933), chap. 8, pp. 213–15. Bodies were no longer given up for burial; prisoners were killed; acts of ferocity were committed by all parties. As to night attacks, one section alone of Diodorus Siculus (16.38 from 352/1) tells of a successful attack by the Boeotians on the Phocians camp at Abai in which great numbers were slain (16.38.4) and a second night fray at Narya in which 200 were killed with their general, Mnaseas (16.38.7).

2 Of the seventy-seven examples listed by Pritchett in his three tables, twenty-two have to do with night attacks on a walled city or escape from a city through the ranks of the encircling besiegers: Pritchett, vol. 2, table 3 Surprise attacks, p. 161; vol. 2, table 4 Night attacks, Herodotus, p. 161; vol. 2, table 5 Night attacks in Thucydides, pp. 165–7. Of the twenty-two, only six were unsuccessful proving the effectiveness of the strategy. Pritchett includes every important military movement by night and he considers his tables complete. His table 6 (vol. 2, pp. 168–9) includes examples from the period 408–362 BC.

3 See Herodotus 1.76.4 where a fierce battle takes place with many on both sides fallen. They separated at nightfall without either side having won a victory.

4 H. Immerwahr, *Form and Thought in Herodotus* (Cleveland: Press of Western Reserve University, 1966), p. 240 who also believes Herodotus was uninterested in battle descriptions. This would explain why they were also short or lacking entirely. He argues that Herodotus was uninterested in military action per se, but used tactical situations to characterise people and events (ibid. chap. 6).

5 The one example I have left out is the early battle (585 BCE) between Alyattes of Lydia and Cyaxares of Media related in Herodotus 1.74.2. This battle was famous because of an eclipse which Thales had predicted. Herodotus says that day had been turned into night, and thus he calls it a kind of night battle. We, however, are discussing only those encounters where 'night' came at the usual time and was used as a cover for a manoeuvre. On the disagreements over this battle see Immerwahr, p. 242, n. 14; A. R. Burn, *Persia and the Greeks* (London: Arnold, 1962) p. 31, n. 16.

6 Herodotus 4.128.3. For a Roman example, see *BG* 4.32.

7 Herodotus 4.135–136 says that Scythians still beat them to the river because they were more familiar with the terrain.

8 See the case at Artemesium in Herodotus 8.11.3. Cf. Thucydides 4.134.2

(Laodoceum) and 4.129.5 (the Athenians against the Mendaeans of Pallene).

9   Herodotus 5.121. The Persian generals Daurises, Amorges and Sisimaces died along with Myrsus, son of Gyges. Heraclides of Mylassus is identified as son of Ibanollis of Lylasa.

10   Herodotus 6.45.1. The tribe supposedly lived between the Strymon and Mount Athos. Pritchett, vol. 2, p. 170, n. 32.

11   Polyaenus 2.2.10. 402–401 BCE.

12   Herodotus 6.16.2. Note a similar attack in the fourth century when the Spartans attack the Theban Cadmeia during the festival of the thesmophoria, but not at night. The unexpected and unprovoked nature of the attack, and the violation of the widely revered religious festival, plus the continued Spartan occupation of the Cadmeia, roused the Greeks against the Spartans.

13   Herodotus 7.217–19. See Herodotus, *The Landmark Herodotus: The Histories*, new trans. by Andrea L. Purvis, ed. by Robert B. Strassler, introduction by Rosalind Thomas (New York: Pantheon Books, 2007), p. 590 on the geography.

14   Herodotus 8.13.

15   Herodotus 8.71.1.

16   Herodotus 9.10.

17   Herodotus 9.47. For a discussion of this manoeuvre as a 'brilliant improvisational response to a mess . . .' see Ray, pp. 95–6.

18   Herodotus 9. 58.2–4. Aubrey de Selincourt trans.

19   Herodotus 9.118.

20   Herodotus 8.27–28; Cf. Pausanias 10.1.11 who supplies a moon which is necessary for the due effect.

21   Thucydides 7.43–44.

22   Thucydides 7.44.1: 'the only one that took place in this war between large armies'. See the comments of Dué and Ebbott, pp. 65–6.

23   Thucydides 7.43.1.

24   Thucydides 7.43.1–2. Epipolae was enclosed with walls some twelve miles (nineteen kilometres) long by the tyrant Dionysius I (c.430–367 BCE). The southern wall, of which considerable remains exist, was probably often restored. Epipolae narrows to a ridge about 180 feet (55 m) wide at one point. Here are the ruins of the most imposing fortress to survive from the Greek period. On the attack, see Roisman, *The General Demosthenes*, pp. 52–70. On the building of the counterwalls, see Ray, pp. 219–21.

25   Thucydides 7.43.2. Lazenby, *The Peloponnesian War*, p. 157.

26   Thucydides 7.43.2–3. The three camps were made up of the Syracusans, the other Sicilians and their allies.

27   Thucydides 7.43.5.

28   Thucydides 7.43.4–7; Lazenby, *The Peloponnesian War*, p. 158.

29   Thucydides 7.43.4–5; Kagan, *The Peloponnesian War*, p. 307.

30   Thucydides 7.43.6.

31   Kagan, *The Peloponnesian War*, p. 307

32   Thucydides 7.44.2.

33   Thucydides 7.44.4.

34   Thucydides 7.44.7.

35   Thucydides 7.44.1.

36   Thucydides 7.44.2–8; Lazenby, *The Peloponnesian War*, p. 158.

37   Kagan, *The Peloponnesian War*, p. 308

38   Thucydides 7.44.1.

39   Thucydides 7.43.5. There is huge problem in locating the defences during these
     events. There is a big divide between scholars over the placement of the Athenian
     wall. Peter Green writes: 'No topographical problem has puzzled students of
     the Syracuse campaign more than determining the location of Trogilus': Peter
     Green, *Armada from Athens* (Garden City, NY: Doubleday, 1970), pp. 196–7.
     Traditionally it has been put in the north, as does A. W. Gomme, A. Andrewes and
     J. K. Dover, *A Historical Commentary on Thucydides* (Oxford: Oxford University
     Press, 1956–81, 5 vols); John Lazenby agrees with them, locating Trogilos at
     the Santa Panagia cove. Cf. H. W. Parke, 'A note on the topography of Syracuse',
     JHS 64 (1944), pp. 100–2. R. B. Strassler (ed.), *The Landmark Thucydides: A
     Comprehensive Guide to the Peloponnesian War*, introduction by Victor Davis
     Hanson (New York, NY: Free Press, 1996), p. 8, on the other hand, follows Green,
     Armada from Athens, pp. 194–5 and locates Trogilus by the Lysimeleia marsh in the
     east. This is based on Thucydides, who writes that Trogilus is 'on the shortest line
     for their blockading wall, which was to extend from the Great Harbour to the sea at
     the other side'. Therefore the shortest route round the city walls between the Great
     Harbour and the outer sea will follow a route, not north but eastsoutheast, along
     the lines of the southern cliffs of Epipolae, reaching the coast a half mile (1 km) or
     so north of St Lucia in the little bay known as I Cappuccini. On the identification
     and the erosion there see Green, *Armada from Athens,* pp. 196–7.

40   Thucydides 3.112.4.

41   Lazenby, *The Peloponnesian War*, p. 159.

42   Thucydides 7.80.3; cf. 4. 125.1.

43   Thucydides 4.135. Rex Warner trans. For such scaling ladders, see Aeneas Tacticus
     36.1 and Whitehead's note. On Brasidas as a general, see Wylie, 'Brasidas – great
     commander or whiz kid?', pp. 423–43.

44   Thucydides 4.135. Gomme, *HCT* 3, 626. Cf. Pritchett, vol. 2, p. 163; Lazenby,
     The Peloponnesian War, p. 100.

45   Aristophanes, *Birds* 842.

46   N. Dunbar in her *Birds* commentary (*Aristophanes' Birds*, Oxford: The Clarendon
     Press, 1998) merely notes that Thucydides 4.135 seems to 'reflect a different system'
     from that in the *Birds*.

47 Thucydides 3.112.4. Cf. 1.51.5 (Kerkyra). On night fighting, see 2.4. On the role of light-armed troops in rough terrain, see 3.97–98.

48 Thucydides 1.116.

49 Thucydides 2.82. See Hornblower, *A Commentary on Thucydides*, vol. 1, p. 364.

50 Thucydides 3.22 . Hornblower, *A Commentary on Thucydides*, vol. 1, p. 406. There seems to be a religious aspect to the one-sandal motif; see Vidal-Naquet, *The Black Hunter*, p. 64 and W. Deonna, 'Les cornes gauches', *Revue des Etudes Anciennes* (1940), pp. 111–26.

51 Thucydides 3.22.

52 Thucydides 3.106.3. The sites of the towns of this area are uncertain. On the possible location of Amphilochian Argos, see Strassler, *The Landmark Thucydides*, p. 214. See also Hammond, 'The campaign of Amphilochia during the Archidamian war', pp. 129–40.

53 Thucydides 3.107.3; Losada, p. 42.

54 Thucydides 4.103.

55 The bridge seems to have been only lightly guarded. We are told nothing about the troops available to Eucles.

56 Thucydides 4.104.2.

57 On the topography around Amphipolis, see Grundy, *Thucydides and the History of His Age*, vol. 2, pp. 136–8; Thucydides 4.104.4.

58 Diodorus 12.68.3. The time frame for this event is telescoped. Henderson thinks it all happened in one winter's day. See Wylie, 'Brasidas – great commander or whiz kid?', p. 430 who finds this improbable.

59 Thucydides 4.103. One must take into consideration that the weather was stormy and even snowing at one point.

60 *The Landmark Thucydides*, trans. by Crawley.

61 Thucydides 4.125.1. Steup and Hornblower agree with W. Schmid that this passage by Schmid – 'Das Alter der Vorstellung vom panischen Schrecken', *RhM* 50 (1895), pp. 310–11 – conceals a Thucydidean polemic against popular superstition: Julius Steup, *Thukydides, erklärt von J. Classen* (Berlin: Weidemann, 1914); Simon Hornblower, *A Commentary on Thucydides*, vol. 2, Books IV–V.24 (Oxford: Oxford University Press, 1996). Cf. Pritchett, vol. 3, pp. 45, 148, 163. P. Borgeaud, *The Cult of Pan in Ancient Greece* (Chicago: University of Chicago Press, 1988), chap. 5 on panic. Cf. E. R. Dodds (ed.), *Euripides' Bacchae* (Oxford: The Clarendon Press, 1960), pp. 109–10; C. P. Segal, 'Gorgias and the psychology of the logos', *HSCPh* 66 (1962), p. 108, n. 50. On Perdiccas, see Grundy, *Thucydides and the History of His Age*, vol. 1, p. 371.

62 Cf. Thucydides 4.124–128. V. D. Hanson, 'Hoplite battle as ancient Greek warfare. When, where and why?', in H. van Wees, *War and Violence in Ancient Greece* (London: Duckworth, 2000), pp. 213 does not seem to take the barbarians as seriously as Brasidas did. He also leaves out the night attack.

63 Thucydides 4.120.2.

64 Thucydides 4.131.3. The generals offer generous terms to the people of Mende, perhaps recognising that most of them had not supported the revolt (ibid. 4.123). They were also anxious to keep Mende loyal so that they could concentrate on Scione.

65 Thucydides 5.58–59. Nemea is some four miles (six kilometres) southeast of Phlius, where the Spartan allies were assembling, and about thirteen miles (twenty kilometres) (as the crow flies) north of Argos. The plain is the Argive plain, north of the city of Argos. See Strassler, *The Landmark Thucydides*, p. 338, n. 5.58.5a. Anderson, *Military Theory and Practice*, p. 67 believes Agis was trying to trap the Argives between three columns marching separately at night.

66 Thucydides 6.7.2. Orneae is some twelve miles (nineteen kilometres) north of Argos. It was an ally of Argos in 418 (see Thucydides 5.67) and Sparta had clearly retained control of it since Mantinea.

67 Thucydides 7.73.2.

68 Thucydides 7.74.1.

69 Thucydides 7.74.2.

70 Thucydides 3.91.3. Oropus is on the northern coast of Attica, opposite Euboea.

71 Thucydides 3.30.3, Rex Warner trans.

72 Thucydides 5.115.4, Rex Warner trans.

73 Thucydides 4.110.1, Rex Warner trans. On the location see Hornblower, *A Commentary on Thucydides*, vol. 1, 1534–35. B. D. Merritt, 'Scione, Mende and Torone', *AJA* 27 (1923), pp. 447–60. The site of Torone has been excavated by a joint Greek and Australian team led by A. Cambitoglu, J. K. Papadopoulos and O. Tudor (eds), *Torone I: The Excavations of 1975, 1976 and 1978* (Athens: He en Athenais Archaiologik e Hetaireia, 2001), 3 vols. See also A. S. Henry, *Torone, The Literary, Documentary and Epigraphical Testimonia* (Athens: Archaeological Society at Athens, 2004); W. R. Connor, *Thucydides* (Princeton: Princeton University Press, 1984), p. 127, n. 43 sees a general parallel here with Pylos which was also a dawn operation. Losada, p. 44.

74 See Wylie, 'Brasidas – great commander or whiz kid?', p. 85; Best, p. 31.

75 Thucydides 4.110–116.

76 Thucydides 2.2.1. On the motives of the group letting in the Thebans, see Losada, vol. 1, p. 107 4n.

77 Thucydides 7.28.2.

78 Thucydides 7.6.2–4.

79 Thucydides 8.35.4.

80 Thucydides 5.56.4.

81 Immerwahr, chap. 4 on the *apaté* motif.

82 Aeneas Tacticus 10.25–26; 22.1–8. He is more concerned with the danger from within, but such operations depended on the use of small units and light-armed

troops for the attack.

83   Thucydides 2.2.1; Aeneas Tacticus 2.3.

84   Thucydides 4.67.2–4.

85   Thucydides 4.103.

86   Thucydides 4.110–113.2.

87   Plutarch, *Alcibiades* 30.2.

88   Xenophon, *Hellenica* 1.3.20; Diodorus Siculus 13.67.1; Plutarch, *Alcibiades* 31.3.

89   Thucydides 4.103.1–2.

90   Thucydides 4.103.5.

91   Thucydides 2.5.2–3.

92   On the lack of guards, see Thucydides 2.2.3. The weather was also a factor in the ultimate failure of the betrayal. It delayed the rest of the Thebans who were supposed to arrive while it was still night, Thucydides 2.5.1–3.

Chapter 7: Surprise Landings, and Assault by Sea

1   Ducrey claims ancient navies reluctantly sailed in the dark, but they dared not fight in the dark. A large-scale *nuktomachia*, however, occurred at Epipolai.

2   B. Strauss, *The Battle of Salamis. The Naval Encounter that Saved Greece – and Western Civilization* (New York: Simon and Schuster, 2004), p. 15.

3   Strauss, *The Battle of Salamis*, p. 21.

4   Herodotus 6.29; Ray, pp. 44–5.

5   Strauss, *The Battle of Salamis*, pp. 193–4.

6   P. Green, *The Greco-Persian Wars* (Berkeley: University of California Press, 1996), p. 180.

7   The figure of 400 Persians on Psattaleia comes from Pausanias 1.36.2. See Burn, *Persia and the Greeks*, p. 453.

8   Herodotus 8.76. J. F. Lazenby, *The Defence of Greece, 490–479* (Warminster, Wilts: Aris and Phillips, 1993), pp. 181–3 doubts the Persians could have entered the channel at night without the Greeks knowing about it. If they had gotten that close, they should have attacked at night before the Greeks could deploy or man their fleet, i.e. they should have done the same thing the Spartans did to the Athenians at Aegospotami (see chap. 8). Certainly the slightest leak for intelligence could turn this operation into a death trap.

9   On Psatteleia, see G. B. Grundy, *The Great Persian War and its Preliminaries* (London: John Murray, 1901), pp. 392–3; W. W. How and J. Wells, *A Commentary on Herodotus* (Oxford: The Clarendon Press, 1968, reprinted edn), vol 2, pp. 382–4; Burn, *Persia and the Greeks*, pp. 455–7; Lazenby, *The Defence of Greece*, pp. 181–2.

10   Herodotus 8.107.1.

11   Thucydides 2.33, who describes the Cranians as 'deceitful'. Ray, p. 154.

12　Thucydides 3.90; Diodorus Siculus 12.54.4–5 claims that Messana lost 1,000 hoplites in the fight at Mylae and that another 600 gave up. This figure is probably inflated since they had nearby refuge and were not pursued by mounted troops: Ray, pp. 163–4.

13　Thucydides 3.103.

14　Thucydides 3.91.

15　Thucydides 2.83.1. The two colleagues were Isocrates and Agatharcidas.

16　Thucydides 2.83.2.

17　Thucydides 2.83.3.

18　Thucydides 2.83.3.

19　Thucydides 2.83.5.

20　Thucydides 2.84.2.

21　Thucydides 2.84.2.

22　Thucydides 2.84.3.

23　Thucydides 2.84.4.

24　The pivot on the gunwale that supports and guides an oar, and provides a fulcrum for rowing; an oarlock (US): Thucydides 2.93.2.

25　See Leebaert, p. 55.

26　Thucydides 2.94.3 on the condition of the ships. On the one hand it is important to regularly dry out trireme hulls to maintain their speed and performance, but excessive dryness would be leaky until the hulls absorbed enough water for the planks to swell and close the joints between them. See Strassler, *Landmark Thucydides*, appendix G on trireme warfare.

27　Thucydides 2.93.1–4, Landmark edn ed. by Strassler, trans. by Crawley; A. J. Beattie, 'Nisaea and Megara', *RhM* 163 (1960), pp. 21–43.

28　For pelting with the rooftiles, see Thucydides 3.74.3. Hornblower, *A Commentary on Thucydides*, vol. 1, p. 472. On women in warfare, see P. Loman, 'No woman, no war: Women's participation in ancient Greek warfare', *G&R* 51, 1 (2004), pp. 34–54; on fighting with roof tiles, see Barry, pp. 55–74.

29　Thucydides 3.81.1, 427, escape of the fleet. According to Hornblower, *A Commentary on Thucydides*, vol 1, p. 476 at some periods in antiquity the channel between Leucas and the mainland was navigable. Today there is a canal between Leucas and the mainland.

30　Thucydides 4.26.6.

31　Thucydides 4.31–32.

32　Thucydides 4.42.4.

33　See Simon Hornblower, *The Greek World 479–323* (New York: Routledge, 1983), p. 121; Stroud, p. 287 seeing the episode from the Corinthian point of view, notes how much Thucydides seems to know about Corinthian plans and movements. On military security generally see Hornblower, *A Commentary on Thucydides*, vol. 3, p. 91 citing Hermocrates at 6.72.5 for awareness of the problem. J. P. Vernant, *Myth and Society in Ancient Greece* (New York: Zone Books, 1988), p. 37 denies the existence of a concept of military security in ancient Greek strategy.

34   Thucydides 4.66.3. J. E. Lendon, *Song of Wrath*, pp. 1–5 begins his book with this incident.

35   Gomme, *HCT 3*, 532; Kagan, *The Archidamian War*, p. 273; A.J. Holladay, 'Athenian strategy in the Archidamian war', *Historia* 27 (1978), p. 417; Roisman, *The General Demosthenes*, p. 42.

36   On the location of Minoa see T. Spratt, 'The supposed situation of Minoa and Nisaea', *Journal of the Royal Geographical Society of London* 8 (1838), pp. 205–9; A. G. Laird, 'Nisaea and Minoa', *CP* 29, 2 (April 1934), pp. 89–100; and Beattie, pp. 21–43.

37   Every night for some time they had been carefully preparing for opening of the gates by regularly assuming the guise of pirates and taking a sculling boat, drawn on a cart, through the ditch and down to the sea, where they would put out. Now the cart was already at the gates, which had been opened in the usual way for the boat. When the Athenians, by whom this had been arranged, saw it, they ran at top speed from the ambush in order to reach the gates before they were shut again, and while the cart was still there to prevent the gates being closed.

38   For the literature on this episode, see N. Geske, *Nicias und das Volk von Athen im Archidamischen Krieg* (Stuttgart: Steiner, 2005), n. 526.

39   Thucydides 6.65.2.

40   Thucydides 7.22.

41   Thucydides 7.22–23.

42   Thucydides 8.41.1.

43   Thucydides 8.42.3.

44   Thucydides 8.41–42.

45   Thucydides 8.101.

46   Thucydides 8.102.

47   Polyaenus 1.48.1. Krentz and Wheeler trans. This incident is not reported by any other extant historian. Conon was admiral in each of the three years 407–405. In 406 he was defeated by the Spartans and blockaded in Mytilene. He was rescued following the Athenian victory at Arginusae (August 406). But, upon the defeat of Athens' fleet at Aegospotami (405), he fled to Cyprus. On the outbreak of the war between Sparta and the Persians (400), Conon obtained joint command, with Pharnabazus, of a Persian fleet. It was in this capacity that he triumphed six years later at Cnidus. Imprisoned by the Persians when he was on an embassy from Athens to the Persian court to counteract the intrigues of Sparta, Conon probably died in Cyprus.

48   Xenophon, *Hellenica* 5.1.27.

49   Xenophon, *Hellenica* 5.1.8. This passage suggests they angled their oars into the water rather than striking the water at right angles so as to make less noise. Xenophon does not say so but perhaps he was also aware that splashes and foam at sea can give

off a visible phosphorescent light. This chapter uniquely mentions some important details about ancient naval military practices: van Wees, *Greek Warfare*, p. 224.

50   Xenophon, *Hellenica* 5.1.9.

51   Polyaenus 3.11.9.

52   Xenophon, *Hellenica* 5.1.10.

53   Polyaenus 5.38.

54   Entries in Polyaenus are notoriously hard to date. Perhaps this Diotimus is the fifth-century admiral mentioned by Thucydides 1. 45.

55   Polyaenus 5.22.2.

56   The crew of a trireme were arranged in three rows. The lowest tier consisted of twenty-seven oars per side and was called *thalamites*; the middle tier also had twenty-seven oars per side and was called *zeugites*; and the oars on the top were called *thranites*.

57   Polyaenus 5.22.4.

58   Polyaenus 1.40.2. See also Frontinus 3.11.3; Diodorus Siculus 13.66–67; Plutarch, *Alcibiades* 31.

59   Polyaenus 5.39.

60   Thucydides 7.29.3; 7.30.4.

61   Aeneas Tacticus 23.6–11; Losada, p. 102.

62   Diodorus Siculus 13.67.1–3; Plutarch, *Alcibiades* 31.1–3.

63   Van Wees, *Greek Warfare*, p. 224.

64   Van Wees, *Greek Warfare*, p. 224.

65   The nearest market was several miles away and 95 per cent of the captured ships were severely undermanned or unmanned; Xenophon, *Hellenica* 2.1.22–8. Van Wees, *Greek Warfare*, p. 224.

66   Vidal-Naquet, *The Black Hunter*, p. 93.

67   Van Wees, *Greek Warfare*, p. 224.

68   Van Wees, *Greek Warfare*, p. 224.

Chapter 8: The Age of Light-Armed

1   On Aegospotami, see Xenophon, *Hellenica* 2.1.22–30; Diodorus Siculus 13.105–106; Plutarch, *Lysander* 10–11; *Alcibiades* 36–37; Frontinus 2.1.18; Polyaenus 1.45.2; Pausanias 9.32.9; Cornelius Nepos, *On Great Generals. On Historians*, trans. by J. C. Rolfe (Cambridge, MA: Harvard University Press, 1929), p. 8. For modern commentaries, see B. S. Strauss, 'Aegospotami re-examined', *AJPh* 104 (1983), pp. 124–35; Kagan, *The Fall of the Athenian Empire*, pp. 386–94.

2   Ducrey, *Warfare in Ancient Greece*, p. 119.

3   P. Baker, 'Les mercenaires', in F. Prost (ed.), *Armées et Societies de la Grèce Classique* (Paris: Ed. Errance, 1999), pp. 240–55. Ducrey, *Warfare in Ancient Greece*, p. 120.

4   Ducrey, *Warfare in Ancient Greece*, p. 119. This is not to imply that Greeks only

served as mercenaries in large numbers beginning in the fourth century. See N. Luraghi, 'Traders, pirates, warriors: The proto-history of Greek mercenary soldiers in the eastern Mediterranean', *Phoenix* 60 (2006), pp. 21–47 who shows that Greek mercenary soldiers served for a number of powers in the southeastern Mediterranean during most of the Archaic Age.

5   Best, p. 115.

6   Thucydides 4.94.1 states that no organised unit of light-armed (*psiloi*) existed in Athens at the time of the Battle of Delium (424 BCE). In 411, however, a Spartan attack on Athens was repulsed by horsemen, hoplites, light-armed men (*psiloi*) and archers (Thucydides 8.71.2). That the Athenians had developed light-armed soldiers in the interim is confirmed by Xenophon, who reports that a Spartan attack on the walls of Athens was repulsed and light-armed troops killed a number of the Spartans rearguard: Xenophon, *Hellenica* 1.1.33–34; Ducrey, *Warfare in Ancient Greece*, p. 108; Best, p. 38.

7   These have been treated in a superb study by Losada. For an example from 395 in Asia of an ambush laid along the line of march, see Xenophon, *Hellenica* 3.4.20–24; Plutarch, *Agesilaus* 1.28–32. For a different version, see *Hellenica Oxyrhynchia* 6.4–6. Cf. Diodorus Siculus 14.80. On the historicity of the event, see Anderson, *Military Theory and Practice*, p. 302, n. 27.

8   The standard work on peltasts is still Best. For illustrations of peltasts on Greek ceramics and in the archaeological record, see Best (ibid.) after p. 6. They were named after the shield, the *pelte*, generally designed in the shape of a crescent moon. It was lightweight, with a wooden frame and no form of reinforcement either in the middle or around the edge. It was covered with a goat or sheep skin and sometimes decorated with an apotropaic device or identifying sign (a nose, a mouth, an eye, etc.). There is a tendency to confuse the light-armed with peltasts. Not every peltast is a light-armed skirmisher. The peltasts who served in the Peloponnesian war were always described as skirmishers, fighting at a distance with their javelins, but this applies only to Greek peltasts. Thracian peltasts are recorded as being able to fight to a limited degree in close combat. The Thracian peltasts Xenophon encountered in Asia could fall upon men crossing a river in addition to their usual skirmishing mode of fighting: Xenophon, *Anabasis* 6.3. Thucydides records Thracians fending off Theban cavalry by charging them (Thucydides 7.30). In the early second century BCE élite Macedonian pikemen were called peltasts (or to Latin authors like Livy, *caetrati*) on account of their relatively small shields. But these troops had no skirmishing capability whatsoever when massed in a pike phalanx.

9   Arrian's *Tactica* divides soldiers into three categories: (1) the heavily-armed hoplites; (2) the light-armed soldiers equipped with a bow, a javelin or a sling, but without cuirass, shield or greaves, used as skirmishers; (3) the peltasts who fell midway between the two with their shields and offensive weaponry who could fight to a

limited degree in close combat: Arrian, 'Ars tactica', in *L'arte Tattica: Trattato di Tecnica Militare: Testo Greco a Fronte, Lucio Flavio Arriano; a Cura di Antonio Sestili* (Roma: Aracne, 2011), p. 3; Best, pp. 3–4; Ducrey, pp. 109–10.

10 The Thracians had always used this style of fighting. There is evidence that as early as the sixth century in Athens Peisistratos used Thracian mercenaries: Best, p. 5. Best (ibid. p. 40) argues that the excessively high cost of recruiting Thracian mercenaries led Athens to set up a force of its own peltasts for overseas expeditions.

11 Best, p. 3; Ducrey, *Warfare in Ancient Greece*, p. 110; Herodotus 7.75 describes the Thracian peltasts: 'The Thracians who marched with the army wore fox-skin caps, and tunics with colorful *zeiras* thrown over them; on their feet and shins they wore fawn-skin boots. They carried javelins, small light shields, and small daggers': Herodotus, *The Landmark Herodotus*, trans. by Andrea Purvis; Anderson, *Military Theory and Practice*, p. 113 quotes Xenophon's *Anabasis* 5.2.29 which shows peltasts, hidden on a scrub-covered hill, flashing their shields in the sunlight to make it appear that they were a much larger force in ambush.

12 At least up to the time of Delium. See Thucydides 4.94; Grundy, *Thucydides and the History of His Age*, vol 1, p. 275. The importance of light-armed troops would become apparent in the Corinthian war. By that time Athens had its own light-armed force, not just mercenaries. Citizens in Athens served as light-armed soldiers as early as the end of the fifth century, and although there is debate over which troops were mercenaries and which native, it is not in dispute that they served well and that their style of fighting was becoming more important: Best, pp. 93–7. Some Attic orators complained that Athens relied almost exclusively on mercenaries in the fourth century, but this is not true. Athenian citizens served in many campaigns in the second and third quarters of the fourth century, and they adapted by training a new type of soldier.

13 S. Yalichev, *Mercenaries in the Ancient World* (London: Constable, 1997), p. 118.

14 Cornelius Nepos, *Iphicrates* 1; Diodorus Siculus 15.44. There is a debate over whether Iphicrates' reformed troops were hoplites or indeed real peltasts. Scholars have sometimes even rejected both Nepos and Diodorus. When we see a soldier carrying a *pelta*, does it mean he is a light-armed skirmisher (i.e. fighting at a distance with their javelins) or lighter-armed hoplites fighting at close range? Some prefer to call these new troops Iphicratean hoplites rather than peltasts. See Parke, *Greek Mercenary Soldiers*, pp. 79–81.

15 On the debate over the reforms of Iphicrates and Chabrias, see Best, pp. 102–10. All theories concerning the reform are based on the information provided by Diodorus Siculus 15.44.2–4 and Cornelius Nepos, *Iphicrates* 11.1.3–4. According to Diodorus Siculus, he lengthened the spear by 50 per cent; according to Nepos he doubled it. Best, p. 13 argues that the Greeks discovered the usefulness of this type of warfare when setting up colonies in Thrace, long before peltasts started to appear on Greek vases (c. 550 BCE). The majority of the peltasts were probably recruited

from the Greek states in the Hellespontine region. Cf. Parke, *Greek Mercenary Soldiers*, p. 80; Lippelt, p. 66.

16   Best, p. 85 argues that Iphicrates did not change hoplites into peltasts (as suggested by Diodorus Siculus and Cornelius Nepos) but instead armed a new type of peltast based on his experiences in Thrace (ibid. p. 102). The fact that both Diodorus Siculus and Nepos had never heard of peltasts before Iphicrates' reforms is no reason to doubt the reforms themselves (ibid. p. 104).

17   Grundy, *Thucydides and the History of His Age*, vol 1, p. 276. N. Bagnall, *The Peloponnesian War. Athens, Sparta and the Struggle for Greece* (New York: St Martin's Press, 2004), p. 141; H.D. Westlake, *Individuals in Thucydides* (London: Cambridge University Press, 1968), pp. 138–9.

18   J. Roth, 'War', in *CHGRW*, vol. 1, p. 391; on cavalry see R. E. Gaebel, *Cavalry Operations in the Ancient Greek World* (Norman, OK: University of Oklahoma Press, 2003), p. 123 who says the fact that the Greeks of this period made more use of peltasts than cavalry to increase the versatility of their armies could be justified on economic grounds as well as by the fact that they were effective.

19   Vidal-Naquet, *The Black Hunter*, p. 94 points out that Athens did not have light-armed troops trained for combat before 424, citing Thucydides 4.94. On archers see A. Plassart, pp. 151–213. During the Sicilian expedition the slingers were Rhodian, the archers were Cretan and the light-armed soldiers were Megarians; see Thucydides 6.43. Specialists in military affairs made their appearance: see, for example, the sophists Euthydemus and Dionysodorus who turn up in the dialogues of Plato and Aristotle: Vidal-Naquet, *The Black Hunter*, p. 103, n. 64.

20   As Chaniotis points out, regional studies of the context of mercenary service have led to different conclusions: A. Chaniotis, *War in the Hellenistic World* (Oxford: Blackwell, 2005), p. 80; M. Launey, *Recherches sur les Armées Hellénistiques* (Paris: de Boccard, 1987), pp. 104–615. The phenomenon is complex and local peculiarities abound.

21   See Luraghi, pp. 21–47. On mercenaries at Sparta, see W. Lengauer, *Greek Commanders in the 5th and 4th Centuries BC* (Warsaw: Wydawnictwa Uniwersytetu Warszawskiego, 1979), p. 80.

22   Chaniotis, *War in the Hellenistic World*, pp. 81–2.

23   Pritchett, vol. 2, p. 103.

24   Kinzl, p. 483.

25   In warfare, the *pilos* cap was a felt hat often worn by the peltast light infantry. The *pilos* cap was sometimes worn under the helmet by hoplites, but usually they preferred not to use a helmet along with the cap before the fifth century for reasons of mobility. The *pilos* helmet was made in the same shape as the original cap. It probably originated from Laconia and was made from bronze. The *pilos* helmet was extensively adopted by the Spartan army in the fifth century BCE and worn by them until the end of the Classical era. This helmet presumably

provided better vision and hearing for the phalanx. An example of the conical *pilos* helmet can be seen in the helmet in the Carapanos Collection in the National Museum of Athens, which is presumably from Dodona. It is mentioned in Arrian, '*Ars tactica*' 3.5.

26   N. Sekunda, *The Ancient Greeks, Armies of Classical Greece 5th and 4th Centuries* BC (London: Osprey, 1986), p. 60.

27   Xenophon, *The Art of Horsemanship*, trans. by M. H. Morgan (London: Allen, 2004), 9.7; Sekunda, *The Ancient Greeks*, p. 53. It seems that his recommendation was implemented very soon afterwards. At the Battle of Mantinea, Diodorus Siculus 15.85.4 tells us that the Athenian cavalry on the left flank were defeated by their Theban opponents, not because of inferior mounts or horsemanship but because the greater numbers, better equipment and better tactical skill of the *psiloi* fighting for the Thebans. This implies that the *psiloi* (or *hamippoi*) were already present fighting alongside the Athenian cavalry. On *psiloi* see Thucydides 5.57.2. Cf. Sekunda, *The Ancient Greeks*, p. 53; L. J. Worley, *Hippeis: The Cavalry of Ancient Greece* (Boulder and Oxford: Westview Press, 1994), p. 62; Gaebel, p. 140.

28   Thucydides 5.57.2.

29   Sekunda, *The Ancient Greeks*, p. 53.

30   Sekunda, *The Ancient Greeks*, p. 53.

31   Pritchett, vol. 2, pp. 59–116 on *condottieri* and mercenaries. The eight generals studied by Pritchett are Iphicrates of Athens, Chabrias of Athens, Chares of Athens, Charidemos of Oreos, Agesilaus of Sparta, Pammenes of Thebes, Diopeithes of Athens and Timoleon of Corinth.

32   One of the alleged changes was a divorce between political and military leadership that caused writers to complain about 'freebooters' and 'banditti chieftains' determining the foreign policy of Athens. Attic orators and many a modern commentator have believed that a general's loyalty to his troops now transcended his fidelity to the state. See, for example, Isocrates 8, *On the Peace* 54–55; Plutarch, *Phocion* 7.3. The Italian word *condottieri* was used for leaders of such mercenary groups, as H. R. Hall, in *CAH*, vol. 6 (1933), p. 151. See Pritchett, vol. 2, pp. 60–1; Pritchett considers Demosthenes worthless as a source on the subject of mercenaries: ibid. pp. 105–7; cf. Griffith, p. 11; A. H. M. Jones, *Athenian Democracy* (Oxford: Blackwell, 1957), p. 128 is among the modern scholars who doubted the loyalty of fourth-century generals.

33   This is a trait that Thucydides seems to admire. See Lengauer, pp. 47, 93–4, 118.

34   Pritchett, vol. 2, p. 97. Pritchett's survey of eight such generals shows, however, that there is little evidence to support the generalisation that the loyalty of fourth-century generals to their city-states was questionable.

35   The Athenians, for one, actively supported the activities of men such as Chares and Charidemos and they were not convicted of anything on their return. We learn from various passages in Demosthenes, especially from the oration *On the*

Chersonese, how the Athenian generals of this period, sent out with inadequate supplies, were driven to commit acts of plunder and violence to maintain their armaments. Demosthenes himself sums up the situation: 'For how else do you suppose that a man who has received nothing from you and has nothing of his own to pay withal can maintain his troops?': Pritchett, vol. 2, p. 101.

36 Polyaenus 3.9.30 on Iphicrates; 31, 35, 36, 27, 51, 59; Polyaenus 3.10.1 on Timotheos, 5, 9, 10, 11, 14. Polyaenus 3.11.5, 8, 9. 10 on Chabrias; Polyaenus 3.14 on Charidemos. See Parke, *Greek Mercenary Soldiers*, p. 78 on putting too much faith in the 'stratagems' attributed to Iphicrates.

37 Polyaenus 6.1.1–7. Stratagems by which generals secured money for their troops are also touched upon in pseudo-Aristotle: Aristotle, *Oeconomicus* 2.2.5, 8, 10, 14, 15, 16, 20, 24, 25. On Jason of Pherae and his army see J. E. Lendon, *Soldiers and Ghosts*, pp. 98–102.

38 US Army Field Manual (hereafter FM) 7–70, *Light Infantry Platoon/Squad* (Washington, DC: Department of the Army, 1986), p. iv.

39 Polyaenus 3.9.32.

40 FM 7–70 p. iv.

41 See especially J. E. Lendon, 'Xenophon and the alternative to realist foreign policy: "Cyropaedia" 3.1.14–31', *JHS* 126 (2006), pp. 82–98 who points out that even the characters in the work, Persians, Assyrians, etc., think and act like Greeks (ibid. pp. 82–3). Cf. S.W. Hirsch, *The Friendship of the Barbarians* (Hanover, NH: University Press of New England, 1985), pp. 61–97.

42 Xenophon, *Cyropaedia* 5.4.1–5.

43 Xenophon, *Cyropaedia* 6.3.30.

44 Polyaenus 2.37 who may be describing the Tissamenus from Herodotus 9.33–35 and his five great victories. Birds hovering over ridge disclosed ambush. The same story appears in Frontinus 1.2.7 who confuses Aemilius Papus, consul of 282 and 278 BC, with Aemilius Paulus – as does Pliny the Elder, *Natural History* 3.138.

45 Polyaenus 2.2.8, Krentz and Wheeler trans. This event only appears in Polyaenus.

46 Polyaenus 2.2.6, 8 and 10. See Best, pp. 52–3 and Walbank, p. 95.

47 Xenophon, *Anabasis* 7.2.22 says that the Thynoi, another Thracian tribe, were the most warlike of all men – by night. Nocturnal surprise attacks were, in fact, a favourite tactic of other Thracian tribes. We heard of these tactics in Herodotus when he described how Mardonius' army suffered heavy losses during such an attack by the Thracian Brygians in 492: Herodotus 6.45.1; Best, p. 53; Xenophon, *Anabasis* 7.2.22. Cf. 4.14–19; Best, p. 53.

48 Polyaenus 2.2.6.

49 Polyaenus 2.2.8; Best, pp. 53–4.

50 Xenophon admired him as man *aner kai polemikos kai filopolemos esxatos*. Xenophon, *Anabasis* 2.6.1–15; Best, p. 54; Parke, *Greek Mercenary Soldiers*, pp. 97–9.

51 Isocrates 4, *Panegyrikos* 115.

52 Plutarch, *Lycurgus* 22.5; Moralia 228F.

53 Xenophon, *Hellenica* 3.5.17–21.

54 Lechaeum was the northwest port of Corinth on the Corinthian Gulf. Long Walls were built from Corinth c.450 BCE. During the Corinthian war, Spartans were admitted to the long walls by treachery. Lechaeum was captured and Corinthian exiles used as a base for raids on the rest of Corinthian territory. See J. B. Salmon, p. 178; Parke, *Greek Mercenary Soldiers*, pp. 53–4.

55 The men of Amyclae always returned home for the festival of the Hyacinthia, whether on active service or not. So Agesilaus left behind all the Amyclaeans serving in any part of his army at Lechaeum. The general in command of the garrison there had posted the garrison troops of the allies to guard the walls during his absence, and put himself at the head of his division of heavy infantry with that of the cavalry, and led the Amyclaeans past the walls of Corinth. When he arrived at a point within three miles (five kilometres) or so of Sicyon, the polemarch turned back himself in the direction of Lechaeum with his heavy infantry regiment, 600 strong, giving orders to the cavalry commandant to escort the Amyclaeans with his division as far as they required, and then to turn and overtake him. The Lacedaemonians were not ignorant of the large number of light troops and heavy infantry inside Corinth, but because of their former successes they arrogantly presumed that no one would attack them.

56 Xenophon, *Hellenica* 4.5.14. John Marincola trans.

57 Xenophon, *Hellenica* 4.5.11ff. Ducrey, *Warfare in Ancient Greece*, p. 124; Anderson, *Military Theory and Practice*, pp. 124–5; J. E. Lendon, *Soldiers and Ghosts*, pp. 93–4.

58 Xenophon, *Hellenica* 4.5.11–17. John Marincola trans. Lazenby, *The Spartan Army*, pp. 148–9.

59 Polyaenus 3.9.24.

60 Xenophon, *Hellenica* 4.5.19.

61 J. B. Bury and Russell Meiggs, *A History of Greece to the Death of Alexander the Great* (New York: St Martin's Press, 1975, 4th edn), p. 342; Best, p. 88.

62 Parke, *Greek Mercenary Soldiers*, p. 54; Best, p. 89.

63 Frontinus 2.1.6. For attacks against encamped forces at mealtime, see ibid. 2.1.5.

64 On Dercylidas as a mastery of trickery, see Xenophon, *Hellenica* 3.1.8. Maricola trans. p. 81 note on 3.1.8.

65 Xenophon, *Hellenica* 4.8.35–39. Frontinus 2.5.42 relates the same incident. Parke, *Greek Mercenary Soldiers*, p. 55.

66 The soldiers in the middle of the column were probably Anaxibius' mercenaries. Sparta had given him enough money to pay for 1,000 mercenaries but Xenophon is sketchy on the numbers Xenophon, *Hellenica* 4.8.32–33; 8.35; See Best, pp. 90–1. Cf. Parke, *Greek Mercenary Soldiers*, p. 55.

67 As Xenophon had also done. See Parke, *Greek Mercenary Soldiers*, pp. 55–6;

Best, p. 92.

68   Diodorus 14.92.2. On Chabrias, see Parke, *Greek Mercenary Soldiers*, pp. 56–7.

69   Parke, *Greek Mercenary Soldiers*, p. 56, n. 4; Best, p. 92.

70   Grundy, *Thucydides and the History of His Age*, vol 1, p. 273.

71   Best, p. 101. For the traditional arrangement of peltasts and their tactics, see Xenophon, *Hellenica* 7.4.22 and Plutarch, *Phocion* 12.13; Demosthenes 9.57.

72   From the scant evidence Xenophon gives, these troops were organised in *taxeis* (sing. *taxis*), roughly translatable as battalions. See Lee, pp. 87, 95. For ease of marching a manoeuvre, the large peltast *taxeis* must have been broken down into smaller units and bands, perhaps along ethnic lines. Xenophon, *Hellenica* 6.4.5 writes of peltasts and archers organised in *lochoi*, suggesting the existence of smaller tactical units for light infantry. C. Tuplin (ed.), *Xenophon and his World* (Stuttgart: Steiner, 2004), pp. 22–3 remarks that Xenophon's use of *taxis* to describe *ad hoc* tactical groupings makes matters fuzzier. His varied use of the term *taxis* renders it impossible to retrieve the details of non-hoplite organisation.

73   Lee, esp. table 2.

74   Lee, pp. 153–5. See the night rendezvous to avoid an ambush in Xenophon, *Anabasis* 3–4.336–37.

75   Those who have concluded that peltasts could be used only against barbarians, however, are incorrect, as argued by Lippelt, p. 64, n. 2: 'Die Aufstellung von Leichtbewaffneten vor der Phalanx (Xenophon, *Anabasis* 4.8.15) und zwischen den Lochen (ibid. 5.4.12) sind sicher keine weitreichenden Neuerungen des Xenophon, da sie nur Barbaren gegenüber anwendbar waren, niemals aber Griechen gegenüber zur Anwendung gekommen sind.' Best, p. 73 disputes this as does B. Mueller, *Beiträge zur Geschichte des Griechischen Söldnerwesens bis auf die Schlacht von Chaeronea* (Frankfurt: Gottlieb and Müller, 1908) who believes Xenophon invented these tactics. Best, p. 74 does not go this far.

76   Xenophon, *Anabasis* 4.1.22; cf. 6.17.

77   Xenophon, *Anabasis* 4.4.15–18.

78   Xenophon, *Anabasis* 4.4.14.

79   Xenophon, *Anabasis* 4.4.15.

80   Xenophon, *Anabasis* 4.4.16.

81   Xenophon, *Anabasis* 4.4.16. Brownson trans.

82   Xenophon, *Anabasis* 4.4.17.

83   Xenophon, *Anabasis* 4.4.18.

84   Xenophon, *Anabasis* 4.4.19.

85   Xenophon, *Anabasis* 4.4.20.

86   Xenophon, *Anabasis* 4.4.21.

87   Xenophon, *Anabasis* 4.4.20.

88   Xenophon, *Anabasis* 4.6.17.

89   Best, pp. 56–67; Yalichev, p. 138.

90 Xenophon, *Anabasis* 4.6.14.

91 Xenophon, *Anabasis* 4.6.13. Xenophon, the Athenian and the Spartan
Cheirisophos then engage in some good-natured bantering in 4.6.14–16 about
how such a 'theft' – skilful, successful and publicly admired stealing (*kleptein*) is a
product of the educational system in which the other was reared. See the comments
of Whitehead, 'Klope Polemou', p. 292. On the night attack and the mountain pass,
see Yalichev, pp. 138–9.

92 Xenophon, *Anabasis* 4.4.18ff. Yalichev, p. 140.

93 Yalichev, p. 140.

94 Xenophon, *Anabasis* 5.2.1–3.

95 Xenophon, *Anabasis* 6.2.13–19; Yalichev, pp. 142–3.

96 Here we have not a Greek commander engaging Thracian peltasts but a Thracian
king enlisting Greek hoplites: Xenophon, *Anabasis* 7.2.18–22.

97 Xenophon, *Anabasis* 7.7.23, and Best, p. 70, n. 154 who describes the relative size
of Seuthes' force.

98 Xenophon, *Anabasis* 7.3.34ff.

99 See the description by Best, pp. 70–2 and Xenophon, *Anabasis* 7.5.

100 Xenophon, *Hellenica* 2.4.2; Cornelius Nepos, *Thrasybulus*, 8.2.1; Xenophon's use
of the term peltast here is confusing. See Best, pp. 41–3 on Thrasybulus and ibid.
pp. 43–7 on Xenophon's confusion of peltasts with light-armed.

101 Xenophon, *Hellenica* 7.1.25. This incident is not narrated or exploited further by
Xenophon.

102 Phlius occupied a site of great strategic importance to Sparta because it was on the
road from Arcadia to Nemea, Cleonae and Corinth. It also commanded the route
from Stymphalos to the Argive Plain. See P. Cartledge, *Agesilaus and the Crisis of
Sparta* (Baltimore: Johns Hopkins University Press, 1987), figure 2.2.

103 Xenophon, *Hellenica* 4.4.15. They were previously unwilling to admit Spartans
within their walls because they feared that the Spartans would bring back with
them the Phliasian exiles who had been driven out because of their pro-Spartan
sympathies. But the Spartans, for as long as they had control of the city, never
mentioned restoring the exiles even though they were sympathetic to them. Instead
they left the city once it was secured and handed back the city and its laws to the
Phliasians in the same condition as they found it.

104 There is a debate over whether this raid was the impetus for Athens forming the
Second Athenian League, or if the establishment of the League led to the raid. The
dates cannot be determined with sufficient certainty to be sure which one of these
events came first. Scholars have not reached a consensus: Strassler, p. 208.

105 Xenophon, *Hellenica* 5.4.20. Cf. Plutarch, *Pelopidas* 14; Xenophon, *Agesilaus*
24.3–6 gives a more detailed account but is in accord with Xenophon.

106 Xenophon, *Hellenica* 5.4.14; Best, pp. 97–8.

107 Xenophon, *Hellenica* 5.4.59.

108 Cf. Thucydides 2.96.4; 4.101.5; Aeneas Tacticus, *Aineias the Tactician*, pp. 139–40 places the incident in 376/5, citing Diodorus Siculus 15.36.1–4. There are considerable divergences in the accounts including a sudden defection of the Thracians, leaving the Abderites left to fight alone. See Aeneas Tacticus, *On the Defense of Fortified Positions*, trans. by the Illinois Greek Club. Loeb Classical Library (Cambridge: Harvard University Press, 1948), p. 78, n. 1. The credibility of Diodorus' version cannot extend to the part allegedly played in it by the Athenian general Chabrias. On the death of Chabrias, see Diodorus who places incorrectly here as well as correctly in 16.7.4 eighteen years later in 358/7. Cf. Cornelius Nepos, *Chabrias* 4; Plutarch, *Phocion* 6.1; Pritchett, vol. 2, p. 72–7.

109 Aeneas Tacticus, *Aineias the Tactician*, 15.9.

110 Xenophon, *Hellenica* 6.4.26. Xenophon suggests that the polemarchs first told the men to be ready for a midnight march through Plataea to Cithaeron but then, suspecting Theban treachery, had the men leave right after dinner and take a different route.

111 Xenophon, *Hellenica* 6.5.11–17.

112 According to Diodorus Siculus 15.62.1 some 1,000 Spartan hoplites and 500 Argive and Boeotian exiles had also gone with Polytropus to defend Orchomenus. Parke, *Greek Mercenary Soldiers*, p. 87.

113 Diodorus Siculus 15.62.2.

114 Xenophon, *Hellenica* 6.5.17. In ibid. 6.5.18–19 he realises his peril in the morning and skilfully manoeuvred his army from the valley. For a discussion of where the peltasts on the Spartan side came from, see Best, pp. 101–2

115 I.e., Castor and Polydeuces, sons of Tyndareus, also mentioned at 6.36. Pausanias 3.16.2 mentions the Temple at Amyclae and the supposed House of the Dioscuroi. How 300 men could fit in a temple this small is not explained.

116 Xenophon, *Hellenica* 6.5.30–32.

117 Strassler, p. 288 accepts the emendation of Schneider, reading 'Proxenos' as the name of a person. Several other translations render the phrase as 'captured their *proxenoi* in Pellene'. The problem is that it is difficult to see what would be generous or brave about the Pheiasians forgoing a ransom for setting free their own *proxenos*, whereas doing so for a captured Pellenian named 'Proxenos' would make sense.

118 Xenophon, *Hellenica* 7.2.17.

119 Diodorus Siculus 15.82.6; Polybius 9.8.3; Plutarch, *Agesilaus* 31, 32.

120 Diodorus Siculus' account diverges from the others here in that he names the king as Agis rather than Agesilaus. No Spartan king named Agis is known for this date. See Diodorus Siculus, p. 183, n. 1.

121 Diodorus 15.82.6.

122 Polybius 9.8.3; cf. Agesilaus 34.

123 Polyaenus 2.3.7.

124 See Whitehead, 'Klope Polemou', p. 295 who points out that this characterisation of Epaminondas is probably not authentic, but rather a later opinion made once again for purposes of making a moral point. The bias of Xenophon for Agesilaus is well known. See Diodorus Siculus, p. 183, n. 1.

125 See Losada, pp. 125–45. Losada lists twenty-seven attempts at betrayal of places during the course of the Peloponnesian war. However, the affirmation of Gomme, *HCT* and Adcock, *The Greek and Macedonian Art of War* concerning the relative infrequency of surprise attacks, criticised by Losada, pp. 100–15 are, in truth, correct if one understands them to refer to hoplite armies. Moreover, it is not necessary to attribute all sources of information about the enemy and the terrain to 'fifth column' activity, as common as such treachery was in Greek siege warfare.

126 Fortification becomes more important than hoplite morale. Y. Garlan writes that the *ville-foyer* from which the citizen-soldier sallied forth to defend his fields and vineyards and ravage those of his enemies becomes the *ville-bastion* offering protection against would-be besiegers: Garlan, *Recherches de Poliorcetique Grecque*, p. 277. Cf. E. Will, 'Le territoire, la ville et la poliorcétique grecque', *Revue Historique* 253 (1975), pp. 298–318.

127 Diodorus Siculus 13.72.2–4.

128 Diodorus Siculus 13.113.1.

120 Diodorus Siculus 14.9.9.

130 Diodorus Siculus 14.82.6.

131 Plutarch, *Pelopidas* 8–13.

132 Cf. Cornelius Nepos, *Pelopidas* 3. For other examples of intelligence received and ignored, see Plutarch, *Div. Jul.* 65 who reports that Artemidorus handed him a scroll revealing the plot. Caesar, however, because of the great crowds that always approached him as he travelled the streets of Rome, was unable to read it. Aeneas Tacticus 31.33 reports that Astyanax, tyrant of Lampsacus, received a letter informing him about an assassination plot against him but he failed to read it and laid it aside. By the time he finally opened it, the conspirators were upon him.

133 Xenophon's account of this same incident in Xenophon, *Hellenica* 5.4.1–12 does not mention Epaminondas or Pelopidas.

134 Griffith, p. 195; Parke, *Greek Mercenary Soldiers*, pp. 21–2, 61–72; Polyaenus 5.6 is the only ancient evidence for this practice. Dionysius I recruited from a wide range of areas including Sicily, mainland Greece and Campania. See Diodorus Siculus 14.8.9, 61–62; Aristotle, *Oeconomicus* 2.1349ff. From Messenia, Diodorus Siculus 44.2, 58.1, 62.1, 34.3. Celt-Iberians Diodorus 15.70.1ff; from Locri and Medymna 14.78.5.

135 Diodorus Siculus 14.88.2.

136 Diodorus Siculus 14.52.6.

137 Diodorus Siculus 14.52; Parke, *Greek Mercenary Soldiers*, pp. 70–1.

138 Diodorus Siculus 14.90.5.

139 Xenophon, *Hellenica* 4.4.8. Anderson, *Military Theory and Practice*, pp. 155–8.

140 Diodorus Siculus 15.93.3. Night escape from besieged city.

141 Diodorus Siculus 16.19.

142 Plutarch, *Dion* 30.

143 The date of the first payments for military service in Athens remains a matter of controversy and cannot be established with certainty. See Ducrey, *Warfare in Ancient Greece*, p. 231. It has been suggested that the practice of paying soldiers was probably connected with that of paying a fee to court judges and members of the Council of 500 in Athens. Just as these civic responsibilities were accompanied by some remuneration, probably from the mid-fifth century, so were the military obligations of the citizens.

144 Griffith, p. 1; Vidal-Naquet, *The Black Hunter*, p. 85.

145 Thucydides 1.70.6.

146 The first explicit mention of a wage (*misthos*) paid to Athenian soldiers is made by Thucydides who records that, during the siege of Potidaea, the hoplites received two drachmas a day – one for themselves and one for their valet. Sailors received an identical amount. M. Trundle, *Greek Mercenaries from the Late Archaic to Alexander* (London and New York: Routledge, 2004), pp. 165–6; Ducrey, p. 232.

147 Ducrey, p. 232.

148 Chaniotis, p. 19; Trundle, *Greek Mercenaries*, p. 164

149 Vidal-Naquet, *The Black Hunter*, p. 94.

150 Xenophon, *Cyropaedia* 3.3.47; Cf. Thucydides 6.11.6. J. E. Lendon, 'Xenophon and the alternative to realist foreign policy', p. 88.

151 On the 'fair and open' attitude see Xenophon, *Hellenica* 6.5.16; Cf. Andocides 3.18 (*On the Peace with Sparta*); Isocrates 15.118 (*On Winning Just Wars*). On defeat not being considered real unless done fairly on a battlefield, see Herodotus 1.212; Demosthenes 60.21; Plutarch, *Pelopidas* 15.4–5; Polybius 13.3.3; Arrian 3.10.3.

152 Griffith, p. 239; Best, p. 110.

153 Best, p. 110; Griffith, p. 239.

154 Aeneas Tacticus 1.2, 15.5–10, 16.4, 24.10.

155 Aeneas Tacticus 16.7.

156 Aeneas Tacticus 23.7–11.

157 Aeneas Tacticus 16.5–6.

158 Aeneas Tacticus 23.2–3.

159 Aeneas Tacticus 28.5, 6–7; 29.3–10, 11–12 and 12.

160 Aeneas Tacticus 15.

161 Xenophon, *Spartan Constitution*, Introduction, text, commentary by Michael Lipka (Berlin and New York: De Gruyter, 2002), 12.2.

162 Xenophon, *Hellenica* 3.4.13.

163 Xenophon, *Anabasis* 6,3.17–18 cf. 6.3.19

164 David Whitehead, *Aineias the Tactician* (Oxford: The Clarendon Press, 1990), p. 36.

165 Xenophon, *Cyropaedia* 1.6.39.

166 Frontinus 1.4.2, 3; 1.8.12; 1.10.3; 1.11.5; 1.9.17; 2.6.6; 3.11.2.

167 Polyaenus 2.1–33.

168 Grundy, *Thucydides and the History of His Age*, vol. 1, p. 275.

169 Grundy, *Thucydides and the History of His Age*, vol. 1, p. 276.

170 J. E. Lendon, *Soldiers and Ghosts*, p. 114.

171 Grundy, *Thucydides and the History of his Age*, vol. 1, p. 4.

172 Cartledge, *Agesilaus and the Crisis of Sparta*, p. 207; Cf. Vidal-Naquet, *The Black Hunter*, pp. 140–1.

173 Pritchett, vol. 2, p. 59; G. Norlin in Loeb edition of Isocrates 8 *On the Peace*, p. 4 held up Chares, the leading general of Athens, as having 'no mind for moral scruples'. On the 'degenerate' nature of the world, see Anderson, *Military Theory and Practice*, p. 1.

174 J. E. Lendon, *Soldiers and Ghosts*, p. 86.

175 J. E. Lendon, *Soldiers and Ghosts*, p. 89 argues that the tension between the 'rules' and ruthless advantage taking was a conflict between two sets of ideals – those of the hoplite and those of the generals. I see them, however, as working as a team with the same ideals.

Chapter 9: The Successor States and into the Hellenistic Age

1 Chaniotis, *War in the Hellenistic World*, p. 71. He points out that Egypt was in a state of dynastic warfare from 132 BCE onwards (ibid. p. 166). See also M. M. Austin, 'War and culture in the Seleucid Empire', in T. Bekker-Nielsen and L. Hannestad (eds), *War as a Cultural and Social Force: Essays on Warfare in Antiquity* (Copenhagen: Det Kongelige Danske Videnskabernes Selskab, 2001), pp. 90–1.

2 Austin, 'War and culture in the Seleucid Empire', p. 91; E. J. Bickerman, *Institutions des Séleucides* (Paris: Paul Geuthner, 1938), pp. 12–17; M. M. Austin, 'Hellenistic kings, war and the economy', *CQ* 36 (1986), pp. 450–66; A. N. Sherwin-White and A. Kuhrt, *From Samarkhand to Sardis: A New Approach to the Seleucid Empire* (London: Duckworth, 1993), pp. 53–9.

3 To this we can add material from later, indirect sources like Livy (late first century CE), Appian (early second century CE) and in Plutarch's *Lives*. On the monumental historiography of war in the Hellenistic Age, see Chaniotis, *War in the Hellenistic World*, pp. 220–7. He argues convincingly that war was 'a central theme of the Hellenistic culture of commemoration' (ibid. p. 241).

4 See the comments of Chaniotis, *War in the Hellenistic World*, pp. xxi, 2; also: 'Even to compile a list of the wars which were fought between 332 and 31 BC, and of the regions which were affected by these wars, is beyond the possibilities of a modern historian' (ibid. p. 5)

5   See Polybius 22.4.10–13 for second-century examples, and Ma, 'Fighting polis of the Hellenistic world', p. 353.

6   Chaniotis, *War in the Hellenistic World*, p. *79*. Cf. Will, pp. 298–317.

7   As reported in Xenophon, *Hellenica* 6.1.5, trans. by John Marincola. See Strassler (ed.), *Landmark Xenophon's Hellenika*. Pritchett, vol. 2, p. 213. See Ma, 'Fighting *poleis* of the Hellenistic world', p. 354 on training in the *gymnasion*.

8   Ma, 'Fighting *poleis* of the Hellenistic world', p. 354.

9   Chaniotis, *War in the Hellenistic World*, p. 51.

10   Chaniotis, *War in the Hellenistic World*, p. 78.

11   Chaniotis, *War in the Hellenistic World*, p. 78.

12   Chaniotis, *War in the Hellenistic World*, p. 78.

13   See Polybius 27.11.1–7; Livy 42.65.9–11; Pritchett, vol. 5, p. 37; Chaniotis, *War in the Hellenistic World*, p. 99.

14   We know of the existence of military trainers primarily from the honorary decrees of the Athenian ephebes. On the *ephebeia* in the Hellenistic period see J. F. Lendon, 'War and society in the Hellenistic world and the Roman Republic', in *CHGRW*, vol. 1, p. 506; see the discussion of the decline of the *ephebeia* in Athens in the fourth century in Chaniotis, *War in the Hellenistic World*, pp. 48–9.

15   See Chaniotis, *War in the Hellenistic World*, p. 50; Philippe Gauthier, 'Notes sur la rôle du gymnase dans les cités hellénistiques', in M. Wörrle and P. Zanker (eds), *Stadtbild und Bürgerbild im Hellenismus* (Munich: Beck, 1995).

16   Chaniotis, *War in the Hellenistic World*, p. 51; M. M. Austin, *The Hellenistic World from Alexander to the Roman Conquest: A Selection of Ancient Sources in Translation* (Cambridge: Cambridge University Press, 1981), p. 215; Philippe Gauthier, 'Notes sur trois décrets honorant des citoyens bienfaiteurs', *Revue de Philologie* 56 (1982), pp. 215–31.

17   Chaniotis, *War in the Hellenistic World*, p. 51; A. Magnelli, 'Una nova iscrizione da Gortyna (Creta). Qualche considerazione sulla neotas', *Annuario della Scuola Italiana di Archeologia d'Atene*, 70/71 (1992/3), pp. 291–305.

18   H. van Effenterre, 'Fortins Crétois', in *Mélanges d'archéologie et d'Oistoire Offerts à Charles Picard à l'occasion de son 65ème Anniversaire* (Paris: Presses Universitaires de France, 1949), pp. 1033–46. On men manning the forts on the frontier and patrolling (*peripoloi* = patrollers) in Akarnania and Epeiros, see L. Robert, 'Péripolarques', *Hellénica* 10 (Paris, 1955), pp. 283–92; P. Cabanes, 'Recherches épigraphiques en Albanie; péripolarques et peripoloi en Grèce du Nord-Ouest et en Illyrie à la période hellénistiques', *CRAI* (1991) pp. 197–221.

19   Chaniotis, *War in the Hellenistic World*, p. 51. For Athens, see M. V. Taylor, *Salamis and the Salaminioi. The History of an Unofficial Athenian Demos* (Amsterdam: Gieben, 1997), pp. 235–7.

20 Chaniotis, *War in the Hellenistic World*, p. 51; D. Knoepfler, 'Les kryptoi du stratège Epicharès à Rhamnous et le debut de la guerre de Chrémonidès, *BCH* 118 (1993), pp. 327–41.

21 Chaniotis, *War in the Hellenistic World*, p. 51; L. Robert, *Études Anatoliennes. Recherches sur les Inscriptions Grecques de l'Asie Mineure* (Paris: de Boccard, 1937), pp. 106–8.

22 Chaniotis, *War in the Hellenistic World*, p. 51; P. Étienne and P. Roesch, 'Convention militaire entre les cavaliers d'Orchomène et ceux de Cheronée', *BCH* 102 (1978), p. 363.

23 Chaniotis, *War in the Hellenistic World*, p. 51; Vidal-Naquet, *The Black Hunter*, pp. 107–8; although see J. Ma, 'Oversexed, overpaid, and over here: A response to Angelos Chaniotis', in A. Chaniotis and P. Ducrey (eds), *Army and Power in the Ancient World* (Stuttgart: Steiner, 2002), p. 115.

24 A. Chaniotis, following Ducrey, considers them to be the best example: Chaniotis, *War in the Hellenistic World*, p. 81; Ducrey, *Warfare in Ancient Greece*, pp. 130–2. See also A. Petropouliou, *Beiträge zur Wirtschafts-und Gesellschaftsgeschichte Kretas in Hellenistischer Zeit* (Frankfurt: Lang, 1985), pp. 15–31; Launey, pp. 248–86.

25 *Greek Anthology*, trans. by W. R. Paton (Cambridge: MA: Harvard University Press, 1916–18), 7.654: 'The Cretans are ever brigands and pirates and never just'; Chaniotis, *War in the Hellenistic World*, p. 251; P. Perlman, 'Κρηιες αει ληιβιαι? The marginalization of Crete in Greek thought and the role of piracy in the outbreak of the First Cretan War', in V. Gabrielsen *et al.* (eds), *Hellenistic Rhodes: Politics, Culture and Society* (Aarhus: Aarhus University Press, 1999), pp. 132–61. David Whitehead defines *klopas polemion* in Polybius as meaning 'theft' whereas W. R. Paton in the Loeb edition (Polybius, *The Histories*, trans. by W. R. Paton, Cambridge, MA: Harvard University Press, 1960, 6 vols) translates it as 'trick played on the enemy'.

26 Xenophon, *Hellenica* 7.1.23; Trundle, 'Identity and Community', p. 490.

27 Roth, p. 391.

28 Ducrey, p. 130.

29 Parke, *Greek Mercenary Soldiers*, pp. 3–6 on mercenaries abroad before 500 BCE and pp. 7–13 on mercenary service under the ancient Greek tyrants. Cf. Ducrey, *Warfare in Ancient Greece*, p. 130.

30 An example might be the ones who scratched the celebrated graffito on the leg of a temple statue in Egypt in 591. R. Meiggs and D. Lewis, *A Selection of Greek Historical Inscriptions to the End of the Fifth Century BC* (Oxford: The Clarendon Press, 1969), p. 12.

31 Pritchett, vol. 2, pp. 101–4; Runciman, p. 743; Luraghi, pp. 21–47. Although see the caveat about assuming all mercenaries in these regions were driven by poverty in C. Morgan, 'Symbolic and pragmatic aspects of warfare in the Greek world of

the 8th to 6th centuries BC', in T. Bekker-Nielsen and L. Hannestad (eds), *War as a Cultural and Social Force* (Copenhagen: Det kongelige Danske Videnskabernes Selskab, 2001), pp. 20–44.

32 No less than 8,000 men were left unemployed in the aftermath of Alexander's conquests and gathered at Cape Tainaron in 323 BCE. See Diodorus Siculus 18.9.1; cf. Launey, p. 105, n. 1 and Chaniotis, *War in the Hellenistic World*, p. 82. The standard view is that the emergence of mercenaries was a sign of widespread social and economic crisis. This was the general view of Parke's *Greek Mercenary Soldiers*; M. Bettalli's *I Mercenari Nel Mondo Greco* (Pisa: ETS, 1995), pp. 23–9. André Aymard's influential article 'Mercenariat et histoire grecque', in *Études d'Histoire Ancienne* (Paris: Publications de la Faculté des Lettres de Paris, 1967), pp. 487–98; and Baker, pp. 240–55. More recently, however, see Luraghi, p. 21 and Van Wees, *Greek Warfare*, p. 273, n. 48.

33 Chaniotis, *War in the Hellenistic World*, p. 85. On the effect of mercenaries on local populations, see A. Chaniotis, 'Foreign soldiers – native girls? Constructing and crossing boundaries in Hellenistic cities with foreign garrisons', in A. Chaniotis and P. Ducrey (eds), *Army and Power in the Ancient World* (Stuttgart: Steiner, 2002), pp. 99–113. On the identity of Greek mercenaries abroad, see Trundle, 'Identity and community among Greek mercenaries', pp. 481–91. Runciman, p. 743.

34 Chaniotis, *War in the Hellenistic World*, p. 83 who calls the position 'parasitic'.

35 Chaniotis, *War in the Hellenistic World*, p. 80. For the numbers, see Launey, pp. 8–11. On their pay scales, see Chaniotis, *War in the Hellenistic World*, p. 116. P. Bresson, 'Hellenistic military leadership', in H. van Wees, *War and Violence in Ancient Greece* (London: Duckworth, 2000), pp. 319–21 on training.

36 Isocrates 8.44–48 includes these points in his tirade against mercenaries.

37 On the political unrest and the behaviour of soldiers, especially the brutality and greed of Thracians, see Best, pp. 127–33.

38 Isocrates, *Panegyricus* 4.166–68 and *On the Peace* 46–48.

39 Aristotle, *Nichomachaean Ethics* 1116b.

40 Isaeus, *Isaeus* 2.6.3 (On the Estate of Menecles); Aeschines 2.149 (On the Embassy).

41 Runciman, p. 743.

42 The Phocians looted Delphi and enabled themselves, even for a short period, to increase their military potential out of all proportion to the size of their own citizen body. See Runciman, p. 744. On the *miles gloriosus* see S. C. Humphreys, *Anthropology and the Greeks* (London: Routledge, 1978), p. 174 citing T. B. L. Webster, *Studies in Later Greek Comedy* (Manchester: Manchester University Press, 1953), p. 39.

43 Demosthenes 9.49–51.

44 Runciman, p. 744 calls ambushes and stratagems conspicuously absent from the wars of the earlier periods but, as we have seen, they always existed.

45 Griffith, p. 5; Best, pp. 118–19 disagrees. He believes Thracian peltasts continued to serve in Greek armies. They disappeared from Athenian vases because they became such a common sight that artists' interest in them waned.

46 Runciman, p. 745.

47 Polybius 4.8.11. On the wars in Crete during the Hellenistic period, see ibid. pp. 9–12. Dué and Ebbott, pp. 260–1 discuss the possibility that ambush was a Cretan speciality already by the time of the *Iliad*.

48 Ducrey, *Warfare in Ancient Greece*, p. 130.

49 Ducrey, *Warfare in Ancient Greece*, p. 130.

50 A number of these treaties, inscribed in stone, have come down to us either intact or in fragmentary form. The longest one is between Rhodes and Hierapytna, but Rhodes concluded an almost identical treaty with a neighbouring city, the little Olons on the north of the gulf of Mirabello. For a list of the treaties, see Ducrey, *Warfare in Ancient Greece*, p. 195.

51 Polyaenus 4.2.18.

52 Polyaenus 4.2.22.

53 The war was caused by a large fine imposed on the Phocians in 357 for cultivating sacred land. Refusing to pay, the Phocians instead seized the Temple of Apollo in Delphi, and used the accumulated treasures to fund large mercenary armies. Although the Phocians suffered several major defeats, they were able to continue the war for many years, until eventually all parties were exhausted. Philip II used the distraction of the other states to increase his power in northern Greece, in the process becoming ruler of Thessaly. In the end, Philip's growing power, and the exhaustion of the other states, allowed him to impose a peaceful settlement of the war, marking a major step in the rise of Macedon to pre-eminence in ancient Greece.

54 Polyaenus 2.38.2. The event occurred some time between 356 and 353 when Onomarchus was defeated and slain by Philip, who had his body ignominiously hung up for the sacrilege against the Temple of Delphi. On Onomarchus, see Aristotle, *Politics* 5; Diodorus Siculus 16.60.2; Parke, *Greek Mercenary Soldiers*, pp. 136–7.

55 Arrian, 3.10.2.

56 Q. Curtius Rufus, *History of Alexander*, trans. J. C. Rolfe (Cambridge, MA: Harvard University Press, 1985), 4.13.3–10 has a more long-winded version. See Plutarch's version in *Alexander* 31.10ff where he suggests striking at night would be easier and remove the 'fear' of attacking them in daylight whereas, in reality, a night attack would be neither easy nor fear-reducing.

57 Thus argues A. B. Bosworth, *A Historical Commentary on Arrian's History of Alexander* (Oxford: The Clarendon Press, 1980), vol. 1, pp. 295–6 who says the story is characteristic of the heroic portrait of the younger Alexander. The king is portrayed on every occasion as engaging the enemy frontally and under the most adverse circumstances. This moralising on the part of later authors portrays failure

to face the enemy as shameful and the use of underhanded stratagems to achieve victory even more so. See Whitehead, 'Klope Polemou', p. 295.

58   Arrian 5.10.3. For the same stratagem see Quintus Curtius Rufus 8.13.18–19; Polyaenus 4.3.9; Frontinus 1.4.9. Only Arrian emphasises that the diversionary manoeuvres took place at night: Bosworth, *A Historical Commentary*, vol. 2, p. 273.

59   Polyaenus 4.3.12 335 concealed force attacked walls in opposite quarter.

60   Diodorus Siculus 15.16.1.

61   Diodorus Siculus 16.38.4.

62   Diodorus Siculus 16.38.7.

63   On this struggle for power, see F. E. Peters, *The Harvest of Hellenism. A History of the Near East from Alexander the Great to the Triumph of Christianity* (New York: Simon and Schuster, 1970), pp. 66–118.

64   Polyaenus 4.11.4.

65   Diodorus Siculus 19.27.2–28.4. A. M. Devine, 'Diodorus' account of the Battle of Paraitacene (317 BCE)', *The Ancient World* 12 (1985), pp. 76–9. Cf. J. E. Lendon, *Soldiers and Ghosts*, pp. 143–4.

66   For a discussion of the Battle of Paraetacene, see J. Romm, *Ghost on the Throne. The Death of Alexander the Great and the War for Crown and Empire* (New York: Knopf, 2011), pp. 252–6. Cf. A. B. Bosworth, *The Legacy of Alexander: Politics, Warfare and Propaganda under the Successors* (Oxford: Oxford University Press, 2002), chap. 4; Devine, pp. 75–96.

67   Brennus was supposedly one of the leaders of the Gallic invasion that sacked Delphi although the ancient sources do not support this. Both the historians who relate the attack on Delphi (Pausanias 10.23 and Justin 24.7–8) say the Gauls were defeated and driven off. See Barry Cunliffe, *The Ancient Celts* (Harmondworth: Penguin, 2000), pp. 80–1.

68   The story is narrated later by Pausanias 10.23.1–10. Cf. Justin 24.8 after the original nucleus had been enriched with typical elements of similar narratives. See Chaniotis, *War in the Hellenistic World*, p. 158.

69   Polybius 2.53.

70   Polybius 4.25.3.

71   Polybius 5.13.4–5. For attacks on rearguard, see Cestius Gallus at the Beth Horon pass where the Jews attacked the Romans in this manner: B. Bar-Kochva, 'Seron and Cestius Gallus at Beit Horon', *PEQ* 108 (1976), pp. 13–21. M. Gichon, 'Cestius Gallus' campaign in Judaea', 113 *PEQ* (1981), pp. 39–62. See an attack on Antony's rearguard in Armenia: R. M. Sheldon, *Rome's Wars in Parthia* (London: Valentine Mitchell, 2010), chap. 4. For a similar ambush in the battle of Sellasia, see Polybius 2.66–67; Walbank, vol. 1, p. 280 with a diagram on p. 276 based on Kromayer.

72   Peters, p. 95.

73   Chaniotis, *War in the Hellenistic World*, p. 119.

74   Polybius 4.63.9.

75   Polybius 4.59.3.

76   Polybius 5.95.8; Walbank, vol. 1, p. 625.

77   Polybius 5.70.7. See E. H. Cline, *The Battles of Armageddon: Megiddo and the Jezreel Valley from the Bronze Age to the Nuclear Age* (Ann Arbor: University of Michigan Press, 2000), p. 101.

78   On signalling and Polybius, see D. Woolliscroft, *Roman Military Signalling* (Stroud: Tempus, 2001), pp. 159–71. Cf. Walbank, vol. 2, p. 144 on signalling.

79   Polybius 8.14.7–8. On the occupation of Lissus and its part in Philip's western policy, see J. M. F. May, 'Macedonia and Illyria 217–216 BC', *JRS* 36 (1946), pp. 48–56.

80   Polybius 16.37.7. Walbank, vol. 2, p. 545.

81   Griffith, p. 320.

82   Griffith, p. 324.

83   Leosthenes was perhaps the last famous general produced by Ancient Athens.

84   Theodotus was an Aetolian who was in command of Coele-Syria under Ptolemy Philopater (221–204 BCE): Polybius 5.40. Scopas was a general who served both the Aetolian League in the Social war and Ptolemaic Egypt against the Seleucids. He was executed in 196 BCE at Alexandria for conspiring to seize power for himself: Polybius 13.1–3; 16.18–19, 39; Josephus, *Jewish Antiquities* 12.3.3; St Jerome, *Commentary on Daniel* 11.15–16.

85   Griffith, p. 320; Livy 37.41.9.

86   J. E. Lendon, *Soldiers and Ghosts*, p. 146.

Chapter 10: Why the Greeks Used Ambush

1   See the examples listed by Pritchett, vol. 2, p. 184. Unlike ancient armies, modern armies calculate the opponent force ratios that are required to attack or defend an objective. It is generally assumed that the force ratio of about 5:1 is required to attack an enemy who has fortified himself. T. N. Dupuy *et al.*, *International Military and Defense Encyclopedia* (Washington, DC: Brasseys, 1993), vol. 5, p. 2033. Van Wees, *Greek Warfare*, p. 132.

2   Ambush by light-armed troops. Even modern training manuals say that light infantry forces train to defeat the enemy on terrain where its unique abilities can be used: FM 7–70, p. iii.

3   See Pritchett, vol. 2, pp. 117–25 on Corinthian peltasts. FM 7–70, 5–1; FM 7–70, p. v states that light infantry has always been different from regular infantry in their use of skills and training to find the best way to solve a problem. They operate in dispersed formations; they lead attacks with limited support and increased freedom of action.

4   On surprise and psychological shock, see FM 7–70, 5–1.

5   FM 7–70, 5–28.

6   FM 7–70, 5–28, 5–29. See Xenophon, *Hellenica* 4.8.35–39 on Iphicrates ambushing in mountain terrain.

7   Grundy, *Thucydides and the History of His Age*, pp. 242–4; Holladay, 'Hoplites and heresies', p. 97.

8   On surprise and speed as security for your own unit: FM 7–70, 4–25.

9   Polyaenus 1.43.2.

10 Xenophon, *Anabasis* 4.1.22; cf. 4.6.17.

11 On ambush as deception, see FM 7–70, 5–2.

12 See Thucydides 2.81.5, 3.90.2 and n. 43.

13 The template figure is 10 per cent for casualties that will cause a unit to be rendered ineffective. See T. N. Dupuy, *Understanding War* (New York: Paragon House, 1987), pp. 225–30.

14 See the comment in FM 7–70 about light infantry leaders needing to take chances and trying new tactics. Best, p. 25 believes the abilities that Mao Tse Tung demanded of guerrilla fighters and those Demosthenes required of his light infantry were almost identical. On Demosthenes as an audacious general, see Kagan, *The Peloponnesian War*, pp. 132–3.

15 Xenophon, *Hellenica* 4.8.35–38.

16 Y. Yadin, *The Art of Warfare in Biblical Lands. In the Light of Archaeological Study* (New York: McGraw Hill, 1963), vol. 1, p. 110; van Wees, *Greek Warfare*, p. 132.

17 FM 7–70, 4–25.

18 Tyrtaeus, F. 12.10–11 West. Van Wees, *Greek Warfare*, p. 290, pt 5, n. 2.

19 FM 7–70, p. vii: 'The duty of the men assigned to light infantry squads and platoons is to kill the enemy in battle ...'.

20 FM 7–70, 5–28.

21 Thucydides 3.112.

22 The Greeks had no problem with slaughtering their enemies. In 392 at the battle between the Corinthian long walls, the Spartans killed so many Corinthians that Xenophon commented on the 'piles of corpses' visible (Xenophon, *Hellenica* 4.4.12). In 368 the Spartans killed more than 10,000 Arcadians without losing a single man in what was called 'the Tearless Battle' – at least from the Spartan point of view: Xenophon, *Hellenica* 7.2.31; Diodorus Siculus 15.72.3.

23 Herodotus 5.121.

24 Thucydides 3.112.

25 Thucydides 7.32.2.

26 Polyaenus 1.39.1.

27 Polybius 16.37.7.

28 Xenophon, *Hellenica* 4.4.15.

29 Xenophon, *Hellenica* 4.8.35–39.

30 Polyaenus 3.9.24.

31 Thucydides 1.65.2.
32 Xenophon, *Hellenica* 5.1.10.
33 Polyaenus 2.8.
34 Aeneas Tacticus 15.9
35 The Triballi are from mid-Danubian Thrace. On the Triballi, see Thucydides 2.96.4, 4.101.5. Whitehead, *Aeneas the Tactician*, p. 140.
36 Polyaenus 4.11.4.
37 Polybius 5.95.8.
38 As in Thucydides 2.81.5 where Stratians ambushed the Chaonians, and ibid. 3.90.2 where Laches fought off the Messanians.
39 Thucydides 3.107.
40 Xenophon, *Hellenica* 6.5.31.
41 Xenophon, *Anabasis* 4.7.22.
42 Xenophon, *Hellenica* 5.1.10. Cf. Polyaenus 3.11.9.
43 Polybius 5.95.8.
44 Polyaenus 4.2.18. See the parallel from the Peloponnesian war when the women and slaves of besieged Plataea got up on the roof tops, screamed and threw stones and heavy terracotta roof tiles down on the heads of the Thebans, who became panic stricken and turned to flee: Thucydides 2.4; Barry, pp. 55–74.
45 Polyaenus 2.382.
46 Thucydides 7.32.2 on the Sicels and Aeneas Tacticus 15.9 on the Triballi.
47 See Trittle, p. 212.
48 Ardant du Picq, p. 46.
49 FM 7–70, p. iv.
50 Polyaenus 3.9.32.
51 FM 7–70, p. iv.
52 Grundy, *Thucydides and the History of His Age*, pp. 246–9. See Anderson, 'Hoplite weapons and offensive arms', p. 5.
53 Gomme, *HCT* 1, 10.
54 Aristotle, *Politics* 1297b.16–28 holds the theory that hoplite reform was connected with the trend to more democratic constitutions because it removed military supremacy from the horse-owning aristocracy. See Greenhalgh, p. 150. Cartledge, 'Hoplites and heroes', p. 27 believes the Spartan state supplied armour and weapons to citizens as well as to helots and ex-helots. K. Chrimes, *Ancient Sparta* (Manchester: Manchester University Press, 1949), p. 14 argues for the individual supply system.
55 FM 7–70, p. v.
56 FM 7–70, 2–27.
57 FM 7–70, 4–32.
58 Herodotus 5.121; 6.87 (naval); Thucydides 3.110–112.6; 7.32.2; *Hellenica Oxyrhynchia* 6.4–6; Xenophon, *Anabasis* 4.7.22; Xenophon, *Hellenica* 4.4.15;

4.8.35–39; 5.1.27 (naval); Polybius 4.63.9; 5.13.4; Polyaenus 1.48.1; 2.8; 2.37; 3.9.24.

59 Thucydides 1.65.2; 3.94.1; 4.67.4; Xenophon, *Hellenica* 5.1.10; 6.5.31; Aeneas Tacticus 15.9; Polybius 5.70.7; 8.14.7–8; 9.17.4; Polyaenus 1.15, 3.11.9, 4.3.12, 4.11.4, 5.10.4, 5.38, 8.3.2, 8.53.4.

60 Herodotus 6.37; Thucydides 2.81.5; 3.90.2; 5.115.1; Polyaenus 4.2.18.

61 Thucydides 3.107 (Olpae); Polybius 4.59.3 (Achaea); 16:37.7 (Scotitas); Polyaenus 2.38.2 (same as first example).

62 Polybius 5.95.8; Polyaenus 4.2.22; 5:39.

63 Four examples Herodotus 6.138.1; Polyaenus 1.39.1; 1.40.2; 5.22.4.

64 Polybius 5.17.3.

65 Frontinus 2.5; 15, 42, 44–47. Passage 2.5.42 refers to the same ambush as that described in Xenophon, *Hellenica* 4.8.32ff.

66 Pritchett, vol. 2, p. 184.

67 Aeneas Tacticus 15.7–10.

68 Aeneas Tacticus 23.10–11.

69 F. S. Russell, *Information Gathering in Classical Greece*, pp. 10–22 on the Greek use of scouts and reconnaissance in Greek warfare.

70 The *skiritai* were Laconian *periokoi*. As noted in Pritchett's chapter on scouts there are passages that testify to the use of *skiritai* to prevent ambush: Pritchett, vol. 1, pp. 128–9. The use of the *skiritai* is discussed by Gomme, *HCT*, pp. 4, 104. Kromayer and Veith, p. 39; Xenophon, *Lac Pol* 13.6 states that, when a *basileus* leads, no one precedes him except the *skiritai* and cavalry scouts. Pritchett, vol. 2, p. 188. The *skiritai* and cavalry deployed together at Tanagra in 377: Xenophon, *Hellenica* 5.4.52.

71 Herodotus 7.206.2. In Herodotus 9.14 some 1,000 Lacedaemonian *prodromoi* are sent to Megara. See also ibid. 1.60.4, 4.121, 122.1, 7.203.1. 7.206.2.

72 The *prodromoi* have been studied by A. F. Pauli, in *R-E* (1957), Band 23,1 'Prodromos' cols. 102–104; Pritchett, vol. 2, p. 189, quoting Photios who characterises these units as *adoxoi* ('held in no esteem'). They are thought to have been *thetes* who replaced the early *hippotoxitai*. See A. Breuckner, 'Zu Athenischen Grabreliefs', *Archaologische Jahrbuch des Kaiserlich Deutschen Archaeologischen Instituts, Berlin* 10 (1895), p. 209.

73 Kromayer and Veith, pp. 52–3.

74 *Hipparchos* 4.4–6.

75 Xenophon, *The Cavalry General*, trans. by H. G. Dakyns, The Project Gutenberg text; available at http://www.gutenberg.org/etext/1172; accessed February 2012.

76 Aristotle, *Athenaion Politeia* 49.1.

77 On the early horse archers, see Xenophon, *Memorabilia* 3.3.1; Gaebel, p. 178; Bugh, pp. 221–4; Spence, p. 58.

78   Aristotle, *Constitution of the Athenians* 49.1–2. M. Sage, *Warfare in Ancient Greece. A Sourcebook* (London and New York: Routledge, 1996), p. 52.

79   Aeneas Tacticus 6.7.

80   Arrian 2.32.3. In the army of Alexander, there were light-armed equestrian *prodromoi* made up in part of Paionians, who seem to have been used as cavalry patrols: Arrian 1.12.7, 1.13.1, 1.14.1, 6; 2.9.2; 3.7.7; 3.8.1; 3.12.3. Cf. D. G. Hogarth, 'The army of Alexander', *Journal of Philology* 17 (1888), p. 17.

81   Mao Tse Tung, *Mao Tse Tung on Guerrilla Warfare*, trans. by Samuel B. Griffith (New York: Praeger, 1961), p. 46.

82   It was described as such by Lippelt, p. 54 nn. 3 and 4.

83   Woodcock, pp. 105–6.

84   Losada, p. 104.

85   Thucydides 4.67.2.

86   Thucydides 4.110.1, 123.2.

87   Xenophon, *Hellenica* 1.3.18.

88   Thucydides 4.68.4.

89   Thucydides 4.68.6.

90   Thucydides 4.76.203.

91   Thucydides 4.89.1.

92   Losada, p. 105; Westlake, *Individuals in Thucydides*, pp. 111–21.

93   Losada, p. 105; Westlake, *Individuals in Thucydides*, pp. 111–21.

94   Losada, p. 107 who points out that the betrayal of Selymbria was the only example in which the betrayal became known ahead of time, but still succeeded.

95   This was done at Mytilene to thwart a surprise attack by the Athenians: Thucydides 3.3.5.

96   Thucydides 4.68.6.

97   Thucydides 2.79.2. In other examples, the Athenians sailed to Camarina to forestall its betrayal to Syracuse (Thucydides 4.25.7). The Boeotians marched to Siphae and Chaeronea when the impending betrayals became known (ibid. 4.89.2). The pro-Spartan government of Tegea called in the Spartans to thwart the betrayal to the allied forces of Argos, Athens and Mantinea (ibid. 5.64.1–2). Conon and 600 Messenians from Naupactus were sent to Corcyra to prevent its betrayal to the Spartans (Diodorus Siculus 13.48.5–6).

98   Some 600 Messenians and the Corcyraean democrats attacked the pro-Spartans, arrested some, killed others and drove more than 1,000 into exile (Thucydides 13.48.7). At Messina, the pro-Syracusan party executed the fifth columnists when Alcibiades informed them of the planned betrayal (ibid. 6.74.1). Chian leaders executed Tydeus and his followers for pro-Atticism (ibid. 8.38.3). Alcibiades had 300 people arrested on Argos for pro-Spartan sympathies (ibid. 5.84.1). The following winter, the Argives themselves arrested more suspected pro-Spartans (ibid. 5.116.1). See Losada, pp. 108–9.

99   At Siphae, Chaeronea, Nichomachus, a Phocian from Phanotis informed the Spartans about the impending betrayals (Thucydides 4.89.1). At Messina, the plot was betrayed by Alcibiades when he fled from recall (ibid. 6.74.1); Plutarch, *Alcibiades* 22.1. At Athens, Theramenes revealed the plans for his former associates (Thucydides 8.90.3; 91.1–2). At Megara, an unnamed fifth columnist betrayed the planned ambush (Thucydides 4.68.6). Losada, pp. 109–10. In other instances such as Spartolus, Camarina, Tegea, Chios and Corcyra, we do not know how the plots were discovered.

100 Aeneas Tacticus 10.5.

101 Losada, p. 110;

102 Gomme, *HCT* 1, pp. 17–18.

103 Adcock, pp. 40–1; Losada, p. 114.

104 Cf. Losada, p. 114.

105 On intelligence gathering in ancient Greece, see F. S. Russell, *Information Gathering in Classical Greece*.

106 Losada, pp. 134–5.

Conclusion: The Complexity of Greek Warfare

1   Wheeler, *Stratagem and the Vocabulary of Military Trickery*, p. 82; Pritchett, vol. 2, p. 156. Whitehead, '*Klope Polemou*', p. 292.

2   Van Wees, *Greek Warfare*, p. 116.

3   See Euripides, *Rhesus* 510–11, 709.

4   Hornblower, 'Warfare in ancient literature: The paradox of war', in *CHGRW*, vol. 1, p. 50. On women in warfare, see E. Kearns, 'Saving the city', in O. Murray and S. Price, *The Greek City from Homer to Alexander* (Oxford: The Clarendon Press, 1990), pp. 323–44 and J. B. Connelly, 'Parthenon and *parthenoi*: Mythological interpretation of the Parthenon frieze', *AJA* 100 (1996), pp. 53–80.

5   Adcock, pp. 40ff; Gomme, *HCT* 1, pp. 17ff; Pritchett, vol. 2, pp. 156, 174ff; Losada, p. 114 who asserts that surprise was extensively used in cases other than betrayals. Roisman, *The General Demosthenes*, p. 71 disagrees.

6   Pritchett, vol. 2: 'The rarity of ambuscades in hoplite battle on Greek terrain is striking. Only one battle during the Peloponnesian war was decided by ambuscade' (ibid. p. 185). On attitude of mind, see ibid. p. 187.

7   Whitehead, '*Klope polemou*', p. 50.

8   See the discussion in Krentz, 'Deception in Archaic and Classical Greek warfare', pp. 172–4.

9   In the Classical as well as the Hellenistic period, for example, Boeotian raiders crossed into Attica in times of hostilities. See Ma, 'Fighting *poleis* of the Hellenistic world', p. 356. R. Osborne, *Classical Landscape with Figures: The Ancient Greek City and its Countryside* (London: Phillip, 1987), pp. 137ff. Local imperialism in

the Classical and Hellenistic ages created violence when one side tried to annex
another's territory.

10   Ma, 'Fighting polis of the Hellenistic world', pp. 357–8.

11   Ober, 'The rules of war in Classical Greece', pp. 63–9. See also Heza, pp. 235–44.

12   V. D. Hanson, *The Other Greeks. The Family Farm and the Agrarian Roots of Western
Civilization* (Berkeley: University of California Press, 1999), pp. 271–89.

13   V. Gabrielson, 'The impact of armed forces on government and politics in Archaic
and Classical Greek *poleis*: A response to Hans van Wees', in A. Chianotis and
P. Ducrey, *Army and Power in the Ancient World* (Stuttgart: Steiner, 2002), p. 83.

14   Griffith, p. 6 argues that the effect of mercenary service upon the warfare of the
Greeks was to make it less stereotyped, but also less decisive.

15   Clausewitz, p. 203.

16   Krentz, 'Deception in Archaic and Classical Greek warfare', p. 177.

17   For a list of these mythological and historical figures see Krentz, 'Deception in
Archaic and Classical Greek warfare', pp. 175–7. Even a revered figure such as Solon
was portrayed as beating the Megarians by a cunning trick: Plutarch, *Solon* 8.

18   Xenophon, *The Cavalry Commander* 5.9–11, trans. by E. C. Marchant, Loeb edn.

19   Krentz, 'Deception in Archaic and Classical Greek warfare', p. 169.

20   Stefan T. Possony in introduction to Waldemar Erfurth, *Surprise*, trans. by Stefan
T. Possony and Daniel Vilfroy (Harrisburg, PA: Military Service Publishing,
1943), p. 1.

21   Thucydides 4.126.

22   Thucydides 4.86.6.

23   Thucydides 5.9.5. See Krentz, 'Deception in Archaic and Classical Greek warfare',
pp. 167–200, including the Brasidas example on p. 174. In the Peloponnesian war
Krentz identifies thirty-seven instances of attacks based on deception or surprise,
outnumbering the two set-piece infantry battles at Delium and Mantinea. The
Achilles/Odysseus ethos is discussed in Wheeler, *Stratagem and the Vocabulary
of Military Trickery*, p. xiv. Deception and surprise are discussed further in J. D.
Montagu, *Greek and Roman Warfare: Battle, Tactics and Trickery* (London:
Greenhill, 2006), pp. 67–81.

24   Pausanias 1.13.5.

25   Plutarch, *Moralia* 238.25 [*On the Spartans*] notes that, when the Spartans defeated
their enemy's by a stratagem, they sacrificed a bull to Ares, but when they won in
open battle they sacrificed a cock, making their leaders not only great fighters but
tacticians as well. See A. S. Bradford, 'The duplicitous Spartan', in A. Powell and
S. Hodkinson (eds), *The Shadow of Sparta* (London and New York: Routledge,
1994), pp. 59–85.

26   Polybius 3.18.9.

27   Herodotus 7.9.1.

28   Polybius 13.3.2–6.

29 Demosthenes, *Philippic* 3.47–50. Vidal-Naquet, *The Black Hunter*, p. 94 points out that the short treatise by Aeneas Tacticus is, in itself, a comment on the violent world of the fourth century.

30 Polybius quotes the ban against missiles and that fact that declarations of war were made first and place of battle of announced ahead of time (Polybius 13.3.2–6). See Anderson, *Military Theory and Practice*, p. 1, who accepts the historicity of the ban.

31 Wheeler, *Stratagem and the Vocabulary of Military Trickery*, p. 25.

32 Detienne and Vernant, p. 26. Van Wees, *Greek Warfare*, pp. 116–17.

33 Porter, p. 77.

34 Xenophon, *Lac. Pol.* 2.6–9. See also Xenophon, *Anabasis* 4.14–15; Plutarch, *Lycurgus* 17; *Moralia* 237ff.

35 N. M. Kennell, *The Gymnasium of Virtue* (Chapel Hill, NC: University of North Carolina Press, 1995), pp. 122–3 argues for the ritual activity of the ephebes. Answered by Krentz, 'Deception in Archaic and Classical Greek warfare', p. 180. A. Powell, 'Mendacity and Sparta's use of the visual', in A. Powell (ed.), *Classical Sparta: Techniques Behind Her Success* (Norman, OK: University of Oklahoma Press, 1989), p. 186 is correct that 'ambush and living off the land by stealth do not sound like elements of warfare for the hoplite phalanx' but this would support my argument that there was more than one kind of fighting going on.

36 Xenophon, *The Cavalry Commander* 5.9, 11; Xenophon, *Cyropaedia* 1.6.27; Dio Cassius 71.3.1.

37 Xenophon, *Anabasis* 3.1.1–2.

38 J. E. Lendon, 'Xenophon and the alternative to realist foreign policy', p. 84.

39 Porter, p. 77.

40 Porter, p. 77.

41 Hanson, *The Wars of the Ancient Greeks*, p. 158.

42 Hornblower, 'Warfare in ancient literature', p. 42.

43 J. Rich and G. Shipley (eds), *War and Society in the Greek World* (London and New York: Routledge, 1993), p. 23.

44 P. Hunt, 'Military forces', in *CHGRW*, vol. 1, p. 126.

45 On hoplite snobbery see Hanson, *The Wars of the Ancient Greeks*, p. 158.

46 Van Wees, *Greek Warfare*, pp. 71–6.

47 Xenophon, *Cyropaedia* 7.4.15.

48 See Xenophon, *Hellenica* 3.4.2.

49 Pritchett, vol. 5, pp. 37, 46–7.

50 See the comments of Whitehead, 'Klope Polemou', p. 296 who thinks that the basic meaning of *klope* is theft and that the moral implications of the use of this word never changes, since theft is a crime. On the battlefield, therefore, it could never be anything but a shameful backdoor route to success. It was 'cheating, breaking the hallowed rules of the great game that was war'. I would respond that if there are any such rules they are always negotiable when the circumstances require.

51 This posture is attacked also by Whitehead in 'Klope Polemou', p. 297.

52 *Dolos:* Homer, *Iliad* 7.142ff, 197–98; *Lochos:* Homer, *Iliad* 1.225–28; Homer, *Odyssey* 14.217ff.

53 Homer, *Iliad* 13.276.

54 Whitehead, 'Klope Polemou', p. 298.

55 Wheeler, *Stratagem and the Vocabulary of Military Trickery*, p. 24.

56 The most thorough study of the vocabulary is still Wheeler, *Stratagem and the Vocabulary of Military Trickery*, p. 81; and ibid. pp. 82–3 on Latin terms for surprise attack.

57 Valerius Maximus 7.3; Wheeler, *Stratagem and the Vocabulary of Military Trickery*, p. 16.

58 Wheeler, *Stratagem and the Vocabulary of Military Trickery*, p. 93.

59 Yalichev, p. 119.

60 Krentz, 'Fighting by the rules', p. 122; this is in reaction to J. Ober's delineation of these rules in Ober, 'The rules of war in Classical Greece', pp. 53–71.

61 Whitehead, 'Klope Polemou', p. 294.

62 The classic discussion is, of course, Edward Said's *Orientalism*. He has not been without his critics. See the discussion in Porter, pp. 14–15.

63 Porter, p. 2.

64 K. Booth, *Strategy and Ethnocentrism* (New York: Holmes and Meier, 1979), p. 33 listing the British underestimation of the Russians in the Crimea, or of the Boers in South Africa. On the American side in Vietnam.

65 Porter, p. 2.

66 Porter, p. 27.

67 See for example, Herodotus 1.1, 3.38, 7.83, 7.223; Porter, pp. 3, 27.

68 Porter, p. 5. See Whatley's observation that Marathon 'certainly was not one of the decisive battles of the world': Whatley, p. 313.

69 Porter, p. 2.

70 V. D. Hanson, *Carnage and Culture: Landmark Battles in the Rise of Western Power* (New York: Doubleday, 2001).

71 See V. D. Hanson, *Fields Without Dreams: Defending the Agrarian Idea* (New York: Free Press, 1996); Hanson, *The Other Greeks*; V. D. Hanson, *The Soul of Battle: From Ancient Times to the Present Day. How Three Great Liberators Vanquished Tyranny* (New York: Anchor Books, 2001). Du Bois, pp. 34–8 provides a critique of Hanson's views. See also Arthur J. Pomeroy, 'The vision of a Fascist Rome in Gladiator', in M. Winkler, *Gladiator: Film and History* (Oxford: Blackwell, 2004), pp. 121–2.

72 As Porter, p. 57 points out: 'You don't need to be Edward Said to see the problem here'.

73 Hanson, *The Western Way of War*, esp. pp. 9–19, 227–8. See the comments of Porter, pp. 5–6; and J. A. Lynn, *Battle: A History of Combat and Culture from*

Ancient Greece to Modern America (Boulder, CO: Westview Press, 2003), p. 13 on John Keegan and Geoffrey Parker as adherents to Hanson's claims.

74 Basil Liddell Hart, *The British Way of Warfare* (London: Faber and Faber, 1932); R. Weigley, *The American Way of War* (Bloomington: University of Indiana Press, 1973); Porter, p. 10.

75 G. Parker (ed.), *The Cambridge History of Warfare* (Cambridge: Cambridge University Press, 2005), esp. pp. 1–15; Porter, p. 11.

76 Lynn, pp. 12–15.

77 Porter, p. 72 who points out D-Day was a massive deception operation and uses the Duke of Wellington and the Spanish irregulars of the Peninsular war as an example of strategies of diversion and concealment, and effective light infantry.

78 Morillo, Black and Lococo, vol. 1, p. 43.

79 Herodotus 9.90.3. Amit, p. 134.

80 Herodotus 8.94. Amit, p. 134 depicts the story as an Athenian slander against the Corinthians.

81 For other examples where there are no wars and no enemies, see Amit, p. 134.

82 See especially Porter's chapter on the Japanese, pp. 85–110.

83 Porter, p. 75. Cf. John Keegan, 'In this war of civilizations, the West will prevail', *Daily Telegraph* (8 October 2001). Lynn, p. 20.

84 Porter, p. 76. Quote is from Philip Sabin, *Lost Battles: Reconstructing the Great Clashes of the Ancient World* (London: Hambledon Continuum, 2007), pp. xi and 29.

85 N. Dixon, *On the Psychology of Military Incompetence* (New York: Basic Books, 1976), p. 266.

86 Yalichev, p. 136.

87 Porter, p. 15

88 Porter, p. 15.

89 Hanson, 'Hoplite battle as ancient Greek warfare', p. 201.

90 See similar comments in a modern context in Col. Thomas X. Hammes, *The Sling and the Stone* (St Paul, MN: Zenith Press, 2004), p. 3.

91 Porter, p. 18.

92 Niccolo Machiavelli, 'Discourses on the first ten books of Titus Livius', in Niccolò Machiavelli, *The Historical, Political and Diplomatic Writings*, trans. by Christian Detmold (Boston: Osgood, 1882), 3.40.

93 Porter, p. 73.

94 See E. Kam, *Surprise Attack* (Cambridge: MA; Harvard University Press, 2004); R. K. Betts, *Surprise Attack. Lessons for Defense Planning* (Washington, DC: The Brookings Institution, 1982).

95 Porter, p. 74.

96 Booth, p. 99. Porter, p. 75.

97   Porter, p. 81. Cf. Colin Gray, 'Out of the wilderness: Prime time for strategic culture', *Comparative Strategy* 26, 1 (January 2007), p. ii.
98   Porter, p. 81.
99   Booth, p. 15.
100 Ardant du Picq, p. 46.
101 Ardant du Picq, p. 43.
102 Ardant du Picq, p. 46.
103 For the relevant passages and discussion see R. Sorabji and D. Roden, *The Ethics of War* (Aldershot, Hants: Ashgate, 2006), pp. 13–15.
104 See the comments of Whatley, p. 321.
105 J. E. Lendon, *Soldiers and Ghosts*, p. 159.
106 Nasty tricks like lying: Frontinus 1.11.6; fabricating religious manifestations: Frontinus 1.11.16 and 1.12.5–7; disguising their troops as women: Frontinus 3.2.7; making covert retreats: Frontinus 3.11.5, or surrender tricks: Polyaenus 4.3.20.
107 C. Morgan, 'Symbolic and pragmatic aspects of warfare in the Greek world of the 8th to 6th centuries BC', p. 20.

Bibliography

Ancient Texts

Aelian, *On the Characteristics of Animals*, trans. by A. F. Schofield, Cambridge, MA: Harvard University Press, 1958.

Aelius Aristides, P., *The Complete Works*, trans. by Charles A. Behr, Leiden: Brill, 1981, 2 vols.

Aeneas Tacticus, *Aineias the Tactician*, trans. by D. Whitehead, with commentary, Oxford: The Clarendon Press, 1990.

Aeneas Tacticus, *On the Defense of Fortified Positions*, trans. by The Illinois Greek Club, Loeb Classical Library, Cambridge: Harvard University Press, 1948.

Aeschines, *The Speeches of Aeschines* with trans. by C. D. Adams, London: Heinemann; New York, G. P. Putnam's Sons, 1919.

Aeschylus, *Persians*, English trans. by Herbert Weir Smyth, Cambridge, MA: Harvard University Press; London: Heinemann, 1922, 2 vols.

Aeschylus, *Prometheus Bound*, English trans. by Herbert Weir Smyth, Cambridge, MA: Harvard University Press; London: Heinemann, 1922, 2 vols.

Andocides, English trans. by K. J. Maidment, in vol. 1 of *Minor Attic Orators*, Cambridge: Cambridge University Press, 1941–54, 3 vols.

Appian, *Appian's Roman History*, trans. by Horace White, Cambridge, MA: Harvard University Press, 1958, 4 vols.

Arrian, 'Ars tactica', in *L'arte tattica: trattato di tecnica militare: testo Greco a fronte, Lucio Flavio Arriano; a Cura di Antonio Sestili*, Roma: Aracne, 2011.

Aristarchus of Samothrace, in K. Lehrs, *De Aristarchi Studiis Homeriicis*, Leipzig: S. Hirzelium, 1882, 3rd edn.

Aristophanes, *Birds*, ed. with trans. and notes by Alan H. Sommerstein, Warminster, Wiltshire: Aris and Phillips, 1987.

Aristophanes, *Birds*, trans. by Nan Dunbar, Oxford: The Clarendon Press, 1998.

Aristotle, *The Complete Works of Aristotle*, ed. by Jonathan Barnes, rev. Oxford trans., Bollingen Series LXXI.2, Princeton: Princeton University Press, 1984, 2 vols.

Aristotle, *Constitution of the Athenians*, trans. by F. G. Kenyon, Union, NJ: Lawbook Exchange, 2003, 3rd rev. edn.

Aristotle, *Oeconomicus*, trans. by Hugh Tredennick, in vol. 2 of Aristotle, *Metaphysics*, Cambridge, MA: Harvard University Press, 1947, 2 vols.

Arrian, *The Landmark Arrian. The Campaigns of Alexander: Anabasis Alexandrou*, trans. by Pamela Mensch, ed. by James Romm, New York: Pantheon Books, 2010.

Arrianus, Flavius, *The Campaigns of Alexander*, trans. by P. A. Brunt, with Greek and English text, Jeffrey Henderson (ed.), Cambridge, MA: Harvard University Press, 1983–9, books I–IV.

Arrianus, Flavius, *Scripta Minora et Fragmenta*, A. G. Roos (ed.), Leipzig: B. G. Teubner, 1968.

Caesar, Julius, *The Gallic War*, trans. by H. J. Edwards, Cambridge, MA: Harvard University Press, 1917.

Demosthenes, *Demosthenes*, English trans. by J. H. Vince, Cambridge, MA: Harvard University Press; London: Heinemann, 1926–1949, 7 vols.

Dio, Cassius, *Dio's Roman History*, trans. by E. Cary, Cambridge, MA: Harvard University Press, 1954, 9 vols.

Diodorus Siculus, *The Library of History of Diodorus of Sicily*, trans. by C. H. Oldfather, Cambridge, MA: Harvard University Press, 1933–1967, 12 vols.

Dionysius of Halicarnassus, *The Roman Antiquities*, trans. by E. Cary, Cambridge, MA: Harvard University Press, 1948, 7 vols.

Euripides, *Andromache*, trans. by David Kovacs, Cambridge, MA: Harvard University Press, 1995.

Euripides, *Bacchae, Iphigenia at Aulis, Rhesus*, trans. by David Kovacs, Cambridge, MA: Harvard University Press, 2003.

Euripides, *Hercules*, trans. by Tom Sleigh, with introduction and notes by Christian Wolff, Oxford and New York: Oxford University Press, 2001.

Euripides, *Trojan Women, Iphigenia among the Taurians, Ion*, trans. by David Kovacs, Cambridge, MA: Harvard University Press, 1999.

Eutropius, *Eutropi Breviarum ab Urbe Condita*, C. Santini (ed.), Leipzig: B. G. Teubner, 1979.

Frontinus, *The Stratagems*, trans. by Charles E. Bennett, Cambridge, MA: Harvard University Press, 1925.

Greek Anthology, trans. by W. R. Paton, Cambridge: MA: Harvard University Press, 1916–18, 5 vols.

Hellenica Oxyrhynchia, ed. and trans. by P. McKechnie and S. Kern, Warminster, Wilts: Aris and Phillips, 1988.

Herodian, *History of the Empire*, trans. by C. R. Whittaker, Loeb Classical Library No. 454, Cambridge, MA: Harvard University Press, 1969–70, 2 vols.

Herodotus, *The Histories,* ed. and trans. by A. D. Godley, Cambridge, MA: Harvard University Press, 1931, 4 vols.

Herodotus, *The Landmark Herodotus; The Histories*, new trans. by Andrea L. Purvis, ed. by Robert B. Strassler, introduction by Rosalind Thomas, New York: Pantheon Books, 2007.

Hesiod, *The Works and Days. The Shield of Herakles*, trans. by Richmond Lattimore, Ann Arbor: University of Michigan Press, 1965.

Homer, *Iliad,* trans. by A. T. Murray, Cambridge, MA: Harvard University Press, 1934–7, 2 vols.

Homer, *Iliad. Homeri Ilias*, recensuit, testimonia congessit Martin L. West, Leipzig: Teubner, 1998–2000, 2 vols.

Homer, *Odyssey*, trans. by A. T. Murray, Cambridge, MA: Harvard University Press, 1931, 2 vols.

Homer, *The Odyssey*, trans. by Robert Fagles, New York: Viking, 1996.

Hyginus, *Fabulae*: *The Myths of Hyginus,* trans. by Mary Grant, Lawrence: University of Kansas Publications, 1960.

Isaeus, *Isaeus* with an English trans. by Edward Seymour Forster, Cambridge: MA: Harvard University Press, 1927.

Isocrates, *Isocrates,* trans. by George Norlin, Cambridge, MA: Harvard University Press, 1928–45, 3 vols.

Josephus, *Jewish Antiquities*, trans. by H. St J. Thackeray, Cambridge, MA: Harvard University Press, 1961, 6 vols.

Josephus, *The Jewish War*, trans. by H. St J. Thackeray, Cambridge, MA: Harvard University Press, 1956, 2 vols.

Justinus, Marcus Junianus, *Epitoma historiarum Philippicarum Pompei Trogi*, ed. by Otto Seel, Stuttgart: Teubner, 1972.

Lesches, *The Little Iliad*, 1. trans. by H. G. Evelyn-White, Loeb edition of *Hesiod, the Homeric Hymns and Homerica*, Cambridge, MA: Harvard University Press, 1914.

Libanius, *Autobiography and Selected Letters*, trans. and ed. by A. F. Norman, Cambridge, MA: Harvard University Press, 1992, 2 vols.

Livy, *Ab Urbe Condita*, Cambridge, MA: Harvard University Press, 1961; vols 1–5 trans. by B. O. Foster; vols 6–8 trans. by F. G. Moore; vols. 9–11 trans. by E. T. Sage; vols. 12–14 trans. by A. G. Schlesinger.

Nepos, Cornelius, *On Great Generals. On Historians*, trans. by J. C. Rolfe, Cambridge, MA: Harvard University Press, 1929.

Ovid, *The Metamorphoses of Ovid*, trans. and with an introduction by Mary M. Innes, Harmondsworth, Middlesex: Penguin Books, 1955.

Pausanias, *Pausanias' Description of Greece*, English trans. by W. H. S. Jones, Cambridge, Harvard University Press; London, Heinemann,1918–35, 3 vols.

Pliny the Elder, *Natural History*, trans. by H. H. Rackham, vols 1–4; trans. by
   W. H. S. Jones, vols 5–8; trans. by D. E. Eichholz, vol. 10, Cambridge, MA:
   Harvard University Press, 1958–62.

Plutarch, *Lives*, trans. by Bernadotte Perrin, Cambridge, MA: Harvard University Press,
   1959, 11 vols.

Plutarch, *Moralia*, English trans. by Frank Cole Babbitt, Cambridge, MA: Harvard
   University Press; London: Heinemann, 1949–1976, 10 vols.

Polyaenus, *Stratagems of War*, ed. and trans. by Peter Krentz and Everett L. Wheeler,
   Chicago: Ares, 1994.

Polybius, *The Histories*, trans. by W. R. Paton, Cambridge, MA: Harvard University
   Press, 1960, 6 vols.

Procopius, *The Secret History*, trans. by H. B. Dewing, Cambridge, MA: Harvard
   University Press, 1960.

Quintus Curtius Rufus, *History of Alexander*, trans. J. C. Rolfe, Cambridge, MA:
   Harvard University Press, 1985, 2 vols.

Quintus of Smyrna, *Posthomerica (Fall of Troy)*, trans. by A. S. Way, Cambridge, MA:
   Harvard University Press, 1913.

Quintus of Smyrna, *The War at Troy; What Homer Didn't Tell*, trans. and with an
   introduction and notes by Frederick M. Combellack, Norman, OK: University of
   Oklahoma Press, 1968.

Sallust, *The War with Jugurtha*, trans. by J. C. Rolfe, Cambridge, MA: Harvard University
   Press, 1920.

Silius Italicus, Tiberius Catius, *Punica*, English trans. by J. D. Duff, London: Heinemann
   and Cambridge, MA: Harvard University Press, 1934, 2 vols.

Simonides fragment, in Ernest Diehl (ed.), *Anthologia Lyrica Graeca*, Leipzig: Teubner,
   1949, 3 vols.

Strabo, *The Geography of Strabo*, trans. by Horace Leonard Jones, Cambridge, MA:
   Harvard University Press, 1982–9.

Sun Tzu, *The Art of War*, trans. with introductions and commentary by Ralph D.
   Sawyer; with the collaboration of Mei-Chün Lee Sawyer, Boulder: Westview
   Press, 1994.

Thucydides, *The Landmark Thucydides: A Comprehensive Guide to the Peloponnesian
   War*, trans. by Richard Crawley, ed. by R. B. Strassler, introduction by Victor
   Davis Hanson, New York, NY: Free Press, 1996.

Thucydides, *The Peloponnesian War*, trans. by Walter Blanco, ed. by Walter Blanco and
   Jennifer Tolbert Roberts, New York: Norton, 1998.

Tyrtaeus, *The War-elegies of Tyrtæus, Imitated and Addressed to the People of Great Britain,
   with Some Observations on the Life and Poems of Tyrtæus*, trans. by Henry James
   Pye, London: printed for T. Cadell, jun. and W. Davies, successors to Mr Cadell,
   1795.

Tzetzes, John, *Antehomerica et Posthomerica*, Charleston, SC: Nabu Press, 2010.

Valerius Maximus, *Memorable Doings and Sayings* (*Factorum et Dictorum Memorabilium*), trans. by Dr Shackleton-Bailey, Cambridge, MA: Harvard University Press, 2000, 2 vols.

Vergil, *The Aeneid*, trans. by Stanley Lombardo, introduction by W. R. Johnson, Indianapolis, IN: Hackett, 2005.

Xenophon, *Agesilaus*, also contained in *Xenophon, Hiero the Tyrant and Other Treatises*, trans. by Robin Waterfield, introduction of Paul Cartledge, London: Penguin Books, 1997.

Xenophon, *Anabasis*, trans. by Carleton L. Brownson, Cambridge, MA: Harvard University Press, 1961, 2 vols.

Xenophon, *The Art of Horsemanship*, trans. by M. H. Morgan, London: Allen, 2004.

Xenophon, *How To Be a Good Cavalry Commander*, trans. by Robin Waterfield, London: Penguin Books, 1997.

Xenophon, *Cyropaedia*, trans. by Walter Miller, Cambridge, MA: Harvard University Press, 2000–2001, 2 vols.

Xenophon, *Hellenica*, trans. by Carleton L. Brownson, Cambridge, MA: Harvard University Press, 1961.

Xenophon, *Hiero the Tyrant and Other Treatises*, trans. by Robin Waterfield, Introduction of Paul Cartledge, London: Penguin Books, 1997.

Xenophon, *The Landmark Xenophon's Hellenika*, trans. by John Marincola, ed. by R. B. Strassler, introduction by David Thomas, New York: Pantheon, 2009.

Xenophon, *Memorabilia, Oeconomicus, Symposium, Apologia*, trans. by E. C. Marchant and O. J. Todd, Cambridge, MA: Harvard University Press, 1979.

Xenophon, *Spartan Constitution*, Introduction, text, commentary by Michael Lipka, Berlin and New York: De Gruyter, 2002.

Xenophon, *Xenophon on Government*, ed. by Vivienne J. Gray, Cambridge and New York: Cambridge University Press, 2007. This work includes both the *Respublica Lacedaemoniorum* and the *Respublica Atheniensium*.

Commentaries and Reference Works

Ameis, K. F. and Hentze, C., *Homer's Odyssey*, Leipzig: Teubner, 1879.

Atkinson, J. E., *A Commentary on Q. Curtius Rufus' Historiae Alexandri Magni*, Amsterdam: J. C. Gieben, books 3 and 4, 1980.

Bettalli, Marco, *La Difesa di una Città Assediata: Poliorketika, Enea Tattico; Introduzione, Traduzione e Commento a Cura di Marco Bettalli*, Pisa: ETS, 1990.

Bosworth, A. B., *A Historical Commentary on Arrian's History of Alexander*, Oxford: The Clarendon Press, 1980, vols 1 and 2.

Bruce, A., *A Historical Commentary on the Hellenica Oxyrhynchia*, Cambridge: Cambridge University Press, 1967.

Cartwright, David, *A Historical Commentary on Thucydides, A companion to Rex Warner's Penguin translation*, Ann Arbor: University of Michigan Press, 1997.

Connor, W. R., *Thucydides*, Princeton: Princeton University Press, 1984.

Daremberg, C. and Saglio, E., *Dictionnaire des Antiquités Grecques et Romaines*, Paris, 1877–1919; available at: http://dagr.univ-tlse2.fr/sdx/dagr/index.xsp; accessed February 2012.

Gomme, A. W., *A Historical Commentary on Thucydides*, Oxford: Clarendon Press, 1970.

Gomme, A. W., Andrewes, A. and Dover, K. J., *A Historical Commentary on Thucydides*, Oxford: Oxford University Press, 1956–81, 5 vols.

Hainsworth, J. B., *The Iliad: A Commentary*, Cambridge: Cambridge University Press, 1993, 3 vols.

Heubeck, A., West, Stephanie and Hainsworth, J. B., *A Commentary on Homer's Odyssey*, Oxford: The Clarendon Press, 1988, 3 vols.

Hornblower, S., *A Commentary on Thucydides*, Oxford: The Clarendon Press, 1991, 2 vols.

Hornblower, S., *A Commentary on Thucydides Vol. II*, Books IV–V.24, Oxford: Oxford University Press, 1996.

Hornblower, S., 'Warfare in ancient literature: The paradox of war', in *CHGRW*, vol. 1, p. 42.

How, W. W. and Wells, J., *A Commentary on Herodotus,* Oxford: The Clarendon Press, 1968, reprinted edn.

Immerwahr, Henry R., *Form and Thought in Herodotus*, published for the American Philological Association, Chapel Hill, NC, by Cleveland: Press of Western Reserve University, 1966.

Jones, P., *Homer's Odyssey: A Commentary Based on the English Translation of Richmond Lattimore*, Carbondale, IL: Southern Illinois University Press, 1989.

Jong, I. J. F. de, *A Narratological Commentary on the Odyssey*, Cambridge: Cambridge University Press, 2001.

Kirk, G. S., *The Iliad: A Commentary*, Cambridge: Cambridge University Press, 1985–93, 6 vols.

Leaf, Walter, *Commentary on the Iliad*, London: Macmillan, 1883.

MacLeod, C. W., *Homer: Iliad, Book XXIV*, Cambridge: Cambridge University Press, 1982.

Meiggs, R. and Lewis, D., *A Selection of Greek Historical Inscriptions to the End of the Fifth Century BC*, Oxford: The Clarendon Press, 1969.

Machiavelli, Niccolò, 'Discourses on the first ten books of Titus Livius', in Niccolò Machiavelli, *The Historical, Political and Diplomatic Writings*, trans. by Christian Detmold, Boston: Osgood, 1882, 4 vols.

Pauly, August and Wissowa, Georg, Kroll, Wilhelm, Witte, Kurt, Mittelhaus, Karl and Ziegler, Konrat (eds), *Paulys Realencyclopädie der Classischen Altertumswissenschaft: Neue Bearbeitung*, Stuttgart: J. B. Metzler, 1894–1980.

St Jerome, *Commentary on Daniel*, trans. by Gleason L. Archer, Jr, Grand Rapids, MI: Baker Book House, 1958.

Schmid, W., 'Das Alter der Vorstellung vom panischen Schrecken', *Rh. Mus.* 50 (1895), pp. 310–11.

Steup, Julius, *Thukydides*, erklärt von J. Classen, Berlin: Weidemann, 1914, 2 vols.

Walbank, F. W., *A Historical Commentary on Polybius*, Oxford: The Clarendon Press, 1957, 3 vols.

Field Manuals

British Army Field Manual, vol. 1, *Combined Arms Operation*, pt 9, *Tactics and Stabilizing Operations*, Army Code 71658, 2005.

British Army Field Manual, vol. 1, *Combined Arms Operation*, pt 10, *Counterinsurgency Operations*, Army Code 71749, 2001.

FM 2–1, *US Marine Corps Intelligence*, Washington, DC: US Department of the Army, 1980.

FM 3–24, *The US Army/Marine Corps Counterinsurgency Field Manual*, Washington, DC: US Department of the Army, 2006.

FM 3–33.5, *Marine Corps Warfighting*, foreword by David H. Petraeus and James F. Amos, Washington, DC: US Department of the Army, 2006; foreword to the University of Chicago Press edn by John A. Nagl, with a new introduction by Sarah Sewall.

FM 7–8, *Infantry Rifle Platoon and Squad,* Washington, DC: US Department of the Army, 1992.

FM 7–70, *Light Infantry Platoon/Squad*, Washington, DC: Department of the Army, 1986.

FM 30–5, *Combat Intelligence*, Washington, DC: US Department of the Army, 1971.

FM 30–96C, *Interrogator,* Washington, DC: US Department of the Army, 1977.

FM 30–97B, *Counterintelligence*, Washington, DC: US Department of the Army, 2007.

FM 34–3, *Intelligence Analysis,* Washington, DC: US Department of the Army, 1990.

FM 90–2, *Tactical Deception*, Washington, DC: US Department of the Army, 1978.

MOS 97B, *Counterintelligence Agent*, Washington, DC: US Department of the Army, 1978.

US Marine Corps, *Small Wars Manual* (Washington, DC: 1940); available at www.au.af. mil/au/awc/awcgate/swm/full.pdf (accessed 6 February 2012)

Modern Works

Adams, W. L. T., 'Antipater and Cassander, generalship on restricted sources in the 4th century', *Ancient World* 10 (1984), pp. 79–88.

Adcock, F. E., *The Greek and Macedonian Art of War*, Berkeley: University of California Press, 1957.

Adcock, F. E. and Moseley, D. J., *Diplomacy in Ancient Greece,* New York: St Martin's Press, 1975.

Adkins, A. W. H., *Merit and Responsibility; A Study in Greek Values*, Oxford: The Clarendon Press, 1960.

Albracht, Franz, *Battle and Battle Description in Homer: A Contribution to the History of War*, trans. and ed. by Peter Jones, Malcolm Willcock and Gabriele Wright, London: Duckworth, 2005.

Allison, J. W., *Power and Preparedness in Thucydides*, Baltimore: The Johns Hopkins University Press, 1989.

Amit, M., 'Hostages in ancient Greece', in *Rivista di Filologia e di Istruzione Classica* 98 (1970), pp. 129–47.

Anderson, J. K., 'Cleon's orders at Amphipolis', *JHS* 85 (1965).

Anderson, J. K., 'Hoplite weapons and offensive arms', in V. D. Hanson (ed.), *Hoplites: The Classical Greek Battle Experience*, London and New York: Routledge, 1991, pp. 15–37.

Anderson, J. K., 'Hoplites and heresies: A note', *JHS* 104 (1984), p. 152.

Anderson, J. K., *Military Theory and Practice in the Age of Xenophon*, Berkeley: University of California Press, 1970.

Anderson, J. K., *Xenophon*, London: Duckworth, 1974.

Andersen, Oivind, 'Odysseus and the Wooden Horse', *Symbolae Osloenses* 52 (1977), pp. 5–18.

Applegate, Rex, *Scouting and Patrolling, Ground Reconnaissance Principles and Training*, Boulder, CO: Paladin Press, 1980.

Archibald, Z. H., *The Odrysian Kingdom of Thrace*, Oxford: The Clarendon Press; New York: Oxford University Press, 1998.

Ardant du Picq, J. J., *Battle Studies: Ancient and Modern Battle*, trans. from the 8th edn in the French by Colonel John N. Greely and Major Robert C. Cotton, Harrisburg, PA: The Military Service Publishing Co., 1947. Originally published in 1870.

Armstrong, James, 'The arming motif in the Iliad', *AJPh* 79 (1958), pp. 337–54.

Austin, M. M., 'Hellenistic kings, war and the economy', *CQ* 36 (1986), pp. 450–66.

Austin, M. M., *The Hellenistic World from Alexander to the Roman Conquest: A Selection of Ancient Sources in Translation*, Cambridge: Cambridge University Press, 1981 [2nd edn 2006].

Austin, M. M., 'War and culture in the Seleucid Empire', in T. Bekker-Nielsen and L. Hannestad (eds), *War as a Cultural and Social Force: Essays on Warfare in Antiquity*, Copenhagen: Det Kongelige Danske Videnskabernes Selskab, 2001, pp. 90–109.

Austin, Norman, *Archery at the Dark of the Moon: Poetic Problems in Homer's Odyssey*, Berkeley: University of California Press, 1975.

Austin, N. J. E. and Rankov, B., *Exploratio: Military and Political Intelligence in the Roman World from the Second Punic War to the Battle of Adrianople*, New York and London: Routledge, 1995.

Aymard, A., 'Mercenariat et histoire grecque', in *Études d'Histoire Ancienne*, Serie 'Études et Methodes' 16, Paris: Publications de la Faculte des Lettres de Paris, 1967, pp. 487–98.

Bader, F., 'L'art de la fugue dans l'Odyssée', *REG* 89 (1976), pp. 18–39.

Bagnall, Nigel, *The Peloponnesian War: Athens, Sparta, and the Struggle for Greece*, New York: St Martin's Press, 2004.

Baillie Reynolds, P. K., 'The shield signal at the Battle of Marathon', *JHS* 49 (1929), pp. 100–5.

Baker, P., 'Les mercenaries', in F. Prost, *Armée et Sociétés de la Grèce Classique. Aspects Sociaux et Politiques de la Guerre aux Ve et IVe s. av. J.-C.*, Paris: Ed. Errance, 1999, pp. 240–55.

Bar-Kochva, B., *The Seleucid Army*, Cambridge: Cambridge University Press, 1976.

Bar-Kochva, B., 'Seron and Cestius Gallus at Beit Horon', *PEQ* 108 (1976), pp. 13–21.

Barry, W. D., 'Roof tiles and urban violence in the ancient world', *GRBS* 37, 1 (1996), pp. 55–74.

Beattie, A. J., 'Nisaea and Minoa', *Rh. Mus.* 163 (1960), pp. 21–43.

Bengtson, H., *Die Strategie in der Hellenistischen Zeit*, Munich: Beck, 1937–52.

Bennett, B. and Roberts, M., *The Wars of Alexander's Successors 323–281 BC*, Barnsley: Pen and Sword, 2008.

Berve, Helmut, 'Staat und Staatsgesinnung der Griechen', *Neue Jahrbücher für Antike und Deutsche Bildung* 1 (1938), pp. 3–15.

Best, J. G. P., *Thracian Peltasts and Their Influence on Greek Warfare*, Groningen: Wolters-Noordhoff, 1969.

Beston, P., 'Hellenistic military leadership', in H. van Wees (ed.), *War and Violence in Ancient Greece*, London: Duckworth, 2000, pp. 315–35.

Bettalli, Marco, 'Enea tattico e l'insegnamento dell'arte militare', *AFLS* 7 (1986), pp. 73–89.

Bettalli, Marco, *I Mercenari Nel Mondo Greco*, Pisa: ETS, 1995.

Betts, Richard K., *Surprise Attack. Lessons for Defense Planning*, Washington, DC: The Brookings Institution, 1982.

Bickerman, E., *Institutions des Séleucides*, Paris: Paul Geuthner, 1938.

Booth, Ken, *Strategy and Ethnocentrism*, New York: Holmes and Meier, 1979.

Borgeaud, P., *The Cult of Pan in Ancient Greece*, Chicago: University of Chicago Press, 1988.

Borza, Eugene, 'Alexander's communications', in *Ancient Macedonia*, vol. 2, 1977, pp. 295–303; reprinted in *Makedonika*, Claremont, CA: Regina Books, 1996.

Bose, Partha, *Alexander the Great's Art of Strategy*, London: Penguin, 2003.

Bosworth, A. B., *The Legacy of Alexander: Politics, Warfare and Propaganda under the Successors*, Oxford: Oxford University Press, 2002.

Bowden, Hugh, 'Hoplites and Homer: Warfare, hero cult, and the ideology of the polis', in J. Rich and G. Shipley (eds), *War and Society in the Greek World*, London and New York: Routledge, 1993, pp. 45–63.

Bracken, Paul, *Fire in the East: The Rise of Asian Military Power and the Second Nuclear Age*, New York: Harper Collins, 1999.

Bradford, A. S., 'The duplicitous Spartan', in A. Powell and S. Hodkinson (eds), *The Shadow of Sparta*, London and New York: Routledge 1994, pp. 59–85.

Bresson, P., 'Hellenistic military leadership', in H. van Wees, *War and Violence in Ancient Greece*, London: Duckworth, 2000, pp. 319–21.

Breuckner, A., 'Zu Athenischen Grabreliefs', *Archaologische Jahrbuch des Kaiserlich Deutschen Archaeologischen Instituts, Berlin* 10 (1895).

Brice, Lee L. and Roberts, Jennifer T. (eds), *Recent Directions in the Military History of the Ancient World*, Claremont, CA: Regina Books, 2011.

Brizzi, Giovanni, *I Sistemi Informativi dei Romani. Principi e Realtà Nell' Età Delle Conquista Oltremare (218–168 a.C.)*, Historia Einzelschriften 39, Wiesbaden: Steiner, 1982.

Brown, Truesdell S., 'Aeneas Tacticus, Herodotus and the Ionian revolt', *Historia* 30, 4 (1981), pp. 385–93.

Buckler, J., 'Epameinondas and the Embolon', *Phoenix* 39 (1985), pp. 134–43.

Bugh, Glenn R., *The Horsemen of Athens*, Princeton: Princeton University Press, 1988.

Burkert, Walter, 'Das Lied von Ares und Aphrodite, Zum Verhältnis von Odyssee und Ilas, *RhM* 103 (1960), pp. 130–44.

Burn, A. R., 'The Generalship of Alexander the Great', in *Greece and Rome* 12 (1963), pp. 140–54.

Burn, A. R., *Persia and the Greeks*, London: Arnold, 1962.

Bury, J. B., Cook, S. A., Adcock, F. E. *et al.* (eds), *Cambridge Ancient History*, New York: Macmillan, 1924–1966, 12 vols, 5 vols of plates.

Bury, J. B. and Meiggs, Russell, *A History of Greece to the Death of Alexander the Great*, New York: St Martin's Press, 1975, 4th edn.

Buxton, R. G. A., *Persuasion in Greek Tragedy; A Study of Peitho*, Cambridge: Cambridge University Press, 1982.

Cabanes, P., 'Recherches épigraphiques en Albanie; péripolarques et peripoloi en Grèce du Nord-Ouest et en Illyrie à la période hellénistiques', *CRAI* (1991), pp. 197–221.

Cairns, D. L., *Aidos: The Psychology and Ethics of Honour and Shame in Ancient Greek Literature*, Oxford: The Clarendon Press, 1993.

Callwell, Col. C. E., *Small Wars: Their Principles and Practice*, London: 1896; Wakefield: E. P. Publishing, 1976, 3rd edn.

Cambitoglu, A. and Papadopoulos, J. K. and Tudor, O. (eds), *Torone I: The Excavations of 1975, 1976 and 1978*, Athens: He en Athenais Archaiologik e Hetaireia, 2001, 3 vols.

Carlisle, Miriam and Levaniouk, Olga (eds), *Nine Essays on Homer*, Lanham, MD: Rowman and Littlefield, 1999.

Carman, J. and Harding, A. (eds), *Ancient Warfare:* Archaeological Perspectives, Stroud: Sutton, 1999.

Carney, T. F., *The Shape of the Past: Models and Antiquity*, Lawrence, KS: Coronado Press, 1975.

Cartledge, P., 'Hoplites and heroes: Sparta's contribution to the technique of ancient warfare', *JHS* 97 (1977), pp. 11–27.

Cartledge, Paul, *Agesilaus and the Crisis of Sparta*, Baltimore: Johns Hopkins University Press, 1987.

Cartledge, Paul, 'The politics of Spartan pederasty', *Proceedings of the Cambridge Philological Society* 27 (1981).

Cassidy, Robert M., *Counterinsurgency and the Global War on Terror; Military Culture and the Irregular War*, Stanford, CA: Stanford Security Studies, 2008.

Cawkwell G. L., 'Orthodoxy and hoplites', *CQ* 39 (1989), pp. 375–89.

Chaniotis, A., 'Foreign soldiers – native girls? Constructing and crossing boundaries in Hellenistic cities with foreign garrisons', in A. Chaniótis and P. Ducrey (eds), *Army and Power in the Ancient World*, Stuttgart: Steiner, 2002, pp. 99–113.

Chaniotis, A., *War in the Hellenistic World*, Oxford: Blackwell, 2005.

Chaniotis, Angelos and Ducrey, Pierre (eds), *Army and Power in the Ancient World*, Stuttgart: Steiner, 2002.

Chrimes, K., *Ancient Sparta*, Manchester: Manchester University Press, 1949.

Chroust, A. H., 'Treason and patriotism in ancient Greece', *Journal of the History of Ideas* 15 (1954), pp. 280–8.

Cimbala, S. J. (ed.), *Intelligence and Intelligence Policy in a Democratic Society*, Dobbs Ferry, NY: Transnational Publishers, 1987.

Clausewitz, Carl von, *On War*, ed. and trans. by Michael Howard and Peter Paret, Princeton, NJ: Princeton University Press, 1976.

Clay, J. S., *The Wrath of Athena*, Lanham, MD: Rowman and Littlefield, 1997.

Cline, E. H., *The Battles of Armageddon: Megiddo and the Jezreel Valley from the Bronze Age to the Nuclear Age*, Ann Arbor: University of Michigan Press, 2000.

Coffee, N., *The Commerce of War: Exchange and Social Order in Latin Epic*, Chicago: University of Chicago Press, 2009.

Coker, Christopher, *Waging War without Warriors? The Changing Culture of Military Conflict*, Boulder, CO: Lynne Rienner, 2002.

Collins, Leslie, *Studies in Characterization in the Iliad*, Beiträge zur klassische Philologie 189, Frankfurt am Main: Athenaeum, 1988.

Connelly, J. B., 'Parthenon and *parthenoi*: Mythological interpretation of the Parthenon frieze', *AJA* 100 (1996), pp. 53–80.

Connolly, Peter, *Greece and Rome at War*, Englewood Cliffs: Prentice-Hall; London: Macdonald Phoebus, 1981.

Connolly, Peter, *The Greek Armies*, Morristown: Silver Burdett, 1977.

Connor, W. R., 'Early Greek land warfare as symbolic expression', in E. L. Wheeler, *The Armies of Classical Greece*, Aldershot, England and Burlington, VT: Ashgate, 2007, pp. 83–109; reprint edition of W. R. Connor, 'Early Greek land warfare as symbolic expression', *P&P* 119 (1978), pp. 3–28.

Cooper, G., 'Thucydides 8.33.3–4 and the use of torture by the Spartan Astyochus and Pedaritus during interrogations at Erythrae in the late fall of 412', in E. Livrea and S. Provitera (eds), *Studi in Onore di Anthos Ardizzaoni*, Milan: *Filologiae e Critica* 25, 1978, pp. 223–9.

Cooper, J. F., *The Deerslayer*, New York: President Publishing Co., 1940.

Crotty, K., *The Poetics of Supplication: Homer's Iliad and Odyssey*, Ithaca, NY: Cornell University Press, 1994.

Cunliffe, Barry, *The Ancient Celts*, Harmondworth: Penguin, 2000.

Danek, George, *Studien zur Dolonie*, Wiener Studien Beiheft 12, Vienna: Österreichische Akademie der Wissenschaften, 1988.

D'Arms, E. F. and Hully, K. K., 'The Oresteia story in the Odyssey', *TAPA* 77 (1946), pp. 207–13.

Darmstaedter, Ernst, 'Feuer-telegraphie im altertum', *Die Umschau* (1924), pp. 505–7.

Davidson, O. M., 'Dolon and Rhesus in the *Iliad*', *Quaderni Urbinati di Cultura Classica* 30 (1979), pp. 61–6.

Davie, M. R., *Evolution of War*, New Haven, Yale University Press, 1929.

Davies, M., 'Dolon and Rhesus', *Prometheus* 31 (2005), pp. 29–34.

Dawson, D., *The Origins of Western Warfare: Militarism and Morality in the Ancient World*, Boulder, CO: Westview Press, 1996.

Delbrück, Hans, *History of the Art of War*, vol. 1, *Warfare in Antiquity*, trans. by Walter J. Renfroe, Jr, Lincoln, NE and London: University of Nebraska Press, 1990.

Deonna, W., 'Les cornes gauches', *Revue des Etudes Anciennes* (1940).

DeSouza, Philip, *Piracy and the Graeco-Roman World*, Cambridge: Cambridge University Press, 1999.

Detienne, M., 'La phalange: Problèmes et controversies', in J. P. Vernant, *Problèmes de la Guerre en Grèce Ancienne*, Paris: La Haye Mouton, 1968, pp. 119–42.

Detienne, M. and Vernant, J. P., *Cunning Intelligence in Greek Culture and Society*, trans. from the French by Janet Lloyd, Hassocks, Sussex: Harvester Press; Atlantic Highlands, NJ: Humanities Press, 1978.

Devine, A. M., 'Diodorus' account of the Battle of Paraitacene (317 BCE)', *The Ancient World* 12 (1985), pp. 75–86.

Ditte, LTC Alfred, *Observations sur les Guerres dans les Colonies*, Paris: Henri Charles-LaVauzelle, 1905.

Dixon, N., *On the Psychology of Military Incompetence*, New York: Basic Books, 1976.

Dodds, E. R. (ed.), *Euripides' Bacchae*, Oxford: The Clarendon Press, 1960.

Dornseiff, F., 'Doloneia', in *Mélanges Henri Grégoire*, *Annuiare de l'Institut de philologie et d'histoire Orientales et Slaves* 10 (1950), pp. 239–52.

Droysen, H., *Heerwesen und Kriegführung der Griechen*, Freiburg: Mohr, 1889.

Du Bois, Page, *Trojan Horses. Saving the Classics from Conservatives*, New York: New York University Press, 2001.

Ducrey, Pierre, *Le Traitement des Prisoniers de Guerre dans la Grèce Antique*, Paris: Editions E. de Boccard, 1999.

Ducrey, Pierre, *Warfare in Ancient Greece*, trans. by Janet Lloyd, New York: Schocken, 1986.

Dué, Casey and Ebbott, Mary, *Iliad 10 and the Poetics of Ambush*, Washington, DC: Harvard University Press, 2010.

Dupuy, T. N., *Understanding War*, New York: Paragon House, 1987.

Dupuy, T. N. *et al.*, *International Military and Defense Encyclopedia*, Washington, DC: Brasseys, 1993.

Dvornik, Francis, *The Origins of Intelligence Services*, New Brunswick, NJ: Rutgers University Press, 1974.

Echols, E. C., 'The ancient slinger', *CW* 43 (1950), pp. 227–30.

Edgeworth, R., 'Ajax and Teucer in the Iliad', *Rivista di Filologia e di Instruzione Classica* 113 (1985), pp. 27–31.

Edwards, Anthony T., *Achilles in the Odyssey*, Königstein: Anton Hain, 1985.

Ehrhardt, C., 'Xenophon and Diodorus on Aegospotami', *Phoenix* 24 (1970), pp. 225–8.

Eichhorn, F., *Die Dolonie*, Garmisch-Partenkirchen: Moser, 1973.

Engels, Donald W., *Alexander the Great and the Logistics of the Macedonian Army*, Berkeley: University of California Press, 1978.

Engels, Donald W., 'Alexander's intelligence system', *CQ* 30 (1980), pp. 327–40.

Erbse, H., 'Betrachtungen über das 5 Buch der Ilias', *Rheinisches Museum* 104 (1961), pp. 156–89.

Erfurth, Waldemar, *Surprise*, trans. by Stefan T. Possony and Daniel Vilfroy, Harrisburg, PA: Military Service Publishing, 1943.

Étienne, P. and Roesch, P., 'Convention militaire entre les cavaliers d'Orchomène et ceux de Cheronée', *BCH* 102 (1978), pp. 359–74.

Everson, Tim, *Warfare in Ancient Greece: Arms and Armour from the Heroes of Homer to Alexander the Great*, Stroud: Sutton, 2004.

Farron, S., 'Attitudes to military archery in the *Iliad*', in A. F. Basson and W. J. Dominik (eds), *Literature, Art, History: Studies on Classical Antiquity and Tradition. In Honour of W. J. Henderson*, Frankfurt am Main: Peter Lang, 2003, pp. 169–84.

Fenik, B., *Studies in the Odyssey*, Hermes Einzelschriften 30, Wiesbaden: Steiner, 1974.

Fenik, Bernard, *Iliad X and the Rhesus*, Collection Latomus vol. 73, Brussels: Berchem, 1964.

Fenik, Bernard, *Typical Battle Scenes in the Iliad: Studies in the Narrative Techniques of Homeric Battle Description*, Wiesbaden: Steiner, 1968.

Ferrill, Arther, *The Origins of War: From the Stone Age to Alexander the Great*, New York: Thames and Hudson, 1985.

Feyel, M., *Polybe et l'histoire de Boéotie au IIIe Siècle Avant Notre Ère*, Paris: E. de Boccard, 1942.

Fichtner, D. P., 'Intelligence assessment in the Peloponnesian war', *Studies in Intelligence* 38 (1994), pp. 59–64.

Finley, J. H., *Homer's Odyssey*, Cambridge, MA: Harvard University Press, 1978.

Finley, M. I., *Ancient Sicily*, New York: Viking Press, 1969.

Fisher, Nick (ed.) *Archaic Greece: New Approaches and New Evidence*, London: Duckworth and The Classical Press of Wales, 1998.

FitzGerald, Augustine, *Peace and War in Antiquity; A Selection of Passages from Ancient Greek and Latin Authors*, Presented in English, with the Originals Appended, London: The Scholar's Press, 1931.

Flaumenhaft, Mera, 'The undercover hero: Odysseus from dark to daylight', *Interpretation* 10 (1982), pp. 9–41.

Forves, R. J., *Studies in Ancient Technology*, Leiden: Brill, 1955.

Fowler, Robert, *The Cambridge Companion to Homer*, Cambridge: Cambridge University Press, 2004.

Franz, J. P., *Krieger, Bauern, Bürger: Untersuchungen zu den Hopliten der Archaischen und Klassischen Zeit,* Europäische Hochschulschriften, Reihe III, Bd. 925, Frankfurt, 2002.

Fraser, A. D., 'The myth of the phalanx-scrimmage', *CW* 36 (1942), pp. 15–16.

French, Shannon, *Code of the Warrior*, Lanham, MD: Rowman and Littlefield, 2003.

Frontisi-Ducroux, F., *Dédale: Mythologie de l'Artisan en Grèce Ancienne*, Paris: Maspero, 1975.

Fuller, J. F. C., *The Generalship of Alexander the Great*, New Brunswick, NJ: Rutgers University Press, 1960.

Gabriel, R. A. and Metz, K., *From Sumer to Rome: The Military Capabilities of Ancient Armies*, New York: Greenwood Press, 1991.

Gabrielsen, V., 'The impact of armed forces on government and politics in Archaic and Classical Greek *poleis*: A response to Hans van Wees', in A. Chianotis and P. Ducrey, *Army and Power in the Ancient World*, Stuttgart: Steiner, 2002.

Gabrielsen, V., 'Naval warfare: Its economic and social impact on Greek Cities', in T. Bekker-Nielsen and L. Hannestad (eds), *War as a Cultural and Social Force: Essays on Warfare in Antiquity*, Copenhagen: Det Kongelige Danske Videnskabernes Selskab, 2001, 72–89.

Gaebel, R. E., *Cavalry Operations in the Ancient Greek World*, Norman, OK: University of Oklahoma Press, 2002.

Galinsky, G. K., *The Herakles Theme*, Oxford: Blackwell, 1972.

Garlan, Y., *Recherches de Poliorcétique Grecque*, Paris: Boccard, 1974.

Garlan, Y., *War in the Ancient World*, trans. by Janet Lloyd, London: Chatto and Windus, 1975.

Gaunt, D. M., 'The change of plan in the "Doloneia"', *G&R* 18, 2 (1971), pp. 191–8.

Gauthier, Philippe, 'Notes sur la rôle du gymnase dans les cités hellénistiques', in M. Wörrle and P. Zanker (eds), *Stadtbild und Bürgerbild im Hellenismus*, Munich: Beck, 1995, pp. 1–11.

Gauthier, Philippe, 'Notes sur trois décrets honorant des citoyens bienfaiteurs', *Revue de philologie* 56 (1982), pp. 215–31.

George, D. B., 'Euripides' *Heracles* 140–235: Staging and the stage iconography of Herakles' bow', *GRBS* 35 (1994), pp. 145–57.

Gernet, Louis, 'Dolon le loup', *Mélanges Franz Cumont*, Bruxelles: Secrétariat de l'Institut. Annuaire de l'Institut de Philologie et d'Histoire orientales et slaves 4, 1936, pp. 189–208.

Geske, Norbert, *Nicias und das Volk von Athen im Archidamischen Krieg*, Stuttgart: Steiner, 2005.

Gichon, M., 'Cestius Gallus' campaign in Judaea', *PEQ* 113 (1981), pp. 39–62.

Goldsworthy, A. K., 'The othismos, myths and heresies: The nature of hoplite battle', *War in History* 4, 1 (1997), pp. 1–26.

Gomme, A. W., 'A forgotten factor in Greek naval strategy', *JHS* 53 (1933), pp. 16–24.

Gomolka-Fuchs, Gudrun, *La Guerre en Grèce à l'Epoque Classique*, Rennes: Presses Universitaires, 1999.

Graf, F., 'Women, war, and war-like divinities', *ZPE* 55 (1984), pp. 245–54.

Gray, Colin, 'Out of the wilderness: Prime time for strategic culture', *Comparative Strategy* 26, 1 (January 2007).

Green, Peter, *Armada from Athens*, Garden City, NY: Doubleday, 1970.

Green, Peter, *The Greco-Persian Wars*, Berkeley: University of California Press, 1996.

Greenhalgh, P. A. L., *Early Greek Warfare*, Cambridge: Cambridge University Press, 1973.

Griffith, G. T., *Mercenaries in the Hellenistic World*, New York: AMS Press, 1977 (reprint edn).

Grundy, G. B., *The Great Persian War and its Preliminaries*, London: John Murray, 1901.

Grundy, G. B., *Thucydides and the History of His Age*, Oxford: Blackwell, 1948, 2 vols.

Hackett, Sir John, *Warfare in the Ancient World*, New York: Facts on File, 1989.

Hamel, Debra, *Athenian Generals: Military Authority in the Classical Period*, Mnemosyne Supplement 182, Leiden: Brill, 1998.

Hamilton, Charles and Krentz, P. (eds), *Polis and Polemos*, Claremont: Regina Books, 1997.

Hammes, Col. T. X., *The Sling and the Stone. On War in the Twenty-First Century*, St Paul, MN: Zenith Press, 2004.

Hammond, N. G. L., *Alexander the Great: King, Commander and Statesman*, Park Ridge, NJ: Noyes Press, 1980.

Hammond, N. G. L., 'The campaigns in Amphilochia during the Archidamian war', *BSA* 37 (1936–7), pp. 128–140.

Hansen, W. F., *The Conference Sequence, Patterned Narrative and Narrative Inconsistency in the Odyssey*, Classical Studies 8, Berkeley and Los Angeles, CA: University of California, 1972.

Hanson, Victor Davis, *Carnage and Culture: Landmark Battles in the Rise of Western Power*, New York: Doubleday, 2001.

Hanson, Victor Davis, *Fields Without Dreams: Defending the Agrarian Idea*, New York: Free Press, 1996.

Hanson, Victor Davis, 'Hoplite battle as ancient Greek warfare: When, where and why?', in H. van Wees, *War and Violence in Ancient Greece*, London: Duckworth, 2000, pp. 167–200.

Hanson, Victor Davis, 'Hoplite technology in hoplite battle', in V. D. Hanson, *Hoplites*, London and New York: Routledge, 1991, pp. 63–84.

Hanson, Victor Davis (ed.), *Hoplites: The Classical Greek Battle Experience*, London and New York: Routledge, 1991.

Hanson, Victor Davis, *The Other Greeks. The Family Farm and the Agrarian Roots of Western Civilization*, Berkeley: University of California Press, 1999.

Hanson, Victor Davis, *The Soul of Battle: From Ancient Times to the Present Day. How Three Great Liberators Vanquished Tyranny*, New York: Anchor Books, 2001.

Hanson, Victor Davis, *The Wars of the Ancient Greeks*, London: Cassell, 1999.

Hanson, Victor Davis, *The Western Way of War: Infantry Battle in Classical Greece*, New York: Knopf, 1989.

Hart, Basil Liddell, *The British Way of Warfare*, London: Faber and Faber, 1932.

Hatzfeld, Jean, *Alcibiade: Étude sur l'Histoire d'Athènes à la Fin du Ve Siècle*, Paris: Presses Universitaires de France, 1951.

Hatzopoulos, M. B., *L'Organization de l'Armée Macédonienne sous les Antigonides*, Athens: Centre de Recherches de l'Antiquité grecque et romaine; Paris: Diffusion de Boccard, 2001.

Havelock, Eric, 'War as a way of life in Classical culture', in *Classical Values and the Modern World,* Vannier Lectures 1970–1, Ottawa: University of Ottawa Press, 1972, pp. 19–78.

Helbig, Wolfgang, *Les Hippeis Atheniens*, Paris: Klincksieck, 1902.

Henderson, B. W., *The Great War between Athens and Sparta*, London: Macmillan, 1927.

Henry, A. S., *Torone, The Literary, Documentary and Epigraphical Testimonia*, Athens: Archaeological Society at Athens, 2004.

Henry, R. M., 'The place of the Doloneia in epic poetry', *CR* 19 (1905), pp. 192–7.

Heubeck, A., *Der Odyssee, Dichter und die Ilias*, Erlange: Palm and Enke, 1954.

Heusinger, H., *Stilistische Untersuchungen zur Dolonie*, Leipzig: Druck von C. and E. Vogel, 1939.

Heymont, I., *Combat Intelligence in Modern Warfare*, Harrisburg, PA: Stackpole, 1960.

Heza, E., 'Ruse de guerre – trait caracteristique d'une tactique nouvelle dans l'oeuvre de Thucydide', *Eos* 62 (1974), pp. 227–44.

Hijmans, B. L., Jr, 'Archers in the Iliad', in J. S. Boersma (ed.), *Festoen; Opgedragen aan A. N. Zadoks-Josephus Jitta bij Haar Zeventigste Verjaardag*, Scripta Archaeologica Groningana 6, Groningen: H. D. Tjeenk Willink, 1976, pp. 343–52.

Hinckley, L. V., *Ajax and Achilles: Their Literary Relationship from Homer to Sophocles*, Diss, Chapel Hill: University of North Carolina, 1972.

Hirsch, S. W., *The Friendship of the Barbarians*, Hanover, NH: University Press of New England, 1985.

Hoelscher, U., '*Die Atriden Saga in der Odyssee*', in R. Alewyn, H. Singer and B. von Weise (eds), Festschrift für Richard Alewyn, Köln und Graz: Böhlau, 1967, pp. 10–16.

Hogarth, D. G., 'The army of Alexander', *Journal of Philology* 17 (1888).

Holladay, A. J., 'Athenian strategy in the Archidamian war', *Historia* 27 (1978), pp. 399–427.

Holladay, A. J., 'Hoplites and heresies', in *JHS* 102 (1982), pp. 94–103.

Holoka, J., 'Looking darkly (UPODRA ILWN): Reflections of status and decorum in Homer', *TAPA* 113 (1983), pp. 1–16.

Hornblower, Simon, *The Greek World 479–323*, New York: Routledge, 1983.

Hornblower, Simon and Spawforth, Anthony, *The Oxford Classical Dictionary*, New York: Oxford University Press, 1996, 3rd edn.

Howald, Ernst, *Der Mythos als Dichtung*, Zürich and Leipzig: Niehans, 1937.

Hudson, Harris Gary, 'The shield signal at Marathon', *AHR* 42 (1936–7), pp. 359–443.

Humble, Richard, *Warfare in the Ancient World*, London: Cassell, 1980.

Humphreys, S. C., *Anthropology and the Greeks*, London: Routledge, 1978.

Hunt, P., 'Military forces', *CHGRW*, vol. 1.

Hutchinson, Geoffrey, *Xenophon and the Art of Command*, London: Greenhill Books, 2000.

Iapichino, Linda, *La 'Guerra Psicologica' dell'Anabasi di Senofonte*, Wien: Holzhausen, 2000.

Ilari, V., *Guerra e Diritto Nel Mondo Antico*, Milan: A. Giuffrè, 1980.

Jackson, A. H., 'Hoplites and the Gods: The dedication of captured arms and armour', in V. D. Hanson, *Hoplites: The Classical Greek Battle Experience*, pp. 228–49, London and New York: Routledge, 1991.

Jackson, A. H., 'War and raids for war booty in the world of Odysseus', in J. Rich and G. Shipley (eds), *War and Society in the Greek World*, London and New York: Routledge, 1993, pp. 64–76.

Jens, W., 'Die Dolonie und ihr Dichter', *Studium Generale* 8 (1955), pp. 616–25.

Johnston, Sarah Iles, 'Myth, festival, and poet: The Homeric hymn to Hermes in its performance context', *CP* 97 (2002), pp. 109–32

Jones, A. H. M., *Athenian Democracy*, Oxford: Blackwell, 1957.

Kaegi, Walter E., 'The crisis in military historiography', *Armed Forces and Society* 7 (1981), pp. 299–316.

Kagan, D., *The Archidamian War*, Ithaca, NY: Cornell University Press, 1974.

Kagan, D., *The Fall of the Athenian Empire*, Ithaca, NY: Cornell University Press, 1987.

Kagan, D., *The Peloponnesian War*, New York: Viking, 2003.

Kam, Ephraim, *Surprise Attack*, Cambridge, MA: Harvard University Press, 2004 (revised edn).

Kearns, E., 'Saving the city', in O. Murray and S. Price, *The Greek City from Homer to Alexander*, Oxford: The Clarendon Press, 1990, pp. 323–44.

Keegan, John, *The Face of Battle*, New York: Viking Press, 1976.

Keegan, John, *A History of Warfare*, New York: Knopf, 1993.

Keegan, John, 'In this war of civilizations, the West will prevail', *Daily Telegraph* (8 October 2001).

Kennell, N. M., *The Gymnasium of Virtue*, Chapel Hill, NC: University of North Carolina Press, 1995.

Kern, P. B., *Ancient Siege Warfare*, Bloomington: Indiana University Press, 1999.

Kilcullen, David, *The Accidental Guerrilla; Losing Small Wars in the Midst of a Big One*, Oxford and New York: Oxford University Press, 2009.

Kinzl, Konrad, *A Companion to the Classical Greek World*, Malden, MA: Blackwell, 2006.

Kirk, G. S., *Homer and the Epic: A Shortened Version of the Songs of Homer*, London: Cambridge University Press, 1965.

Kirk, G. S., *The Iliad: A Commentary*, Cambridge: Cambridge University Press, 1985–93, 6 vols.

Kirk, G. S., *The Songs of Homer*, Cambridge: Cambridge University Press, 1962.

Kirk, G. S., 'War and warrior in the Homeric poems', in J. P. Vernant, *Problèmes de la Guerre en Grèce Ancienne*, Paris: La Haye, Mouton, 1969, pp. 93–117.

Klingner, F., 'Über die Dolonie', *Hermes* 75 (1940), pp. 337–68.

Knoepfler, D., 'Les kryptoi du stratège Epicharès à Rhamnous et le debut de la guerre de Chrémonidès, *BCH* 118 (1993), 327–41.

Korfmann, M., 'The sling as a weapon', *Scientific American* 229, 4 (1973), pp. 34–42.

Krentz, Peter, 'Casualties in hoplite battle', *GRBS* 26, 1 (1985), pp. 13–20.

Krentz, Peter, 'Continuing the Othismos on Othismos', *AHB* 8 (1994), pp. 45–9.

Krentz, Peter, 'Deception in Archaic and Classical Greek warfare', in H. van Wees (ed.), *War and Violence in Ancient Greece*, London: Duckworth, 2000, pp. 167–200.

Krentz, Peter, 'Fighting by the rules: The invention of the hoplite *agôn*', in E. L. Wheeler, *The Armies of Classical Greece*, Aldershot, Hants and Burlington, VT: Ashgate, 2007.

Krentz, Peter, 'The nature of hoplite battle', *ClAnt* 4, 1 (1985), pp. 50–61.

Kromayer, J. and Veith, G., *Heerwesen und Kriegführung der Griechen und Romer*, Munich: C. H. Beck, 1928.

Laird, A. G., 'Nisaea and Minoa', *CP* 29, 2 (April 1934), pp. 89–100.

Latacz, J., *Kampfparänese Kampfdarstellung und Kampwirklichkeit in der Ilias, bei Kallinos und Tyrtaios,* Zetemata 66, Munich: Beck, 1977.

Launey, M., *Recherches sur les Armées Hellénistiques,* reimpression avec addenda et mise à joure en postface par Y. Garlan, P. Gauthier and C. Orrieux, Paris: de Boccard, 1987.

Lawrence, A. W., *Greek Aims in Fortification,* Oxford: The Clarendon Press, 1980.

Laser, S., 'Über das Verhältnis der Dolonie zur Odyssee', *Hermes* 86 (1958), pp. 385–425.

Lazenby, J. F., *The Defence of Greece, 490–479,* Warminster, Wilts: Aris and Phillips, 1993.

Lazenby, J. F., 'The killing zone', in V. D. Hanson, *Hoplites,* London, 1991, pp. 87–109.

Lazenby, J. F., *The Peloponnesian War. A Military Study,* London and New York: Routledge, 2004.

Lazenby, J. F., *The Spartan Army,* Warminster, Wilts: Aris and Phillips, 1985.

Lazenby, J. F. and Whitehead, David, 'The myth of the hoplite's *hoplon*', *CQ* 46, 1 (1996), pp. 27–33.

Lee, John W. I., *A Greek Army on the March, Soldiers and Survival in Xenophon's Anabasis,* Cambridge: Cambridge University Press, 2007.

Leebaert, Derek, *To Dare to Conquer,* New York: Little, Brown, 2006.

Lehrs, K., *De Aristarchi Studiis Homericiis,* Leipzig: Teubner, 1882.

Leighton, A. C., 'Secret communications among the Greeks and Romans', *Technology and Culture* 10, 2 (1969), pp. 139–54.

Lendon, J. E., 'Homeric vengeance and the outbreak of Greek wars', in H. van Wees (ed.), *War and Violence in Ancient Greece,* London: Duckworth, 2000.

Lendon, J. E., *Soldiers and Ghosts. A History of Battle in Classical Antiquity,* New Haven: Yale University Press, 2005.

Lendon, J. E., *Song of Wrath. The Peloponnesian War Begins,* New York: Basic Books, 2010.

Lendon, J. E., 'Xenophon and the alternative to realist foreign policy; "Cyropaedia" 3.1.14–31', *JHS* 126 (2006).

Lendon, J. F., 'War and society in the Hellenistic world and the Roman Republic', in *CHGRW,* vol. 1, pp. 498–516.

Lengauer, W., *Greek Commanders in the 5th and 4th Centuries BC,* Warsaw: Wydawnictwa Uniwersytetu Warszawskiego, 1979.

Leveque, P., 'La guerre à l'époque hellénistique', in J.-P. Vernant (ed.), *Problèmes de la Guerres en Grèce Ancienne,* Paris: La Haye, Mouton, 1968, pp. 261–87.

Lewis, I. E. S. *et al.* (eds), *Cambridge Ancient History,* London: Cambridge University Press, 1970 – 19 vols, 5 vols of plates.

Liddell, Henry George and Robert Scott, *A Greek-English Lexicon,* Oxford, Clarendon Press, 1968.

Lippelt, O., *Die Griechischen Leichtbewaffneten bis auf Alexander den Grossen,* Weida in Thuringia: Thomas and Hubert, 1910.

Lissarague, F., *L'autre Guerrier: Archers, Peltastes, Cavaliers dans l'Imagerie Attique*, Paris: Découverte; Rome: Ecole française de Rome, 1990.

Lissarague, F., 'Iconographie de dolon le loup', *RA* (1930), pp. 3–30.

Littauer, M. A. and Crouwel, J. H., *Chariots in Late Bronze Age Greece*, Oxford: Antiquity Publications, 1983.

Loman, P., 'No woman, no war: Women's participation in ancient Greek warfare', *G&R* 51, 1 (2004), pp. 34–54.

Lonis, R., *Guerre et Religion en Grèce à l'Époque Classique*, Paris: Les Belles Lettres, 1979.

Lord, Albert, *The Singer of Tales*, Cambridge: Cambridge University Press, 1960, 2nd edn 2000.

Lorimer, H. L., 'The hoplite phalanx with special reference to the poems of Archilochus and Tyrtaeus', *ABSA* 42 (1947), pp. 76–138.

Losada, L. A., *The Fifth Column in the Peloponnesian war*, Leiden: Brill, 1972.

Luginbill, R. D., 'Othismos: The importance of the mass-shove in hoplite warfare', *Phoenix* 48, 1 (1994), pp. 651–61. Reprinted in E. L. Wheeler, *The Armies of Classical Greece*, Aldershot, Hants and Burlington, VT: Ashgate, 2007, pp. 323–33.

Lung, Col. Huang Ngoc, *Intelligence: Indochina Monographs*, Washington, DC: US Army Center of Military History, 1982.

Luraghi, N., 'Traders, pirates, warriors: The proto-history of Greek mercenary soldiers in the eastern Mediterranean', *Phoenix* 60 (2006), pp. 21–47.

Luttwak, E., *Strategy: The Logic of Peasce and War*, Cambridge: Cambridge University Press, 1987.

Lynn, John A., *Battle: A History of Combat and Culture from Ancient Greece to Modern America*, Boulder, CO: Westview Press, 2003.

Ma, J., 'Fighting *poleis* of the Hellenistic world', in H. van Wees, *War and Violence in Ancient Greece*, London: Duckworth, 2000, pp. 337–76.

Ma, J., 'Oversexed, overpaid, and over here: A response to Angelos Chaniotis', in A. Chaniotis and P. Ducrey (eds), *Army and Power in the Ancient World*, Stuttgart: Steiner, 2002, pp. 115–22.

McKechnie, P., 'Greek mercenary troops and their equipment', *Historia* 43 (1994), pp. 297–305.

McKechnie, P., *Outsiders in the Greek Cities and the Fourth Century BC*, London and New York: Routledge, 1989.

McLeod, W., 'The bow at night: An inappropriate weapon?', *Phoenix* 42 (1988), pp. 121–5.

Magnelli, A., 'Una nova iscrizione da Gortyna (Creta). Qualche considerazione sulla neotas', *Annuario della Scuola Italiana di Archeologia d'Atene*, 70/71 (1992/3), pp. 291–305.

Manganaro, G., 'Kyme e il disastro Phoiletairos', *Chiron* 30 (2000), pp. 403–14.

Mao Tse Tung, *Mao Tse Tung on Guerrilla Warfare*, trans. by Samuel B. Griffith, New York: Praeger, 1961.

Marsden, E. W., *Greek and Roman Artillery*, Historical Development and Technical Treatises, Oxford: The Clarendon Press, 1969, 2 vols.

May, Elmer C., Stadler, Gerald P. and Votaw, John. F., *Ancient and Medieval Warfare*, The West Point Military History Series, Wayne, NJ: Avery Publication Group, 1984.

May, J. M. F., 'Macedonia and Illyria 217–216 BC', *JRS* 36 (1946), pp. 48–56.

Mendelsohn, J. (ed.), *Covert Warfare; Intelligence, Counterintelligence and Military Deception During the World War II Era*, vol. 2, *The Spy Factory and Secret Intelligence*, New York: Garland Press, 1989.

Merritt, B. D., 'Scione, Mende and Torone', *AJA* 27 (1923).

Miller, M. C., *Athens and Persia in the Fifth Century BC: A Study in Cultural Receptivity*, Cambridge: Cambridge University Press, 1997.

Milns, R. D., 'Alexander's Macedonian cavalry and Diodorus 17.4', *JHS* 86 (1966), pp. 167–8.

Montagu, J. D., *Greek and Roman Warfare: Battle, Tactics and Trickery*, London: Greenhill, 2006.

Morgan, C., 'Symbolic and pragmatic aspects of warfare in the Greek world of the 8th to 6th centuries BC', in T. Bekker-Nielsen and L. Hannestad (eds), *War as a Cultural and Social Force*, Copenhagen: Det Kongelige Danske Videnskabernes Selskab, 2001, pp. 20–44.

Morillo, Stephan, Black, Jeremy and Lococo, Paul, *War in World History. Society, Technology and War from Ancient Times to the Present*, New York: McGraw Hill, 2009, 2 vols.

Morris, Ian, *Burial and Ancient Society: The Rise of the Greek City-State*, Cambridge: Cambridge University Press, 1987.

Morris, Ian and Powell, B. B., *A New Companion to Homer*, Leiden: Brill, 1997.

Morrison, J. S. and Coates, J. F., *The Athenian Trireme: The History and Reconstruction of an Ancient Greek Warship*, Cambridge: Cambridge University Press, 1986.

Mueller, B., *Beiträge zur Geschichte des Griechischen Söldnerwesens bis auf die Schlacht von Chäronea*, Frankfurt: Gottlieb and Müller, 1908.

Mueller, Martin, *The Iliad*, London and Boston: Allen & Unwin, 1984.

Murnaghan, Sheila, *Disguise and Recognition in the Odyssey*, Princeton: Princeton University Press, 1987.

Murray, O. and Price, S., *The Greek City from Homer to Alexander*, Oxford: The Clarendon Press, 1990.

Myers, J. L., 'Akhruktos Polemos' (Herodotus V.81), *CR* 57 (1943), pp. 66–7.

Naiden, F., 'Homer's leopard simile', in M. Carlisle and O. Levaniouk (eds), *Nine Essays on Homer*, Lanham, MD: University Press of America, 1999, pp. 177–203.

Nagler, M., *Spontaneity and Tradition: A Study in the Oral Art of Homer*, Berkeley: University of California Press, 1974.

Nagy, Gregory, *The Best of the Achaeans*, Baltimore: Johns Hopkins University Press, 1981.

Nitsche, Adolf, *Untersuchung über die Echtheit der Doloneia*, Marburg: E. Janschitz, 1877.

Ober, Josiah, 'Hoplites and obstacles', in V. D. Hanson, *Hoplites: The Classical Greek Battle Experience*, London and New York: Routledge, 1991.

Ober, Josiah, 'The rules of war in Classical Greece', in *The Athenian Revolution: Essays on Ancient Greek Democracy and Political Theory*, Princeton: Princeton University Press, 1996, pp. 53–71. Originally published in M. Howard, G. J. Andreopoulos and M. R. Shulman (eds), *The Laws of War: Constraints on Warfare in the Western World*, New Haven, Yale University Press, 1994, pp. 12–26, 227–230. Trans. by J. Odin as 'Les règles de guerre en Grèce à l'époque classsique', P. Brulés and J. Oulen (eds), Rennes, 1999, pp. 219–39.

Ollier, F., *Le Mirage Spartiate*, Paris: de Boccard, 1933.

Oman, Charles, *A History of the Art of War in the Middle Ages*, New York, Franklin, 1959, 2 vols.

Orszulik, Karl, *Über das Verhältnis der Doloneia zu den ubrigen Theilen der Ilias und zur Odyssee*, Prog. Teschen, 1883.

Osborne, R., *Classical Landscape with Figures: The Ancient Greek City and its Countryside*, London: Phillip, 1987.

Ostwald, M., *Nomos and the Beginnings of the Athenian Democracy*, Oxford: The Clarendon Press, 1969.

Page, D. L, 'Stesichorus: the Geroneis', *JHS* 93 (1973), pp. 138–54.

Parka, Marilyne G., *Ptocheia or Odysseus in Disguise at Troy*, Papyrus Köln, vol. 6, no. 245, Atlanta: Scholar's Press, 1992.

Parke, H. W., *Greek Mercenary Soldiers from the Earliest Times to the Battle of Ipsus*, Chicago: Ares, 1981; reprint of Oxford, 1933 edn.

Parke, H. W., 'A note on the topography of Syracuse', *JHS* 64 (1944).

Parke, H. W., 'Polyaenus VI 18', *CR* 42 (1928), pp. 120–1.

Parker, G. (ed.), *The Cambridge History of Warfare*, Cambridge: Cambridge University Press, 2005.

Pauly, A. and Wissowa, G., *Real-Encyclopädie der Klassischen Altertumswissenschaft*, Stuttgart: Metzler, 1957.

Pearson, L., *The Greek Historians of the West*, Atlanta, GA: Scholars Press, 1987.

Pelekidis, C., *Histoire de l'Éphébie Attique,* Paris: de Boccard, 1962.

Perlman, P., 'Κρηιες αει ληιβιαι? The marginalization of Crete in Greek thought and the role of piracy in the outbreak of the First Cretan War', in V. Gabrielsen *et al.* (eds), *Hellenistic Rhodes: Politics, Culture and Society*, Aarhus: Aarhus University Press, 1999, pp. 132–61.

Petegorsky, D., *Context and Evocation: Studies in Early Greek and Sanskrit Poetry*, PhD dissertation, University of California Berkeley, 1982.

Peters, F. E., *The Harvest of Hellenism. A History of the Near East from Alexander the Great to the Triumph of Christianity*, New York: Simon and Schuster, 1970.

Petropouliou, A., *Beiträge zur Wirtschafts-und Gesellschaftsgeschichte Kretas in Hellenistischer Zeit*, Frankfurt: Lang, 1985.

Plassart, A., 'Les archers d'Athènes', *REG* 26 (1913), pp. 151–213.

Pomeroy, Arthur J., 'The vision of a Fascist Rome in *Gladiator*', in M. Winkler, *Gladiator: Film and History*, Oxford: Blackwell, 2004.

Poole, J. H., *Phantom Soldier: The Enemy's Answer to US Firepower*, Emerald Isle, NC: Posterity Press, 2001.

Poole, J. H., *Tactics of the Crescent Moon*, Emerald Isle, NC: Posterity Press, 2004.

Porter, Patrick, *Military Orientalism. Eastern War Through Western Eyes*, New York: Columbia University Press, 2009.

Powell, A., 'Mendacity and Sparta's use of the visual', in A. Powell (ed.), *Classical Sparta: Techniques Behind Her Success*, Norman, Oklahoma: University of Oklahoma Press, 1989, pp. 173–92.

Pritchett, W. K., *The Greek State at War*, Berkeley: University of California Press, 1971–91, 5 vols.

Raaflaub, Kurt A., 'A historian's headache. How to read "Homeric society"', in N. Fisher and H. van Wees (eds), *Archaic Greece: New Approaches and New Evidence*, London: Duckworth and The Classical Press of Wales, 1998, pp. 169–93.

Rabel, R. (ed.), *Approaches to Homer: Ancient and Modern*, Swansea: The Classical Press of Wales, 2005.

Rabel, R., 'The theme of need in *Iliad* 9–11', *Phoenix* 45 (1991), pp. 288–91.

Ranke, Fritz, *Homerische Untersuchungen I: Die Dolonie*, Leipzig: Teubner, 1881.

Ray, Fred Eugene, *Land Battles in 5th Century BC Greece*, Jefferson, NC: McFarland, 2009

Redfield, James M., *Nature and Culture in the Iliad: The Tragedy of Hector*, Chicago: University of Chicago Press, 1975.

Reinhardt, Karl, *Die Ilias und ihr Dichter*, Göttingen: Vandenhoeck und Ruprecht, 1961.

Rich, J. and Shipley, G. (eds), *War and Society in the Greek World*, London and New York: Routledge, 1993.

Richmond, J. A., 'Spies in ancient Greece', *G&R* 45 (1998), pp. 1–18.

Ridley, R.T., 'The hoplite as citizen: Athenian military institutions in their social context', *AC* 48 (1979), pp. 508–48.

Risch, E., *Wortbildung der Homerischen Sprache*, Berlin: de Gruyter, 1974, 2nd edn.

Robert, L., *Études Anatoliennes. Recherches sur les Inscriptions Grecques de l'Asie Mineure*, Paris: de Boccard, 1937.

Robert, L., 'Péripolarques', *Hellénica* 10 (Paris, 1955), pp. 283–92.

Rodgers, William Ledyard, *Greek and Roman Naval Warfare*, Annapolis: Naval Institute, 1937.

Roisman, Joseph, *The General Demosthenes and His Use of Military Surprise*, Stuttgart: Steiner, 1993.

Roisman, Joseph, 'Kallikratidas. A Greek patriot?' *CJ* 83, 1 (Oct.–Nov. 1987), pp. 21–33.

Romilly, J. de, 'Guerre et paix entre cités', in J. P. Vernant, *Problèmes de la Guerre en Grèce Ancienne*, Paris: La Haye Mouton, 1968.

Romm, James, *Ghost on the Throne. The Death of Alexander the Great and the War for Crown and Empire*, New York: Knopf, 2011.

Runciman, W. G., 'Greek hoplites, warrior culture, and indirect bias', *Journal of the Royal Anthropological Institute* 4, 4 (Dec. 1998), pp. 731–51.

Russell, A. G., 'The Greek as a mercenary soldier', *G&R* 11 (1942), pp. 103–12.

Russell, Frank Santi, *Information Gathering in Classical Greece*, Ann Arbor: University of Michigan Press, 1999.

Rüter, K., *Odysseeinterpretationen: Untersuchungen zum ersten Buchund zur Phaiakis*, Göttingen: Vandenhoeck, 1969.

Rutherford, R. B., *Homer*, Greece and Rome New Surveys in the Classics 26, Oxford: Oxford University Press, 1996.

Sabin, Philip, 'Land battles', in *CHGRW*, vol. 2, pp. 399–433.

Sabin, Philip, *Lost Battles: Reconstructing the Great Clashes of the Ancient World*, London: Hambledon Continuum, 2007.

Sabin, P., Wees, H. van and Whitby, M. (eds), *Cambridge History of Greek and Roman Warfare*, Cambridge: Cambridge University Press, 2007, 2 vols.

Sage, Michael, *Warfare in Ancient Greece; A Sourcebook*, London and New York: Routledge, 1996.

Said, Edward, *Orientalism*, New York: Vintage Books, 1978.

Said, S., 'Les crimes des prétendents la maison d'Ulyse et les festin de l'Odysée', *Études de la Litterature Ancienne*, 1979, pp. 9–49.

Salmon, J., 'Political hoplites', *JHS* 97 (1977), pp. 84–101.

Salmon, J. B., *Wealthy Corinth, A History of the City to 338 BC,* Oxford: The Clarendon Press, 1984.

Sanders, L. J., *Dionysius I of Syracuse and Greek Tyranny*, NY: Methuen, 1987.

Sankey, Charles, *Spartan and Theban Supremacies*, New York: Charles Scribner, 1886, p. 34.

Schadewaldt, W., 'Hector and Andromache', in G. M. Wright and P. V. Jones, *Homer. German Scholarship in Translation*, Oxford: The Clarendon Press, 1997, pp. 124–42; trans. from *Von Homers Welt und Werk*, Stuttgart: K. F. Koehler, 1957 (3rd edn), pp. 207–29.

Schaps, D., 'The women of Greece in wartime', *CP* 77, 3 (July 1982).

Schnapp-Gourbeillon, Annie, *Lions, Héros, Masques et Représentations de l'Animal chez Homère*, La Découverte, coll. 'Textes à l'appui', 1981.

Schnapp-Gourbeillon, Annie, 'Le lion et le loup. Diomédie et Dolonie dans l'Iliade', *Quaderni di Storia* 8 (1982), pp. 45–77.

Schwien, Col. E., *Combat Intelligence: Its Acquisition and Transmission*, Washington, DC: Infantry Journal, 1936.

Segal, C. P., 'Gorgias and the psychology of the logos', *HSCPH* 66 (1962).

Sekunda, N, *The Ancient Greeks, Armies of Classical Greece 5th and 4th Centuries BC*, London: Osprey, 1986.

Sekunda, N, *Greek Hoplite 480–323 BC*, London: Osprey Élite, 2000.

Sekunda, N., *The Persian Army 560–330 BC*, London: Osprey, 1992.

Sekunda, N., *The Spartan Army*, London: Osprey, 1998.

Sekunda, N., and P. de Souza, 'Military forces', in *CHGRW*, vol. 1, p. 339.

Sheldon, R. M., 'The ancient imperative: Clandestine operations and covert action', *IJIC* 10, 3 (1997), pp. 299–315.

Sheldon, R. M., 'The Ill-fated Trojan spy', *Studies in Intelligence* 31, 1 (1987), pp. 35–9; reprinted in *American Intelligence Journal* 9, 3 (Fall 1988), pp. 18–22.

Sheldon, R. M., *Intelligence Activities in Ancient Rome: Trust in the Gods, But Verify*, New York and London: Frank Cass, 2005.

Sheldon, R. M., 'The Odysseus syndrome: Ambush and surprise in ancient Greek warfare', in *European History: Lessons for the Twenty-First Century*, Essays from the 3rd International Conference on European History, ed. by Gregory T. Papanikos and Nicholas C. J. Pappas, Athens: ATINER, 2007, ch. 8.

Sheldon, R. M., *Rome's Wars in Parthia*, London: Valentine Mitchell, 2010.

Sheldon, R. M., 'Tradecraft in ancient Greece', *Studies in Intelligence* 30, 1 (1986), pp. 39–47.

Sherwin-White, A. N. and Kuhrt, A., *From Samarkhand to Sardis: A New Approach to the Seleucid Empire*, London: Duckworth, 1993.

Shewan, Alexander, *The Lay of Dolon (The Tenth Book of Homer's Iliad); some notes on its language, verse and contents, with remarks by the way on the canons and methods of Homeric criticism*, London, Macmillan, 1911.

Simonyan, R. G. and Grishin, S. V., *Tactical Reconnaissance: A Soviet View*, Washington, DC: Department of the Air Force, 1990.

Smith, Peter Mullen, *The Relevance of the Doloneia*, BA honours thesis, Harvard University.

Snodgrass, A. M., *Arms and Armour of the Greeks*, Ithaca, NY: Cornell University Press, 1967.

Snodgrass, A. M., 'The hoplite reform and history', *JHS* 85 (1965), pp. 110–22.

Snodgrass, A. M, 'The hoplite reform revisited', *DHA* 19, 1 (1993), pp. 47–61, reprinted in E. L. Wheeler, *The Armies of Classical Greece*, Aldershot, Hants and Burlington, VT: Ashgate, 2007, pp. 3–61.

Sorabji, Richard and Roden, David, *The Ethics of War*, Aldershot, Hants: Ashgate, 2006.

Souza, Philip de, 'Towards thalassocracy? Archaic Greek naval developments', in N. Fisher and H. van Wees (eds), *Archaic Greece: New Approaches and New Evidence*, London: Duckworth and The Classical Press of Wales, 1998, pp. 271–94.

Spaulding, Oliver, *Pen and Sword in Ancient Greece*, Princeton: Princeton University Press, 1937.

Spaulding, Oliver Lyman and Nickerson, Hoffman, *Ancient and Medieval Warfare*, London: Constable, 1994.

Spence, I. G., *The Cavalry of Classical Greece. A Social and Military History with Particular Reference to Athens*, Oxford: The Clarendon Press, 1993.

Spratt, T., 'The supposed situation of Minoa and Nisaea', *Journal of the Royal Geographical Society of London* 8 (1838), pp. 205–9.

Stagakis, G., 'Athena and Dolon's spoils', *Archaiognosia* 5 (1987–8), pp. 55–71.

Stagakis, G., 'The hippoi of Rhesus', *Hellenika* 37 (1986), pp. 231–41.

Stahl, P., *Thukydides, die Stellung des Menschen im geschichtlichen Prozess*, Zetemata 40, Munich: Beck, 1966.

Stanford, W. B., *Homer's Odyssey*, London and New York: 1971, 2 vols.

Starr, Chester G., *Political Intelligence in Classical Greece*, Mnemosyne Supplement 31, Leiden: Brill, 1974.

Strauss, Barry S., 'Aegospotami reconsidered', *AJPh* 104, 1 (1983), pp. 24–35.

Strauss, Barry S., *The Battle of Salamis. The Naval Encounter that Saved Greece – and Western Civilization*, New York: Simon and Schuster, 2004.

Strauss, Barry S., 'A note on the topography and tactics of the Battle of Aegospotami', *AJPh* 108 (1987), pp. 741–5.

Stroud, R. S., 'Thucydides and Corinth', *Chiron* 24 (1994).

Suess,Wilhelm, 'Über antike Geheimschriftmethoden und ihr Nachleben', *Philologus* 78 (1922), pp. 142–75.

Sutton, Dana, *The Lost Sophocles*, Lanham, MD: University Press of America, 1984.

Taplin, Oliver, *Homeric Soundings. The Shaping of the Iliad*, Oxford: The Clarendon Press, 1992.

Taylor, M. V., *Salamis and the Salaminioi. The History of an Unofficial Athenian Demos*, Amsterdam: Gieben, 1997.

Thornton, A., *Homer's Iliad: Its Composition and the Motif of Supplication*, Hypomnemata 81, Göttingen: Vandenhoeck and Ruprecht, 1983.

Thornton, A., *People and Themes in Homer's Odyssey*, London and Dunedin: Methuen, 1970.

Treu, M., 'Der stratege Demosthenes', *Historia* 5 (1956), pp. 420–47.

Trittle, Lawrence, 'Warfare in Herodotus', in Carolyn Dewald and John Marincola (eds), *The Cambridge Companion to Herodotus*, Cambridge University Press, 2006, pp. 209–23.

Trundle, M. T., *Greek Mercenaries from the Late Archaic to Alexander*, London and New York: Routledge, 2004.

Trundle, M. T., 'Identity and community among Greek mercenaries in the Classical World 700–322 BCE', in E. L. Wheeler, *The Armies of Classical Greece*, Aldershot, Hants and Burlington, VT: Ashgate, 2007, pp. 481–91.

Tuplin, C., 'Aeneas Tacticus Poliorketika 18.8', *LCM* 1 (1976), pp. 127–31.

Tuplin, C. (ed.), *Xenophon and His World*: papers from a conference held in Liverpool in July 1999, with contributions from V. Azoulay et. al., Stuttgart: Steiner, 2004.

Van Creveld, Martin, *The Transformation of War*, New York: Free Press, 1991.

Van Effenterre, H., 'Fordins Crétois', in *Mélanges D'archéologie et d'Histoire Offerts à Charles Picard à l'Occasion de son 65eme Anniversaire*, Paris: Presses Universitaires de France, 1949, 2 vols.

Van Wees, H., 'The development of the hoplite phalanx: Iconography and reality in the seventh century', in H. van Wees (ed.), *War and Violence in Ancient Greece*, London: Duckworth, 2000, pp. 125–66.

Van Wees, H., 'Greeks bearing arms: The state, the leisure class, and the display of weapons in archaic Greece', in N. Fisher and H. van Wees (eds), *Archaic Greece: New Approaches and New Evidence*, London: Duckworth and The Classical Press of Wales, 1998, pp. 333–78.

Van Wees, H., *Greek Warfare: Myths and Realities*, London: Duckworth, 2004.

Van Wees, H., 'Heroes, knights and nutters: Warrior mentality in Homer', in Alan B. Lloyd, *Battle in Antiquity*, Swansea: Classical Press of Wales, 1996, pp. 1–86.

Van Wees, H., 'The Homeric way of war: The *Iliad* and the hoplite phalanx', *G&R* 41 (1994), pp. 1–18, 131–55.

Van Wees, H., 'Kings in combat: Battles and heroes in the Iliad', *CQ* 38, 1 (1988), pp. 1–24.

Van Wees, H., 'Leaders of men? Military Organisation in the Iliad', *CQ* 36 (1986), pp. 285–303.

Van Wees, H., 'Men of bronze: The myth of the middle class militia', in H. van Wees, *Greek Warfare: Myths and Realities*, London: Duckworth, 2004.

Van Wees, H., 'The myth of the middle-class army: Military and social status in ancient Athens', in T. Bekker-Nielsen and L. Hannestad, *War as a Cultural and Social Force. Essays on Warfare in Antiquity*, Copenhagen: Det Kongelige Danske Videnskabernes Selskab, 2001, pp. 45–71.

Van Wees, H., *Status Warriors: War, Violence and Society in Homer and History*, Dutch Monographs on Ancient History and Archaeology, Amsterdam: J. C. Gieben, 1992.

Van Wees, H., 'Tyrants, oligarchs and citizen militias', in Angelos Chaniotis and Pierre Ducrey, *Army and Power in the Ancient World*, Heidelberger Althistorische Beiträge und Epigraphische Studien 37, Stuttgart: Steiner, 2002, pp. 61–82.

Van Wees, H. (ed.), *War and Violence in Ancient Greece*, London: Duckworth, 2000.

Vermeule, E., *Aspects of Death in Early Greek Art and Poetry*, The Sather Classical Lectures 46, Berkeley and Los Angeles: University of California Press, 1979.

Vernant, J. P., *Myth and Society in Ancient Greece*, trans. by Janet Lloyd, New York: Zone Books, 1988.

Vernant, J. P., *Problèmes de la Guerre en Grèce Ancienne*, Paris: La Haye Mouton, 1968.

Vian, F., 'La function guerrière dans la mythologie grecque', in J.-P. Vernant (ed.), *Problèmes de la Guerre en Grèce Ancienne*, Paris: La Haye, Mouton, 1968, pp. 53–68.

Vidal-Naquet, P., 'The black hunter and the origin of the Athenian Ephebia', *Proceedings of the Cambridge Philological Society* 14 (1968), pp. 49–64.

Vidal-Naquet, P., *The Black Hunter. Forms of Thought and Forms of Society in the Greek World*, Baltimore and London: The Johns Hopkins University Press, 1986.

Von Wilamowitz-Moellendorf, U., 'Sphakteria', *Sitzungber. Der Preuss. Akad der Wiss* 17 (1921), pp. 306ff.

Walcot, P., 'Odysseus and the art of lying', *Ancient Society* 8 (1977), pp. 1–19.

Warry, John Gibson, *Warfare in the Classical World*, London: Salamander, 1980.

Wathelet, P., 'Rhésos ou la Quête de l'immortalité', *Kernos* 2 (1989), pp. 213–31.

Webster, T. B. L., *Studies in Later Greek Comedy*, Manchester: Manchester University Press, 1953.

Weigley, R., *The American Way of War*, Bloomington: University of Indiana Press, 1973.

Westlake, H. D., *Individuals in Thucydides*, London: Cambridge University Press, 1968.

Westlake, H. D., 'Seaborne raids in Periclean strategy', *CQ* 39 (1945), pp. 75–84.

Westlake, H. D., *Thessaly in the Fourth Century BC*, London: Methuen, 1935.

Whatley, N., 'On the possibility of reconstructing Marathon and other ancient battles', in E. L. Wheeler, (ed.), *The Armies of Classical Greece*, Aldershot, Hants and Burlington, VT: Ashgate, 2007, pp. 301–21.

Wheeler, E. L., *The Armies of Classical Greece*, Aldershot, Hants and Burlington, VT: Ashgate, 2007.

Wheeler, E. L., 'Ephorus and the prohibition of missiles', *TAPA* 117 (1987), pp. 157–82.

Wheeler, E. L., 'The general as hoplite', in V. D. Hanson, *Hoplites: The Classical Greek Battle Experience*, London and New York: Routledge, 1991.

Wheeler, E. L., 'The legion as phalanx in the Late Empire', pt 1, in Y. Le Bohec and C. Woolf (eds), *L'Armée Romaine de Diocletian à Valentinian*, 1ère Actes du Congrès de Lyon, 12–14 Sept 2002, Paris: CERGR, 2004, pp. 309–58.

Wheeler, E. L., *Stratagem and the Vocabulary of Military Trickery*, Leiden: Brill, 1988.

Whitehead, David, *Aineias the Tactician*, Oxford: The Clarendon Press, 1990.

Whitehead, David, 'Klope Polemou. "Theft" in ancient Greek warfare', in E. L. Wheeler, *The Armies of Classical Greece*, Aldershot, Hants and Burlington, VT: Ashgate, 2007, pp. 289–99.

Whitehead, David, 'Who equipped mercenary troops in Classical Greece?', *Historia* 40, 1 (1991), pp. 105.

Will, E., 'Le territoire, la ville et la poliorcétique grecque', *Review Historique* 253 (1975), pp. 298–318.

Williams, D., 'Dolon', in P. Müller *et al.* (eds), *Lexicon Iconographicum Mythologia Classicae*, Zürich: Artemis and Winkler, 1981–1997, vol. 3, pp. 660–4.

Williams, Mary Frances, 'Crossing into enemy lines: Military intelligence in *Iliad* 10 and 24', *Electronic Antiquity* 5, 3 (Nov. 2000), pp. 1–41.

Wilson, D., 'Demodocus' *Iliad* and Homer's', in R. Rabel (ed.), *Approaches to Homer: Ancient and Modern*, Swansea: The Classical Press of Wales, 2005, pp. 1–20.

Wilson, D., *Ransom, Revenge and Heroic Identity in the Iliad*, Cambridge: Cambridge University Press, 2002.

Wilson, J. B., *Pylos 425 BC, A Historical and Topographical Study of Thucydides' Account of the Campaign*, Warminster, Wilts: Aris and Phillips, 1979.

Winter, Frederick E., *Greek Fortifications*, Toronto: University of Toronto Press, 1971.

Wiseman, J., *The Land of the Ancient Corinthians*, Goteborg: Paul Åstrom, 1978.

Woodcock, E. C., 'Demosthenes, son of Alcisthenes', *HSCPh* 39 (1928), pp. 93–108.

Woolliscroft, D., *Roman Military Signalling*, Stroud: Tempus, 2001.

Worley, L. J., *Hippeis: The Cavalry of Ancient Greece*, Boulder and Oxford: Westview Press, 1994.

Wylie, G., 'Brasidas – great commander or whiz kid?', in E. L. Wheeler (ed.), *The Armies of Classical Greece*, Aldershot, Hants and Burlington, VT: Ashgate, 2007, pp. 423–43.

Wylie, G., 'Demosthenes the general – protagonist in a Greek tragedy', *G&R* 40, 1 (April 1993), pp. 20–30.

Yadin, Y., *The Art of Warfare in Biblical Lands. In the Light of Archaeological Study*, New York: McGraw Hill, 1963.

Yalichev, S., *Mercenaries in the Ancient World*, London: Constable, 1997.

Index

273